CEREMONIAL SWORDS OF BRITAIN

STATE AND CIVIC SWORDS

LIEUTENANT COLONEL (RETD) EDWARD BARRETT MBE

CEREMONIAL
SWORDS
OF BRITAIN

STATE AND CIVIC SWORDS

FOREWORD BY GENERAL THE LORD DANNATT, GCB, CBE, MC, DL

The
History
Press

A Sword, a Cap of Maintenance, a Mace
Great and well gilt, to do the Town more grace:
Are borne before the Mayor, and Aldermen,
And on festivities, or high days then,
Those Magistrates their scarlet gowns do wear,
And have six Sergeants to attend each year.
John Taylor, 'Verry Merry Wherry Ferry Voyage' (1622)

First published 2017

The History Press
The Mill, Brimscombe Port
Stroud, Gloucestershire, GL5 2QG
www.thehistorypress.co.uk

British Library Cataloguing in Publication Data.
A catalogue record for this book is available from the British Library.

ISBN 978 0 7509 6244 5

Typesetting and origination by The History Press
Printed and bound in India by Replika Press Pvt. Ltd.

CONTENTS

Summer Silk or Velvet Cap – Other Forms of Headgear – Sword-bearers'
Apparel

FOREWORD

By General the Lord Dannatt, GCB, CBE, MC, DL

This is a fascinating book and is unique, in that the subject matter, though culled from a wide variety of sources, has never before been consolidated into a single volume. I am sure it will be a most useful addition to the libraries of the many organisations and local authorities who have so kindly given permission for the details of one of their prized possessions to be published, or in one case six items.

I am delighted to have been asked to comment on this work for three reasons. First, I am the current Constable of Her Majesty's Royal Palace and Fortress, better known as the Tower of London, and a Trustee of Historic Royal Palaces. Eight of the swords included in the book are housed and displayed in the Tower.

The two longest swords, both over 600 years old, are in the White Tower or keep, which is some 400 years older. The most intrinsically valuable sword, The Sword of Offering, which plays a central part of the coronation ceremony, is seen by the nearly 3 million visitors a year to the Crown Jewels in the Jewel House in Waterloo Barracks. I am well aware of the time and courtesy of staff of the Tower in providing advice for this publication.

It is worth noting that the author spent his first three months in the Army in Waterloo Barracks doing his basic military training.

My second reason is that I am Chairman of the Royal Armouries. The main museum is at Leeds and it is a truly enthralling place to visit. Again, the staff there were most generous in providing information and advice on the content of this book.

Third, since becoming a peer I have the privilege of being present at the State Opening of Parliament and being able to witness the historic procession where the sovereign is preceded by the Sword of State borne by one of my ex-Service colleagues. It is an extremely solemn, significant and truly British occasion.

The author has gone to considerable lengths to make this an interesting read for those who are not sword buffs. He has managed to make the history easy to follow and has, sensibly, included a lengthy glossary at the back for those who may not be familiar with some of the more ancient words.

Setting aside the historical parts, much attention has been paid to the descriptions of the swords and to the scabbards. Although this must be judged a reference book, it nonetheless informs any reader of the intricate work of the manufacture of these swords and how each differs from the others, and, in particular, what makes each sword special. There can be no doubt that some of these swords are mighty, some are magnificent and one quite beautiful.

This book is a great read, in that it brings together in single volume a very noteworthy part of our heritage. It is informative and has an easy-to-read manner. The years spent in research, the miles driven both in Great Britain and Ireland to visit each sword and the hours spent collating and standardising the layout are praiseworthy. I commend this book equally to the expert enthusiast and to the general reader.

The City of Lincoln Sword-Bearer

INTRODUCTION

Preamble

A ceremonial sword is used to display power or authority. Although descended from swords used in actual combat, they are not used as such. The aim is to show status and to be an impressive sight rather than have practicality as a weapon. Often their construction is of different, lighter or more precious metals which are too delicate for combat and such a sword will be poorly balanced. Similarly the scabbard, though essentially to protect the blade, is decorated to ensure the sword is noticed, a very outward and visible display.

They say never volunteer – perhaps I should have taken notice. Having been the prime-mover in a complete rewrite of the *Manual of the Mace*, the bible for the Guild of Mace-Bearers in 1999, I volunteered in 2004 to produce a section about Swords of State and civic swords. I finally started this in autumn 2007 and finished in June 2009. However, the amount of research involved meant that I had far too much information for the small section of fairly general text required. Many of those who helped me suggested that I produce a much fuller version. This necessitated the inspection, measurement and photographing of each sword and scabbard, and investigating the sword-bearer's outfits. Over seven years later, the book is now complete.

Sources

The information comes, in the main, from two primary sources, published a century apart. The first, a monumental undertaking, is a two-volume opus *The Corporation Plate and Insignia of Office of the Cities and Corporate Towns of England and Wales*, originally researched by Llewellyn Jewitt and later completed and edited by Sir William St John Hope in 1895, referred to throughout as *J&H*.[1]

The second main source is *The Sword Catalogue*, which is part of *The Crown Jewels*, published in 1998, another very large two-volume publication referred to throughout as *TSC*.[2] It was edited by the late Claude Blair OBE, MA, FSA, the doyen of sword knowledge in Britain and further afield and author of countless books, papers and articles about swords.

Two further sources have been of enormous help, and both are by Claude Blair. The first is the opening chapter of *European and American Arms (c. 1100–1850)*, published in 1962.[3] The second is the general introduction, written in 1988 by Claude Blair, to *The Dublin Civic Swords*; this was a collaborative effort with Ida Delamer, whose work forms the basis of the details of the Dublin swords.[4]

By Christmas 2009, a long list of questions to be put to Claude Blair had been amassed, but unfortunately, emails were not sent until early February 2010. The emails went unanswered and he died two weeks later.

It is important to acknowledge the work of R. Ewart Oakshott, who died in 2002, who produced many learned books on swords. He has been particularly useful for the sterling work in trying to provide a technical description and classification of each type of blade, each cross-piece and each pommel. These ceremonial swords do not, by and large, follow his descriptions, but nonetheless these have been very helpful.[5]

The two main sources have been extensively plundered, frequently verbatim, to produce a single tome about these swords. With *J&H*, each extract has had to be almost completely rewritten.

In *J&H*, in the editor's preface, Sir William St John Hope states:

> The present work in no sense claims to be an exhaustive treatise on municipal history and antiquities, but is a descriptive account of the insignia of the office and plate in the possession of the cities and towns of England and Wales. Swords of State and caps of maintenance … are properly included. Every effort has been made to obtain full and accurate descriptions of all the [items], but as much of the information has naturally been contributed by mayors, town clerks, and other officials who have no special antiquarian knowledge, and do not always fully understand what is desired, it is possible that some articles may be found imperfectly and even wrongly described.

Some of the information collected came from a number of other publications. However, a considerable amount of the information contained in these works can be attributed to *J&H*, which was obviously the starting point for most of the later works.

It is now over a century since this extremely detailed record was produced by *J&H*, and several changes have occurred. Some swords have been lost and new ones acquired, scabbards have been lost, altered, refurbished or replaced, museum staff and archivists have devoted more time to researching their treasures and, surprisingly, relevant charters have been discovered. Furthermore, there has been a tendency to embellish history! As mayors change and each new person joins the mayor's staff, the details have been retyped or written, anecdotes passed on – not always accurately – and conjecture has become fact.

Visits

The information garnered about the additional swords from the twentieth century, together with the details about sword-bearers' uniforms and costumes and the current forms of headdress worn, are the result of several years of intermittent research. Each sword was inspected and photographed during a five-week, 3,500-mile trek around the country, ranging from Exeter to Edinburgh and from Carmarthen to Canterbury, in 2010.

An additional week was in London, with visits to Buckingham Palace, St James's Palace, the Tower of London, Westminster Abbey, the Guildhall, the Mansion House and the Old Bailey. When researching the coronation ceremony, it proved impossible to obtain a copy of that Coronation 'Order' and so a considerable amount of time was devoted, at the British Film Institute, watching seven hours of the BBC film record of the day, now luckily converted to video tape – thank goodness for fast forward and instant rewind!

Rather late in the day, further reading showed that there were a further twelve bearing-swords in Ireland – as they were granted in a similar manner to the others, they have been included. This resulted in a week driving some 1,000 miles around Ireland, to inspect, measure and photograph each one, from Dublin to Galway and Waterford to Derry, in 2011.

By June 2012, the text was finished but it was not until September 2013 that the text and all the images were delivered to the publishers. However, after some time, it became obvious that some images were not of sufficient quality. So, in July 2015, another few days were spent travelling around several towns and cities retaking a number of photographs.

Synopsis

The layout of the book tries to build up the knowledge of those who have little previous familiarity of the subject, and therefore the next chapter is a general introduction to the history and manufacture of the sword and of the scabbard. The third chapter covers the history of ceremonial swords and deals with the Royal Collection; the Swords of State and the coronation swords.

This is followed by a chapter devoted to municipal swords and covers carriage, limitations of use, sword and scabbard decoration and the protocol involved with surrendering the sword when the sovereign visits. The fifth chapter is about the Cap of Maintenance and the uniform or costume worn by those who bear these swords. The final chapter, and the bulk of the book, identifies and gives details of each of the swords, all ninety-six of them, together with a photograph(s) of each sword and scabbard where one exists. Where possible, a reasonably standard form of description and layout has been followed. A diagram of a sword and scabbard is included at the beginning of the chapter as, to some, the nomenclature will not be familiar.

Additionally, there are ten appendices. Much of the book deals with the history of swords and details are frequently tied to the coronation or reign of a particular king or queen – hence Appendix 1, which lists our kings and queens from Edward the Confessor, the earliest mentioned, to our current sovereign. It also includes a chronological list of the towns or cities granted a charter and/or gifted a sword and those that have had a sword donated by someone other than the monarch.

Age is important, so Appendix 2 lists the swords by age, from before 1367 to 2003, a span of at least 636 years, together with other criteria. Size is also important; thus Appendix 3 gives a summary of the measurement of each sword, from almost 6ft down to just under 3ft in imperial measurements, while Appendix 4 lists the same facts but in metric measurements.

Appendix 5 gives a brief history of the English influence in Ireland, while Appendix 6 has details of the swords used in Freemasonry. Appendix 7 gives details of non-bearing swords known to be in amongst civic insignia. Appendix 8 offers guidance on the care and preservation of these swords and scabbards. An extensive and quite detailed glossary is given in Appendix 9, as only those particularly interested in swords and history will be familiar with many of the terms used. Indeed some of the English in *J&H* seems rather stilted in today's world. Appendix 10 is a bibliography of the other sources consulted or used and acknowledgements of all those individuals who have helped in the research and production of this book.

Clarifications

There are occasional references to 'double' years, as in 'the charter of 1404–05'. This is because the charters were issued in a certain year of the king's reign that necessarily covers two years.

In both main references, the use of the original Latin in charters is frequent. However, as few now speak Latin all such quotations have been translated into English and are now printed in italics, as have three in French. Where Latin is part of the decoration on a sword or scabbard, it has been left in the original but a translation has been added in brackets.

Then there are simple anomalies. For example – is our head of state a sovereign or a monarch? *J&H* uses 'sovereign' while *TSC* uses 'monarch'.

According to the *Shorter Oxford English Dictionary*:

Sovereign – the recognised supreme ruler of a people or country under monarchical government: a monarch: a king or queen.

Monarch – a sole and absolute ruler of a state. In modern use, a sovereign bearing the title of king, queen, emperor, or empress, or the like.

They are obviously interchangeable!

Another key element is the collective noun covering items held. According to the *OED*:

Regalia – a ceremonial emblem of Royalty.

Insignia – an emblem of dignity or office.

In general, *TSC* uses 'regalia', as this is primarily what the *TSC* is about, and *J&H* uses 'insignia', as civic accoutrements are such. Therefore, throughout this book 'regalia' has been used to describe items that are part of the Royal Collection and 'insignia' those items which belong to civic authorities.

One further word requires some clarification. It is the word 'arms'. There are three primary meanings. The most common use is to describe the upper limbs of a body (used only once). The next most common use is to describe weapons. It is used a number of times in the phrase 'a trophy of arms' – used thirteen times and covered in the glossary at the end of the book. .

The third meaning comes in the term to 'bear arms', which has two interpretations. It is now in common parlance due to the Second Amendment to the US Constitution concerning the right 'to keep and bear arms', i.e. weapons.

However, its most frequent use in this book, over 270 times, is where the right to 'bear arms' means the right to display armorial bearings – the official heraldic symbols of a family, town or city or the state (in these cases to the head of state, i.e. the sovereign or monarch). Such symbols are more often referred to in everyday use as a 'coat of arms'.

There will appear to be many mis-spellings and much use of poor English. The reader is asked to bear in mind that most of the quotations are translations from Latin, and others use various forms of the English language in use at the time of the original writing and the ancient scribes were not all educated at the same school!

Municipal swords have been categorised as either Swords of State or civic swords. The difference is simple. Swords of State are those where the town or city has been granted the right to bear the sword before the mayor by royal prerogative, or in the case of some of the older swords where the sword has been the gift of the sovereign.

Civic Swords are more recent and are those for which there is no royal authority or direct connection to the sovereign.

Local Government

Some councils still have sword-bearers who are members of the mayor's retinue, while others have staff who have other council duties but who carry the sword on special occasions. Many smaller councils have honorary but permanent sword-bearers. However, four councils differ. Canterbury has a Sword of State but uses a soldier from the local regular unit. Stratford upon Avon and Ipswich both have civic swords but use a soldier from the local yeomanry and a local military cadet respectively. While this may look quite smart, it is feared that, with the probability of a different person bearing the sword on each occasion, the history and traditions of that town or city are in danger of being lost.

The fourth is Preston, which has a civic non-bearing sword of Indian origin with seemingly no relevance to the city except the donor. For some reason, now lost in the mist of time, it is, inappropriately, processed before the mayor by a member of the local constabulary at the 'at ease' position. As one of the newest cities in the country, it might be considered more appropriate for the city to acquire a proper bearing-sword and invite the beadle or his assistant to bear such before the mayor, lodging the current sword in the museum.

Perhaps these councils might reconsider this practice and change to a permanent but honorary sword-bearer, often an ex-soldier or a member or ex-member of the council staff. The cost is reasonable. A new bi-corn or tri-corn, of good quality with a Goss body rather than steamed felt, would cost only about £450–£500, including a gold flash on the side, and a simple black academic gown would be about £200. It must be borne in mind that, because these items are only worn very occasionally, they will, if looked after well, last a very long time. Perhaps a hat previously worn by the mayor might be appropriated?

In a few other councils, the practice of wearing a winter fur hat has lapsed, possibly due to economies. A new hat made of synthetic musquash fur, from a company such as Patey Hats, would cost about £1,000. In some councils, the outgoing mayor donates an article to mark their year in office – might this not be an appropriate gift? Thought might be given to an approach to the local university that may well have a spare unused gown!

One fact became obvious. In a number of cases, swords have been effectively neglected, either due to a lack of diligence, or of ignorance, or where conservators, trying to assist in one area, actually caused harm in another. These swords are very special and must be taken out of their scabbards and inspected on a regular basis.

Exclusions

Some explanation has been included about swords used in ceremonies by Freemasons in Appendix 6, yet there are most certainly other swords that are used in ceremonies but have not been included. These range from swords used in livery company and university rituals to items held in museums and private collections.

Nine non-bearing swords were presented by or to corporations: Kingston upon Hull – the second sword obtained about 1636; Much Wenlock – a small sword obtained about 1757; Norwich – a Spanish naval sword surrendered to Admiral Nelson in about 1797; Exeter – a naval sword presented to Admiral Lord Nelson in 1801; Liverpool – a naval sword presented in remembrance of Admiral Lord Nelson in 1805; Preston – a Maharatta infantry sword presented to the Corporation in 1845; Rochester – a naval dress sword presented to the Corporation in 1871; Crewe – a German sword presented to the Corporation in 1877; and Exeter – a cavalry sabre presented to General Buller in 1901. Their importance is irrelevant to this book but brief details of these nine swords are given in Appendix 7.

Exhibitions

One interesting fact, which does not fit anywhere else, is that over the last 150 years or so four exhibitions of civic insignia have taken place. The first was at the Art Treasures' exhibition in Manchester in 1857; the second was in Burlington House, Piccadilly, the home of the Society of Antiquaries, on 20 June 1888, where twenty-four Swords of State were among the items exhibited; the third was at the Mansion House on 12 July 1893, where twenty-seven Swords of State and three caps of maintenance were exhibited; and the fourth was an exhibition of Corporation Plate in the Goldsmiths' Hall in London in 1953.

Conclusion

Significantly, the overall numbers have changed. In 1895 there were forty-six swords in thirty-one towns and cities. Today there are seventy-three bearing-swords in forty-eight towns and cities, though it must be quickly added that not all are currently used. Some are merely treasures among the insignia, with no civic function. Together with four ancient bearing-swords with royal connections, six in the Royal Collection, the Sword of Scotland, the two Manx swords and one in a museum, there are a total of eighty-seven ceremonial bearing-swords. Four others have non-bearing swords. Three other cities – Calais, Oxford and Salisbury – no longer have swords.

This book attempts to gather all the information together and tries to indicate the norms and standards which should pertain and which have been eroded over a long period of time.

The book is aimed at three groups of people in particular. First are the sword-bearers of this realm, be they sword-bearer to HM the Queen or to a town mayor – all have an important role to play. The second group are the many civic authorities who have swords as part of their insignia. The last group are those individuals who are interested in swords generally. It is hoped that it will be a useful reference book for all.

Acknowledgements

Before getting into the detail of the book, it is important to acknowledge and thank the city councils, unitary authorities, borough councils and town councils, and the staff of the lord mayors', lord provosts' and mayors' offices of the fifty-five cities and towns for the assistance they have given in providing extra information for their entry and, except where specifically mentioned, for giving their kind permission for their sword(s), cap(s) of maintenance and sword-bearer's uniform to be inspected, measured, weighed, photographed and included in this book.

THE HISTORY AND MANUFACTURE OF THE SWORD AND THE SCABBARD

'The history of the sword is the history of humanity'[6]

The History of the Sword

Before going into the details of the various swords held throughout the country, it is necessary to explain something of the origins of the implement itself.

The evolution of man into a hunter resulted in the need for weapons. Man's first effective weapon was the club, a branch or large bone, which could, with the aid of sharp-edged flint, be fashioned into better weapons, including ones with a cutting edge.

So what is a sword? The word *swer-* comes from a Proto-Indo-European root meaning to wound or cut. Its origins are many: *sweord* (Old English), *swert* (Old High German), *swaert* (Middle Dutch), *sverd* (Icelandic), *swærd* (Danish), *sverd* (Norwegian), *swärd* (Swedish), *swerd* (Old Frisian and Old Saxon), *zwaard* (modern Dutch) and *schwert* (German). There is no equivalent in French. This definition and the quotation/observation above are taken from *The Book of the Sword* by Richard Burton in 1884.[6]

By definition, a sword is a long, edged piece of forged metal, used in many civilisations throughout the world, primarily as a cutting or thrusting weapon and occasionally for clubbing. It is fundamentally a blade, with one or two edges for striking and cutting, and a point for thrusting, and a hilt, consisting of a cross-guard or quillons, a grip or handle and a pommel. The blades vary in length and width and are of different shapes. The sword is longer than a dagger and the handle or hilt usually has a cross-guard. The hilt is moulded around the tang, the tapered bottom end of the blade.

The most important single advance in weapon development came with the discovery of the malleability of metal. The mixture of copper and tin produced a weapon of durability and strength. During the Bronze Age (3000–1200 BC), man learned to fashion various tools and manufacture metal blades to make efficient weapons, including swords.

The advent of iron around 1200 BC heralded the beginning of the Iron Age (1200 BC–AD 500) and revolutionised the sword. The Romans exploited this to manufacture weapons of different designs, which had great strength and remained sharp for longer. The short, stabbing Roman sword could also cut. It is thought that the Roman knowledge came from the Phoenicians (the Canaanite people of Lebanon and Syria). The Latin word for iron is *ferrum*, which was the common name of a sword.

In the Bible, Tubal-cain was 'an instructor of every artificer in brass and iron'. It is believed that the ancient Egyptians were acquainted with iron, but no trace of it has ever been discovered in excavations.

From the earliest times, iron came from India, whilst the manufacture of steel there had been practised from time immemorial. Despite this, the Greeks continued to prefer and to employ bronze for a long period after the art of tempering steel became known to them. Homer states that the Greeks were acquainted with the method of tempering steel in a similar way to the modern one.

In the ancient process in India, the iron ore was put into furnace and heated for several hours. The red-hot mass was then divided into pieces, which were sold on to blacksmiths. This iron piece was converted into steel by returning it to the furnace, where it was melted into some twenty small cakes. These cakes of steel, called 'wootz', were sent to what we now call the Middle East, where it was manufactured into sword-blades, razors and other articles of cutlery. One cake, weighing about 2lb, was insufficient to make a sword-blade; every blade needed at least three, while a heavy blade would probably require eight or more.

The blade was manufactured by drawing the cakes into bars, then welding them by repeated firing and hammering which produced, with the addition of a little carbon, a form of mild steel. Some blades were made by laminating strips of iron, which is done by frequent folding and then hammering them together again. The Vikings (AD 700–1000) made blades from strips of iron twisted and hammered out many times to ensure an even distribution of strength.

In the process of forging the blade, the laminae or plates were necessarily thin. By increasing the number of laminae, the beauty and the quality of the blade would be improved proportionally.

Blades were double-edged with one or more fullers running down the centre. This was to reduce weight and to give the blade more flexibility – not to allow the blood to flow!

By the European Middle Ages (AD 500–1500), the sword had developed into a major and most important weapon in a battle. A good sword was a priceless possession, and many were known by name and handed down from father to son.

Swords are much in evidence in the Bayeaux Tapestry commemorating the Norman Conquest in 1066. Norman swords were similar to those of the Vikings. Between 1096 and 1291, the Holy Wars, or Crusades, took place. There were seven separate Crusades in just under 200 years, and they showed how European weaponry fell short of that of the Muslims. European blade tips were rounded, indicating a cutting rather than thrusting weapon. It had a long one-handed hilt. The cross-guard consisted of simple short quillons; the grip was normally wood bound in leather or wire and ended with a domed pommel.

The development of plate armour was partly responsible for the changes to the sword. The heavy broadsword of medieval times was double-edged and straight. Blades were made to taper to a sharp point so they could be used for thrusting as well as cutting, and the grips were often lengthened so the weapon could be used with two hands. These swords are usually referred to as one hand and a half or bastard swords. The cross-guard was quite long and very strong, in order to stop the opponent's weapon from sliding down and slicing through the fingers or wrist. Swords of this size were needed to defeat the heavy body armour worn by knights.

The curved blade originated in Asia. It was a popular weapon in India and Persia (modern Iran) and was put to good use by the Turks, particularly during the Crusades. Sound blades needed to be strong and sharp, and Damascus in Syria was formally celebrated all over the world for its manufacture of sword blades which were found to be infinitely superior in temper and quality to those of other countries. The razor-sharp scimitars of the Muslims appeared much better than the blunt broadswords of the Crusaders. Better weapons make better soldiers, so returning soldiers brought with them the spoils of war, which included examples of Muslim weaponry. This taught the armourers of Europe that blade-making could be a fine art.

At the other end of Asia, the Japanese developed a long bladed, slightly curved version with a two-handed grip, now known in the West as a Samurai sword.

During the twelfth and thirteenth centuries, the blades were gradually made longer and so were the quillons, but a new wheel or disc pommel was introduced. Some soldiers carried falchions, which were swords with great curved blades rather like a modern machete (many had a cusped end that formed a point). Very few survived the Middle Ages.

Improvements in armour during the fourteenth and fifteenth centuries continued, but as battles became more fluid the use of body armour became a hindrance. More agile soldiers now needed shorter, lighter swords.

No longer was the blacksmith the man who made the ploughs or horseshoes. A good smith became well known. Fine blade-smiths kept their skills secret and this created excellent competition. As early as 1340, one group of blade-smiths were given the right to mark their blades with an emblem which was an early trademark. In due course the makers of weapons were elevated to be on a par with those who wielded them.

This resulted in the creation of cutlers, the men who made the blades and fashioned the finely decorated and embellished hilts. The combination of a fine blade with attractive jewellery made a sword both beautiful and effective. However, the blade is the most important part of the weapon as the blade is the weapon of incapacitation – all the rest is adornment.

The advent of the musket and hand gun in the fourteenth century changed this. The importance of guns in warfare resulted in the decline of the armoured knight. The reign of Henry VIII (1509–47) marks the close of the Middle Ages and the beginning of modern Britain. By 1544, full armour was seldom seen on the battlefield as most soldiers preferred to trust their safety to mobility and luck. Battles were now fought at a longer range and the sword slowly gave way to the rifle and the pistol. The Turkish scimitar was modified in the West to become the single-edged cavalry sabre and naval cutlass. The traditional straight sword became single-edged and was used by the infantryman.

However, the sword evolved then into a duelling weapon. The thrusting swords, the rapier style, were very elaborate, and as the art of fencing grew in popularity so did the style and embellishment of the weapon. These later developed into sports weapons, with the foil, epee and sabre. Nowadays, traditional swords are carried only on ceremonial occasions.

The Locations of European Blade-Smiths

The rise of the European edged weapons industries started from about the twelfth century as technology progressed. During this period, the finest swords were produced on the continent and weapons of superior quality could only be purchased from the first blade-making centres. These sites came about due to the proximity to the natural materials needed to make iron into steel (iron, charcoal and water) and they became expert in creating blades of the finest quality.

Certain towns from an early date specialised in the manufacture of edged weapons and exported their wares in large quantities. In the Middle Ages, many towns were famous for their swords: Pavia in Italy, Poitou and Bordeaux in Savoy in France, Valencia in Spain, and Cologne, Passau and Solingen in Germany. These last two places retained their eminence until long after the Middle Ages, and from the sixteenth century to the early nineteenth century Solingen in particular supplied blades of appropriate national styles to most European and many non-European countries. Toledo in Spain was particularly noted for the fine blades in the sixteenth and seventeenth centuries, with the result that the signatures of the smiths of that city were among those most commonly imitated by the German cutlers. However, Toledo was not quite as important as is popularly believed, and the best German blades were not in any way inferior to the best Spanish ones. Other sword-making centres that should be mentioned were Vienne in Dauphine in France, Milan, Brescia and Bergamo in Italy and Toloseta in Spain.

The above may be regarded as the international centre for the manufacture of edged weapons, but there were also certain national centres that were probably virtually unknown outside their own countries. Among these, reference must be made here to two minor English workshops, both operated by immigrant German smiths. One of these, founded, possibly after a tentative start in London, at Hounslow in the 1630s, seems barely to have survived the Civil War; the other was established in Shotley Bridge, County Durham, shortly before 1687 and survived with difficulty until 1832. Neither workshop, as far as is known, produced anything of outstanding quality.

The two great modern English centres of the cutlery trade, Sheffield and Birmingham, are known to have produced edged implements and weapons from the Middle Ages onwards. Their rise to pre-eminence did not, however, commence until the second half of the eighteenth century, and it was not until the nineteenth century that they became serious rivals to Solingen in the markets of the world.

The Evolution of Sword Types

There are enormous gaps in our knowledge, and it is no exaggeration to say that of the many swords surviving from before the end of the seventeenth century only a comparatively small number can be dated more than approximately or assigned to a definite country of origin. The problems of dating and identification are rendered particularly difficult by a number of factors.

Firstly, most of the important sword-making centres exported their wares in large quantities, especially detached blades: it cannot therefore be assumed that because a sword bears the mark or signature of, say, a German smith on the blade, the hilt is also German.

Secondly, a number of centres, notably in Solingen in Germany, produced many imitations of the work of the best foreign masters, complete with signatures and marks, and it is often very difficult to distinguish the imitation from the real thing.

Thirdly, a blade might remain in use over a long period, and then appear equipped with a much later hilt.

Fourthly, hilt-makers rarely signed or marked their products, so that, though the names of many of these craftsmen are known from documentary sources, their products can rarely be identified.

Finally, there is the difficulty, encountered in all branches of archaeology, caused by conservatism: certain styles were retained in some areas longer than in others, and sometimes there were even deliberate revivals of old styles.

The characteristic sword of the Middle Ages, from AD 1100 onward, was therefore designed almost exclusively as an offensive weapon. It was of simple form with only a single bar as a cross-guard; the cross was sometimes straight and sometimes bent or arched upwards (throughout this book, the usual modern practice of describing the sword as though held point upward in the right hand ready for use has been followed). The blade was usually straight and double-edged, though single-edged examples do occur, and was balanced at the bottom of the hilt by a shaped pommel made of metal or, more rarely, crystal or some semi-precious stone. The grip was normally of wood covered with leather or bound with cord or wire, but grips of more valuable materials were also used.

Between AD 1100 and 1500, the most popular form of sword was one designed primarily to be used on horseback with one hand, though after about 1250 the hilt was often made long enough to gripped with both hands if necessary. The usual length of one of these weapons was about 35–40in, but from the end of the thirteenth century, a much larger type with a total length of about 45–55in was also used. This larger type of sword – which seems to have been called a bastard sword in the fifteenth and sixteenth centuries – is usually referred to as a hand-and-a-half sword by modern collectors and was always made with a hilt that could be used with one or two hands, as the occasion demanded. The true two-handed sword, which sometimes achieved a total length of 6ft or more, was known at least as early as the second quarter of the fourteenth century, but actual examples dating from before the sixteenth century are rare, except in ceremonial bearing-swords.

After the Middle Ages, from the early years of the sixteenth century, the history of the sword becomes increasingly complex. The old method of settling a quarrel by formal combat in the lists was replaced by the duel, and gentlemen for the first time began to wear their swords as part of their everyday dress. These influences, affecting the design of the post-medieval sword, led to the appearance of a wide variety of forms which can be classified into six main groups. Only one, the post-medieval cruciform sword, is considered here.

Sword Typology

One of R. Ewart Oakeshott's greatest and most enduring accomplishments, arguably, is his categorisation of various elements of the medieval and early Renaissance sword.[5] He was not the first to organise swords into classes, though his work is perhaps the most complete system of typology for the medieval sword. Oakeshott refined an earlier system of seven types by adding two transitional types, VIII and IX. A key difference between the Oakeshott system and those that came before lies in the fact that it does not limit its focus simply to the hilt or the blade alone, but looks at the whole of the sword. Viking age swords tended to vary very little in terms of blade form, leading others to use hilt styles as defining characteristics for their classifications. Medieval swords, however, show great variety in blade form. This information is included for those who might wish to enquire further.

The Manufacture of the Sword

The detailed description of the manufacture of the blade comes from *The Engines of War* by Henry Wilkinson, written in 1841.[7] The descriptions concerning the manufacture of the hilt, the cross-guard, grip and pommel are taken from *European and American Arms* by Claude Blair (1962).[3]

It is likely that, in the Middle Ages at least, some swords were entirely the work of a single craftsman. Normally, however, a sword complete with its sheath and belt was the work of at least five people: the cutler or blade-smith, the hilt-maker, the sheather, the girdler and finally the furbisher, who assembled all the parts and usually sold the complete weapon. Sometimes the furbisher also did the work of the hilt-maker. By the end of the eighteenth century, many of the people who traded under the name of cutler were in fact only furbishers who assembled and sold swords, or were even only retailers. The presence of a particular cutler's name on a sword, therefore, frequently means nothing more than that he had retailed it.

It is important to stress at this stage that the following descriptions are based on 'arming' swords, i.e. those designed and made for battle. The swords described in this book are, by nature, ornamental and thus, with few exceptions, they do not follow convention.

The Blade

In 1841, Henry Wilkinson[7] wrote:

> The present method of manufacturing sword-blades of the best quality in England is very simple. The steel is made in Sheffield, and sent to the sword cutlers in Birmingham in lengths sufficient to form two blades; the best cast steel is employed; each end is then drawn out by forging to about half the thickness of the bar; leaving a few inches in the centre the original size, each end in its turn serving as a handle to hold it by while forging the other; it is afterwards notched and broken in two at the centre, and the tang, which is of iron, is welded onto the thick end, by splitting open one end of the tang, or that part which enters the handle, and the forging of the blade is completed to the desired pattern; after which it is hardened by passing it backwards and forwards through a large hollow forge fire until of bright red heat, when it is instantly plunged into a tub of water by a cutting movement, edge foremost, which is directly changed to a perpendicular one.
>
> The blade in this state is quite brittle, and often very much set or cast sideways; it is again passed through the fire until a certain colour or appearance comes on the blade, known only by long experience, and it is set as straight as possible, by the eye, in a fork fixed on the anvil, and laid aside to be ground and polished, which operations require no description.

The ornamenting of the blade is preformed in various ways, first by embossing as it is called; the design is drawn on the polished blade with a composition of vermilion and turpentine, or stopping; the fine lines intended to represent shading, or engraving, are scratched in with a needle; all those parts intended to remain bright being covered with stopping. The blade is then washed over those parts with diluted nitric acid, which, in minutes removes the bright polished surface; and when the whole is washed off with water and the stopping removed, the pattern drawn is perfectly bright and the ground a dead white.

If gilding be desired, the design is faintly scratched in, and then carefully gone over with a fine brush dipped in a solution of sulphate of copper. The copper is immediately precipitated, in its metallic state, on the bright surface of the steel. An amalgam of gold being prepared by dropping fine gold into mercury while hot, a portion of this is put into a piece of crape and dabbed over those parts where the copper has been precipitated; it adheres to the copper, leaving it of a silvery colour.

The blade is then blued over a charcoal fire, which effects two purposes at the same time; for the heat, necessary to blue the steel, drives off the mercury and leaves the gold only on the surface of the copper; as the amalgam will not adhere to the steel at all. It does not, however, assume the appearance of gold until it has been polished up with putty powder and burnished. This operation finishes the ornamental part, unless an admixture of dead white is required on the blue ground, in which case the design is traced on the blue with a camel's hair brush and much diluted muriatic acid, which instantly removes it and the blade is then washed. The combined effect of blue, gold and dead white and polished steel produces a very pleasing and beautiful appearance, if skilfully done and is the only ornament put on English blades.

Today, many blades come from India, using traditional methods, and are made to an ISO standard. Most swords are now solely for ceremonial purposes, but the manufacture of blades for knives, bayonets, daggers and other like weapons means that there is plenty of work to keep the art alive and ensure that the traditional methods are passed on to another generation. There is also a sizable re-enactment market.

However, modern times call for modern methods. In Britain today, firms such as Crisp and Sons utilise both traditional and modern methods in the manufacture of their blades. Blades are profiled from high-performance carbon steel before being rough ground and then milled using modern equipment. The blade is then hardened, tempered and straightened before being hand ground to the desired shape and, after a second tempering, the blade is finally mirror-polished and then acid-etched in the traditional manner.

Crisp and Sons, of Framfield near Uckfield, are true sword manufacturers of all the component parts used in the production of their bespoke swords, from blades to hilts and scabbards. This company employs past employees of Wilkinson's as well as training the future generation in the art of sword-making.

The Hilt

The simple cruciform hilt seems to have gone almost completely out of use in the third decade of the sixteenth century, except for four special groups of swords: the bearing-sword, the claymore, an Irish version of the claymore and executioners' swords – the latter three are not discussed further. But in the late sixteenth and early seventeenth century, it once again had a limited vogue, possibly as a result of the artificial revival of 'chivalry'. Henceforth, until the nineteenth century it survived as part of the full dress of certain knightly orders.

From very early times, the normal method of attaching the blade of a sword or dagger to its hilt was by passing its tang through the cross-guard until engaged with the shoulders of the blade. Next, the grip is either slid on or fixed to each side of the tang and bound. Then the pommel is added. The tang end is then either hammered flat against the pommel like a rivet or the end is threaded and a nut screwed on to keep all the parts firmly together. Finally a button was often added to hide the end.

The majority of Swords of State and civic swords (ceremonial bearing-swords) are of this style. Included in this category are swords which, from as early as 1365 until the late eighteenth century, were blessed by the Pope and given to selected rulers and noblemen whom the Church wished to honour.

Though the simple cruciform hilt went out of general use in the third decade of the sixteenth century, swords that were basically cruciform continued to be made in large quantities until the early years of the seventeenth century. The bastard sword of the sixteenth century retained the proportions of its medieval precursor. The quillons were sometimes straight and sometimes recurved either vertically or horizontally. The two-handed sword, which remained in use throughout the sixteenth century, usually had a simple cross-guard, often arched, and one or two side-rings. The blades of many of these swords had a long leather-covered ricasso with two projecting lugs above so that the user could bring a hand forward on to the blade if necessary.

The Cross-guard or Quillons

Throughout the Middle Ages, the form of the cross-guard was varied quite arbitrarily, and this part of the hilt is of comparatively little use in determining the date of any given sword. Nevertheless, a few general trends are discernible. The beginning of the twelfth century saw the end of a vogue for very short, thick quillons. Apart from this, it is broadly true to say that from about 1100 to about 1350 the majority of swords had fairly long quillons that were either straight or only very slightly arched. From the third quarter of the fourteenth century, an increasing number of swords had quillons with upturned tips, which from the early fifteenth century were often scrolled. The early fifteenth century also saw the widespread adoption of a feature found occasionally at an

Cross-guards or quillons

City of Bristol – Mourning – pre-1367

City of Coventry – State – 1430

City of Lincoln – Mourning – 1486

City of Hereford – Mourning – late fifteenth century

earlier date, namely the so-called écusson, a small triangular extension projecting from each side of the centre of the cross. From the middle of the fifteenth century, strongly arched quillons became common. Before 1500, it was known as a cross or cross-guard; after this, the term used has been quillons.

The Grip

There is evidence to show that as early as the late Bronze Age, a firmer grip was sometimes obtained on the sword by hooking the forefinger over the base of the blade. One sword of about 1150 has a rectangular unsharpened section (modern ricasso) for the finger at the base of the blade. In the fourteenth century, the practice of holding the sword this way became widespread, and from about 1350 rather more blades seem to have had a ricasso, though the feature only became widely used in the sixteenth century.

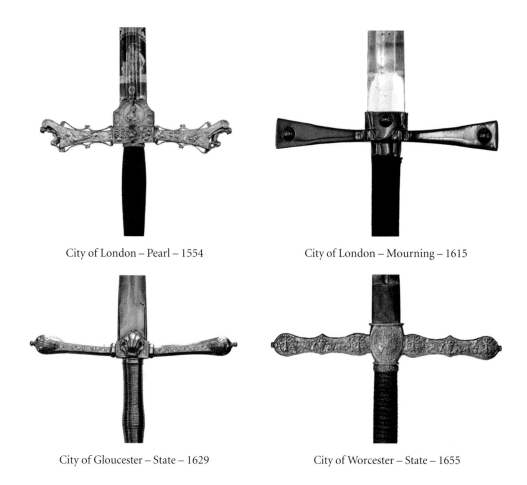

City of London – Pearl – 1554

City of London – Mourning – 1615

City of Gloucester – State – 1629

City of Worcester – State – 1655

A few thrusting swords of the first half of the fifteenth century have a ricasso that extend from a quarter to a third of the way up the blade. This was presumably to enable the swordsman to grasp the blade with his left hand when fighting at close quarters on foot.

In general, the grip or handle is in two forms. It is either a single shaped piece of wood through which a hole is bored for the tang, or it is made of two pieces of wood hollowed out and sandwiched over the tang and then bound.

The Pommel

The part of the medieval sword-hilt most subject to change was the pommel. The two commonest forms at the beginning of our period were the 'mushroom' or 'tea-cosy' and the 'Brazil nut' shapes. The former was in use until about 1150, but the other remained popular, particularly in Germany, until the third quarter of the thirteenth century. A few

Pommels

Ovoid – City of Bristol – Mourning – pre-1367

Scent stopper – King's Lynn – *c.*1446

Heart-shaped – City of Hereford – Mourning –
late fifteenth century

Disc – City of London – Mourning – 1615

Wheel – City of Gloucester – State – *c.*1627

Globular – City of London – State – 1670

Pear drop – Thetford – 1678

Globular – City of Lincoln – George II – 1730

twelfth- and thirteenth-century swords were equipped with lozenge-shaped pommels. The most common of the medieval pommels was the so-called 'wheel' pommel, which started to come into wide use after about 1150, though it had been introduced at least a century earlier. At first simply a flat disc, it developed a narrow chamfered border to each face in about 1200. After about 1250, the chamfer was usually made concave and the pommel thicker, so producing the effect of a raised circular plane in the centre of each face. This form survived, with minor variations, until the second quarter of the fifteenth century, when it tended to become flatter again, finally reverting to the simple disc shape – often of lenticular section – after about 1450.

The remaining principal types of medieval pommel stemmed from three basic shapes:

Triangular: this type appeared in the second quarter of the fourteenth century as a simple flat triangle with its truncated apex at the top. A related form, in use from about 1435, was shaped like a lozenge with concave sides; it developed into a flat pear-shape during the third quarter of the century.

Conical: the so-called 'scent-stopper' type was usually of polygonal section – the truncated apex of the cone at the top, the base domed. Introduced in about 1350, this form was especially popular during the first quarter of the fifteenth century. After about 1450, it developed into the fig or pear shape.

Globular or ovoid: this was found occasionally from the thirteenth century onwards, but rarely before the sixteenth century, when it became the commonest form.

Finally, before leaving the medieval pommel, it should be mentioned that from the middle of the thirteenth century, a prominent 'button' was often fitted between the pommel and the riveted-over tip of the blade-tang.

From the early sixteenth century, the pommels on all types of sword were, with few exceptions, either globular, ovoid, fig-shaped or some variation thereof.

As most of the swords described in this book were manufactured for a ceremonial purpose, they do not follow the conventions above in terms of time. Today, their pommels follow the shapes above, namely, wheel or circular flattened disc, though a few are hexagonal, lozenge or diamond-shaped, triangular or heart-shaped, conical or pear drop, globular or spherical, mushroom and ovoid.

The Manufacture of the Scabbard

The scabbard is a case or sheath for a sword blade. It serves a dual purpose. First, it protects the blade, and particularly the sharpened edges and point, from damage. Second, it protects the user from injury from the sword itself. Scabbards are usually worn suspended from a sword belt or from a shoulder-belt or baldric by hangers. However, there are a

Chapes

| King's Lynn – 1446 | City of London – Pearl – 1554 | City of Gloucester – State – 1629 | City of Bristol – State – 1752 |

number that were worn across the back, necessitating the sword to be drawn over the shoulder from behind the head. Over the years, scabbards have been manufactured from a variety of materials, but the most common are leather, wood and metal. Some ancient ones even had fur linings, which were oiled to protect the blade from rust. Some had a waxed linen foundation under the velvet covering.

The Greek and Romans favoured lightweight scabbards which were designed simply to hold and support the sword. However, from the second century onwards, the decoration on both the swords and the scabbards became much more intricate.

The normal sword or dagger sheath from about 1100 onwards was made of thin slats of wood covered with leather, parchment, rich material or, more rarely, sheets of gold or silver. The tip was reinforced with a metal ferrule (chape), which was sometimes little more than a u-shaped binding.

Over the years, ceremonial scabbards have been subject to decoration in the form of chapes, mounts, lockets and bands. One of the prime reasons for these decorations is to hide joins and stitching. It can be very difficult to date many of the old scabbards, as the mounts have been transferred to later scabbards and no record is held of the date of refurbishment.

One unusual feature occurs on several scabbards. Some swords have a pointed or convex quillon block called an écusson. This necessitates a concave cut-out in the mouth

Mouth-lockets

City of Coventry – State – 1430   City of Gloucester – State – 1627

City of Hereford – State – 1667   City of Lincoln – State – 1902

of the scabbard, which is reflected in the mouth-locket. Some other swords have a protecting plate which is part of the quillon block and projects out over the scabbard. The mouth-locket is necessarily thin to allow the protecting plate to pass over it.

On three swords there are a set of 'hooks' above the quillons. All three have scabbards; with two the scabbard ends at the 'hooks', while on the third the mouth-locket is nearer the point and the bottom few inches are split to pass over the 'hooks'.

Leather

For the leather scabbard, a piece of treated rawhide is cut to just over double the width required and then soaked to make it soft and supple. It is then split and the back part discarded. The remaining piece is then curved round a metal mount, called a mandrel, which is just slightly larger than the blade. The two edges are then stitched together to form a leather sleeve. The scabbard is then placed in a low-temperature oven until it is dry and has taken the shape of the mandrel. When dry, the leather is sanded down and then rubbed with bone to create a smooth finish. Finally, it is painted with a black acrylic dye to achieve a shiny finish.

Leather scabbards survived in military use as late as the American Civil War (1861–65). They were also used as a form of truncheon. They are still in use today, though now the scabbard is principally used for decoration and not for war.

Wood

Wooden scabbards are usually fashioned and then covered. The scabbard is made from a strong lightweight wood. The piece is roughly sized and is then split. Each half is then hollowed out by chisel to the width and length of the blade and to half its depth. The two halves are then glued together and, when dry, the outside is shaped and sanded down to the required external measurements. It is then covered in fabric, usually velvet, or pigskin leather. For the last few decades, the hollowing out has been done by machine. For wooden and leather scabbards, a 'forme of woode' was made. This was a blank wooden sword to maintain the shape of the scabbard when the metal sword was being used. Today it might cost some £150 to re-cover in velvet.

Metal

Metal scabbards became popular in Europe in the early nineteenth century. Metal was more durable than leather and stronger than wood. It was therefore more suited to the rigours of battle, particularly for mounted horsemen.

Most had a ring attached to the throat locket and another attached part way down the scabbard to enable the scabbard to be attached to the belt by straps or hangers. Some were fitted with a frog stud for use in a frog.

Perspex

A new scabbard for the Exeter Sword of State was made by city conservators using unorthodox materials in 2009. Silicon rubber mouldings were taken of the chape, crown and mouth-locket. Wax positives were then made and then these were sent to Niagara Falls Casting in Warwickshire, who cast silver replicas. A roughly shaped sheet of Perspex was hollowed out in a horseshoe-shape to fit the blade. This was then dowelled and glued between two other pieces of Perspex. The finished sheath was then ground down to the required length and thickness. A piece of calico was then sewn around the scabbard. Hand & Lock, embroiderers of London, provided a swatch of crimson leather which was then embroidered with an exact copy of the intricate work on the current scabbard.

This was then fitted over the calico and stitched on. The newly cast chape, crown and mouth-locket were then added to complete the new scabbard. While the costs of this new scabbard are high in comparison to those of several hundred years ago, the scabbard itself will last an extremely long time, with only the covering and embroidery needing replacement, but not for many years to come.

Hangers

Until the middle of the thirteenth century, the sword-sheath was usually attached to the belt with laces. But from about 1250 it became customary for the belt to be made in two pieces with the ends laced round the sheath at different points, so causing the hilt of the sword to tip towards the front. Sometimes the two parts of the belt were linked on the sheath by a diagonal thong, which prevented them from sliding apart.

Shortly after about 1300, it became increasingly common for the sword-sheath to be fitted with one or more metal bands towards the mouth, to which metal terminals on the two parts of the belt were linked by rings. This form of attachment remained in use until the middle of the fourteenth century, after which it became customary for the belt to be worn horizontally, with the sword-sheath attached to it by a loop or a hook at the reverse of the top locket. In the second decade of the fifteenth century, the ring attachment came back into favour and, in a variety of forms, remained in general use until the second quarter of the sixteenth century. In the third quarter of that century, this developed into the form of hanger that was triangular in shape and normally consisted of two broad straps linked at the top by a metal mount terminating in a small hook: this last was hung on a small metal loop on the belt, at this date usually called a girdle.

The triangular form of hanger was gradually replaced in the third decade of the seventeenth century by a broad shoulder-belt or scarf, worn diagonally from the right shoulder to the left hip, with one or two slings for the sword included in its construction. More rarely, a broad waist-belt of similar shape was worn. At the end of the seventeenth century, a waist-belt with slings came back into general favour but was now made to be unobtrusive, but from about 1740 it tended to be supplanted by a flat metal hook from which the sheath was suspended on two chains.

Frogs

The sword frog is a simple attachment to a belt. It consists of a short sleeve into which the scabbard is inserted. A short strip of leather is attached to the scabbard, this is bent over the top of the frog and a button hole in it is clipped over the frog stud to hold the scabbard in place. Two adjustable straps are fitted to the outside corners of the frog, and these are used to attach the frog to the belt through rings that are part of the lower edge of the belt. The scabbard in a frog retains it in an upright position. The straps permit movement to allow for the drawing and sheathing of the sword.

THE HISTORY OF
CEREMONIAL SWORDS

The Sword as a Symbol of Royal Authority

The sword is a very obvious symbol of authority, and has probably been used as such from the beginning of its history. The following account of the general history of state swords is taken from *The Dublin Civic Swords* by Claude Blair (1988)[4] and was largely based on chapter 8 of Lord Twining's *European Regalia* (London, 1967);[8] however, most of the remainder of the chapter comes from *TSC.*[2] The details of the coronation ceremony are mainly from a study of the film record of the event.

The formal investment of a king or prince with a sword as part of his coronation ritual, and the carrying of a sword before him on state occasions, seem to be customs of Germanic origin that started to become general only during the Middle Ages (AD 500–1500). At first the weapon with which the ruler was invested was his own sword, but eventually a special sword, often elaborately decorated, came to be included in the state regalia. This was sometimes associated with the national hero or saint, and sometimes called merely the Sword of State; nevertheless, a popular tradition persisted that it was the king's personal weapon. The role of the ruler's sword-bearer was therefore important, and the position was regarded as one of great honour. In England, this led to rivalry between the chief magnates, with the result that by the coronation of Richard I in 1189, several swords had been brought into use for the ceremony, so that the right of more than one magnate to carry a sword was established. The act of carrying the monarch's sword for him on any occasion came, in fact, to be regarded as one of feudal service.

In coronations, the sword was usually girded on the king by the officiating priest, who had previously blessed it. This originally signified that the king had received temporal and military domination within his realm, including the duty of administering justice. Thus in the coronation of the German Emperor – to quote the late Lord Twining – 'the investiture with the sword signified that the Emperor had received total domination with God's authority, and in token of this had been given a weapon for use against the heathen and the heretic … to protect the Church and the faithful … to defend widows and orphans and … as an instrument of justice'. During the Investiture Controversy, which was a dispute about lay investiture between the Holy Roman Empire and the papacy in the eleventh and twelfth centuries, much was made of the doctrine of the two swords, the spiritual in the hands of the *sacerdotium* and the temporal in the hands of the *regnum*. The Church's view was that both belonged to her, but that she employed the temporal one in the hands of the prince while reserving the spiritual one for the priest: In Lord Twining's words, 'the Church was satisfied that the prayers used during the delivery of the sword to the Emperor and kings of Europe at their coronation effectively implied that its delivery at the hands of the clergy indicated the supremacy of the Church'.

A weapon is an obvious choice as a symbol both of manhood and of authority. The giving of arms to a boy as part of the rite of passage into manhood is an ancient and widespread custom amongst primitive societies, as is the use of a particular weapon – spear, sword, axe or club (sceptre) – as a symbol of chieftainship.

Kings have had Swords of Estate for over 1,400 years. The first definitive evidence is provided by a scene in relief on the gilt copper-alloy brow-plate of a late sixth-century Lombardic helmet, now in the Museo Nazionale del Bargello, Florence. This bears the name of the Lombard King Agilulf (crowned 591, died 616), who is depicted receiving two crowns, presumably those of the Lombards and of Byzantine Italy, enthroned, and holding a sword across his left knee, clearly as his main symbol of authority.

In 781, Louis the Pious, then just 3 years old, was girded with a sword when he was given the Kingdom of Aquitaine by his father, Charlemagne, and was girded again by his father in 791 'cause he had reached the threshold of adolescence'.

All these ceremonies seem to have been secular, but by the same period the Church was also becoming involved. Louis the Pious girded his son, Lothar, with a sword at his coronation as Emperor by the Pope in 823. He later girded his other son, Charles the Bald, with a sword in 838 when he was crowned King of Francia and other parts of the Holy Roman Empire. The regalia Louis the Pious gave to his son, Lothar, on his deathbed in 840 included a sword. The Emperor Lothar I is depicted in his psalter, executed shortly after 842, prominently girt with a sword on which he rests his left hand. Lothar's son, later Emperor Louis II, at his father's instigation, was also crowned by the Pope in 844. In a manuscript of 845–46 the sword of the enthroned King Charles the Bald (later Emperor Charles II) is shown held, sheathed, by one bearer, and his spear and shield by another.

The earliest English evidence for the use of what was presumably an official royal sword appears to be Abbot Ælfric's vernacular life of St Edmund, which cites the king's sword-bearer as a source of information. In a late eleventh-century English manuscript illumination of the coronation of St Edmund in 855, two sword-bearers appear.

Louis II (The Stammerer) on his deathbed in 879 also sent a sword to his son, the future Louis III.

It seems likely that these are examples of the familiar process of a previously pagan ceremony being taken over by the Church.

The sword as a symbol of sovereign power and authority has been associated with our kings and queens since very early times. From the coronation of King Æthelred in 978 to that of Queen Elizabeth II in 1953, a period of nearly 1,000 years, an important part of the ceremony has been the blessing of a sword and its formal delivery to the sovereign, who, after putting on the crown and ring, offers it upon the altar. It is then redeemed and carried unsheathed by a noble during the rest of the ceremony, which is covered in more detail at the end of the chapter.

In a manuscript of 1039–43, the German King Henry III (1039–56) and future Emperor (1046–56) is shown entering a church, crowned and holding an orb and sceptre, and followed only by a sword-bearer holding the sword point upwards in the manner that is now normal for such officers.

Shortly after the Battle of Hastings, it is claimed in the *Carmen de Hastingae Proelio* of Guy, Bishop of Amiens, that Harold on his ill-fated visit to Duke William of Normandy, probably in 1064, took with him from Edward the Confessor a ring and a sword as tokens that the duke was to succeed the latter as king. Even if this claim was merely a piece of pro-Norman propaganda, its inclusion by the author is an indication of the significance of the sword at the period in question as a secular symbol of royal authority.

On the Bayeux Tapestry (1066–84?), the representation of Harold enthroned after his coronation includes a courtier standing near him, gesturing towards him and holding what must be the royal sword point upwards in one hand, while in the scene showing Harold being told of the appearance of Halley's Comet his informant is apparently his sword-bearer, since he holds a sword.

According to French chroniclers, Richard I had a bodyguard. Their duty was 'to watch round the King's tent in complete armour, with a mace, a bow, arrows, and a sword'.

On the obverses of all the English great seals, from Edward the Confessor to the first seal (1218) of Henry III, and in pictures down to Edward III, our kings are shown holding the sword, but after the fourteenth century the sword is generally represented as carried by an attendant sword-bearer. It was also borne before the sovereign on all state occasions.

In about 1450, the Pope presented to Henry VI a sword 'richly garnished' and a cap of maintenance, and in 1507, Pope Julius II presented a sword and cap to James IV of Scotland. The Ottoman ruler, Suleiman the Magnificent (1495–1566) had a sword-bearer, an extremely important personage with much power.

There can be no serious doubt that the swords thus shown symbolise the monarchs' own weapons: the sword with which they were invested at their coronations, which eventually came to be known as 'The Sword of Offering'. It seems certain that from an early date the investiture sword was further symbolised by a sword that accompanied the ruler on all formal occasions, being carried either by him or by a sword-bearer.

The Sword of Estate

The earliest evidence of a Sword of Estate being used by an English monarch for anything other than for his coronation is contained in a list of precious objects deposited in the City of London in 1380.

The use of a Sword of Estate by the monarch on all official occasions is well-attested thereafter, and, in view of this, and of the evidence previously cited about such swords, it is reasonable to assume that it was by then a long-established practice, probably going back to Saxon times.

The iconographic evidence suggests that, during most of the Middle Ages, none of them was made larger than a normal war or tournament sword of their period, the type usually classified, from the early sixteenth century, as an 'arming-sword' to distinguish it from the civilian rapier. The processional function of swords like the coronation swords, however, led to them being classified also as 'bearing-swords', a term first recorded in the fifteenth century and which often, though not always, refers to the large form exemplified by the present Sword of State.

As early as the fifteenth century, the sword was called 'The Sword of Estate' (in the early seventeenth century contracted to 'Sword of State').

The earliest evidence for the use of such a large Sword of Estate by an English monarch comes from Henry VIII's reign (1509–47).

The royal cutler, John Ayland, was commissioned to provide a Sword of Estate for the coronation of Edward VI in 1547. It was described in the Wardrobe Accounts as 'gilt and Enamelled cutt and wroughte with antike work'.

A portrait in Hatfield House of Elizabeth I, dated 1585, shows, in the bottom right corner, part of a bearing-sword which is described as 'the Sword of Estate'. There is a small cartouche on it with '1585', though this is believed to be the date of the portrait rather than the date of the sword. This sword could be described as above and might, therefore, be the same one.

The Sword of Estate is, in fact, a symbol rather than a specific sword, and it is clear that initially any sword carried before the monarch on formal occasions was so called, though, of course, the name came to be applied to a specific sword, perhaps as early as the beginning of the seventeenth century.

Up to and including the coronation of Charles II in 1660, it was customary for the monarch to ride in procession on the eve of the coronation from the Tower of London to Westminster. During this, as on all official occasions, he or she was preceded by someone bearing the Sword of Estate.

An obvious example in the present context is the commencement of the preliminary coronation proceedings in Westminster Hall with the laying of the Sword of State on the table.

A bearing-sword of some kind must have been provided for Charles II immediately after his return to England in 1660. A new sword was ordered on 23 January 1678, and there can be little doubt that it was used at the coronation of James II in 1685 and has been used at all subsequent coronations since then, though we can only be certain of this from that of George IV onwards.

By extension, the Sword of State was itself symbolised in some situations where the monarch was theoretically present in person, but for practical reasons could not be, by other swords which were, in effect, incarnations of the main one, as it was itself an incarnation of the Sword of Offering.

Examples are the Irish Sword of State, which was used by the Viceroy, the sword over the senior judge's bench in the Central Criminal Court at the Old Bailey, and those swords carried before certain lord mayors and mayors of English cities and towns that were acquired in the only legitimate way, that is by royal grant or gift. The idea behind these last is that the head of the community concerned is governing it for the monarch, and some of the swords were, in fact, normally referred to locally as 'The King's (Queen's) Sword'.

The term 'Great Sword of State' to distinguish the main Sword of State was not used before the coronation of George VI in 1937.

In modern times, the fact that the Sword of State is no longer used regularly has obscured its symbolic significance, which is analogous in relation to the monarch to that of the House of Commons mace in relation to the Speaker. It was (and is) the visible symbol of the royal presence, and formal proceedings directly involving the monarch could not take place until it was displayed.

It has been borne before the Queen on such formal occasions as the Prince of Wales's Investiture at Caernarvon Castle in 1969 and at the annual State Opening of Parliament.

The Curtana and Swords of Justice

Besides the Sword of State delivered to the sovereign, three other swords are still borne in the coronation procession by three peers. They are the Curtana, the Sword of Spiritual Justice and the Sword of Temporal Justice. They have certainly been so carried since the first coronation of Richard I in 1189, described by Roger of Howden, a contemporary writer, and at his second Coronation in 1194 by three different peers.

There is no doubt that, for the coronation of Charles I in 1625, specific swords were supplied, and these are the present Curtana and Swords of Justice. There are good reasons to believe that after the coronation the king personally instructed that they be deposited with the other regalia at Westminster.

The form and proportion of these swords, and the fact that their cross-guards and pommels are made of iron, show that – in contrast to all the other swords in the Jewel House – they were made in exactly the same way as practical weapons. They represent types that have been used in the coronation ritual since the Middle Ages but, unfortunately, they cannot themselves be identified positively in any publication or document prior to the Restoration.

The Sword of Offering

There can be no serious doubt that the swords mentioned earlier symbolise the monarch's own weapons: the sword with which they are invested at their coronations, which eventually came to be known as 'The Sword of Offering'.

The Sword of Offering was described in the Coronation 'Order' of James I as 'the King's own sword'. This is the first coronation for which we have definitive evidence of the Sword of Offering being placed in the Abbey beforehand, as later became usual. It is likely that, as now, it was exchanged during the ceremony.

The practice of changing swords during the ceremony, probably first recorded at the coronation of Charles I though the first certain evidence for this practice is at the coronation of James II in 1685, was clearly a practical development brought about by the fact that the official Sword of Estate had become too large to be used for girding and offering.

Subsequent coronations can be easily dealt with, since James II and all his successors have used the present Sword of State – made in 1678 – and the present Curtana and Swords of Justice.

It must be concluded that there is only one true coronation sword, namely that with which the monarch is actually invested. It is as much part of the regalia as, for example, the orb and sceptres, though, because it is the monarch's personal sword, only in 1903 was a permanent Sword of Offering introduced into the Jewel House; until the coronation of George V in 1911, it was always – in theory at least – provided personally by the monarch for his or her coronation. Symbolically, it is the most important of the swords, and, as already pointed out, a Sword of Estate is merely in incarnation of it: the two seem always to have been regarded as interchangeable, as, of course, they are in the modern ceremony.

The magnificent coronation of George IV in 1821 naturally demanded swords of appropriate splendour. The king would have been prevented by protocol of the Coronation 'Order' from using anything other than the now official Sword of State and the Curtana and Swords of Justice for the ceremony, but the design of his personal sword for offering was subject to no restrictions.

It is believed that the sword was used at the coronation but, in accordance with the Coronation 'Order', that it was covered with purple velvet. The sword has been used at all subsequent coronations, though frequently covered. It was not until the coronation of Elizabeth II that this requirement was omitted from the 'Order'.

Rehearsal Replicas

It is worth noting that Westminster Abbey has a rough copy of each of these five coronation swords on display in its museum. These swords, which resemble the real swords, were made in the 1930s (perhaps for the planned coronation of Edward VII), to be used for rehearsals rather than move the very precious real swords. They were used in the many rehearsals that took place before the coronations of George VI in May 1937 and Elizabeth II in June 1953.

The Coronation Ceremony

The coronation procedures are laid down in the *Liber Regalis* or *Royal Book* produced in about 1390. They are generally adhered to but are, on occasion, changed, particularly when a queen regnant is to be crowned. The procedure to be followed at a coronation has been promulgated since 1661 in the Coronation 'Order'. The ceremony consists of six parts: the procession in, the Recognition, the Oath, the Anointing, the Crowning and the procession out. As it is the most recent, the coronation on 2 June 1953 of Elizabeth II is described here.

The procession entered in groups. First were the Chaplains, followed by the Officers of the Orders of Knighthood, and then the Standards. The next group was the members of the royal household – fourth in this group was the Keeper of the Jewel House (the Governor of the Tower of London) bearing a long cushion on which were the jewelled Sword of Offering, sheathed, and the ring and the armills (bracelets). Initially the Sword of Offering was deposited in St Edward's Chapel. The following groups were the Commonwealth Prime Ministers, the Archbishops and the Queen Consort (of a Queen Regnant only). The next group were the bearers of regalia – after St Edward's staff came one of the sceptres and the golden spurs. These were followed by three peers abreast bearing the coronation swords, unsheathed and point upwards. The Curtana was in the centre; the 'second' sword, the Sword of Temporal Justice, was on the right; and the 'third' sword, the Sword of Spiritual Justice, was on the left. This appears to indicate that the Curtana is the 'first' sword; however, that honour may belong to the Sword of State. At this point the peers were bareheaded.

The swords were followed by the Kings of Arms, another sceptre, Black Rod, The Lord Great Chamberlain, The Lord High Steward of Ireland, The High Constable of Scotland, the Great Steward of Scotland, the Earl Marshal and the Lord High Constable of England.

Before the Crowning – the three Coronation Swords and the Sword of State

After the Crowning – the three Coronation Swords and the Sword of Offering

Behind him was the Sword of State, borne, sheathed and point upwards, by another peer. This was followed by the third sceptre, St Edward's Crown, the Orb, the Patten, the Bible and the Chalice. The final group was that of the sovereign. The Queen was preceded by the Clerk and ten Gentlemen at Arms from Her Majesty's Bodyguard of the Honourable Corps of Gentlemen at Arms, formed in 1509 by Henry VIII.

Thereafter, the three coronation swords were carried abreast close to the Queen throughout the ceremony and in the procession out of the abbey. The Sword of State was also carried close to the Queen initially. After the Recognition, the Oath and the Anointing, and the robing ceremony, came the Crowning in the Coronation Chair, St Edward's Chair. The peers now wore their coronets.

The Lord Chamberlain then brought the Sword of Offering, sheathed, from the traverse of St Edward's Chapel to the peer, who carried the Sword of State. The swords were exchanged and the Lord Chamberlain took the Sword of State back to St Edward's Chapel.

The Sword of Offering (previously described as being 'in a scabbard of purple velvet') was then delivered to the Archbishop of Canterbury, who laid it on the altar. The Archbishop, after blessing it, delivered it to the Queen with appropriate injunctions about its use. She took it, and after a prayer, moved to the altar and returned it to the Archbishop, who placed it upon the altar, whence it was redeemed for 100 new shillings – a fee already established in the Middle Ages – by the peer who carried the Sword of State. He then drew it and carried it in place of the latter, unsheathed, for the remainder of the proceedings. When the sovereign was a king, the sword was taken from the altar and girt about him. The king then ungirded it and offered it at the altar again – the last to do this was George IV. Since then it has only been 'offered' and returned to the altar in the 'purple covering', until George VI who received it uncovered, as did Elizabeth II.

At the end of the Crowning, the Sword of Offering was brought back before the Queen, followed by the three coronation swords. They then preceded her to the throne and stood in line at the side. At the end of the ceremony, the Sword of Offering and the three coronation swords preceded the Queen to St Edward's Chapel, where she was re-robed again. Then the procession reformed with the coronation swords abreast and the Sword of Offering (now the Sword of State) preceding the Queen, until she left the abbey and boarded the Gold State Coach.

The State Opening of Parliament

The use of the Sword of State now is normally confined to the annual State Opening of Parliament by the monarch, where it has, since the disappearance of an older sword, been carried regularly before the monarch, historically by the Gentleman Usher of the Sword of State, usually a retired very senior military officer, but since 1998 by an ex-Armed Forces peer of the realm in scarlet robe with broad ermine collar. In 1998, the peer wore white gloves, but sadly no longer. However, the Gentleman Usher still follows tradition.

The royal cap of maintenance is borne before the sovereign on a wand (cushion) by a peer of the realm alongside the Sword of State on only very special occasions such as the State Opening of Parliament.

The State Opening of Parliament – the arrival of the regalia (Photo by Ian Jones)

The State Opening of Parliament – awaiting the Queen's speech (Photo by Ian Jones)

The State Opening of Parliament – guarding the sovereign; with the cap of maintenance
(Ben Stansall/WPA Pool/Getty Images, Inc.)

MUNICIPAL SWORDS
OF STATE AND
CIVIC SWORDS

Obtained as Royal Gift or by Royal Charter

The purpose of this preamble is to make clear something that has generally been forgotten, namely that the ritual carrying of a sword before a magnate (as opposed to a monarch) was originally profoundly symbolic, and that one of the things it symbolised was real and actual power. It was undoubtedly for this reason that the privilege of having such a sword – eventually called a bearing-sword in English – was granted only very sparingly to minor dignitaries during the Middle Ages. A detailed investigation of the extent of the practice on the Continent has not been carried out, but Lord Twining believed that such swords were used there almost exclusively by territorial magnates.[8] The content of this chapter is based primarily on the introduction to *J&H*,[1] but includes extracts from the introduction of Blair's *Dublin Civic Swords.*[4]

In medieval Britain – or at least those parts ruled by the English Crown – there can be no doubt that an official bearing-sword was something that was only permitted to magnates with quasi-supreme jurisdiction within their own particular lordships: obvious examples are the earls of Chester and dukes of Lancaster as rulers of their respective palatine counties.

Despite the fact, as has already been shown, that the sword was a very ancient emblem of municipal authority, the use of it as such in England originated, like that of the mace, independently of any Roman or later foreign influence; there being no record of a Sword of State in any English city or town before the reign of Edward III.

Although it cannot be shown that the mayors of any of our cities and towns were invested with so extensive an authority, the exercise of criminal jurisdiction certainly pertained to them. By the latter half of the fourteenth century, when Swords of State were first allowed to be borne before certain mayors as a special privilege, it may be that the original meaning of the sword had become modified.

In many cases the mayor was also the chief magistrate and presided over the 'bench', whether it was sitting in its judicial or administrative capacity. In some cases he was also a judge of the Courts of Record, of the Assize, of the Quarter Sessions and of Grand Gaol Delivery. His jurisdiction extended over the whole area of the borough and of the county of the town, and the liberties and precincts thereof. Those mayors who were not the chief magistrate were sometimes ordered to have the sword borne behind rather than in front of them.

It is not known for certain when or where the first British mayor started to use an official bearing-sword, since a formal grant does not always seem to have been needed, and the earliest evidence for the existence of mayoral swords predates the earliest known grants. There can be little doubt, however, on the basis of negative evidence, that it was not before the fourteenth century.

A number of towns – Bristol, Norwich, Kingston upon Hull and Gloucester – were granted swords in charters that gave them the status of being a county, and it appears that all medieval towns with county status had swords. But if it was a reason for granting the honour, it cannot have been the only one, since some towns with mayoral swords received them long before they became counties, while others never received the status at all. It is not known what qualifications a town or city had to have before it could acquire a sword, nor why it was that some places received a formal written grant and others only a verbal one. In all, only thirty-nine towns and cities received a sword as a result of a royal charter or royal gift. Today only three, Calais, Oxford and Salisbury, no longer have a sword. However, the other thirty-six, including one in Scotland, one in Wales, one in Northern Ireland and seven in Ireland, each possess at least one sword.

The one obvious thing that many of the towns and cities granted the honour in the fourteenth and fifteenth centuries have in common is that they are all places of great strategic or commercial importance, or both. It seems likely, therefore, that this was the main reason for conferring swords on them, namely to do them honour and strengthen their loyalty to the Crown because they were important. Such a view seems to be supported by the four definitive pieces of evidence in the cases of Newcastle upon Tyne, Dublin, Drogheda and Exeter.

The privilege of having a sword carried before the mayor was very sparingly granted at first, and during the fourteenth century only eight cities and towns received it or are assumed to have received it. That the mayor of London was the first to whom this privilege was granted there can be little doubt, but when or how is not recorded. Indeed, it is only by chance that we know he had a sword at all before the fifteenth century. It was never embodied in a formal document, nor has it ever been confirmed in any charter to the city.

However, in the charter to Coventry in 1387 are the words 'that the mayor of the town may have a man carrying a sword with golden adornment and decoration in his presence in the manner of London'. This is the first recorded mention of a sword-bearer; the first mention of a sword-bearer to the lord mayor of London is eight years later in 1395.

This and other references of a similar kind in later grants of mayoral swords would seem to support the view that the London one was the prototype for all the others.

Amongst the four swords belonging to Bristol, there is still in use a Sword of State – now used as a mourning-sword – of the fourteenth century with the arms of Edward III. The privilege of having it borne before him is believed to have been conferred upon the mayor when the important charter of Edward III in 1373 was granted, giving the city county status, which might have been thought reason for the mayor to have this special honour. The charter itself contains no reference to a sword; however, it appoints the mayor as the king's escheator, which conferred the right to have a sword borne before him.

In 1384, Richard II ordered that the mayor of Coventry have the sword borne behind him 'because he did not do justice', so the privilege must have been initially granted before this. In 1387, the city recovered the privilege of having a sword-bearer carrying before the mayor 'in the manner of London'.

It is recorded that Richard II gave a sword to Lincoln during a visit in 1386. The oldest of the Lincoln swords is certainly as old as the Bristol sword, given it too bears the first arms of Edward III.

Richard II is said to have given a sword from his side to York in 1388. A sword-bearer was first appointed in 1388–89. In the charter dated 1396, the king confirmed to the mayor and his successors the right to have carried before them 'their sword, given by Us'.

The 1391 letters patent from Richard II to Newcastle simply empowers the mayor and his successors to have a sword borne before them, but state specifically that he gave it 'in consideration of the honour of the town'. The king also presented a sword.

At the request of Thomas Mowbray, Earl Marshal and Captain of Calais, in 1392, Richard II granted the right to bear a sword to the town of Calais, then still an English possession. He also gave a sword. The licence granted was vague, but it contains some interesting information as to how the sword should be carried:

> The King, to all those to whom the present letters shall come, Greetings. Know ye
> that of our especial grace and on the supplication of our beloved and faithful blood
> relative, Thomas Mowbray of Nottingham, Earl Marshal and Captain of Calais, we
> have granted to the current Mayor of the said town of our, Calais, and to those
> who shall be our mayors in the same place according to future circumstances, that
> they, for the honour of our said town, may have, carried in their presence, a certain
> sword, with its point upwards. Likewise, that the point of the aforesaid sword, in
> our presence and that of our uncles, and also of the captain of the said town, or
> of anyone holding his place during his absence, shall always be borne downwards.

And in confirmation of our said concession, we have given a sword to the current mayor of our aforementioned town. In testimony of which matter we have caused these letters of ours to become patent. With the King as witness at Westminster on the twenty-second day of March.

No record of any sword exists today and it is not mentioned further.

In Chester, the sword is recorded to have been a gift of Richard II himself in 1394. A charter of confirmation was granted by Henry VII in 1506, following upon the gift of a sword previously. It was couched in the same terms as York.

During the fifteenth century, the privilege was extended to a further ten towns and cities. In 1403, Henry IV granted a charter to Dublin.

A charter from Henry IV in 1404 made Norwich a county and granted the privilege of bearing a sword before the mayor. He also gave a sword. It was couched in the same terms as those of York and Chester.

The charters just quoted do not specify any limitations as to the place where the mayor might have his sword carried, but the charter granted by Henry VI to Kingston upon Hull in 1440 granted county status and the privilege to have a sword borne before the mayor, but restricts the privilege to the town and liberty and precinct of the same. The sword could be borne erect 'out of the presence of the king and his heirs'.

Oxford had a mayoral sword before 1446 – known only from an oblique reference in a King's Lynn document of August 1446. No sword is in existence today and it is not mentioned further.

King's Lynn certainly had a sword in the fifteenth century, and accounts indicate that Henry VI personally granted the privilege in 1446, but no record exists. A charter by Henry VIII in 1524 returned to Lynn the right of the mayor to have a sword borne before him, but there is no record of why the privilege had been lost.

In 1461, Waterford was to have 'a sword as in Bristol' in a charter from Edward IV.

Drogheda, just north of Dublin, was granted the privilege in 1468 by the Irish Parliament for services to the English Crown, confirmed by letters patent in July 1468 and *inspeximus* of Edward IV of February 1470.

According to a mayor's inventory in October 1475, Hereford certainly had a sword, and it is believed that Henry VIII presented a sword during a visit in 1528, but there is no grant or charter to support either of these acquisitions.

The language of the Gloucester charter from Richard III in 1483 shows that the bearing of a sword had become a recognised practise, for the mayor might have his sword borne before him within the town and its liberties 'in the manner and form which prevails in other cities and towns within our kingdom of England'. It also awarded county status to the city.

There is evidence that a sword was given to Exeter by Henry VII in 1497. According to the sixteenth-century account of the circumstances, this was 'to encourage the mayor and citisens to be myndefull of their duties and to continue dutyfull and obedient sub-gects hensforth as tofore they had donne'. It is claimed that another sword was given by Edward IV in 1469.

In the sixteenth century, only three new grants were made. The first, by Henry VIII in 1546, empowered the mayor of Carmarthen to appoint a sword-bearer to carry a sword before him, the only town or city in Wales ever to receive the honour. The second was a charter from Elizabeth I granting a like privilege to the mayor of Thetford in 1573, and the third in 1575 when it was the turn of Limerick to be granted the privilege of having a sword and a sword-bearer by Elizabeth I.

During the seventeenth century, seventeen more towns were empowered to have a sword borne before the mayor. Clonmel and Canterbury received royal charters in 1608, Kilkenny and Edinburgh in 1609 – the latter the only town or city in Scotland to be so honoured – Galway in 1610, Londonderry in 1613 – the only city in what is now Northern Ireland to have the privilege – and Worcester in 1622.

In the charter to Kendal in 1636, the sword is called 'the sword of us and our heirs'. The city of Carlisle had purchased a sword in London in 1535–36 – in anticipation of a grant by royal charter, which was not granted until 1637, a complete century later. In it, the sword is called the sword 'of us and our heirs' and was described in the municipal accounts as 'a sword of honour for ye citie'.

Importantly, Charles I's charter of 1638 to Shrewsbury confers a sword on the mayor in order 'that the said town may shine and be encreased, as well in honour and dignity as privileges and authority, and that the wicked beholding the ensign of justice may be withholden from the lust of sinning'. This last quotation probably sums up what the significance of a municipal Sword of State had always been.

Special mention must be made of Salisbury. In a 1656 charter from Oliver Cromwell, Salisbury was granted the right to bear a sword before the mayor. It was expressly granted that the sword-bearer should bear the sword, and 'wear a Cap of Mayntenance before the Maior of sd Citie for the tyme being'. The charter cost £124 3s 6d, the sword cost £10, the embroidery on the scabbard £2 and the cap of maintenance £7. In June 1659, the charter was declared null and void, and on 14 June 1660, the council decreed that the sword and cap be brought to the council house to be sold. The sword was actually destroyed – by smashing it on the whipping post – and the cap burnt as republican baubles. These are not mentioned further.

After the Restoration, the practice continued with Wigan being granted a charter in 1662, that stipulated that the sword shall be 'inscribed or adorned with our arms and those of our heirs and successors'.

The Hertford charter of 1680 restricts the use to 'everywhere within the borough aforesaid the liberties, bounds and precincts thereof'.

It is believed that the right for the mayor of Bury St Edmunds to bear a sword was included in a Charles II charter of July 1684. Certainly a sword was given by an individual to the corporation in October 1684. However, the charter was recalled in 1687. Thus no record exists.

The sword at Great Yarmouth, adopted as a result of a charter in 1684, is called 'a sword of justice'.

Lichfield was given the privilege in 1686 and Liverpool in 1695.

Thereafter the rarely given privilege ceased for over 200 years, until, in the twentieth century, Durham was so honoured by George V in 1913 as a result of a Prayer to the King.

A municipal Sword of State, then, when legitimately assumed, was a mark of honour and a symbol of justice, but it also had one other symbolic significance that overrode the others. Several cities, are recorded as referring to their sword, or one of them, as 'The King's Sword' or, in the case of London, 'His (Her) Majesty's Sword', and many of these weapons bear the royal arms.

All this points strongly to an underlying assumption that a mayoral sword is an incarnation of the royal Sword of State, held on behalf of the monarch by the mayor for the time being as a visible symbol of the fact that he represents and acts for him or her in everything to do with the governance of, and administration of justice in, his town. The personal nature of this relationship, at least at the beginning, is underlined by the fact that many of the swords are recorded, either in the original grants or by tradition, as personal gifts of the monarch concerned.

In all, just thirty-nine towns and cities received a sword as a result of a royal charter or royal gift. Today only twenty-nine towns and cities in Great Britain still possess a sword(s), as do seven in Ireland: Dublin, Waterford, Drogheda, Limerick, Clonmel, Kilkenny and Galway. The other three cities of Calais, Oxford and Salisbury no longer have a sword.

Limitations of Use, Jealousies and Insecurities

The obscurity that surrounds the extension of the privilege of a Sword of State to a city or town is not lightened by an examination of the royal charters granting it.

We have already seen that in 1384 the mayor of Coventry was ordered to have his sword borne behind him instead of in the usual way. It is interesting to find that a similar punishment was inflicted only the year before upon Henry le Dispenser, Bishop of Norwich, who appears to have had a sword carried before him in right of his lordship of Lynn. The bishop was impeached before Parliament in 1383, and one of the articles of the sentence passed upon him was: 'And the King commands you that from this time henceforth you do not have the sword carried, or allowed to be carried in front of you as it has been done, on pain of the appropriate penalty.'

This matter of the Bishop of Norwich's sword explains certain somewhat obscure passages in the Lynn records concerning the mayor's sword in 1446. It was the custom in Lynn for the sword to be carried behind the mayor, 'contrary to ye custom of London, Oxford and other good Towns of ye Kingdom of England'. Taking advantage probably of the election of a new bishop, the townsfolk (as they did with respect to the mace) obtained the king's leave for the sword to be carried before the mayor with the point erect. An entry in the Hall Book dated 5 August 1446 reads: 'Ordered ye same day yt ye Sworde of ye Mayor shall be carried before him point upwards or erect, as our Lord ye King granted to ye Mayor, ye last time he was in ye town.' To this, the Bishop of Norwich, who was lord of the borough and the town, strongly objected, and there are several items in the Chamberlain's Accounts of 1446 and 1448 about a writ of Privy seal concerning to this matter. The mayor was summoned to London with the sword and four men to argue the town's case. The council lost its appeal and the king annulled his previous permission on 8 November 1446, with 'And howbeit that we were enclyned to youre desire in this behalf, yit is not, nother is not oure entent, to prejudice any ptie and namely ye Chirche, for by oure oth made at oure coronation, we be bounde to supporte and mainteyne ye Chirche, and ye right thereof'. It is thus beyond doubt that the king did give his permission for a sword to be borne before the mayor during his visit. It was not until 1524, a few years before the temporalities of the Bishop of Norwich became vested in the Crown, that leave was given to the mayor by Henry VIII, by charter, to have a sheathed sword borne before him by a sword-bearer.

As in the case of the maces, the authority of the charters for the sword to be carried, i.e. with the point upwards everywhere within the town and its liberties and precincts, has usually been considered to include the right to carry it into church before the mayor when he attended divine service.

At Chester, 'in 1606, in the month of January, the sword being carried before the mayor through the minster church, it was put down by one of the prebends, which was the cause of some controversy, but the same was presently appeased by the bishop'. It was probably with reference to this matter that an award was made the following year over a dispute between the mayor and citizens on the one part, and the dean and chapter of Chester on the other part, touching the right of the former to enter the cathedral church by the great west door, and of the mayor to have the sword properly borne before him. The terms of the award were that the mayor and citizens were to be at liberty to pass and re-pass through the great west door at funerals, and as often as the mayor repaired to the cathedral church to hear divine service or sermons, or upon any just occasion, he was at liberty to have the sword of the city borne before him with the point upwards.

In 1608, the Lord Sheffield, lord president of the north, demanded, as the king's lieutenant, that the city sword should be delivered up to him on his entrance into the City of York and not carried erect 'with the point upwards but abased at all times and in all places in his presence!'. This the lord mayor and commonality refused to do, pleading the right conferred by the charter of Richard II. The case was tried in the Earl Marshal's court and decided in favour of the city.

In 1617, when James I visited York, the Lord Chamberlain asked to carry the king's sword before the king. The Lord Clifford, then Earl of Cumberland, refused, saying that his ancestors had always carried the city sword within the city. The Lord Sheffield suggested that he should carry the king's sword. The king ruled that the Earl of Cumberland should carry the king's sword up to the gates of the city and then should take the city's sword.

The Shrewsbury charter (1638) also directed that the sword be borne sheathed. However, it expressly stipulates that the sword 'is not to be borne erect in any church or chapel consecrated to the worship of God', a restriction due perhaps to the king's views on ecclesiastical matters.

In 1639, due to the absence of the Lord Clifford, the sword of the City of York was carried by the Earl Marshal while the lord mayor bore the mace. Afterwards, the sword was borne by a variety of lords until the Lord Clifford returned and then bore the sword in the absence of his father, the Earl of Cumberland, who was infirm. On the death of the fifth Earl of Cumberland in 1643, the barony of Clifford devolved upon his only daughter and became in abeyance: at which time, we may presume, the singular privilege described also passed away.

On 20 September 1644, during the siege of Chester, the outworks on the eastern side were stormed by the parliamentary army, and part of the city, including the Bars where the mayor resided, fell into the enemy's hands. The city sword and mace were at the time in the mayor's keeping, and thus became part of the spoil; and, says Thomas Hughes, writing in 1872, were 'transmitted as honoured trophies to the Parliament at London'. In 1647, the city having fallen, after a long and heroic defence, into the hands of the Roundheads, a warm partisan of theirs, Colonel and Citizen Edwards, was intruded without election into the mayor's chair. When order was thus temporarily restored, the captured mace and sword, after three years' forced sojourn in London, were sent back to the city.

It has been noted with regard to the maces that they were in no wise laid up during the Commonwealth (1649–59), and the same holds good as to the swords and other emblems of civic insignia.

In Exeter, the old difficulty between the civic officers and the dignitaries of the cathedral church with respect to maces, which was decided in 1447, came to the front in a new form with regard to the sword two-and-a-half centuries later. In 1708, after much contention, it was decided that if divine service had commenced before the mayor reached the cathedral church, the royal sword should be drooped, and the hat of maintenance removed from the wearer's head at the entrance to the choir, but that otherwise the sword should be borne erect and the hat worn before the mayor on entering and leaving the choir, as had for some time past been customary; and that convenient places be appointed and made for placing the sword and hat before or near the right side of the mayor or his successors during divine service.

In Edinburgh, at a meeting of the Council of High Constables on 16 November 1843, the council resolved: 'That in future they discontinue their official attendance at church, and hereby prohibit and discharge their officers from carrying the mace or other insignia to any place of worship in time to come.' An action was raised in the Court of Session in 1843 by a minority of the town council to establish the right of having the mace and sword borne before the town council when officially attending divine service. Interim interdict was granted at the instance of the minority, and the mace and sword are still borne before the lord provost and magistrates when officially attending divine service.[9]

Sword Numbers

Today the number of municipal bearing Swords of State and civic swords in England, Scotland, Wales and Ireland is seventy-three, and they are distributed amongst forty-eight cities and towns.

London has six swords, while Bristol and Lincoln have four each. Exeter has four swords, but only two are bearing-swords. There are two each at York, Newcastle, Dublin, Waterford, Hereford, Gloucester, Worcester, Shrewsbury and Durham. Coventry also has two, though one of these is in a Scottish museum. Norwich, Kingston upon Hull and Liverpool each has two, but only one of each is a bearing-sword. Lichfield has two swords, but one was specifically made for display purposes only. The other towns and cities have but one sword each.

In the twelve cities and towns that have more than one bearing-sword, seven – London, Bristol, Lincoln, Hereford, Gloucester, Exeter and Worcester – have a sword specifically called the 'mourning sword' that is used only on occasions of mourning or great public solemnity.

In days long gone by, where a town only had one sword it was adapted for use on various occasions by the simple plan of furnishing it with more than one scabbard, the spare ones being kept on wooden dummy blades called 'forms' when not in use. At Kingston upon Hull, for example, the sword had three such scabbards: one of cloth-of-gold for state occasion, a second of blue velvet for ordinary use and a third of black velvet for mourning. At London and Bristol, where a number of swords have been preserved, special swords are assigned to particular purposes.

Swords of Note

The Bristol mourning and pearl swords and Swords of State of Dublin and Lincoln are the only fourteenth-century swords now remaining, but from the fifteenth century fifteen Swords of State have been preserved. In their main lines they follow those of actual swords of the period, but the cross-guards and pommels are more or less elaborately wrought or covered with silver-gilt. The hilt of Kingston upon Hull's Sword of State, made in 1440, is an excellent example. The hilt of the Newcastle Sword of State, made in about 1460, shows the ornamentation of a similar sword on a larger scale. Five other good fifteenth-century swords are the Lent sword at Bristol, the Sigismund sword at York and the Swords of State at Coventry, Chester and King's Lynn.

Of the sixteenth-century swords, only thirteen remain, though three – one at Southampton and two at Worcester – are poor examples. The most magnificent of the others is that of Scotland. One fine example is the splendid pearl sword of the City of London. Three other good examples are the Old Bailey sword at London, the Sword of State at Waterford and Sir Martin Bowes's sword at York.

Excluding the three coronation swords, the remaining ten bearing-swords from the first half of the seventeenth century call for no special remark, but the Swords of State at Canterbury, Edinburgh and Gloucester are good examples of their kind. In the second half of the century, there are seventeen bearing-swords. The Swords of State at Shrewsbury and London and the civic sword at Appleby are of very similar pattern. A further five, at Hereford, Thetford, Carmarthen, Bury St Edmunds and Great Yarmouth, were all made to the same pattern. They vary in date from 1669 to 1670, in which year the first was bought, to 1684, the date of purchase of the last sword. The pommel of the Norwich Sword of State is similar to this last group. Although of this same period, the great Sword of State and the Hertford sword are not of this pattern.

Of the six eighteenth-century bearing-swords, only one calls for remark. The Bristol Sword of State (1752) is an inelegant but grandiose giant of a sword with a blade almost twice as wide as any other mentioned. The sword alone weighs more than any other sword and its scabbard combined, while the scabbard is heavier than all but two of these combined weights.

Of the eight of the nineteenth century, the Sword of Offering has been described as 'the most beautiful of swords'. There are six bearing-swords from the twentieth century and just one from the twenty-first century.

Carriage

An ancient writer on armoury wrote:

> [T]he sword is needful to be borne before head officers of the borough or other corporate towns to represent the state and princely office of the king's most excellent majesty, the chief governor. The bearer must carry it upright, the hilts being holden under his bulk, and the blade directly up the middle of his breast and so forth between the sword-bearer's brows: and this is the distinction from bearing the sword for a duke, or an earl, or a baron.

The York and Norwich charters of 1386 and 1403–04 respectively allow the sword to be carried with the point erect in the presence of everyone save the king and his heirs, and while the Carmarthen charter (1546) empowers the election of a sword-bearer to carry a sword before the mayor 'in manner as is accustomed to be done in our City of London', the 1608 charter to Canterbury directed that the sword be borne sheathed.

Randle Holme, writing about Swords of Estate in the seventeenth century, said 'but all Officers of Corporate Cities, and Towns; which have the Honor of a Sword, have the point of it borne up right, as the Charter of those places have, and still do allow of it'.

As has been shown in the preceding paragraphs, all swords should be carried in this manner, i.e. sheathed and upright in two hands on the grip, with the quillons or cross-guard at breast height.

When any sword is laid against the shoulder, this is in the 'at ease' position. When 'at attention' or when on the move, the sword should be carried erect. To bear it in the 'at ease' position dishonours the person before whom it is borne. This fact is very obvious in that the swords borne before the sovereign and the lord mayors of all the cities so entitled are all carried erect.

From the evidence above, it is obvious that any other method of carriage for a bearing-sword is incorrect and that such practice should be discontinued, irrespective of how long it has occurred.

Photographs of the Kingston upon Hull sword-bearer in 1901 show him carrying the sword in the 'at ease' position. Apparently this unusual and rather inconvenient and incorrect position was adopted for a number of years until the correct form of carrying it erect was reintroduced in about 1935. Today just two towns with bearing-swords do not conform. They are Carlisle and Bury St Edmunds. Both have been requested to reconsider the manner in which they carry their swords, as did Kingston upon Hull many years ago.

Most of the charters specifically direct the city or town 'to bear before the mayor of the city one sword or blade covered everywhere within the city', and this is still the usual practice. However, it is the custom in Carmarthen, Great Yarmouth and Bury St Edmunds that, whenever war is declared between England and any other power, the sword is carried unsheathed until peace is declared.

The Sword-Bearer's Oath

Following the 1715 Jacobite rebellion, a number of oaths were introduced in 1723 requiring those holding public office to swear an oath. The principal oaths were of allegiance to the sovereign, the supremacy of the English church and the abjuration of the Catholic faith. All the oaths were based on the requirement to be loyal to the British sovereign and his successors.

One oath dating from that time is that of the City of Worcester sword-bearer, who is required to confirm:

You will be good and true to our Sovereign, to his or her heirs and successors, Kings and Queens of Great Britain and to the mayor of the City of Worcester for the time being. Upon him you shall give diligent attendance and all other things which belong to the Worships of the said city and appertaining to the office of sword-bearer of the said city, you duly do and execute during such time as you shall continue in the office of sword-bearer. So help you God.

The City of Bristol Sword-Bearer

Surrender of the Sword

There has never been a laid-down procedure for the surrender of the sword to the sovereign. Over the years, this has led to a lack of consistency as there are few towns and cities with swords and the frequency of visits to them is extremely limited. It would seem sensible that as the sovereign visits the City of London more often the any other, the procedure followed there[11, 12] should be the one to be followed elsewhere. Due to this lack of consistency there have been occasions when the sword has not been presented at all.

The authority of the mayor in his own domain was supreme, subject only to the sovereign. The sword and the mace form part of the mayor's insignia, and this is indicative that the mayor's authority was derived from, and subject only to, the sovereign.

In specific towns and cities, the privilege to have a sword borne before the mayor was granted upon the express condition of the sovereign that it should be carried with the point erect, except in the presence of the sovereign and, in some cases in times past, the sovereign's close relatives. In most early cases, this privilege was often accompanied by the gift of a sword by the sovereign. The ritual, which can be traced back to the time of Richard II, is also performed by the mayors of other cities when they are visited by the sovereign.

The evidence of early custom is conclusive in that the practice everywhere was for the mayor to surrender the sword on the approach of the sovereign. Historically, the sword was surrendered on the entry of the sovereign and only returned on the departure of the sovereign. Many years ago, after the surrender, in the sovereign's presence, the sword was carried reversed, that is with the point downwards, if borne by an apparitor of the corporation, signifying the subjection of the city to the monarch. If, however, the mayor himself bore the sword before the sovereign, it was held erect, the mayor by this action having, for the time being, surrendered his prerogative and placed himself in the position of apparitor to the Crown. The sword was only borne erect again after the return from the sovereign.

In other towns and cities a similar routine is followed. On the arrival of the sovereign at the appointed place in the town, the sword, like the mace, is to be reversed, i.e. carried point down (see picture of the sword-bearers of York with sword reversed on page 158). The mayor surrenders the token of his/her power whether that token be a sword or mace, or both to the sovereign. This is now usually done by the sword-bearer, by offering the sword hilt-first or sword-sideways to the sovereign – the tip is never pointed at the sovereign.

If the sovereign is satisfied that the mayor can be entrusted with authority in the royal presence, then the sovereign indicates confidence in the mayor by touching the hilt and thereby returning the sword for the mayor to bear; but obeisance had been rendered and the carrying of the sword or mace in the sovereign's presence is only with the sovereign's permission.

The City of York Sword-Bearer surrenders the Sword of State (Photo by *The Press*, York)

The Sovereign accepts the surrender of the sword (Photo by *The Press*, York)

However in London, the lord mayor does, on occasion, continue to bear the sword before the sovereign. At the service in St Paul's Cathedral to celebrate the 90th birthday of Queen Elizabeth II, the lord mayor bore the sword himself, in the upright position, before the sovereign as she entered and left the cathedral.

In later years there came to be scarcely a pause between surrender and return. Today, the sovereign simply touches the sword or hilt; the surrender is merely notional and the ceremony symbolic. Following the symbolic return, the sword is then carried erect and the mace is similarly raised again.

When the reigning sovereign pays a state visit to the City of London, the lord mayor meets the royal party at the boundary with Westminster, the site of the old Temple Bar. All members of the civic party pay appropriate compliments and the sword and mace are reversed. The sword-bearer then hands the sword to the lord mayor, who approaches the royal coach or car and offers to relinquish the mayoral sword to the sovereign, an offer that is always refused.

The hilt is presented, through the open door of the coach or car, to the sovereign, who touches the hilt, signifying acceptance. Upon the return of the sword by the sovereign, the lord mayor returns the sword to the sword-bearer and both sword and mace are raised to the normal position.

When the lord mayor of London goes into a royal law court or into the precinct of a royal palace, where the monarch is symbolically present, his or her sword is borne point downwards.

Sword and Scabbard Decoration

Since the Sword of State is symbolical of certain jurisdiction derived from the Crown, it ought, like the mace, to bear the royal arms in all cases where the sword is a royal gift or held by royal charter.

To place the royal arms or a royal cipher on a civic sword given to, or bought by, towns such as Appleby, Warrington and Ipswich, which have no right to have a Sword of State, was simply, according to *J&H*, 'an impudent assumption of authority', but at least the gift to Appleby was made when charters were still being granted. In all other cases where civic swords have been gifted to towns and cities, the royal arms have been very properly omitted.

The swords which were in use in 1649 and bore the royal arms and badges fell under the ban of the Commonwealth, and at London, Gloucester and other places they were 'altered', i.e. stripped of all symbols of royalty and the 'State's arms' substituted. At the Restoration, the royal emblems were, of course, replaced. In the case of the Gloucester sword, as will be seen in the description of it in the sixth chapter, we are able to note exactly what these alterations were.

Swords of State, being for show and not for use, are more of the nature of 'property swords' than real weapons, with hilts elaborately wrought in silver-gilt, and scabbards covered with velvet and adorned with chapes and lockets, also of silver-gilt. Bristol and Lincoln, however, possess splendid specimens of actual fourteenth-century fighting swords, and one of the swords at York is also a veritable weapon, being the sword that was hung in St George's Chapel, Windsor, over the stall of the Emperor Sigismund on his election as a Knight of the Garter in 1416. The sword given by Richard II to the mayor of York in 1388, now missing, was probably a fighting sword.

The majority of the existing Swords of State (excluding mourning swords) have their scabbards covered with crimson or red velvet. However, in five cases – Lincoln (Charles I), Carlisle, Liverpool (Sword of State), Derby and Durham (Sword of State) – the scabbard is purple. The Swords of State of Kingston upon Hull and Shrewsbury have blue scabbards. The scabbards of the Bristol Lent and Kendal swords are, unusually, black.

Of the seven mourning swords, five have scabbards covered with black velvet. However, the decoration on these scabbards varies enormously – London's is plain but not actually black, with black mounts, while Bristol's is decorated with many silver-gilt mounts. Lincoln's is heavily embroidered and Hereford's has a silver-gilt chape but the remainder of the decoration is of gold lace. Gloucester has an old embroidered black velvet scabbard, probably a second scabbard for the Sword of State, and a new scabbard with silver-gilt mounts on the mourning sword. Exeter's scabbard is of plain black crepe with no mounts, and the Worcester mourning sword has no scabbard at all.

Seven of these bearing-sword scabbards are covered in leather. The Canterbury Vision sword and that at Southampton are brown, at Manx and Bath they are black, at Winchester it is red, at Leeds it is blue and at Stratford upon Avon it is a deep tan.

In a few cases the sheath is covered with embroidery, as at Exeter and Lincoln, which is (or has been) further enriched with pearls at London and Bristol. The two last-named cities furnish examples of swords with inscriptions on the scabbards as part of the decoration. The scabbard of the Sigismund sword at York was originally embroidered with red silk scorpions, which were afterwards replaced in 1586 by the splendid silver-gilt 'pendragons' that now ornament it. Another York sword, the lost one given by Richard II, had its scabbard adorned with silver-gilt scallop shells.

The scabbard of the Sword of Offering is covered in over 3,000 precious stones, including diamonds, sapphires, rubies, emeralds and turquoises.

The Virtues and Other Symbols

Most of the scabbards are decorated with lockets and chapes of silver-gilt, embossed or engraved with various devices. Some are simply for identification. For others, the embellishments were and are much more detailed. Decorations have included coats of arms, engravings, effigies of kings and mythical icons. Many have depicted religious symbols. The most frequent are the royal arms, the emblems of England, Scotland, Wales and Ireland, the crest or arms of the city or town and figures of semi-clad females or 'personifications'. Others have been merely decoration in the form of leaves and flowers. Many have gold lace along each edge or down one face. One scabbard in the royal collection is covered in precious stones.

Nearly all Swords of State bear a representation of the royal arms pertinent to the period when the sword was made, though in some cases there is a second, later set of arms. These later arms appear to have been added when the sword or scabbard was being refurbished and bear the arms of that period. However, there are a number of instances where the arms applied are not those officially in use by the sovereign at the time of acquisition. In most cases where this occurs, the arms appear to predate the date of acquisition of the sword and probably indicated the period when the sword was manufactured.

For example, the royal arms of Edward III, used from 1340 to 1367, appear on the Bristol mourning sword, which is said to have been acquired in 1373. This appears to indicate that the sword was made at least six years earlier and only acquired by the city in 1373. Similarly, Lincoln is said to have received a sword from Richard II in 1386, but this too bears the royal arms of Edward III. It would seem unlikely that the engraver was not aware of the change of the sovereign's arms and so it is possible that, in this case, the sword had been manufactured at least nineteen years earlier.

Personifications

Another frequent decoration is a 'personification', in the form of a semi-naked female figure. The most common is that of Justice, one of the four Cardinal Virtues, which appears forty times, including fourteen times on a single sword and scabbard. Of the other three Cardinal Virtues, Fortitude (or Courage) appears once, Prudence (or Wisdom) twice (but in different guises) and Temperance (or Restraint) once. One scabbard, on the Bristol Lent sword, bears all four Cardinal Virtues. The three theological Virtues Faith and Hope and Charity (or Love) appear once each. Other figures include Fame (five times), Law (five times), Britannia (thrice) and Glory (once). The figures of Commerce, Peace, Philosophy, Prosperity and Trade appear once each on a single scabbard, the Bristol Sword of State, together with Justice, Faith and Charity.

Civic Swords

Apart from Durham in 1913, no further charter has been granted since that to Liverpool in 1695, but twelve swords have been presented by individuals or organisations to a number of towns and cities and are included among their insignia. There was and is, without any shadow of a doubt, no right of the mayors to have them borne before them, and thus they are not entitled to be regarded as Swords of State and are best described as civic swords.

Civic bearing-swords were presented to ten corporations: to Appleby in about 1675, Carrickfergus in 1712, Wootton Bassett in 1812, Derby in 1870, Ipswich in 1887, Warrington in 1897, Bath in 1902, Winchester in 1957, Dewsbury in 1972 and Leeds

The Virtues and
Other Symbols

Prudence & Justice   Temperance & Fortitude

Faith   Charity   Peace   Commerce

in 2003. Bearing-swords were also acquired by Stratford on Avon in around 1500, but it was not used as a civic sword until 1916, and by Southampton, sometime before 1801. Of these twelve swords, seven are processed, while Carrickfergus, Southampton and the three most recently acquired – Winchester, Dewsbury and Leeds – remain on display.

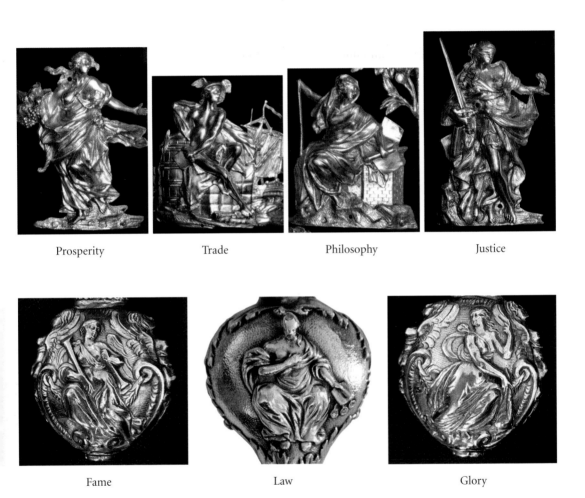

Prosperity   Trade   Philosophy   Justice

Fame   Law   Glory

CAPS OF MAINTENANCE
AND SWORD-BEARERS'
APPAREL

The Royal Cap of Maintenance

The historical parts of this chapter are taken in the main from *J&H*,[1] while the remainder is the result of a questionnaire, numerous telephone calls, observation and inspection.

The cap of maintenance was originally worn as a symbol of dignity by people of high rank, but it may have had a purely practical use to help the crown fit more firmly or to protect the head from the bare metal of the crown. The connection to the sword is obscure.

When the connection between a sword and a cap of maintenance first arose, or for what reason, has not been clearly established. That the two were intimately connected is evident from the fact that an important part of the ceremony of the investiture of a duke was girding him with a sword and the placing of a cap of maintenance on his head.

Thus the record of the creation of John of Ghent as Duke of Lancaster in 1362 states: 'And then our said Lord the King girded his said son John with a sword and put on his head a fur cap and above a circle of gold and jewels and named and made him Duke of Lancaster.' And in 1397, when Henry of Lancaster, Earl of Derby, was created Duke of Hereford, we read: 'And thereupon the King girded the said duke with a sword and put on his head a cap of the honour and dignity of a Duke.'

It was also customary for the popes, when they desired to bestow a special honour on a sovereign prince, to send him a sword and cap of maintenance, as for example in the case of Edward IV (1461–83), 'to him, our Lord Pope Sixtus, the fourth of that name, sent a sword and a cap appropriate for kingly rank'. John Anstis, writing in 1724, quoting from a manuscript in his possession, described the presentation to the king of the Pope's letter 'with a Sword and Cap of maintenance' in St George's Chapel, Windsor, on St George's day, when 'The Archbishoppe of Yorke Chancellor of Englande, redde the Lettre, and declared the effect of the same, and then girte the Sworde aboute the Kinge, and sette the Cappe on the Kinges hedde, and forthwith toke it off ageyne, and so proceded to the Procession, and the foresaid Cappe was borne one the pointe of the said Sworde by the Lorde Standley'.

Henry VII seems to have twice been the recipient of a sword and cap of maintenance, from Pope Innocent VIII in 1488 and Pope Alexander VI in 1496. In 1507, Pope Julius II gave James IV of Scotland a sword, together with a cap of maintenance. Henry VIII received a like honour from Pope Leo X in March 1514.

The sovereign's cap of maintenance is a ceremonial crimson velvet cap turned up with ermine. It is the insignia of the sovereign and is paraded directly before the sovereign during the coronation ceremony (but not for Elizabeth II) and other state occasions such as the State Opening of Parliament. Although the hereditary bearer is the Marquess of Winchester, today it is carried, upon a white wand or cushion, by a nominated peer.

A similar cap is worn inside the coronet of lords. It also survives in the velvet caps turned up with ermine that are sewn as linings to the royal crown and the coronets of princes. The coronet slips over the velvet crown of the cap and rests on the ermine band. Inside the band there are cross straps which rest on the head, so stopping the weight of the coronet from pushing the whole cap down onto the ears.

The Civic Cap of Maintenance

Concurrent with the gift of a Sword of State, where such has been bestowed by the sovereign upon a city or town, was the gift of a special head-covering, to be worn by the sword-bearer when carrying the sword, known as a cap of maintenance. So well was this understood, and so fully was it established by immemorial usage, that the charters and letters patent by which the right of having a sword so carried was conferred contain no reference to the cap.

The cap of maintenance is the official head covering of a sword-bearer and as such it is 'borne' before the mayor. Caps of maintenance and Swords of State are emblems of authority and are inseparable. So strictly is the cap an appendage to the sword that it is never worn by the sword-bearer except when he is actually carrying the sword. The cap is worn now by the sword-bearer on all occasions, even in the presence of the sovereign, and the sword-bearer does not remove the cap till he has set down the sword.

To what extent and in what way the cap of maintenance worn by a sword-bearer was identical with, or similar to, the caps conferred to kings and dukes, it is by no means easy to say. If they are identical, it is difficult to see how the wearing of a cap of such dignity could be extended to so humble a personage as a mayor's sword-bearer. If they are different, it is hard to say whence the sword-bearer's cap is derived. The question is the harder to decide since the earliest record of the grant of a cap of maintenance to a sword-bearer is as far back as 1393, when Richard II is stated (on good authority) to have conferred the privilege on the City of York.

It had probably been granted to the City of London much earlier.

In 1536, Henry VIII gave a sword and a cap of maintenance to Waterford. His letter states, 'And now at this tyme as a remembrance and evident token of our favours we have sent you by this brynger a Capp of mainteynance to be borne at tymes thought by you necessarie before you the Maior being our officer of that our said Citie and your successors officers of the same. Given under our signet at our Manor of Greenewich the last day of Aprill in the xxviiith years of our reigne. To our right trustie and welbeloved the Maior and Cominality of our Citee of Waterford in our land of Ireland'.[10] Both the sword and the cap still exist and are the oldest surviving evidence of the tradition of the sovereign providing a cap to accompany a sword.

In the fifteenth century, we find record of the making of the sword-bearer's hat at Norwich in 1406–07; the Norwich accounts referred to it as 'a hat for the office of mayor' in the same way that the sword is termed 'the sword of the Mayor'. There are records of a new hat at Kingston upon Hull in 1443–44, and of a new one at York in 1446. At King's Lynn, it is stated that Henry VI, in 1446, granted 'yt he who shall carry ye Sword of ye Mayor before him, shall have his hat upon his head agreeable to ye King's writ'.

In other places, where a cap of maintenance is or was worn by the sword-bearer, a search of the records would probably show that one was obtained (as at Norwich and Kingston upon Hull) at the same time as the sword.

Perhaps it was a gift in the same manner as that of the popes to princes and was intended for the mayor; yet in several charters specific mention is made of a cap 'for the sword-bearer'.

Winter or Summer?

In days gone by there were two distinct styles of cap; the tall brimless fur cap used in winter and the wide-brimmed low-crowned silk or velvet cap used in summer. There is no reason whatever why the use of the two caps, for summer and winter wear respectively, should not be revived.

It was the custom at London and elsewhere for the sword-bearer to have two caps, one 'of Grey ffurr for winter', the other 'of Sylk for Somer'. The silk cap, however, seems to have been superseded in 1546 by 'a very goodly and Riche hat', probably of velvet. This custom, though we have no earlier record of it than 1520 at London, was undoubtedly an ancient one, for Kingston upon Hull had two caps before 1450. There were also two caps, one of velvet, the other of fur, at Gloucester, Norwich and Coventry. At Coventry, the two caps still exist. Of the other places that still possess caps of maintenance, the fur one alone survives at London, Bristol, Gloucester and Newcastle, the velvet cap or hat at Coventry, Lincoln, York and Exeter. It is claimed that a cap at Exeter, though externally seventeenth-century, contains the black felt body of the cap of maintenance given with one of the swords by Henry VII in 1497. At Hereford, the hat was sometimes red and sometimes purple, and the sword-bearer also had another hat of black velvet.

Current Caps of Maintenance

As to the patterns of the existing caps and hats, there is much diversity. In only thirteen towns and cities does the sword-bearer now wear a cap or hat of maintenance; in London, Bristol, Coventry, Lincoln, York, Newcastle upon Tyne, Kingston upon Hull, Exeter, Gloucester, Hereford, Worcester, Hertford and Bath. At Hereford and Kingston upon Hull, its use had been discontinued, but following a comment made by Jewitt and Hope in 1895 that they 'might with perfect propriety resume their ancient and most honourable privilege', both have now reverted to wearing fur hats. Norwich, unfortunately, has since replaced the velvet hat with a top hat. It must be presumed that Chester, King's Lynn and Carmarthen would have followed this tradition, given the era in which the privilege was granted to them, but there is no evidence to support this.

The Winter Fur Cap

The fur cap is a high cylindrical and brimless hat of sable, mink or squirrel that resembles the conical hats worn by persons of quality before about 1400. Nowadays, many of these hats are made from synthetic fur. The crown can be of silk, velvet or fur. The crown is wider than the headband. The caps of London, Bristol, Coventry, Newcastle upon Tyne, Kingston upon Hull, Gloucester, Hereford, Hertford and Bath are of this style. The Bristol and Gloucester caps have rolled brims, a pattern that has been followed at Bristol since at least the reign of Edward IV. The Coventry and Newcastle upon Tyne caps have gold braid round the headband and gold braids hanging from this with tassels at the ends. The Worcester cap is of this style but is manufactured from beige felt and sports ostrich feathers.

Winter Caps of Maintenance

City of Bristol

City of Coventry – (1606) 1858

City of Newcastle upon Tyne – (1391)

City of Gloucester – 1933

The Summer Silk or Velvet Cap

The velvet caps are, properly speaking, hats, with low flat crowns and broad brims. They are of red or crimson velvet, embroidered with gold and with pendant cords and tassels. This Tudor hat is in the shape fashionable in the time of Henry VIII and is similar to that worn by the Queen's Bodyguard of the Yeomen of the Guard and by the Yeoman Warders of Her Majesty's Royal Palace and Fortress of the Tower of London since about 1485. In olden times some of these hats were made of red felt.

Nowadays, these hats are traditionally made from goss, formed from linen coated with coodle, a shellac-based paste, which is left for some five months to cure. The goss is cut into strips and ironed by hand onto the wooden block of the shape required. The body is left for a week to dry and the block removed. The hat is then trimmed and the finished hat can be steam-heated to allow a perfect fitting to the head. In the meantime, a piece of crimson velvet is elaborately embroidered, this fitted over and stitched onto the hat.

Very few of this civic type still exist and they are very precious. Waterford has the oldest cap, but it is now a museum item. Coventry, Lincoln and Exeter are the only cities to still use this style, and the latter two both have had a new hat made recently. In Coventry, the hat is now worn by the person bearing the sword on a special occasion. It has a domed crown with tassels on the top, and uniquely the brim is split above each ear. The purpose of the split is not known – it cannot be to fold the hat flat, as the crown will not allow this. It is presumed that the split is to allow the hat band to expand to fit on differing sizes of heads.

At Lincoln, the hat is worn by the sword-bearer, but a superb collection of four previous hats are kept on display. At Exeter, the old hat was in such a worn condition that many years ago it was decided to bear it on a cushion to extend its life. The previous hat is kept on display, but the current new hat is absurdly still borne before the mayor on a cushion rather than on the head of the sword-bearer for whom it is intended. However, it must be noted that at the State Opening of Parliament, the sovereign's cap of maintenance is borne on a wand beside the sword while the sovereign rightly wears the crown.

York has an old hat dating from 1580 very much in the same style as Coventry, but it is covered in very faded deep crimson velvet, ruched over the domed crown, and is no longer worn.

The specification for the Exeter hat was that it should match the original, using silk velvet and gold-plated silver sheet wrapped round the thread cores – the original cores proved impossible to match and are now synthetic. The hat block was made traditionally by Booth & Lane and the hat formed by Patey, hat makers, in the method described above. The silk velvet was embroidered by Hand & Locke, embroiderers, with gold passing and embellishments. These embroidered panels were then stitched to the hat using quilted liners to match the original. Great care was taken to match the stitching, especially the Exeter double-stitch, which is very unusual. The overall cost

Summer Caps of Maintenance

City of Waterford – 1536

City of York – 1580

City of Coventry – 1623

City of Exeter – (1497) 2010

to both Lincoln and Exeter was just over £5,000 each (against two other quotations to Exeter of £20,000 and £67,000 respectively). At Exeter, the sword-bearer and mace-bearers each wear a Tudor hat covered in black velvet but smaller than the ones described above.

A comparison of these various 'Tudor' hats is shown below, in imperial and metric measurements. The diameter of the brim and crown are measured at the widest point (front to back).

Dimensions	Yeomen Traditional	Waterford 1536	York 1580	Coventry 1623	Lincoln 2006	Exeter 2010	Exeter SB Current
Diameter of brim	13¾in	15¾in	15¾in	16in	19½in	16½in	12¾in
Diameter of crown	9¼in	9⅜in	Domed	Domed	10½in	12in	8⅜in
Height of crown	5⅛in	4½in	5½in	6in	5¾in	5¼in	4¾in
Width of brim	2¾in	3⅝in	3⅞in	4in	5½in	4in	2¾in
Weight	2lb 0oz	14oz	1lb 1¾oz	1lb 1oz	3lb 5¼oz	3lb 1oz	15oz
Diameter of brim	34.9cm	39.7cm	40 0cm	41.0cm	49.0cm	41.9cm	32.4cm
Diameter of crown	23.5cm	23.7cm	Domed	Domed	26.8cm	30.5cm	22.2cm
Height of crown	13.1cm	11.4cm	14.0cm	15.2cm	14.6cm	13.3cm	12.0cm
Width of brim	7.0cm	9.2cm	10.0cm	10.2cm	14.0cm	10.2cm	7.0cm
Weight	0.907kg	0.400kg	0.500kg	0.485kg	1.602kg	1.379kg	0.424kg

Other Forms of Headgear

Of the forty-eight cities and towns with bearing-swords, nine (Waterford, Drogheda, Limerick, Derry, Carrickfergus, Southampton, Winchester, Dewsbury and Leeds) do not process their swords and have, therefore, no sword-bearer. The remaining thirty-nine all have a sword-bearer. Thirteen, mentioned above, wear either the traditional fur or velvet hat. Four others (Clonmel, Edinburgh, Liverpool and Derby) are bare headed. Two (Stratford upon Avon and Canterbury) use local Army personnel in uniform, while one (Ipswich) uses a local military cadet in uniform. Two (Dublin and Galway) have a firefighter in uniform. Between them, the other seventeen wear six different forms of headgear, an assortment of bonnets, tri-corns, bi-corns, top hats and peaked caps. York's hat is unique.

The current hat of York has a unusual shape. It is undoubtedly a summer hat in basic style. It has a hard flat-topped crown and wide brim covered in red velvet trimmed with ermine. The sides and back are looped up, leaving a frontal peak. The previous one was presented in 1915. It was replaced by a brand new hat, which was presented by Queen Elizabeth II on Maundy Thursday in 2012.

Other Forms of Headdress

Looped brim City of York – (1915) 2012

Tudor bonnet Thetford

Tri-corn City of Shrewsbury

Bi-corn King's Lynn

The 'Tudor bonnet' or 'round' cap was first introduced as part of the uniform of the Most Noble Order of the Garter by Henry VIII, and was based on a fifteenth-century chaperon which was a circular roll round the head with a floppy crown. Nowadays, it has a stiff wide brim with a loose crown. Black velvet covers the brim and is then gathered to form the headband. The remaining material, which forms the crown of the hat, has no support and is rather floppy in appearance and falls loosely upon the brim. On some there is a tassel fitted to the centre. The caps of Thetford and Durham are of this type.

A top hat is worn by four sword-bearers (Norwich, Wigan, Bury St Edmunds and Great Yarmouth). Six wear tri-corns (Carmarthen, Shrewsbury, Appleby, Lichfield, Royal Wootton Bassett and Warrington) and two more wear bi-corns (Chester, fore and aft, and King's Lynn, side to side). Three (Kilkenny, Kendal and Carlisle) wear a military-style peaked cap. The Manx sword-bearer also wears a peaked military-style cap.

At the State Opening of Parliament, the peer bearing the Sword of State is bare headed. At a coronation the peers bearing the Sword of State and three coronation swords, although initially bare headed, later wear their coronets, which have within them a cap of maintenance similar to the sovereign's. The Keeper of the Jewel House wears a cockaded bi-corn.

Sword-Bearers' Apparel

At a coronation, the five peers bearing swords wear their ceremonial robes. The Keeper of the Jewel House wears his dress uniform.

At the State Opening of Parliament, the Sword of State is taken to Westminster by the Gentleman Usher of the Sword of State, a very senior ex-military officer wearing his military dress uniform. However, it is processed by a former armed services peer in his ceremonial robes.

It has always been considered fitting that the bearer of so important an ensign as the city sword should be distinguished from his fellow officers by a special habit.

From the sixteenth century onward, the civic sword-bearer's 'ceremonial' dress is described as being of damask, with a cap of maintenance. It may be noted that the order put forth in 1463–64 against the wearing of excessive apparel, etc, is expressly stated not to apply to 'swerdberers to Mayers'.

As with the caps, the forms of dress worn by sword-bearers vary enormously. Of the forty-eight cities and towns with bearing-swords, nine (Waterford, Drogheda, Limerick, Derry, Carrickfergus, Southampton, Winchester, Dewsbury and Leeds) have no sword-bearer. Another eight wear uniform; in Canterbury, Ipswich and Stratford upon Avon it is military, in Dublin and Galway it is a fire-fighter while in Kilkenny, Kendal and Carlisle a military-style uniform is worn. The Manx sword-bearer also wears a military-style uniform.

Fifteen sword-bearers wear a robe or gown over a dark suit. Six of these sword-bearers (Coventry, King's Lynn, Shrewsbury, Great Yarmouth, Liverpool and Durham) wear a black academic gown trimmed with gold braid embellishments. At Thetford and Appleby, it is a plain black academic gown. At Gloucester, it is a burgundy super-fine robe with a fur collar. At Exeter, a black superfine robe with a fur collar is worn. At Carmarthen, it is a deep blue superfine robe with a large collar trimmed with scarlet. In Clonmel, a light blue robe is worn. At Wigan, a long black cloak trimmed with red and with a very large collar is worn. At Hertford, a blue superfine robe trimmed with gold piping is worn. At Warrington, a dark blue robe with a collar trimmed with gold lace is worn.

A further eleven wear a frock-coat, tail-coat or morning-coat (the glossary explains the differences between these coats), however the colours and lower garments vary. In Bristol, an open black frock-coat with black waistcoat is worn over black breeches and black stockings. At Norwich, an open black frock-coat with red waistcoat is worn with black trousers. At York, Newcastle upon Tyne and Bury St Edmunds, a buttoned-up black frock-coat is worn over black trousers. At Lichfield, a buttoned-up scarlet frock-coat is worn over black breeches and black gaiters. At Wootton Bassett, an open scarlet frock-coat with scarlet waistcoat is worn over grey breeches and white stockings. In Edinburgh, a black tail-coat with black waistcoat is worn over black trousers. In Lincoln, a dark green morning-coat with red waistcoat is worn over green breeches and white stockings. At Chester, a rust-coloured morning-coat with matching waistcoat is worn over matching breeches and black stockings. At Hereford, a black morning-coat with red waistcoat is worn over black trousers.

Three sword-bearers wear a combination of a gown over a morning-coat or tail-coat. In London, the sword-bearer wears a gown of brocaded satin with black velvet facings over a black morning-coat, with Old Bailey trousers in the morning and Old Bailey breeches in the evening. At Kingston upon Hull, a black gown of brocaded satin and black velvet facings is worn over a dark blue liveried tail-coat. At Worcester, a beige morning-coat with matching waistcoat is worn over matching breeches and white stockings unfortunately a plain black academic gown is worn over this, which obscures the outfit.

The remaining two are very different. At Bath, the sword-bearer wears a green smock over black velvet breeches and black stockings. Derby really is the odd one out – the sword-bearer wears a normal dark suit!

All sword-bearers wear white cotton gloves, except in Bath, where brown leather gloves are worn.

It should be noted that several of the sword-bearers photographed have since retired from their posts.

DETAILS OF SWORDS OF STATE AND CIVIC SWORDS

Introduction

The following descriptions of the swords in the Royal Collection are based primarily on the entries in *The Sword Catalogue*.[2] The descriptions of the municipal swords are taken, by and large, from Jewitt and Hope.[1] However, since 1895 much has changed and the details in *J&H* have required considerable revision as a result of personal inspection and new inclusions, such as the Scottish and Irish swords and the Manx swords. There have been ten new swords with scabbards and four new scabbards since 1895. Two other scabbards have been re-covered. However, since 1895, one sword, two scabbards and three caps have been lost or disposed of.

In 1895, Jewitt and Hope concluded that there were forty-six swords in thirty-one cities and towns, and over the years this has been oft quoted. Today, the number of cities and towns has risen to forty-eight. Thirty-six of these hold swords by royal charter or royal gift, and twelve have bearing swords for which there is no royal authority. Three other cities, Calais, Oxford and Salisbury, were granted the right but no longer have swords.

Between them, they hold seventy-three bearing-swords. To these another fourteen bearing-swords need to be added. They are four ancient bearing-swords with royal connections, the six swords of the Royal Collection, the Sword of Scotland, the two in the Crown Dependency of the Isle of Man and the hilt of one in a museum in Scotland. This gives a grand total of eighty-seven Swords of State and civic swords. The Channel Islands is also a Crown Dependency with a Lieutenant Governor, but has no sword.

Nine non-bearing swords are included in Appendix 7; however, they have no significance except to their own towns or cities.

Age and Dating

One of the main problems uncovered is that of accurately dating the swords and scabbards. The problem of identifying the age of these swords is that frequently they have been updated or modernised. Some of the swords have been re-bladed, while others have had the hilt completely replaced. Some have had part of the hilt replaced or altered. The age of each sword has been based on the oldest identified part of it.

All swords are mentioned under the city or town to which they were first granted, not the title of the current local authority. The towns and cities that possess Swords of State are listed in order of their 'right' to have a sword. In so doing, note has been made of the date of a charter actually granting the privilege or the date of an ancient record of the sovereign giving a sword. This has not been possible in every case, but holds good for the majority. In some cases, the date is unsubstantiated but is part of the city or town's tradition.

Fortunately, all civic swords, with the exception of Appleby in about 1670, were taken into use after the practice of a royal grant had ceased with Liverpool in 1695. The royal grant to Durham over 200 years later in 1913, in answer to a prayer, was very unusual.

Several cities have more than one sword and in some cases the Sword of State is not the oldest. Where more than one sword is held, they have been listed by age – though this may now only apply to a part of the sword. There are, of course, some swords that are older than the date of the grant or of the acquisition. The inclusion of royal arms helps with dating, but cannot be relied upon.

Scabbards are poor indicators of age and are considerably more difficult to date. A large proportion of the swords have received a completely new scabbard. Others have had a new covering but have had some, but not necessarily all, of the mounts transferred from the old to the new one. For some this has occurred a number of times. For a detailed discussion on a single scabbard, see Lincoln – Additional scabbard.

Description

All swords should be carried with the 'point erect' and the descriptions of all the swords, blades and hilts, is based on the sword being held point upwards. Each description of the blade and hilt starts at the point and concludes with the pommel. The same is true of the scabbards, with the description of the mounts starting at the 'top' with the chape. The photographs are similarly portrayed.

There are a large number of swords that can be viewed in either direction as there is no definitive marking. The same is true of only eleven scabbards. However, some swords need to be physically viewed point down; likewise some scabbards have mounts which should be viewed point downwards, which means they are viewed 'upside down'.

Just to make life difficult, there are five swords that have been decorated in both directions, while eight scabbards have a later set of mounts applied in the opposite direction to the original mounts!

Some of these ceremonial swords and scabbards have no distinguishing marks to indicate whether they should be viewed point up or point down. The vast majority have been made to be viewed point up, and this is now an internationally recognised manner.

Of the eight newest swords, i.e. those made in the twentieth and twenty-first centuries, only three of the seven bearing-swords do not follow this norm. The Buller sword (1901) at Exeter is a sabre and therefore hangs down from the belt it is thus correctly viewed point down. Although Bath's civic sword (1902) is viewed point up, it is a replica of a much older sword. The Durham State Sword (1913), made by Wilkinson, is surprisingly viewed point down; similarly, the civic sword (1957) at Winchester, made by Garrard, is viewed point down. The travelling sword (1962) in London, being a copy of an older sword, is viewed point up. The sword at Dewsbury (c. 1972) is viewed point up, though this only applies to two embroidered items on the scabbard. The Vision Sword (1988) at Canterbury, made by Wilkinson, is properly viewed point up. Surprisingly, the sword at Leeds (2003), made by the Royal Armouries, is viewed point down. It seems probable that the designers of the Durham, Winchester and Leeds swords got it wrong or were unaware of the norm, and the swords' makers/assemblers just followed the design. Either way, it is disappointing.

Where possible, a standard format has been used to describe each sword and each scabbard. On some swords and scabbards, it is obvious which is the primary face, yet

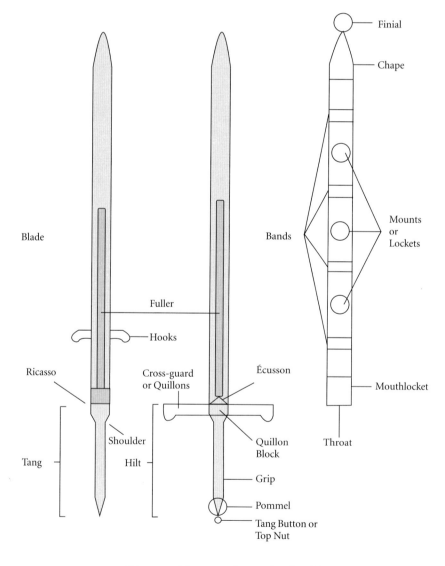

Diagram of the parts of a sword and scabbard

on many it is not possible to determine this, so the sides have been arbitrarily chosen. Each description includes 'obverse' or 'reverse', shortened to (O) and (R) in most cases.

Where it has been possible to obtain photographs of both sides of the sword, these have been shown.

Imperial measurements have been used throughout, but for younger generations and readers in countries where metric measurement is more common, these have been included.

In two cases, Southampton and Bath, the scabbard is much shorter than the blade; this is due to 'hooks' part-way up the blade.

All swords are carried sheathed, with the exception of the three coronation swords and the Manx and Bath swords. All swords are borne in the correct manner, except for Carlisle and Bury St Edmunds.

Batch of Swords

J&H wrote, 'Of the second half of the century there are a dozen swords, no fewer than eight of which are all made after the same pattern, that of the London "Sunday" sword.' They vary in date from 1669, in which year the Shrewsbury one was bought, to 1684, the date of the Yarmouth sword. The Norwich sword was of the same pattern, but has received a new cross-guard. The eight swords of this pattern are the Shrewsbury State (1669), Appleby (*c.* 1675), Hereford State (1677), Thetford (1678), Carmarthen (*c.* 1680), London State (1680), Bury St Edmunds (1684) and Great Yarmouth (1684).

They are between 4ft and 4ft 4⅝in long, and two have a blade marked with 'Ferara' of Toledo in Spain. However, it must be remembered that some blades were marked with another's mark and that the date of the blade's manufacture is not necessarily the date of the sword's assembly. The name 'Ferara' appears on the blade of a Derry sword of 1616 and on the blade of a Manx sword of 1704 or 1724.

With the aid of modern digital photography, it has been possible to compare in considerable detail the form and markings of the hilts of all eight swords, and they clearly break into two groups. The hilts of Shrewsbury (purchased in 1669), Appleby (donated between 1661 and 1679) and the London Sword of State (thought to have been acquired in 1680 or later) have been carefully studied and are as near identical as manufacture will allow. The shape and form of the quillons are identical, the quillon blocks vary only in the arms applied, and pommels are again identical with the figures of Justice and Fame. Due to the length and width of the tangs, the grips differ but are very similar in style.

This leads to the conclusion that they must have been made at virtually the same time. Since only the Shrewsbury sword can be accurately dated, it must be assumed that the swords at Appleby and London were made around 1670.

Batch of Swords

Shrewsbury (State) – 1669

Appleby – *c.* 1670

London (State) – *c.* 1670

The other five swords at Hereford, Thetford, Carmarthen, Bury St Edmunds and Great Yarmouth appear to be another later batch, as the dates are from 1677 to 1684.

Hereford, Carmarthen, Bury St Edmunds and Great Yarmouth have near identical quillon blocks with a rose in repoussé on each side – while that of Thetford is similar but with an inscription on one side and some arms on the other.

The quillon shafts of Hereford and Thetford are very similar, smooth with roses, as are another pair at Carmarthen and Bury St Edmunds, with spirals and no decoration. The shafts at Great Yarmouth are smooth without decoration.

At Hereford, Thetford, Bury St Edmunds and Great Yarmouth, the quillons ends are similar and recurved, i.e. with one head raised and the other lowered. At Carmarthen, the quillons are not recurved but at some stage they have been removed and are now on upside down. Thus both heads are raised. However, if fitted properly, the heads would lowered.

At Thetford, Carmarthen, Bury St Edmunds and Great Yarmouth, the grip is very similar, with the spiral in the same direction – at Hereford the spiral twists in the other direction and is of a bolder pattern.

They all have very similar pommels in shape and decoration. All have the figure of Justice with sword and scales on one side and Law with a book/scroll with attached seals on the other. The pommels of Carmarthen, Bury St Edmunds and Great Yarmouth are virtually the same on each face, though Yarmouth has one less seal. Hereford and

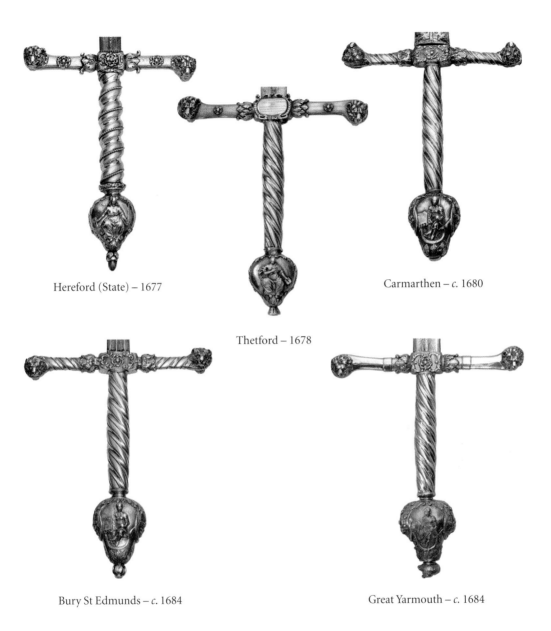

Hereford (State) – 1677

Carmarthen – c. 1680

Thetford – 1678

Bury St Edmunds – c. 1684

Great Yarmouth – c. 1684

Thetford have a differing but almost identical figure of Law, but the figures of Justice are totally different from each other and from the other three swords.

Despite a contradictory inscription on the much later quillon block, the pommel of the Norwich sword is very similar to the five mentioned above, with the figures of Justice and Prudence, though it is on upside down; it appears to be contemporary. The grip is of similar shape but wire-bound. The quillons are unique.

Ancient Bearing-Swords with Royal Connections

Four other enormous bearing-swords with royal connections exist, though none has a scabbard. One might well ask what sort of giant might have wielded these massive weapons but they are just too large to be used on a battlefield and are, therefore, nothing more than Swords of State. They are described in order of age.

St George's Chapel, Windsor Castle – Fourteenth Century

In St George's Chapel at Windsor hangs a sword that belonged to Edward III. Sir Guy Laking[16] said: 'The sword is doubtless that which was suspended over King Edward III's stall in the first Chapel of the Order of the Garter, and was offered at the High Altar on his death in 1377.' In the Precentor's account for 1387–88 the sword is alluded to: 'For the repair of the sword of Edward the Founder of the College. 17*d*'. Later, in 1615, a treasurer's account notes, '2*s* 6*d* – To Noke, for making cleane the Twoe hande sworde whiche hangith by K: Edward the 3: picture'. The sword was hidden in Cromwellian times and not discovered.

In later years the sword has been subjected to an over-rigorous cleaning which has removed the patina of age. The age and authenticity of the sword cannot be questioned, as its provenance is well attested. The workmanship is crude. The blade, which is in good condition, has a rather short double fuller and bears an armourer's mark of a dagger, now somewhat erased. Curiously, the blade is not straight but curves slightly to one side and then straightens again about 2ft from the point. The cross-guard is long, square-sectioned and straight with square ends. The grip has, at some stage, been re-covered in black leather. The pommel is in the form of an ovoid flattened wheel with high centres characteristic of swords of the latter part of the fourteenth century. There is a small tang button and the tang end is hammered flat.

Length of sword	6ft 8¼in – 2.033m	Weight of sword	9lb 12½oz – 4.430kg
Length of blade	5ft 4in – 1.625m – Double-edged	Width of blade	2¼in – 0.057m
Length of hilt	16¼in – 0.416m – Two-handed	Width of guard	16in – 0.410m

Westminster Abbey – Fourteenth Century

The sword in Westminster Abbey is known as 'the sword of Edward III'. It is thought to have been used in the funeral arrangements of Edward III. It used to be held in the Confessor's Chapel but is now on public display in the museum. The sword has been in the possession of the Abbey for many centuries and therefore the attribution of the latter half of the fourteenth century would seem appropriate.

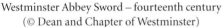

Westminster Abbey Sword – fourteenth century (© Dean and Chapter of Westminster)

St George's Chapel, Windsor Sword – fourteenth century (© Dean and Canons of Windsor)

However, it is said that, when Lord Protector, Oliver Cromwell, who had little truck with such items, gave the original sword to a visiting German count. The shape and style of the original sword indicate that it was a weapon of battle. It bears the emblem of the Order of the Garter and a portcullis on the blade. The pommel has a rock crystal insert covering a fragment of fabric, possibly extracted from the tomb of Edward III. The original is now in a private collection in southern Germany. The count is believed to have courteously donated the sword held in replacement.

The sword on display appears to be of German origin. It was described by Sir Guy Laking[16] as 'a monstrous construction of the crudest workmanship' and 'a poor rusty thing, the make of which is very indifferent'. Although an acknowledged authority, he was well-known for his robust language.

The blade has quite a long fuller but no other marking, and is extremely pitted. The long, straight, square-shaped quillons are square-ended and curve almost imperceptibly towards the point. The wooden foundation of the grip remains, as does the iron collar at each end. The large pommel is in the form of a faceted wheel. There is a small tang button.

Length of sword	7ft 3in – 2.210m	Weight of sword	18lb 0oz – 8.166kg
Length of blade	5ft 4in –1.625m – Double-edged	Width of blade	3½in – 0.089m
Length of hilt	23in – 0.584m – Two-handed	Width of guard	24½in – 0.622m

Tower of London Swords

There are two swords on display in the Tower of London. Although undoubtedly processional bearing-swords, nothing is known of their former use, but they were probably those of early Lancastrian kings either Henry IV or his son Henry V. One of the swords is known to have been in the Tower since at least the eighteenth century, being illustrated in *A Treatise on Ancient Armour and Weapons*, written by Francis Grose in 1786.

Sword 1 – Fifteenth Century

The blade is from Passau and in remarkably good condition. It has a series of four markings along its length on one side – similar to maker's marks – probably once inlaid with brass. There is a quite sizeable notch on one side about 15in from the point and a number of other nicks along both edges. The hilt was probably fitted in England. The cross-guard is straight and of square section, tapering slightly towards the ends. The wooden grip is original and in a baluster shape, each part capable of being gripped by two hands. There are traces of a leather covering. The pommel is flat and hexagonal like a nut (as for a bolt), with a large hole through the middle; the hole is filled with another material.

This is by far the largest sword included in this book. It is the longest sword (by 2in), has the second longest blade (by 1in), the longest hilt (by 3in) and the cross-guard is first equal. However, it is not the heaviest by some 3lb and 10oz.

Length of sword	7ft 7in – 2.312m	Weight of sword	14lb 6oz – 6.501kg
Length of blade	5ft 5in – 1.651m – Double-edged	Width of blade	3⅛in – 0.081m
Length of hilt	26in – 0.661m – Two-handed	Width of guard	24½in – 0.626m

Sword 2 – Fifteenth Century

The blade is from Passau and in remarkably good condition. It has a series of five markings along its length on one side – similar to maker's marks. Some are very similar to those on the other sword. Again there are a number of nicks along each edge. The hilt was probably fitted in England. The cross-guard is straight and of square section, tapering slightly towards the ends. The wooden grip is original and in a baluster shape, each part capable of being gripped by two hands. There are traces of a leather covering with some gilding. The pommel is flat and hexagonal like a nut, with a large hole through the middle filled with another material.

Length of sword	7ft 5in – 2.257m	Weight of sword	14lb 3oz – 6.435kg
Length of blade	5ft 6in – 1.676m – Double-edged	Width of blade	3in – 0.076m
Length of hilt	23in – 0.584m – Two-handed	Width of guard	23¼in – 0.59m

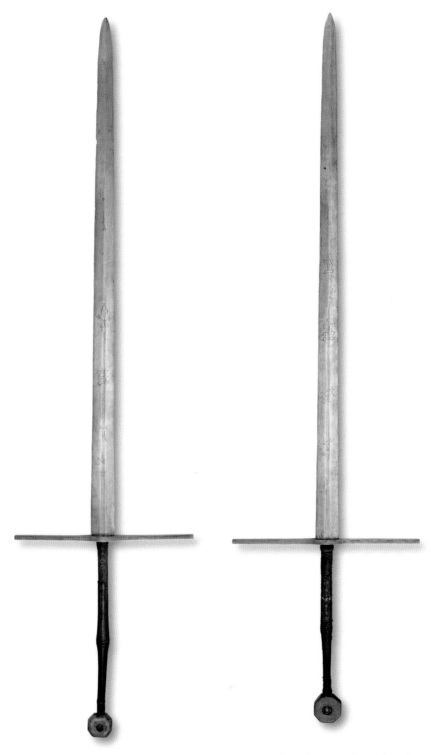

Tower of London Sword 1 – fifteenth century
(© Royal Armouries)

Tower of London Sword 2 – fifteenth
century (© Royal Armouries)

The Royal Collection

The Swords in the Collection

Six swords are exhibited in the Jewel House in the Tower of London, of which only four are specifically coronation ones, namely the Sword of Offering (often incorrectly called the Jewelled State Sword), the Swords of Temporal and Spiritual Justice and the Curtana (Sword of Mercy), though a fifth, the Sword of State, has a role at the coronation. The paragraphs below cover what is known of the actual swords used at coronations since that of Richard III in 1483, the earliest for which there are detailed records. The sixth sword displayed in the Jewel House, the Irish Sword of State, has nothing to do with the coronation and remains permanently on display. All six are classed as Swords of State. The photographs of these swords have been kindly supplied by the Royal Collection Trust/© HM Queen Elizabeth II 2012. Unfortunately for the reader, the pictures only show one side of each sword and scabbard.

All the Royal Collection swords are bearing-swords in that they all are, or have been, borne before the monarch. It is said that the monarch is regarded as the 'protector and defender of the Church of Christ'.

A seventh royal sword is the Sword of State of Scotland, held in Edinburgh Castle but not used.

The Swords of Justice and the Curtana

The characteristic medieval sword form, with simple cruciform hilt, has remained in use continuously for the Swords of Justice and the Curtana for almost 400 years.

The current three swords are all closely similar to each other, and, apart from later alterations, are clearly contemporary products of the same workshop brought together at one time – obviously a specific coronation – to form a set.

The scabbards and grips are all of much later date than anything else, as almost certainly are the silver tang buttons (and the tips of the tangs have clearly been re-threaded in the nineteenth or early twentieth century).

All the evidence available about the Swords of Justice and the Curtana points to them having been produced in England during the earlier years of the seventeenth century. There is therefore no reason for thinking that they are other than contemporary with the coronation of Charles I in 1626. There can be little doubt that all the swords would have been supplied initially for royal service.

For some time during the Middle Ages, the coronation swords were apparently kept permanently in the royal treasury, but from at least as early as the coronation of Richard III in 1483 they were provided new for each occasion. They were still not a permanent part of the regalia when the Westminster 1605 inventory was made, but Charles

I, after his coronation in 1626, handed over the Curtana and two other swords to the bishop and ordered that they be kept with the other regalia and put in the inventory.

The present swords are not, therefore, likely to have been used at any coronation earlier than Charles I's. They can be dated to the period before the Civil War, so it would appear extremely likely that they are, in fact, actually the ones that were supplied for Charles's coronation and, like many other royal possessions, were recovered after the Restoration.

To sum up, there is good substantial evidence pointing to the Swords of Justice and the Curtana having been made for the coronation of Charles I in 1626, probably by Robert South, the King's Cutler, and having been recovered after the Restoration and used at the coronation of Charles II in 1661. The first unequivocal evidence of their existence, however, is at the coronation of James II in 1685. A major refurbishment was carried out for the coronation of George IV in 1821, where the scabbards mentioned were probably the original ones. The scabbards were completely recovered with embroidered crimson silk velvet in 1937 for the coronation of George VI, and this is probably what still covers them.

The Sword of State

There is no record of when a sword was used before the Reformation. The Sword of State was of immense importance as a symbol of royal authority. For this reason, a bearing-sword of some kind must have been provided for Charles II immediately after his return to England in 1660. In January 1678, a 'new' Sword of State was ordered, and thereafter two such swords – sometimes described respectively as 'new' and 'old' – are recorded until 1770. The old sword might, of course, have been acquired at any time in Charles's reign before 1678, but it seems probable that it was the one used at his coronation on 23 April 1661. The absence of any further reference, in a fairly complete set of later Jewel House books, to any other sword being acquired after 1678 leaves no doubt that the Sword of State now in the Jewel House is one of the two that existed then.

The reason why two swords were required was that it must have been convenient for the monarch to have one to hand for his general use, and another at the Houses of Parliament, where royal personal attendances were more frequent than they are now.

The disappearance of one of the swords after 1770 – almost certainly that used at the House of Lords – was no doubt the result of the reduction in the number of such personal appearances after 1776. Symbolically there was only one Sword of State, and each of the two swords was, as it were, merely an incarnation of it: therefore, as well as being of similar size and materials, and decorated using a similar technique – as we know they were from documents – they are likely also to have been made to resemble each other. Support for this is provided by the very close similarities in the design and decoration of the hilts of the existing main Sword of State and the Irish one, of which the latter again was no more than an incarnation of the one Sword of State: it was known as 'The King's (Queen's) Sword' and was held by the Lord Lieutenant of Ireland for the monarch while he or she was absent from the country, and had no independent symbolism of its own.

Further support for the view that all three swords were designed to resemble each other is provided by an examination of the two surviving ones. It would seem that the Irish sword was, in fact, one of two similar swords made at the same period, the other being the old main Sword of State. The only clue to the date of manufacture of the latter is the warrant ordering a case for it, which is dated 23 November 1660, the period when we know the Irish sword was being made.

It is reasonable to assume from this that it had become the main sword as soon as it was made, and that it was the old sword that was relegated to the House of Lords.

The sword was first exhibited in the Jewel House in 1869.

The Sword of Offering

This sword was made especially for the coronation of George IV in 1821. The king was much involved with the design and had many articles of jewellery broken up and re-set. When made in 1820, the sword cost just under £6,000 (equivalent to £215,000 in modern-day currency). There is no doubt that it was used at the coronation, despite the printed Form and Order describing it as being 'in a Scabbard of Purple Velvet' employed in all such documents from the coronation of James II to that of George VI, though not always adhered to in practice. Since, traditionally, the Sword of Offering was the monarch's personal sword, it was retained by him after the coronation. It was finally transferred to the Jewel House in 1903. This is more commonly called the Jewelled State Sword.

Major General Sir Hervey Degge Wilmot Sitwell CB, MC was the keeper of the Jewel House from 1952 to 1968 and wrote extensively about these swords in the *Sitwell Papers* (he is mentioned ten times in *TSC*). According to him, the number of precious stones set in the hilt and the scabbard of this sword are: one large yellow sapphire, one large blue sapphire, two large turquoise, fifteen Burmese rubies, nine other rubies, four large Columbian emeralds, twenty-five smaller Columbian emeralds, five other emeralds, one large yellow diamond, four smaller diamonds, 511 rose diamonds and 2,805 brilliants – a total of 3,383 precious stones. Unfortunately, his handwritten notes do not quite match the totals in his typed work.

The Sword of Spiritual Justice – *c.* 1626

This sword is known as the 'second sword' and originally had an obtuse point.

At a coronation it is carried unsheathed on the right of the three swords by a very senior peer of the realm wearing his ermine-trimmed scarlet robe and coronet. In 1953, it was the Earl of Home.

Length of sword	3ft 10in – 1.168m	**Weight of sword**	2lb 6¼oz – 1.080kg
Length of blade	3ft 3¼in – 0.996m – Double-edged	**Width of blade**	1in – 0.025m
Length of hilt	6¾in – 0.171m – Single-handed	**Width of guard**	7in – 0.177m
Length of scabbard	3ft 4¼in – 1.022m	**Weight of scabbard**	11oz – 0.312kg

Sword

The steel blade has a double fuller, slightly offset from the centre, extending for about a quarter of the length of each face. A running wolf mark, with traces of copper inlay, is incised on one face, while struck near the base of the other, and partly concealed by one écusson, are two marks, one like a letter 'A' with V-shaped cross-bar, followed by a triangular dot, and the other like a circle between two addorsed 'C's. The cruciform hilt is of gilt iron. The quillon block incorporates two triangular écussons, the tips of which are rather sharply pointed; they are decorated with dart-shaped gadroons and project over the centre of the base of the blade on each side. Pieces of leather are wedged between them and the blade to hold the cross-guard firm. The long, straight, ribbon-like quillons are of flattened oblong section and are bent almost imperceptibly towards the blade; they widen in the horizontal plane and end in scrolled tips curved towards the blade, each marked off on the grip side by two lateral grooves and bordered on each edge by a raised rib with a single inner groove. The wooden grip is of oblong section, with the wider faces convex, bound with gilt wire – probably of silver that has been coppered before gilding, but possibly of copper – and with silver-gilt Turks' heads at top and bottom. The flat, octagonal pommel is shaped rather like a large nut: it is of oblong section, the side adjoining the grip longer than the others, and with a central circular hole through which the blade-tang is visible. Each of two diagonally opposite edges of the visible part of the tang is marked with a pair of notches. The knob-shaped silver-gilt button is made in one with a tubular sleeve which is recessed into the enlarged hole in the pommel for the blade-tang, the whole being threaded internally to screw on to the end of this last. A single punched dot – presumably an assembly mark – is visible on the tang through the aperture in the pommel.

Scabbard

The scabbard is of leather covered with crimson velvet embroidered in gold thread with a design of running scrollwork with double and trefoil loops at intervals, with the background partly covered with gilt sequins secured by V-shaped gold-thread stitches: on each edge is a gold galloon. The two silver-gilt mounts comprise firstly a deep tapering chape with a rounded tip terminating in a globular button, and a horizontal inner edge bordered by a row of cut-out fleurs-de-lis, and secondly a mouth-locket, deeply cut out to take the quillon block of the hilt, its lower edge *en suite* with the upper edge of the chape, and with a mushroom-shaped frog-stud, cast and chased as a lion mask, in the centre of the obverse face.

The Sword of Spiritual Justice – *c.* 1626 (The Royal
Collection Trust/© HM Queen Elizabeth II 2012)

The Sword of Temporal Justice – *c. 1626*

This sword is known as the 'third sword'.

At a coronation it is carried unsheathed on the left of the three swords by a very senior peer of the realm wearing his ermine-trimmed scarlet robe and coronet. In 1953, it was the Duke of Buccleuch and Queensferry.

Length of sword	3ft 9in – 1.143m	**Weight of sword**	2lb 5½oz – 1.060kg
Length of blade	3ft 3in – 0.991m – Double-edged	**Width of blade**	1½in – 0.039m
Length of hilt	6in – 0.152m – Single-handed	**Width of guard**	8⅛in – 0.205m
Length of scabbard	3ft 4in – 1.016m	**Weight of scabbard**	11oz – 0.314kg

Sword

The straight steel blade tapers gradually to a leaf-shaped point. It has an oblong ricasso and a single narrow fuller, slightly offset from centre, extending for a quarter of the length of each face. Symbols like open lozenges with wavy edges are stamped in the fullers, together with the name 'ZANDON FRARA (FERARA)', divided between the two faces. The cruciform hilt is of gilt iron. The quillon block incorporates two triangular écussons, the tips of which are rounded, possibly as the result of reshaping after damage; they are decorated with dart-shaped gadroons and project over the centre of the base of the blade on each side. The long, straight, ribbon-like quillons are of flattened oblong section and are bent almost imperceptibly towards the blade; they widen in the horizontal plane and end in scrolled tips curved towards the blade, each marked off on the grip side by two lateral grooves and bordered on each edge by a raised rib with a single inner groove. The wooden grip is of oblong section, with the wider faces convex, bound with gilt wire – probably of silver that has been coppered before gilding, but possibly of copper – and with silver-gilt Turks' heads at top and bottom. The flat, octagonal pommel is shaped rather like a large nut: it is of oblong section, the side adjoining the grip longer than the others, and with a central circular hole through which the blade-tang is visible. A single punched dot – presumably an assembly mark – is visible on the tang through the aperture in the pommel. The knob-shaped silver-gilt button is made in one with a tubular sleeve which is recessed into the enlarged hole in the pommel for the blade-tang, the whole being threaded internally to screw on to the end of this last.

Scabbard

The scabbard is leather covered with crimson velvet embroidered in gold thread with a design of running scrollwork with double and trefoil loops at intervals, and with the background partly covered with gilt sequins secured by V-shaped gold-thread stitches: on each edge is a gold galloon. The two silver-gilt mounts comprise firstly a deep tapering

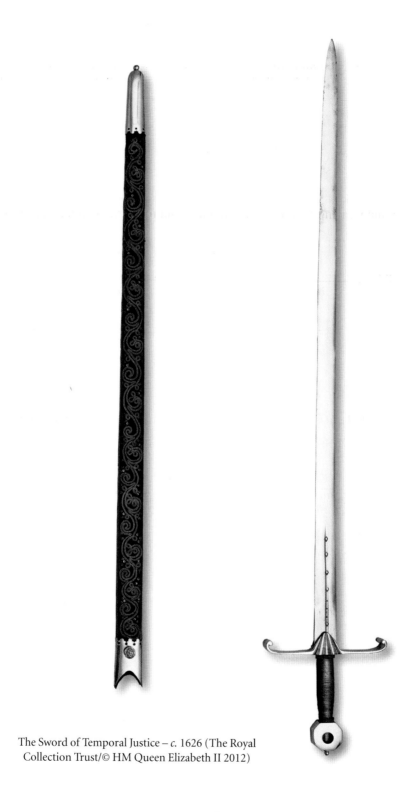

The Sword of Temporal Justice – *c.* 1626 (The Royal
Collection Trust/© HM Queen Elizabeth II 2012)

chape with a rounded tip terminating in a globular button, and a horizontal inner edge bordered by a row of cut-out fleurs-de-lis, and secondly a mouth-locket, deeply cut out to take the quillon block of the hilt, its lower edge *en suite* with the upper edge of the chape, and with a mushroom-shaped frog-stud, cast and chased as a lion mask, in the centre of the obverse face.

The Curtana or Sword of Mercy – *c. 1626*

At a coronation it is carried unsheathed in the centre of the three swords by a very senior peer of the realm wearing his ermine-trimmed scarlet robe and coronet. In 1953, it was the Duke of Northumberland.

Length of sword	3ft 2in – 0.965m	Weight of sword	2lb 10oz – 1.190kg
Length of blade	2ft 7¼in – 0.794m – Double-edged	Width of blade	1in – 0.025m
Length of hilt	6¾in – 0.171m – Single-handed	Width of guard	7½in – 0.191m
Length of scabbard	2ft 9¼in – 0.844m	Weight of scabbard	11¼oz – 0.318kg

Sword

The truncated steel blade, which is the characteristic feature of this sword, started life as a normal pointed one and has merely been cut off straight about 1in from the original point. It is much shorter – about 7in – and considerably broader than the blades of the other two swords, and slightly too wide for the quillon block. It has a wide shallow central fuller for about a third of the length of each face, and one face is inlaid in copper with a running wolf mark (much of the copper missing). The copper foundation for the gilding is visible in places on the gilt-iron cruciform hilt. The quillon block incorporates two triangular écussons, the tips of which are rounded, possibly as the result of reshaping after damage; they are decorated with dart-shaped gadroons and project over the centre of the base of the blade on each side. The long, straight, ribbon-like quillons are of flattened oblong section and are bent almost imperceptibly towards the blade; they widen in the horizontal plane and end in scrolled tips curved towards the blade, each marked off on the grip side by two lateral grooves and bordered on each edge by a raised rib with a single inner groove. The wooden grip is of oblong section, with the wider faces convex, bound with gilt wire – probably of silver that has been coppered before gilding, but possibly of copper – and with silver-gilt Turks' heads at top and bottom. The flat, octagonal pommel is shaped rather like a large nut: it is of oblong section, the side adjoining the grip longer than the others, and with a central circular hole through which the blade-tang is visible. Two dots are punched on the visible part of the tang. The knob-shaped silver-gilt button is made in one with a tubular sleeve which is recessed into the enlarged hole

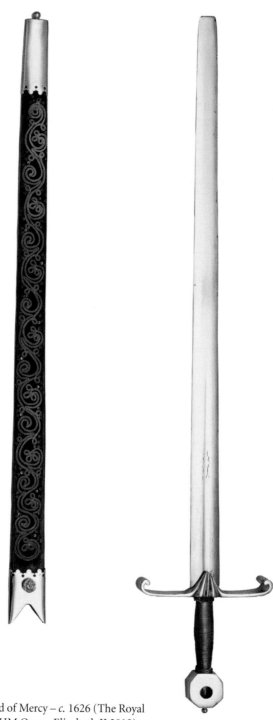

The Curtana or Sword of Mercy – *c.* 1626 (The Royal
Collection Trust/© HM Queen Elizabeth II 2012)

in the pommel for the blade-tang, the whole being threaded internally to screw on to the end of this last.

Scabbard

The scabbard is of leather (not, apparently, on a wood base) covered with crimson velvet embroidered in gold thread with a design of running scrollwork with double and trefoil loops at intervals, and with the background partly covered with gilt sequins secured by V-shaped gold-thread stitches: on each edge is a gold galloon. The two silver-gilt mounts comprise (1) a deep tapering chape which conforms in shape to the end of the blade terminating in a globular button, and a horizontal inner edge bordered by a row of cut-out fleurs-de-lis, and (2) a mouth-locket, deeply cut out to take the quillon block of the hilt, its lower edge *en suite* with the upper edge of the chape, and with a mushroom-shaped frog-stud, cast and chased as a lion mask, in the centre of the obverse face.

The Irish Sword of State – *c*. late 1660 or early 1661

A warrant of 7 August 1660 addressed to the Master of the Wardrobe tasked him to pro-vide also a cap of maintenance. This was the royal Sword of State, 'The King's (Queen's) Sword', used by the English Lord Lieutenant, Chief Governor or Viceroy of Ireland as the sovereign's representative. The sword remained in Dublin until the establishment of the Irish Free State in January 1922. It was placed in the Jewel House in 1959, where it remains.

This sword is no longer processed.

Length of sword	4ft 2⅞in – 1.292m	**Weight of sword**	6lb 9¼oz – 2.985kg
Length of blade	3ft 2½in – 0.978m – Double-edged	**Width of blade**	2¼in – 0.056m
Length of hilt	12⅜in – 0.314m – Single-handed	**Width of guard**	12⅛in – 0.308m
Length of scabbard	3ft 3½in – 1.003m	**Weight of scabbard**	1lb 4¾oz – 0.590kg

Sword

It is similar in form and decoration to the main Sword of State but with a hilt of finer quality. The broad, straight, flat, two-edged, slightly tapering, pointed steel blade is deco-rated with engraving. The blade is decorated on each face with rather coarse engraving, with traces of gilding. Starting from the top, the obverse has: (a) a harp, uncrowned, for Ireland, under a chevron (point upwards) with a pendent scroll on each side; (b) a shield of the royal arms with, unusually, England, Scotland and Ireland respectively in the first three quarters, and France in the fourth, with the Nassau lion, for William III, on a shield of pretence, all within the Garter, surmounted by a crown and with lion and unicorn supporters; and (c) three fleurs-de-lis, flanked by foliated scrolls, above

The Irish Sword of State – *c.* late 1660 or early 1661 (The Royal Collection Trust/© HM Queen Elizabeth II 2012)

a rose and a thistle. The reverse has: (a) a chevron with scrolls, in the same position as the obverse, framing the three lions from the English royal arms; (b) as on the obverse; and (c) a rectangular panel with foliated borders at the bottom and sides, framing a lion rampant on a foliated scroll, presumably intended to represent the arms of Scotland. Across the bottom of each face of the blade is a narrow border of acanthus leaves which is crossed by the other decoration, and is therefore possibly earlier, though it is not obviously different in style. The cruciform hilt is of silver-gilt, including the grip, with cast and chased decoration. The decoration of the hilt was cast integrally with it and chased, the main motifs being in relief against finely matted backgrounds. The hilt is by George Bowers. The rounded oblong quillon block has prominent mouldings above and below, that next to the grip double; the block is hollow and is packed with wood where the blade goes into it. On the obverse of the quillon block is a fleur-de-lis, and on the reverse a Tudor rose, each within a laurel wreath. The long, vertically recurved quillons are formed respectively as a rampant lion and a unicorn (the latter's horn missing), supported on leaf scrolls. The grip is of circular section, tapering towards the pommel, and with a narrow crimped moulding at top and bottom. The grip has rows of acanthus leaves at top and bottom, and the following (from cross-guard to pommel): on the obverse, a portcullis and a fleur-de-lis, the latter between a pair of thistles, and a Tudor rose; and on the reverse the same but instead of a rose a harp with the front formed as a winged harpy. The pommel is globular, rather small in proportion to the rest of the hilt, with a narrow crimped moulding at top and bottom. It has a thistle on the obverse, the royal lion crest on a coronet on the reverse, a Tudor rose on one side and a harp on the other: The prominent button has a similar moulding at the bottom; the tip of the blade-tang is rather roughly riveted over a silver-gilt washer and is formed as a calyx of vine-like leaves enclosing seeds.

Scabbard

The scabbard is of wood covered in deep crimson velvet, with four silver-gilt mounts. There are no belt attachments. The decoration on the scabbard, all of which is chased in relief, is: (1) the chape: a rather roughly executed thistle on each face framed in acanthus foliage; the button is formed as an orb (now lacking its cross); (2) a Tudor rose on each face, linked by a narrow side-band, each pierced for a fixing rivet; (3) a large plaque on each face, each with the full Hanoverian royal arms as borne between 1714 and 1801, and linked by two plain bands, which are merely pressed round the scabbard and left open on one side (this mount is of markedly better quality than the others, although one mount is upside down); and (4) the mouth-locket: on each face is a Tudor rose flanked by acanthus foliage, and on the edges further acanthus foliage; the top and bottom are bordered by acanthus leaves, those towards the point cut out and with a cabled inner moulding.

The Sword of State – 1678

At a coronation it is carried sheathed by a very senior peer of the realm wearing his ermine-trimmed scarlet robe and coronet. In 1953, it was carried by the Marquess of Salisbury.

At the State Opening of Parliament, the Sword of State is borne by an ex-armed forces peer in his scarlet robe with a broad collar.

It is always carried sheathed.

Length of sword	3ft 11¾in – 1.213m	**Weight of sword**	5lb 11oz – 2.581kg
Length of blade	2ft 11¾in – 0.908m – Double-edged	**Width of blade**	1⅝in – 0.041m
Length of hilt	12in – 0.305m – Two-handed	**Width of guard**	12⅝in – 0.321m
Length of scabbard	3ft 2in – 0.965m	**Weight of scabbard**	2lb 5¼oz – 1.057kg

Sword

The Sword of State is similar in form, though slightly smaller all round, and decoration to the Irish Sword of State but with a hilt of inferior quality. The broad, straight, flat, two-edged blade is decorated with etching. Struck on one face, partly concealed by the decoration, is an unidentified blacksmith's (?) mark 'S'. Each face of the forte is etched with an overall design (now slightly rubbed) of foliated tendrils involving birds and, at the base, a monster's head. The birds are mostly the right way up when the blade is point upwards, but some, and the monster's head, are set sideways. The cruciform hilt is of silver-gilt with cast and chased decoration. The decoration of the hilt is cast integrally with it and chased, the main motifs being in relief against finely matted backgrounds. The rounded oblong quillon block has a moulding where it meets the grip, and an extension enclosing the base of the blade; the zig-zag edge of this last engages – only one way round – with the corresponding zig-zag edge of the mouth-locket of the scabbard. On the obverse is a Tudor rose, and on the reverse a fleur-de-lis, each within a laurel wreath. The long, vertically recurved quillons are formed respectively as a rampant lion and unicorn (the latter's horn, which is loose, replaced by Garrard in 1921), each supported on leaf-scrolls. The grip is of circular section, tapering towards the pommel, and with a narrow crimped moulding where it meets it. Each face is decorated with – from cross-guard to pommel – a portcullis, a fleur-de-lis flanked by thistles, and a harp with the front formed as a winged harpy. The globular pommel is cast in one with the grip – a very unusual feature – and is rather small in proportion to the rest of the hilt, with a narrow crimped moulding at top and bottom. It has the royal lion crest on a coronet on the reverse, a thistle on the obverse, and respectively a Tudor rose and an orb at the sides. There is a prominent button, the tip of the blade-tang riveted directly over it, with a similar crimped moulding at the bottom. The button is formed as a calyx of vine-like leaves enclosing seeds.

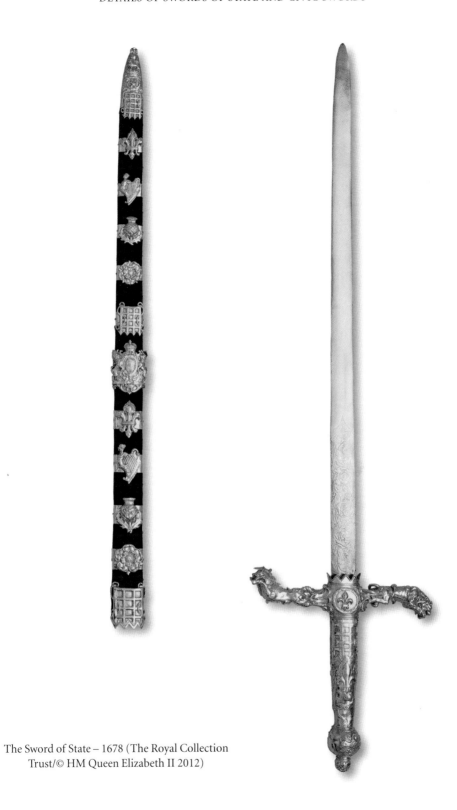

The Sword of State – 1678 (The Royal Collection
Trust/© HM Queen Elizabeth II 2012)

Scabbard

The wooden scabbard is covered with red velvet and fitted with twelve silver-gilt mounts, all chased in relief. One edge is reinforced with a narrow strip of riveted silver-gilt, divided into sections, between the mounts (one section recently replaced). There are no belt attachments. The decoration of the mounts is as follows (unless otherwise stated, the secondary mounts consist of a plain band, riveted to the scabbard at the sides, and with the decorative motif on each face): (1) the chape; at the top an orb, its cross forming the finial to the chape; below, on each face, the royal lion crest on a closed crown, a double scroll of foliage with a scallop shell below, and a portcullis, its spiked lower end cut out and forming the edge of the chape; (2) a smaller fleur-de-lis; (3) a smaller harp with its front formed as a winged harpy; (4) a smaller thistle; (5) a smaller Tudor rose; (6) a portcullis; (7) a plaque, each depicting the full royal arms as borne by William III from 1694 to 1702, with Garter, motto, supporters and crown, above two leaf scrolls. They are joined directly together (by solder?) at the sides and riveted to the scabbard; (8) a large fleur-de-lis; (9) a large harp with its front formed as a winged harpy; (10) a larger thistle; (11) a large Tudor rose; and (12) the mouth-locket is formed as two portcullises, back to back, their spiked lower ends cut out to form a zig-zag edge which engages with the corresponding edge of the quillon block of the sword.

The Sword of Offering – 1820

At a coronation it is initially carried sheathed on a cushion by the Keeper of the Jewel House wearing ceremonial dress. Later, it is exchanged for the Sword of State and carried by that peer of the realm.

Length of sword	3ft 2⅝in – 0.981m	**Weight of sword**	1lb 8oz – 0.680kg
Length of blade	2ft 7⅝in – 0.787m – Double-edged	**Width of blade**	1⅛in – 0.229m
Length of hilt	7in – 0.178m – Single-handed	**Width of guard**	5⅞in – 0.146m
Length of scabbard	2ft 8⅝in – 0.828m	**Weight of scabbard**	2lb 13oz – 1.278kg

Sword

It has a steel blade mounted in gold. It is signed underneath the quillon block 'RUNDELL BRIDGE' and 'RUNDELL FECERUNT'. The straight, narrow, sharply-tapering blade is of flattened diamond section with a central fuller on each face of the forte. The blade is decorated on both faces for 27½in from the hilt with partly blued and gilt-etched strap-work involving foliage and the national emblems of England (roses), Scotland (thistles) and Ireland (shamrocks), and various other devices. These, starting from the point, are as follows. On the obverse: (a) a classical female figure holding a flag bearing the crowned cipher 'WR'; (b) the royal arms of

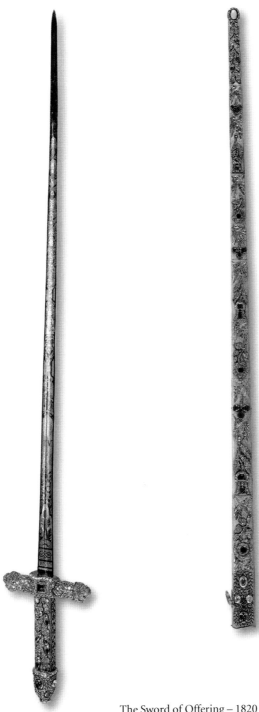

The Sword of Offering – 1820 (The Royal Collection
Trust/© HM Queen Elizabeth II 2012)

George IV, on an oval escutcheon within the Garter, surmounted by the royal crest on a crown, and supported by the lion and unicorn above a straight scroll inscribed 'DIEU ET MON DROIT'; (c) a trophy of arms involving a banner and an oval escutcheon bearing a cross of St George superimposed on a saltire; and (d) a royal crown, its cross in a sunburst, above IV, over a double 'GR' cipher. On the reverse: (a) the standing figure of Britannia; (b) the same as (b) on the front, but with the motto on a U-shaped scroll; and (c) the same as (d) on the obverse. The plain section of the blade towards the point is burnished bright. The cruciform hilt is of gold. The faces of the oblong quillon block are slightly concave at the sides, and shaped as a horizontal flattened-S scroll towards the blade. It is engraved with the maker's name in capitals on the face nearest to the blade. Each face has a narrow border of diamonds framing a reserved central panel. This panel conforms to the outline of the block, is finely chased with scrolling acanthus foliage and set with a large central emerald framed in diamonds, that is on the obverse rectangular and on the reverse octagonal. The short, straight quillons are of thick baluster shape, terminating in cast and chased lion masks. Each quillon is enclosed in a cross-set spiral of diamonds, except for the lion-mask terminal, which is set directly with many small diamonds and has ruby eyes. The straight grip is of oblong section. Each side is set with diamond oak sprays with emerald acorns, and edged with diamond laurel sprays. The pommel is shaped like a deep mushroom-cap with a button and an invected lower edge. It has a lower border of diamonds and, on the main surfaces, diamond laurel festoons, framing eight larger stones set in gold collets, on each face a central emerald, at the side central diamonds, and round the top four rubies. The button is formed from a large diamond in a gold collet set with a ring of smaller diamonds. On the hilt and scabbard, unless otherwise stated, it can be taken that the precious stones, forming the main decoration, are set in applied silver (or platinum?) mounts which provide the basic shape of the motifs represented.

Scabbard

The leather scabbard is lined at the mouth with red baize, and completely encased in sheet gold, made in six sections threaded over the scabbard itself and merely butted together, so that the whole has a certain amount of flexibility. The bottom section is a chape with a rounded tip, and a simulated mouth-locket is chased in the top section. The mouth is shaped to the corresponding face of the quillon block, so that the sword will only fit one way round. Applied respectively to the centre of the reverse of the locket and its upper edge are two small fixed rings, of which that on the edge is attached to a mount in the form of a double oak-leaf spray, and has a larger gold ring threaded through it. These are for attachment to a belt. The reverse, except for on the chape, is chased with roses, thistles, shamrocks and crossed laurel and palm branches, and, on the simulated locket, laurel wreaths, rosettes and acanthus scrolls, all against a finely matted ground. This design is repeated on the obverse, but with the roses, thistles and shamrocks executed in diamonds, the roses with ruby centres, the leaves of the shamrocks emeralds, and the centres of the thistle-heads emeralds and rubies. The obverse of the simulated mouth-locket bears diamond laurel wreathes only, framing two diamonds and, in gold collets, a blue sapphire, yellow sapphire and ruby. Each face of the chape is decorated with diamond oak-leaf sprays with emerald acorns, and it has a diamond shoe embracing, in the centre of each face, a turquoise in a gold collet. This scabbard should be viewed point down.

The Sword of State of Scotland

Although not part of the Royal Collection *per se*, the Scottish Sword of State is an important part of the Honours of Scotland, the country's regalia, which includes the Scottish crown and sceptre. The three items were first used together at the coronation of the 9-month-old Mary Queen of Scots in September 1543. All three items are permanently displayed in the Crown Room in the Royal Palace in Edinburgh Castle. The paragraphs below are extracted from *The Honours of Scotland*:[13]

In 1502, King James IV ordered a Sword of Honour with scabbard. It was carried by the king at a meeting of the Parliament in 1503. However, it was superseded by a munificent gift from Pope Julius II in 1507. James V ordered a refashioning of the sword. The sword was used at the very lavish coronation of Charles I at Holyrood Abbey, Edinburgh, in June 1633. It was last used formally at the coronation of Charles II at Scone in January 1651. In 1652, during the Commonwealth, it was hidden in Dunnottar castle and later buried in Kinneff parish church, where the blade was broken to fit the hole and the scabbard bent in three. It was returned to Edinburgh Castle in December 1660. In 1707, it was locked in a chest in the castle, where it remained for 111 years, until February 1818. In 1941, it was again hidden amid fears of a German invasion. It was taken out again on 24 June 1953, when the newly crowned Queen Elizabeth II made her first formal visit to Scotland.

On 24 June 1953, the sword was taken by the Lord Lyon Kings of Arms, escorted by the Queen's Bodyguard, the Royal Company of Archers, to the High Kirk of St Giles in Edinburgh's High Street, where a service of thanksgiving took place in the presence of the new sovereign, Queen Elizabeth II. At the close of the service, the crown, sword and sceptre were, in turn, presented to Her Majesty, who returned them. They were then returned to the Crown Room at Edinburgh Castle, where they have remained ever since.

The Sword of State of Scotland – 1507

Length of sword	4ft 6¼in – 1.378m	Weight of sword	6lb 0oz – 2.722kg
Length of blade	3ft 3in – 0.991m – Double-edged	Width of blade	1¾in – 0.044m
Length of hilt	15¼in – 0.387m – Two- handed	Width of guard	17¼in – 0.438m
Length of scabbard	4ft 2⅜in – 1.280m	Weight of scabbard	5lb 0oz – 2.268kg

Sword

The sword and scabbard were made by Domenico da Sutri in the period of the so-called High Renaissance, and their sumptuous appearance reflects the decorative style then in vogue in Italy. The slim, steel blade, which was broken in half to shorten it during its period of interment, is etched beneath the protecting plates, with on one side the figure of St Peter and on the other that of St Paul. In the fuller is etched 'JULIUS II PONT MAX' (Julius II Supreme Pontiff). The etched lines of the figures and lettering were originally inlaid with gold. The hilt is silver-gilt and was all of *repoussé* work. The quillon block has two stylised oak leaves (broken at the points) which form a protecting plate over the scabbard. The quillons are dolphin-shaped (with mouth to the block), symbolic of Christ's Church, tapering to the end in three points, the centre one an acorn. At some stage the dolphins have been cast from the originals and replaced. The grip, which is in the form of a double baluster with central collar, is decorated with oak leaves and acorns; symbols of the Risen Christ. The massive pommel is circular and flat and 4in across, and once had inset enamelled plates. It is now somewhat damaged, no doubt from its periods of interment.

The Sword of State of Scotland (© Crown Copyright HES)

Scabbard

The wooden scabbard is covered with dark crimson velvet and the edges are bound in silver-gilt galloons. It is mounted with silver-gilt *repoussé* work. On the obverse, the chape bears a large section of blue enamelling and a small finial. The main length of the scabbard is divided into three roughly equal sections by two bands which once held enamelled plates. The three areas are filled with elaborate decoration (missing in places) of oak leaves, acorns, dolphins and grotesque masks. The mouth-locket has an enamelled panel bearing the arms of Julius II and above the arms is the symbol of the papacy – crossed keys linked by a tasselled cord surmounted by the papal tiara. This form of ornamentation is repeated on the reverse. Quite large sections are missing on both sides due to the folding into three it received during its periods of interment. Unusually, the scabbard is nearly 12in longer than the sword, indicating that they were not made to go together. Uniquely, of all the swords mentioned, this sword has a 4ft 9in (1.499m) sword belt.

The Manx Sword-Bearer

The Manx Swords

Although not part of the Royal Collection, the Manx sword is not a municipal sword as the Isle of Man is not part of the United Kingdom but a self-governing Crown Dependency. HM The Queen is the Lord of Mann.

The Sword of State is carried unsheathed before His Excellency the Lieutenant Governor, who is the Queen's personal representative on the isle. The Lieutenant Governor has been advised that the sword should be carried sheathed, as is the Sword of State before the sovereign, but, as yet, no action has been taken.

In 2003, the late Claude Blair OBE MA FSA undertook 'long-overdue assessment of the old Manx sword' for the Isle of Man Natural History and Antiquarian Society, in order to ascertain the date of acquisition (Volume XI, number 2).[14]

The use of a Sword of State in the island, though certainly of ancient origin, can only be documented with certainty from the Tynwald meeting of 1417, the first to be attended by one of the Stanley Kings, Sir John Stanley II, whose identically named father had obtained the title in 1405. At the meeting, mention was made of 'yor swoard before you, houlden wth the pointe upwards'.

A letter of 1 May 1736 from the then governor to the newly inherited Lord of Mann, the second Duke of Atholl, states: 'The Sword of State might have been a fine thing in the days of yore but now rusty and paultry. Yr Grace should order another. Let it only be glaring it is no matter what metal it is made of'. A second letter on 24 May states: 'Our Sword of State is so rusty and the Scabard ragged that it will be a shame to produce it!' A third letter to the third Duke from his steward on 11 June 1765 states: 'I have according to your Grace's direction taken into my custody the Family Settlement, the old Seal of Office and the Three Swords of State.'

William Harrison, in the preface to his *Records of the Tynwald and St John's Chapel*, published in 1871, refers both to 'The ancient Sword of State, which had so long remained neglected, until the present Lieutenant Governor rescued it from ignoble use, and had it cleaned and placed once more in safe custody' and to another sword.

Harrison also gives a full description of the old sword, beginning with the following passage:

In the Rolls Office is still preserved the old Sword of State which was borne before Sir John Stanley, the King, at his first Tynwald, in 1422. It has lately been sent to London to be cleaned, by order of Henry Brougham Loch, Esq., the Lieutenant Governor, it having become foul by misusage. It is a curious and beautiful specimen, and evidently of ancient date.

Like all Swords of State, including the one carried before HM The Queen on official state occasions, this would have been called a bearing-sword from the late Middle Ages onwards; that is to say, it was designed, not for combat, but to be borne point upwards before a ruler or his representative.

The possession of a Sword of State is the prerogative of an independent ruler, or, as with mayoral swords legitimately assumed, someone representing the ruler. A Sword of State would, therefore, have been required by the revived Kingdom of Man from its inception in 1405, and even though the first King, Sir John Stanley I, never visited the island, one would almost certainly have been displayed during meetings of the Tynwald to represent him. This practise continues today at the ten meetings of the Tynwald each year.

The evidence given below for dating the original parts of the present sword makes it unlikely that it could have been used on that occasion. The probability is that it was made for one or other of the Tynwald meetings of 1417 or 1422, the first attended by Sir John Stanley II. The fact that he found it necessary to ask for information 'about the law and constitution of old time' suggests that the second is the stronger candidate.

The Isle of Man has two swords.

The Sword of State – 1417 or 1422

Length of sword	3ft 6in – 1.067m	Weight of sword	2lb 8¾oz – 1.158kg
Length of blade	2ft 5⅝ in – 0.753m – Double-edged	Width of blade	1⅝in – 0.041m
Length of hilt	12⅜ in – 0.314m – Two-handed	Width of guard	11⅝in – 0.295m
Length of scabbard	2ft 5½in – 0.749m	Weight of scabbard	10oz – 0.286kg

Sword

No evidence is available about the origins of the sword, but it is certainly English, and probably made in London, the main English centre for the manufacture of arms and armour in the Middle Ages. The long, straight, tapering double-edged blade is of very flat oval section with a narrow central fuller of 7½in and a rounded point; it bears no maker's or town mark. The very long iron cross-guard with comma-shaped tips is slightly arched, and is wider in the same plane as the blade than in its cross-section, which is a very flattened oval; in the centre of each face is an écusson which extends slightly over the base of the blade, and is chiselled with the Legs of Man in bas-relief, the resulting broad border being crossed by a number of engraved lines set at intervals. The long grip, circular in section, tapers towards the pommel and is formed of two pieces of plain wood, glued (?) around the tang. It is fitted with a rough iron ferrule where it meets the cross-guard. The iron pommel is hollow and globular, but with two flattened faces corresponding to the two faces of the blade, each similarly chiselled with the Legs of Man within a shallow circular recess; the small tang button is made separately, as is the plinth-like base (stool), encircled by a hollow moulding and fitted to the tip of the grip, which supports the pommel proper.

The iron parts of the hilt have suffered considerably from general wear and tear, and also from over-thorough cleaning with abrasives. As a result, the fine details of the Legs of Man chiselled, rather coarsely, both on the pommel and cross-guard of the sword have been severely abraded. Those on the cross-guard are more worn than the others, and are also mutilated: on one face, the legs now have the appearance of suffering from acute malnutrition, and the point of the écusson containing them has been broken off; on the other, one foot has been amputated; and on both, the central point where the legs join is almost completely illegible. Fortunately, photographs taken in 1871 for Harrison's *Records of the Tynwald* show more details – an indication of the considerable amount of wear that has taken place during the subsequent 145 years – and reveal that a certain amount of reworking appears to have taken place since the photographs were taken. They make it clear-cut that – on the pommel, and therefore elsewhere – the legs are in plate armour, their spurs, which now look like clumsily exaggerated prick-spurs (that is with a single goad), are of the rowels type, with star-shaped rowels and long straight necks, and a central feature resembling a three-bladed propeller is actually the graphic device, found also on modern representations, that enables the legs to fit neatly together at the top. They also reveal that the foot on one of the legs on the cross-guard, which now appears to be wearing an ankle-boot of seventeenth-century type, with a prominent block-shaped heel and an upturned toe, was almost completely illegible in 1871, so the boot must be a product of the subsequent reworking.

The cross-guards of several other swords of roughly the same age are similar – see the second chapter. The sword, therefore, is essentially a fifteenth-century one, but has been subjected to modification since it was made, most significantly by being fitted with a new blade in the late sixteenth century or early seventeenth century.

Scabbard

The leather scabbard is covered with extremely worn velvet. It has two plain iron mounts, comprising a deep, and somewhat pitted chape of 5½in with a rounded tip and a rounded end on its inner end, and a deep mouth-locket of 4½in, again with a rounded end. The mouth-locket is engraved or etched with, on the obverse, the Legs of Man within a circular frame incorporating what looks like a pyramidal-roofed tower at the top, with foliated appendages at the sides and bottom, and inscribed with the Manx motto 'QUOCUNGUE IECERIS STABIT'; and, on the reverse, a sailing ship with sails furled within a scroll inscribed 'REX MANNIÆ ET INSULARUM' (King of Man and the Isles). The end of the mouth-locket has a concave cut-out to match the écusson of the hilt. The style of the devices on the mounts suggests that they, and therefore the whole scabbard, date from the nineteenth century despite the inscriptions. Unfortunately, the mouth-locket was on upside down – this has been corrected. This scabbard should be viewed point down.

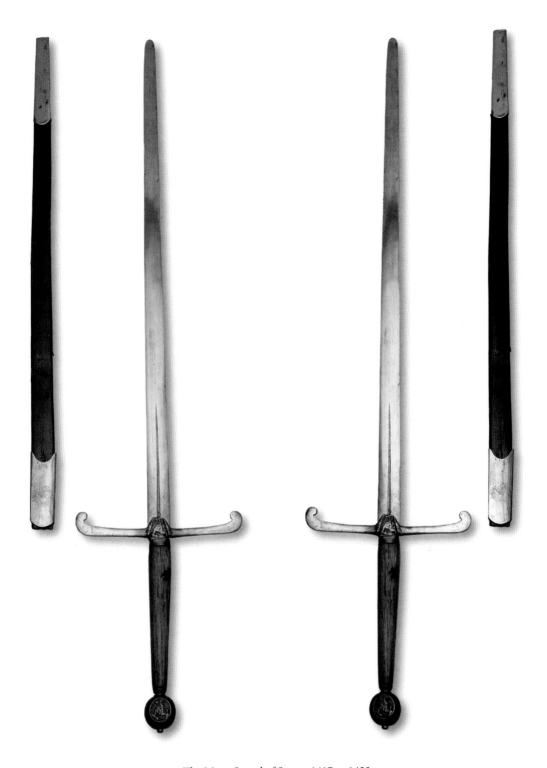

The Manx Sword of State – 1417 or 1422

The Atholl Sword – 1704 or 1724

Length of sword	3ft 7½in – 1.105m	Weight of sword	2lb 6oz – 1.074kg
Length of blade	2ft 9½in – 0.851m – Double-edged	Width of blade	1⅝in – 0.041m
Length of hilt	10in – 0.254m – Two-handed	Width of guard	8½in – 0.216m
Length of scabbard	2ft 11⅛in – 0.892m	Weight of scabbard	9¼oz – 0.265kg

Sword

This second Sword of State has been in the Manx Museum since 1922. The narrow, tapering blade is separated from the cross-guard by a scabbard mouth cap, and has a hollow central fuller on each face, extending for 7½in, each containing the incised name 'ANDREA FERARA' partly defaced by indeterminate later engraving. The copper-alloy (brass?) hilt comprises a short, straight, flat cross-guard with rounded tips which curves upward. The centre and ends of the quillons are finely engraved on both faces with shaped triangular panels framing foliated scrollwork against a fish-roe ground partly sown with quatrefoils. The wooden grip, which tapers towards the pommel, is covered with worn velvet, originally dark blue but now black, and bound with twisted silver (?) wire. The small globular pommel is finely engraved, as with the quillons, and ends with a button.

This type of robe-sword is difficult to date but it seems clear that the sword was made originally as a state sword for an early eighteenth-century Duke of Atholl after he was admitted to the Order of the Thistle, which means either the First Duke (admitted in 1704) or the Second (admitted 1734).

Scabbard

The scabbard is wooden, covered with badly worn velvet, originally dark blue, with a narrow, central strip of lace running down the outer face, and has four brass mounts. These comprise: (1) the mouth-locket, which has a cusped arch inner end and is engraved, on each side, with panels similar to those on the quillons; (2) a locket, with lobe-shaped ends, bearing, on the obverse, the arms (with Ducal coronet and supporters) of a Duke of Atholl, the shield encircled by a band bearing the motto of the Order of the Thistle, 'NEMO ME IMPUNE LACESSIT', and with the first two words of the family motto, 'FURTH FORTUNE AND FILL THE FETTERS', on a scroll below, and on the reverse is engraved, probably by hand, with the Legs of Man encircled by their usual motto 'SHABIT QUOCUN IECERIS', and with the initials 'IDA', for John (or James) Duke of Atholl; (3) a locket, with lobe-shaped ends, bearing, on the obverse, the family crest within another band with the motto of the Order of the Thistle, and on the reverse, the Legs of Man encircled by their usual motto, and with the initial IDA, for John (or James) Duke of Atholl – again probably hand-engraved; and (4) the chape, which has

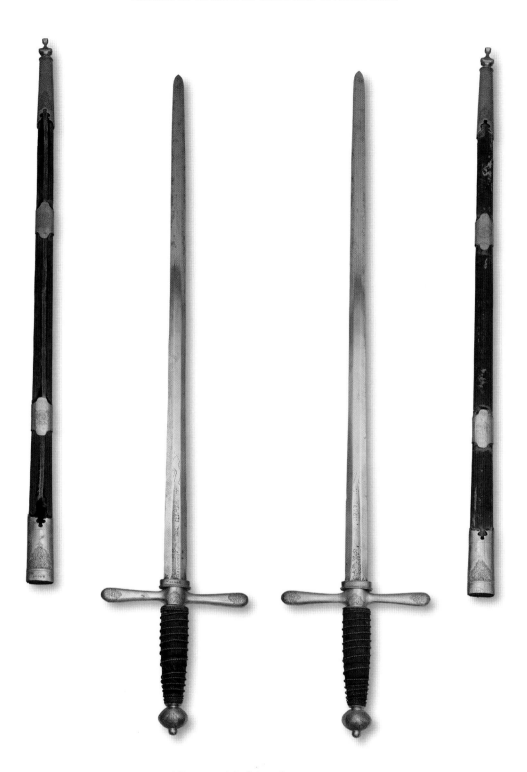

The Manx Atholl Sword – 1704 or 1724

an inner end shaped as cusped arches with an engraved panel similar to that on the quillons on each side, and a terminal formed as an inverted neo-classical lidded urn (a later replacement). This scabbard should be viewed point down.

Cap of Maintenance

There is no cap of maintenance or any record of there being one. The sword-bearer wears a black military-style peaked cap with a broad scarlet band and a cap-badge incorporating the Legs of Man within a crowned Garter. As the current sword-bearer is female, the cap is of the same pattern as worn by a female soldier.

Uniform/Costume

The sword–bearer wears a scarlet tunic with black cuffs and thick gold rope-work around the high collar and cuffs and on the epaulettes, black trousers, black shoes and white cotton gloves. As the current sword-bearer is female, a black skirt is worn.

The City of London Sword-Bearer

London

Prerogative

A Sword of State was certainly carried before 1373. It is inconceivable that London was not the first city to be granted the privilege of a Sword of State.

No mention of the right to have a sword is to be found in the charters of the City of London, and the right of the mayor to have it carried before him is therefore prescriptive. Yet in the history of the mayor's household there is mention of John Blytone, the first known sword-bearer who, on resignation from the office of mayor's esquire, was granted in 1395 the mansion over Aldersgate previously occupied by a sergeant of the chamber (*Studies in London History* by Philip Edmund Jones, 1969).[15]

When a sword was first borne before the mayor of London is unknown, and the minute books are silent on the subject before 1520. The reason for this appears to be that the sword or swords were provided, not by the city, but at the charges of the mayor himself for the time being. There is mention of the purchase of a sword in 1512 with '3 scaberdes perteigning to the same sword, wherof the chief is rychely browdered … The 2de is of cloth of gold, both chaped and gyrdelled with siluer and ouergilt, and the 3de is of blak velivet wt a chape of siluer and ouergilt, wt a lyke crosse and wt a bocle and pendaunt'.

The first entry relating to swords in the minute books is in 1520, which enacts that from henceforth not only the swords but the caps of maintenance worn by the sword-bearer shall be provided by the chamberlain at the cost of the city, and not of the then lord mayor. The sword taken over in 1520 continued in use for the next fourteen years, when either because it and its scabbards had become shabby or worn out, or because they were not thought fine enough, it was replaced by another. In 1534, a new sword was bought, furnished with three scabbards, one of cloth of tissue for state occasions, a second of crimson velvet for ordinary use, and the third of black velvet 'wt gylte chapes' for times of mourning or great solemnity.

Eleven years later in 1545, a new sword was given to the city by Sir Ralph Warren, who was the lord mayor of London, as appears in the following minute:

Item this day Sr Rauf Warren Knight and aldran for the very zeale good wyll and ffavo that he hathe & beareth towarde this honorable Cytie of London hys native countrye hath frely gevyn unto the seid Cytie a very goodly Sworde & a Riche Scaberd of crymsyn velvett garnesed wth golde for the same to be borne before the lords mayors of the Cytie for the tyme beinge when they shall thynke yt mete and convenient.

In 1554, yet another sword was obtained, this time by purchase, but without a scabbard, it being ordered that the city's 'Ryche Scaberds' should be used with it. In 1563, another new sword was given to the city by Richard Matthew, citizen and cutler. Whether these four swords continued in use together, or whether any one was superseded, does not appear, as no further mention of the swords occurs in the minute books for nearly fifty years after the last quoted entry. Within that period, at any rate, the scabbard of the fine sword still existing, known as 'the pearl sword', was procured; for in 1608, the scabbard was already in need of repair and the chamberlain was ordered to effect such repair.

In 1615, a new sword and scabbard was ordered to be bought, to take the place of the one until then carried before the lord mayor, which was declared to be 'verie old and unfitting' to be carried any longer. The new sword was provided by Oliver Plankett, cutler, at a cost of £22. Two years afterwards, an entry occurs which is difficult to believe can refer to the new sword so soon after its purchase, where the sword-bearer was to be refunded for 'new guilding and mending the Lord Maiors sworde'. Only five years later, in 1623, another new sword and scabbard was bought, to be carried before the lord mayor.

In 1649, when the city mace was re-made in obedience to the order of the Parliament, the city swords were stripped of all emblems of royalty, and otherwise 'amended' to suit the altered state of things. Of the alterations made on the Restoration of the monarchy, there does not seem to be any record in the minute books. Besides the entries already quoted, there are many others, which show that the constant wear and tear necessitated the frequent repair and renewal of the swords and their scabbards.

London has six swords.

The Pearl Sword – 1554?

Length of sword	3ft 10¾in – 1.187m	Weight of sword	4lb 6¾oz – 2.007kg
Length of blade	3ft 0in – 0.914m – Double-edged	Width of blade	1¾in – 0.044m
Length of hilt	10¾in – 0.273m – Two-handed	Width of guard	11⅞in – 0.303m
Length of scabbard	3ft 1⅜in – 0.949m	Weight of scabbard	1lb 13oz – 0.819kg

Sword

The pearl sword is so called after the decoration of its sheath. The blade has four parallel fullers, two long and two shorter, with the Solingen or Passau wolf mark, but its original appearance had been greatly marred by blueing it for the first 20½in and etching with various devices. On the obverse it has a bunch of fruit, some leaf-work and three different trophies of arms. On the reverse it has a trophy of arms, with quivers of arrows, a shield of the city arms and a ship in full sail. The quillon block is oblong, with a boldly modelled lion's face and fruit on each side, and the protecting plate has on the obverse the city arms, once enamelled, and on the reverse a bust of Minerva with trophies of arms in the spandrels. In the plate and through the blade is a hole for the scabbard screw. The quillons, which are box-shaped with scrolled bands along each upper and lower

The City of London Pearl Sword – 1554?

edge, are also wrought with trophies of arms in relief on each side. Each end terminates in a vaguely crescent shape but with the lower end shorter. In each 'crescent' is a finely modelled figure of a satyr. The grip is covered with rather tarnished silver wire. The ovoid pommel is of silver-gilt, with a beautifully chased figure of Justice with sword and scales in a medallion on each side, and grotesque masks on the edges. The tang nut is segmented.

This fine sword is said to have been given to the city by Elizabeth I on the opening of the Royal Exchange in 1570; but no mention of such a gift is to be found among the city records, and neither do other writers notice it. The sword is, however, certainly of sixteenth-century date, and is probably that bought in 1554; or possibly it may be that 'verye goodly sworde' given to the city by Sir Ralph Warren in 1545. The silver-gilt portions of the sword and sheath are most beautifully wrought, and are of course original; they are not hallmarked. This sword is only borne before the lord mayor on great occasions.

Scabbard

The scabbard is covered in crimson velvet, bordered with gold lace and embroidered throughout its length on both sides with a guilloche of loops of pearls and spangles inside a border of more pearls. Surprisingly, the decoration is longer on one side than the other and ends some 4in from the end of the scabbard with a band of gold lace. It slims down to fit under the protecting plate. There is a small hole to accommodate the scabbard screw. The chape, which has a segmented finial, is of silver-gilt, with an oval medallion of Minerva with helmet and spear on one side, and the back view of another female figure on the other. There is neither mouth-locket nor throat-locket. The 'rich scaberd of pearle', from which the sword gets its name, was already in existence in 1608, when it was repaired and new trimmed. The present arrangement of the pearl embroidery is quite recent, and the sheath has been so often re-covered and repaired that it is impossible to say how it was originally decorated.

The Old Bailey Sword – 1563?

Length of sword	3ft 10⅝in – 1.184m	Weight of sword	3lb 6¾oz – 1.548kg
Length of blade	2ft 11¾in – 0.908m – Double-edged	Width of blade	1⅝in – 0.041m
Length of hilt	11¼in – 0.286m – Two-handed	Width of guard	8½in – 0.216m
Length of scabbard	3ft 1⅜in – 0.949m	Weight of scabbard	1lb 0¾oz – 0.477kg

Sword

This sword, which is in very good condition, is placed above the lord mayor's chair in the Central Criminal Court (the Old Bailey) on the occasion the lord mayor opens the term and receives Her Majesty's judges, and thereafter above the centre seat in the court

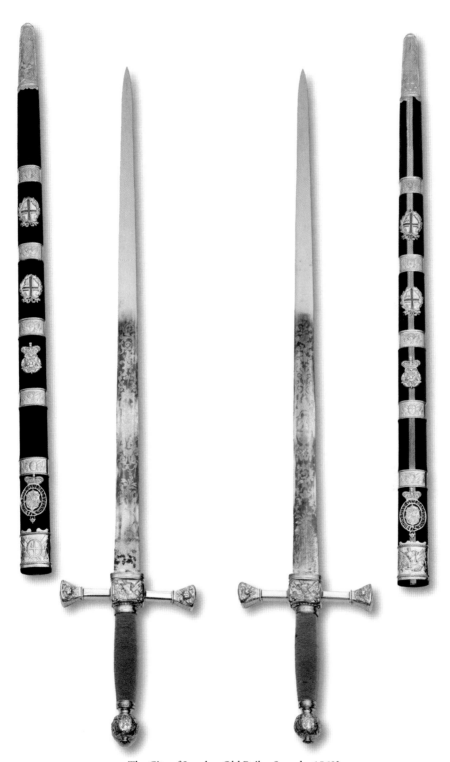

The City of London Old Bailey Sword – 1563?

of the senior judge each day. The blade is of no great antiquity but has sustained damage at some stage in the past. This extends for the first 5in of the point and has been electro-plated over, though the marks are still evident. It is blued for the first 18½in and bears much leaf-work. It has on the obverse the royal arms, probably of George IV, within the Garter and crowned, and on the reverse the arms of the city. It has a scabbard screw hole half an inch from the hilt. The hilt is of copper-gilt. The quillon block has a cup to receive the end of the scabbard and has raised trophies of arms on each side. The quillons are of square section with chamfered edges. They are plain for the first 1½in and broaden with a rose on each face and widen out at the ends, and are wrought with flowers and fruit in relief. The grip is wrapped with silver wire with a chased ferrule at the hilt end. The ferrule at the other end is part of the globular pommel, which has scroll-work and trophies in relief with a grotesque on each side. The pommel is loose. There is a small button screwed onto the tang.

The hilt is apparently of sixteenth-century date, and it may possibly be the 'very fayer & goodly sword well and workmanly wrought & gylded' given to the city in 1563 by Richard Matthew, citizen and cutler.

Scabbard

The scabbard is covered with deep crimson velvet with a gold lace galloon down the obverse and seven copper-gilt mounts (chape, five bands and the mouth-locket) inter-spersed with four later silver-gilt mounts. They are: (1) the chape, which is 4¾in long, has a damaged lower end and has the city arms in an oval, with flags, etc. (O) and military trophies (R); (2) a band with a trophy (O) and the city arms (R); (3) an oval cartouche with the city arms within a laurel wreath (with what appears to be a piece of red tinsel under the cross) on each side; (4) a band with the city arms (O) and trophies (R); (5) an oval cartouche with the city arms within a laurel wreath (as above) on each side; (6) a band with trophies (O) and the city arms (R); (7) a crowned rose on each side; (8) a band with the city arms (O) and trophies (R); (9) a band with trophies (O) and the city arms (R); (10) the Hanoverian royal arms as borne from 1714 to 1801, within the Garter and crowned on each side; and (11) the mouth-locket with trophies (O) and the city arms (R). A small screw hole is below this.

The Mourning Sword – 1615 or 1623?

Length of sword	4ft 2⅜in – 1.280m	Weight of sword	3lb 12oz – 1.700kg
Length of blade	3ft 2⅜in – 0.975m – Double-edged	Width of blade	1⅞in – 0.047m
Length of hilt	12in – 0.305m – Two-handed	Width of guard	11¼in – 0.286m
Length of scabbard	3ft 3¼in – 0.997m	Weight of scabbard	10oz – 0.284kg

The City of London Mourning Sword – 1615 or 1623?

Sword

It has long been the custom in the city of London, as well as in other places, to have a sword painted black and devoid of ornament, which is borne before the lord mayor on occasions of mourning or special solemnity. As early as 1534, the Chamberlain of London was ordered to pay for a sword of black velvet with a gilt chape, and an entry of 1628 which orders the reimbursement of the sword-bearer for trimming the black sword shows that such a sword has continued in use. The blade, which is an old one, is in good condition, though somewhat stained, and has identical markings on each side. It has short ricasso which is gilt for the first 3½in and blued gilt for another 1in from the hilt. It has a broad hollow central fuller which stretches almost the entire length of the blade, with two armourer's marks, one formed of a series of dotted devices and the other a circle with five outward spokes. The hilt is iron and has been japanned black. It is of the most ordinary character, and apparently modern. The quillon block has a protecting cup with a boss on each side. The quillons are straight, flat and spread at the end to 1½in with a similar boss on each face. The grip is covered in very deep maroon velvet with a serrated ferrule at each end. The pommel is circular with domed faces and a boss on each face. There is a small globular tang button.

This sword is borne before the lord mayor on Good Friday, all feast days, the anniversary of the Great Fire of London and all occasions of great solemnity.

Scabbard

The scabbard is covered in velvet: it looks black but is actually a very deep maroon, with a short plain japanned black iron chape with a fleur-de-lis end and a small finial. The velvet is now a little worn in places along the edges. In 1895 there was a mouth-locket – today the scabbard ends with the velvet tucked into the mouth.

The Sword of State – *c.* 1670

Length of sword	4ft 2¼in – 1.276m	Weight of sword	5lb 1¼oz – 2.302kg
Length of blade	3ft 1½in – 0.952m – Double-edged	Width of blade	1⅝in – 0.041m
Length of hilt	12¾in – 0.324m – Two-handed	Width of guard	12¾in – 0.324m
Length of scabbard	3ft 3in – 0.991m	Weight of scabbard	1lb 14½oz–0.866kg

Sword

This sword is usually carried before the lord mayor. The blade, which is in fair condition, has a broad central fuller with, on the obverse, an armourer's mark and the letters '3ANODNAW', and on the reverse the name 'FERARA'. The first 19in has an added damascene pattern in blue and gold (now mostly worn off), with the city arms (O) and the royal arms of George IV, within the Garter and crowned, with supporters (R). Close to the hilt is a scabbard screw hole. The hilt is silver-gilt and richly chased. The quillon

The City of London Sword of State – *c.* 1670

block has the royal arms (probably that of Charles II) within the Garter and crowned on the obverse, with fleurs-de-lis in the spandrels, and the city arms on an oval shield on the reverse. The quillons are wrought with an oak-leaf pattern with acorns, and turn up at the ends in a single lion's head. In the mane, at the back of the head, is a grotesque facing backwards (possibly a bull or a pig?). The grip, which tapers slightly, is bound with silver wire (given the age of the sword, it is probable that the wire has been renewed as it is in such good condition comparatively). The globular pommel, which is a trifle loose, is wrought in *repoussé* with flattened faces, and has the figure of Justice with sword and scales on the obverse and the figure of Fame with two trumpets on the reverse. On each edge is a cherub. There is small chased tang button.

In 1895, *J&H* concluded that 'from comparison with other swords of similar fashion, e.g. those at Thetford, Yarmouth etc., this sword cannot be older than *c.* 1680, but there are no entries in the minute books which can be specially connected with it'. However, with the aid of modern digital photography, the hilts of Shrewsbury (dated in 1669) and Appleby (donated between 1661 and 1679) and this sword are as near identical as manufacture will allow (only the grip of this sword differs). It is therefore probable that this sword and that at Appleby were actually obtained closer to 1670.

Scabbard

The scabbard is covered with crimson velvet, and adorned with twelve mounts. The chape and six silver-gilt bands are older, all richly wrought in *repoussé*, and are designed to be viewed when the sword is point upwards. The five intermediate mounts are all of the same later date, but three have been put on upside down. The mounts are: (1) the chape has a winged but armless figure issuing from foliage on each side, and terminates in an acorn; (2) a broad band with a cherub's head and wings on each side; (3) an oval cartouche, with the city arms on a tinsel field, and encircled by a wreath of laurel on each side; (4) a broad band with a cherub's head and wings on each side; (5) a crowned rose on each side (down); (6) a broad band with a cherub's head and wings on each side; (7) a crowned harp on each side (down); (8) a broad band with a cherub's head on each side; (9) an oval cartouche, with the city arms on a tinsel field, and encircled by a wreath of laurel on each side; (10) a broad band with a cherub's head on each side; (11) the royal arms, of George IV, within the Garter and crowned on each side (down); and (12) a broad mouth-locket with a scabbard screw hole on each side, with, on one side, the city arms with foliage and scroll-work and an acorn above, and, on the other side, the royal arms, probably of Charles II, within the Garter and crowned, with an acorn above and a cherub's head and wings below The bands with cherubs have lost their securing pins and now slide.

In 1962, this sword was considered too valuable to be taken outside the city boundaries and so a 'travelling' sword and scabbard (virtually identical) were purchased for 'daily' use.

The Justice Room Sword – *c.* 1830

Length of sword	3ft 9¾in – 1.163m	Weight of sword	4lb 13oz–2.185kg
Length of blade	2ft 9⅝in – 0.854m – Double-edged	Width of blade	1½in – 0.038m
Length of hilt	11¾in – 0.298m – Two-handed	Width of guard	11⅝in – 0.295m
Length of scabbard	3ft 5¼in – 1.048m	Weight of scabbard	1lb 8oz – 0.678kg

Sword

This sword used to hang in the Justice Room in the Mansion House, but since 1991 it has been displayed in the No. 1 Magistrate's Court in the City of London. The sword is believed to be Portuguese and dates from around 1830. It has a steel blade with a ¾in ricasso and is inscribed 'DONNA MARIA' on both sides, now slightly worn from cleaning, in the 9½in fuller. The hilt is gilt. The quillon block is large and square with a large circular leaf pattern with a raised central portion on each side. The quillons are of oval section with bold acanthus leaves on the underside and terminate in a dragon's head. The grip is covered in much-worn crimson velvet, which badly needs replacement, with gold lace on either side. There is gilt ferrule next to the pommel, which is circular and flat. A medallion with foliage in relief is inset on each face, while the sides and base have raised shoulders, giving an overall impression of a cross. The tang button is tiny.

Scabbard

The wooden scabbard is covered with crimson velvet with gold lace down each edge and eleven silver-gilt mounts with a chape, four bands and mouth-locket, and on the obverse only a further five mounts. The reverse of all the mounts is plain. These are: (1) the chape, which is 9in long with a finial and leaf and scroll-work; (2) a badge of the city arms with a red tinsel field; (3) a band with three narrow longitudinal cartouches; (4) a crowned rose; (5) a band as above; (6) a crowned harp (very loose and with a poor blue field added later); (7) a band as above; (8) a badge of the city arms with a red tinsel field; (9) a band as above; (10) the royal arms, probably of Victoria, set in a diamond shape over a blue tinsel field, within the Garter and crowned; and (11) the mouth-locket which bears the city arms set in relief with a red tinsel field. On the reverse of this locket is a small crown which is viewed up. The velvet is much worn and needs replacement, as the wood can be seen through one gap. The scabbard is some 7in longer than the blade, indicating that it was made for another sword. It should be viewed point down.

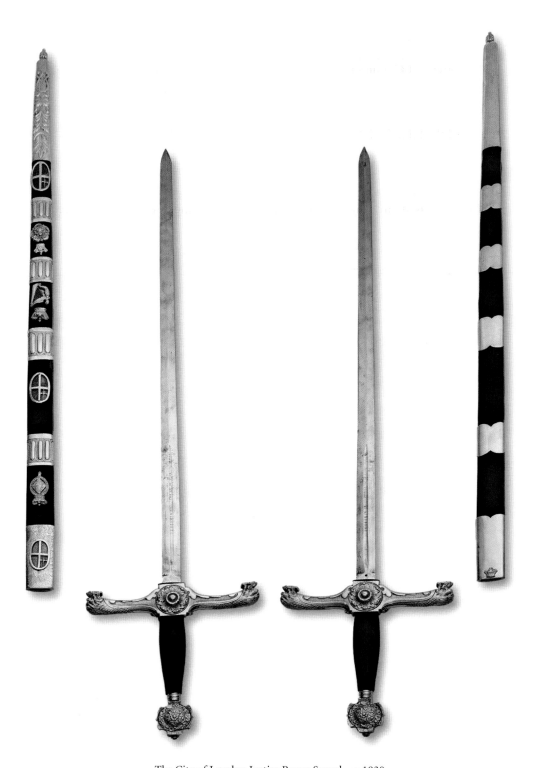

The City of London Justice Room Sword – *c.* 1830

The Travelling Sword of State – 1962

Length of sword	4ft 3¼in – 1.315m	Weight of sword	4lb 0oz–1.816kg
Length of blade	3ft 2⅝in – 0.981m – Double-edged	Width of blade	1⅝in – 0.041m
Length of hilt	12¾in – 0.323m – Two-handed	Width of guard	12¼in – 0.311m
Length of scabbard	3ft 4in – 1.016m	Weight of scabbard	2lb 3¾oz–1.012kg

Sword

The Sword of State is considered to be too valuable to be taken outside the city boundaries. This sword, made by Wilkinson Sword at their Acton works, gives the impression of being an exact copy of the original but is, in fact, markedly different, particularly in the measurements etc. The sword was presented by Sir Ralph Perring, lord mayor in 1962, to mark his year of office. The beautiful modern blade was hand-forged in the finest sword steel and is etched for 17in. On the obverse, it bears the royal arms of Elizabeth II within the Garter and crowned with supporters and the Wilkinson logo. On the reverse, it bears one of the usual Wilkinson patterns with a badge of the city arms with crest, supporters and motto and the Wilkinson logo. It also bears, some 15in from the point, the inscription 'FIRST BORNE BY THE SWORDBEARER BRIGADIER R H S POPHAM OBE 3-5-1963'. A scabbard screw hole is close to the hilt. The hilt is finished in silver-gilt. The hilt is similar to the original, except the quillon block bears an extremely stylised royal arms and the grip is now somewhat tarnished. There is a rather prominent tang button.

Scabbard

The scabbard is covered with crimson velvet with gold lace along each edge and twelve silver-gilt mounts. Most are very similar to the originals, except that the acorn finial on the chape is rather flattened, the city arms on the four lockets are enamelled with a red cross on a white field and the royal arms on the last locket on each side and on the mouth-locket are those of Elizabeth II and are again stylised. Again the crowned rose, crowned harp and royal arms have been applied upside down to mirror those on the original. The velvet is now well-worn in the lowest section. Made in 1962, it should be viewed in both directions.

Cap of Maintenance

Besides a special habit, the sword-bearer wore a cap of maintenance. The earliest entry in the minute books was in 1519. In 1546, it was described as 'a very goodly and Riche hatt for the swordeberer'. The next entry in 1614 shows a sum was to be paid for 'the amendmt and garnishing of a riche hat of Crymson velvett called the cap of mainte-nance', and in 1629 £3 was to be paid 'for the repairing of the riche ymbrodered Capp'. Although no mention of the fur cap for winter occurs in the records during the century after 1520, it certainly continued to be worn by the sword-bearer, and an example of its use in the early part of the seventeenth century may be seen in the curious contemporary picture belonging to the Society of Antiquaries, representing James I and his court, with the judges and the lord mayor, with all the civic authorities, hearing a sermon at St Paul's Cross on 26 March 1620. In 1688, £11 was paid 'for new furring and tassels to the cap of maintenance'. It was repaired in 1746 and in 1777, and again in 1813. The custom of wearing a silk or velvet hat in summer, and a fur cap in winter, has long ceased, and the only cap of maintenance now worn on all occasions is a hat of sable fur. The current fur cap of maintenance is of natural Russian sable with a stiff sable crown. It is 8in high, and widens out from the bottom upwards in the manner of the fur hats worn by persons of quality during the reigns of Richard II and Henry IV; indeed it is possibly derived from a hat at that time. The lining is of black silk. It was presented in 1975. Inside the crown is a small pocket that contains the lord mayor's key to the Christ's Hospital seal. A disappearing strap to enable it to be carried on the arm when not worn on the head has now disappeared!

Uniform

In 1539, it was stated that 'the swordeberer shall have a cote of damask gardyd wt [erased] velvet & viij other Cotes of Russet clothe gardyd wt Russet velvet at the charge of thys Cytye'. In 1553, it was ordered that the sword-bearer should also have a black gown. From the late fourteenth century, it had become an established custom that the sword-bearer's official robe should be of damask, and one typical entry in 1587 states 'a decent gowne of damaske garded and faced with velvet to be made for master Swordbearer'. The wearing of Court Dress with black breeches and black silk stockings was discontinued for the coronation of George IV in 1820. The sword-bearer's ordinary habit is now a gown of brocaded satin, of the same material as the lord mayor's state gown, without the gold lace but with silk lace and tufts and black velvet facing. This is worn over a black morning coat complete with a 'flash', white lace cuffs, a shrieval collar, white jabot, Old Bailey trousers and shoes with silver buckles and white gloves. Old Bailey breeches are worn in the evening.

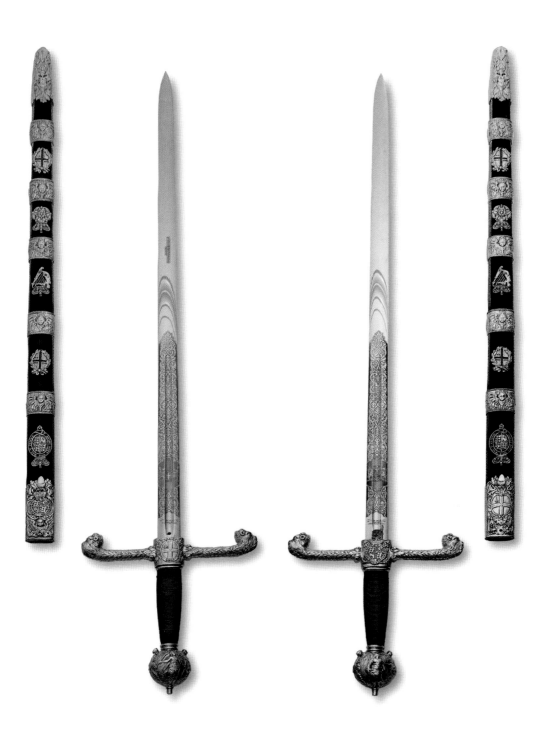

The City of London Travelling Sword of State – 1962

Bristol

Prerogative

In 1373, Edward III granted a charter to the city for services rendered by Bristol ships and men during the siege of Calais. The charter made the city a county, created the mayor and made him the king's escheator in the new county. An escheator was entitled to have a sword borne before him; thus the office of sword-bearer dates from that year. There is no mention of a sword in any of the city charters.

Bristol has four fine processional swords, the quality of which surpasses all other cities.

The Mourning Sword – pre-1367

Length of sword	3ft 11¼in – 1.200m	Weight of sword	5lb 1½oz – 2.314kg
Length of blade	3ft 2⅝in – 0.981m – Double-edged	Width of blade	2⅛in – 0.054m
Length of hilt	8⅝in – 0.219m – Two-handed	Width of guard	14⅛in – 0.359m
Length of scabbard	3ft 3½in – 1.003m	Weight of scabbard	2lb 10oz – 1.190kg

Sword

This sword has a steel blade with an armourer's mark on each side. The hilt is silver-plated and gilt. The six-sided straight quillons are deflected or turned up at the points (the central portion is a clumsy restoration of later date); they are decorated with a chasing of leaf-work. Each end has sustained damage. There is a hexagonal nut between the block and the grip. The grip is wrapped with alternating gilt bands and gilt wire. The pommel is ovoid, 3¼in long by 2¼in wide, and has on either side a sunken panel surrounded by raised cables. One of these bears the device of the city, a ship entering the water-gate, on a ground formerly enamelled; the other, two shields side by side, the dexter bearing the cross of St George, on a diapered field, the sinister bearing the royal arms with France ancient and England quarterly which was used by Edward III up to 1367, the whole having originally been enamelled. The broad edge of the pommel is chased with foliage. The tang end has been hammered flat over a crude washer. The pommel is viewed point down.

There is good reason for supposing that this sword was given to or obtained by the city on the granting of Edward III's charter of 1373; however, the royal arms on the sword ceased to be used in 1367. It is therefore probable that the sword was actually manufactured prior to 1367. In 1895, it was noted that through carelessness in putting together the sword after some repairs, the quillons had been put on upside down. This error has now been corrected. This sword is used only on the death of the sovereign or if the lord mayor dies in office.

The City of Bristol – Mourning Sword – pre-1367

Scabbard

The scabbard is covered in black velvet, richly decorated with seven silver-gilt mounts. All are in very good condition. The mounts are: (1) the chape, with on the obverse four large roses, the reverse is most beautifully chased with foliage (acanthus) in relief; (2) a small star or sun (O), which appears to be part of the original fourteenth-century enrichments of the scabbard, that on the reverse is now lost; (3) a broad band beautifully chased with acanthus leaf and flowers (O), and a large rose (R); (4) a large star or sun on each side; (5) a broad band with a skull and cross-bones between the words 'MEMENTO MORI' (Reminder of Death), and above, 'STATVTVM EST OMNIBVS SEMEL MORI' (It is ordained that for all to die once) (O) and 'IOHN KNIGHT Esqr MAIOR ANNO DOM 1670' (R) – attached to each side is a small mordant with a cherub's head in relief, to which was originally attached a black velvet baldric which laced the lockets in position; (6) a large star or sun on each side; and (7) the mouth-locket has on the obverse, in relief, a figure of Elizabeth I seated on a throne of state, with a lion's head on the end of each arm, with orb and sceptre beneath a canopy and on the reverse the royal arms, probably of Elizabeth I, within the Garter, with helm, crest and mantling, and lion and dragon supporters. It has two rings for the baldric. The locket is of the same date and by the same hand as on the 1594 mounts on the Lent Sword described below. Mounts (1) and (3) form part of the original decoration of the sword, probably late fourteenth or early fifteenth century.

The Pearl Sword – pre-1399

Length of sword	4ft 0½in – 1.232m	**Weight of sword**	4lb 5¼oz – 1.962kg
Length of blade	3ft 0in – 0.915m – Double-edged	**Width of blade**	1½in – 0.038m
Length of hilt	12½in – 0.318m – 1½-handed	**Width of guard**	12⅝in – 0.321m
Length of scabbard	3ft 2⅜in – 0.981m	**Weight of scabbard**	1lb 2oz – 0.505kg

Sword

This sword is one of the most precious examples of English late-medieval metalwork. The steel blade is of a type common between 1350 and 1420 and has an armourer's mark on each side – now almost obliterated. The hilt is silver-gilt. The quillons are straight, plain and six-sided, and terminate with a square cut. The grip has, on the obverse directly under the cross-guard, a small shield bearing the royal arms with France modern and England quarterly, impaled by the cross Fleury and five martlets ascribed to Edward the Confessor: this version used by Richard II ceased in 1399. Below is the first half of an inscription 'Jon wellis of London groc' & meyr'. At the other end of the grip, next to the pommel, is a small shield of the city arms which may have been added later, and above the other half of the inscription 'to Bristow gave this swerd feir'. On the other side of the grip, next to the pommel, is engraved 'w cleve'. Halfway down the grip

The City of Bristol – Pearl Sword – pre-1399

is a collar, indicating that this is a 'bastard' sword, i.e. one-and-a-half handed. Across the flattened pear-shaped pommel on each side is a scroll inscribed with the Wells motto 'mercy and grace'. The sides are chased with three flutes.

This sword was given to the city by Sir John Wells, mayor of London in 1431. There is no record of the reason for the gift of this sword. It is known that Sir John Wells, who was a member of the Worshipful Company of Grocers, lent money to the Crown. Such occasions were by no means rare in the fifteenth century, when one or another of the Crown Jewels was often in pawn. It has been suggested that the sword was a piece of royal property which was acquired by him as an unredeemed pledge, from the Royal Armoury. Alternatively, until 1520 the sword carried before the mayor of London was not provided by the Corporation but paid for by the mayor in office himself, and there is reason to believe that this particular sword was passed on from mayor to mayor from the 1390s, until John Wells decided to buy a new one, no doubt of more fashionable design. Who W. Cleve was is not known; his name does not occur in the lists of mayors or sheriffs.

The use of this sword is reserved for royal visits and other very special occasions.

Scabbard

The original scabbard was replaced in 1574 by one richly embroidered with seed pearls, hence the name, to mark a visit by Elizabeth I. This sheath, which is 3ft 3⅛in long and weighs 1lb 2¼oz, is still held in a cabinet in the lord mayor's office. No traces of pearls are visible on the scabbard, but there were portions of silver embroidery on the crimson velvet. The mounts of the sheath are of silver-gilt, ornamented with foliage and strap-work of Elizabethan character, to which period the silver embroidery also belonged. On one side are two silver-gilt letters, 'r' and 'd', all that remains of the motto, 'mercy and grace', which formed part of the original decoration of the sheath.

A new scabbard was presented to the city in 1953 by Alderman Sir Kenneth Brown, the lord mayor at the time of the coronation of Elizabeth II. The scabbard is covered with crimson velvet; the design is based on traditional English sixteenth-century sources. The three silver-gilt mounts and letters were executed by Leslie Durbin and the embroidery, including the royal cipher, the four national emblems and the Bristol arms and the motto 'Mercy and Grace' interspersing the various decorations, are enriched with seed pearls, by the Royal School of Needlework, all on the obverse. The decorations on the obverse are: (1) the chape, which is plain, ending with a fleur-de-lis edging; (2) the royal cipher 'EIIR'; (3) the letters 'me'; (4) the English rose; (5) the letters 'rcy'; (6) the Scottish thistle; (7) the letters 'and'; (8) the Irish harp; (9) a plain band with fleur-de-lis edging; (10) a Welch griffon; (11) the letters 'gr'; (12) three lions passant; (13) the letters 'ace'; (14) a ship in the form of the city arms; and (15) the mouth-locket, which bears on the obverse the inscription 'This scabbard was given to commemorate the Coronation of QUEEN ELIZABETH II by Alderman K A L Brown Lord Mayor 1953'. On the reverse, the bands are blank and there is an embroidered linear pattern of repeated 's' with pearls and a leaf on each side of a galloon of gold lace. The velvet is now very worn along each edge and several of the pearls are missing.

The Lent Sword – *c.* 1499

Length of sword	4ft 1¼in – 1.251m	Weight of sword	4lb 3½oz – 1.915kg
Length of blade	3ft 3⅞in – 1.013m – Double-edged	Width of blade	2in – 0.051m
Length of hilt	9¾in – 0.248m – Two-handed	Width of guard	11in – 0.279m
Length of scabbard	3ft 10in – 1.169m	Weight of scabbard	4lb 2¼oz – 1.877kg

Sword

This sword gains its name from being borne before the judges at the Lent Assizes, where it is then placed behind the senior judge. However, it was known earlier as the Sunday or 'hollidaye' sword. The steel blade has a maker's mark on each side and a 2¾in ricasso. The hilt is silver-gilt. The straight quillons are of square section and engraved with leaf-work. The ends turn up. The grip is bound with silver wire with a ferrule at each end. The pommel is a slightly oval flattened wheel-shape with a raised circular centre, and has on one side in a circle a shield of royal arms with France modern and England quarterly, possibly of Henry VII, and on the other a shield of St George, originally enamelled, with the date 1583 (engraved subsequently) in chief. The pommel is further ornamented with scrollwork and has, at each end of the oval, a Lombardic T enclosing the letter M and surmounted by a crown of three *fleurons*. Round the edge of the pommel is engraved on one side 'THIS x SWORDE x WE x DID x REPAIER*' and on the other 'THOMAS x ALDWORTH x BEINGE x MAYOR*'. Thomas Aldworth was mayor in 1582–83. There is a fairly prominent tang button.

How Bristol came to acquire this elaborate sword is not known. Tradition links it with the royal charter of 1499 which set the seal on the government of the town until 1835. It is now the sword borne most regularly before the lord mayor.

Scabbard

This very heavy scabbard is covered with black velvet, with on the obverse eight and on the reverse seven rich silver-gilt mounts and mordants, and is encircled by the baldric, which is also of black velvet. The mounts are: (1) the chape with, on the obverse, a falcon standing on the stump of a tree, with a rose bush in bloom trailing over the field – a badge of Queen Anne Boleyn also borne by her daughter, Elizabeth I – and on the reverse, the figures of Prudence (Wisdom) with a serpent round an arm (on the left) and of Justice with scales and a scimitar (on the right) (one pair of Cardinal Virtues), with, above, the royal arms with France modern and England quarterly, within the Garter, again possibly of Edward IV. The chape terminates in a finely modelled royal crown which unscrews and is now slightly out of alignment and leans to one side; (2) a small star or blazing sun on each

The City of Bristol Lent Sword – *c.* 1499

side; (3) a small star or blazing sun on each side; (4) a broad locket, which also belongs to the baldric, has the city arms with the crest and supporters granted in 1569 (O) and a large star or blazing sun (R); (5) a large star or blazing sun on each side; (6) a broad locket of the baldric, which bears a spirited representation of St George overcoming the dragon (O) and a large star or blazing sun (R); (7) a large star or blazing sun (O) and the reverse is blank; and (8) the mouth-locket, which has, on the obverse, a figure of Temperance bearing two vases (on the left) and of Fortitude with a scroll and pillar (on the right) (the other pair of Cardinal Virtues), and on the reverse, the first four verses of 'ROMANES XIII' – 'Let every soul be subject to the higher power, etc.' and 'ANO * 1594 * ANO * EL * REG * 36 * FRANCIS x KNIGHT x MAIOR' (the '5' is the wrong way round, as is the third 'N'). It is similar in style to the mouth-locket on the mourning sword. Locket (4) appears to be slightly later than the other lockets, which are all of the date 1594.

The Sword of State – 1752

Length of sword	4ft 8in – 1.422m	Weight of sword	11lb 6oz – 5.158kg
Length of blade	3ft 5⅜in – 1.051m – Double-edged	Width of blade	4¼in – 0.108m
Length of hilt	15in – 0.381m – Two-handed	Width of guard	17⅛in – 0.435m
Length of scabbard	4ft 2¾in – 1.289m	Weight of scabbard	10lb 0oz – 4.536kg

Sword

This enormous sword is in very good condition and has a long, wide steel blade that is blued for 11½in with various patterns and leaf-work, and has remnants of gilding. The hollow hilt is massively wrought in silver-gilt. The quillon block has a cup to seat the base of the scabbard and has a large rose in relief on each face. The quillons are shaped like an elaborate 'w' and are decorated with acanthus leaves and other swirling leaf-work and a chevron pattern along the top edge. The grip is spirally fluted. The pommel, which is small in comparison to the rest of the sword, is spherical and has decoration similar to the quillons. The tang nut is large and wrought but is somewhat flattened and bent to one side due to the weight when set down (hardly surprising when one considers the total weight is over 21lb).

This outstanding example of the work of a rococo goldsmith was especially commissioned by the council following a resolution in 1751 that 'a handsome scabbard of gilt plate with such arms and devices as shall be directed' should be bought for the use of the mayor. This ended the previous custom of the sheriffs presenting the mayor with a new scabbard on New Year's Day and resulted in the purchase of a sword as well. The commission was placed with Nathaniel Nangles, goldsmith, a freeman of Bristol. However, as with several other pieces of civic insignia, the order was probably passed on to London, as the hilt bears the London hallmarks for 1752–53, and PW with a star above, for Peter Werritzer, the maker, of Foster Lane, London.

Scabbard

The scabbard is covered with crimson velvet and has seven silver-gilt mounts of elaborate character interspersed with a spiral of flowers and foliage throughout the length of the scabbard. This is not continuous but made in sections – small elements are missing. These are: (1) the chape, which has floral decorations beneath shell fluting on each side, complementing the detail on the exuberantly styled hilt, is capped with a not-so-miniature coronet with a cap of velvet turned up with an ermine collar, symbolic of the mayor's role as escheator; (2) a figure of Charity (O) and of Justice (now detached) (R); (3) a figure of Peace (O) and of Prosperity (R); (4) a figure of Faith (O) and of Philosophy (R); (5) a figure of Commerce (O) and of Trade (R); (6) a locket bearing the royal arms of George II within the Garter and crowned with supporters and motto (O) and the city arms (R); and (7) the mouth-locket, which is inscribed 'ANNO REGNI GEORGII SECUNDI VICESIMO QUINTO ANNOQUE SALUTIS 1752' (In the twenty-fifth year of the reign of George II and in the year of salvation 1752) (O). The reverse is plain. The end of the mouth-locket is reduced to fit into the quillon block cup.

The sword and scabbard were purchased by the corporation in 1752. The bill included £176 13s 3d for the silver upon it, which weighed 201oz 13 pennyweights, £3 3s for gold plate and chasing the king's arms, £6 6s for the velvet scabbard and blade and £2 4s for the case and box: a grand total of £188 6s 3d.

For many years, this sword was the one most regularly used, despite its weight. It is no longer carried but is held in the Council House and placed behind the lord mayor at council meetings to show the authority.

Cap of Maintenance

The fur cap of maintenance is of grey Russian squirrel fur with a rolled brim and a deep loose crimson velvet crown.

Uniform

The usual uniform for the sword-bearer is a black moleskin frock-coat over black moleskin breeches with white shirt, white jabot, black stockings and black shoes with silver buckles. Occasionally, the sword-bearer will wear a black academic robe over a dark suit, with white shirt and black shoes, or a short black morning-coat with a black waistcoat over a white shirt, and pinstriped trousers and black shoes. A white jabot and white cotton gloves are worn with each outfit.

The City of Bristol Sword of State – 1752

Coventry

Prerogative

It is not known when the city was first granted the privilege of bearing a sword *before* the mayor, but it must have been in 1384 or prior to that, because in 1384 Richard II ordered the sword be carried *behind* instead of before the mayor, because he did not do justice. It was not carried again before the mayor until July 1387, when, according to Henry Knighton of Leicester, on the occasion of the king's visit: 'And again he granted to them, that the mayor of the town may have a man carrying a sword with golden adornment and decoration in his presence, after the London manner.' In 1471, Edward IV came to Coventry, and on account of the adherence of the citizens to the Lancastrian cause, took away the mayor's sword and the sheriffs' yards or staves; so they lost their privileges, which were not restored until payment of 500 marks. The mayor's sword was stolen during riots in 1481 but recovered some months later.

An inventory of 1704 mentions three swords and four scabbards, but the city now possesses only one of each. It is not known what has become of one of the swords or three of the scabbards, but one other hilt survives.

The exhibit in the Burrell Collection of the hilt of a former Coventry sword claims (Tobias Campbell, 2007):

> This hilt is all that remains of a sword that probably belonged to Edward IV of England. This war-like Yorkist king, who crushed his enemies during the Wars of the Roses, gave this sword to the City of Coventry as a symbol of royal authority and good relations between the city and the crown. The guard bears the famous Yorkist badges of the 'sun in splendour' and the white rose.

There is evidence that Edward IV took away a sword in 1471, but none that he gave one. The second part of the first sentence of this extract is, therefore, pure speculation. The first part of the second sentence is irrelevant, while the second part is unsubstantiated. Only the third sentence is factual and accurate.

The Sword of State – *c.* 1430

Length of sword	4ft 1⅞in – 1.267m	Weight of sword	4lb 6¼oz–1.994kg
Length of blade	3ft 2⅛in – 0.968m – Double-edged	Width of blade	2in – 0.051m
Length of hilt	11¾in – 0.298m – Two-handed	Width of guard	15in – 0.381m
Length of scabbard	3ft 3¼in – 0.997m	Weight of scabbard	2lb 6oz – 1.076kg

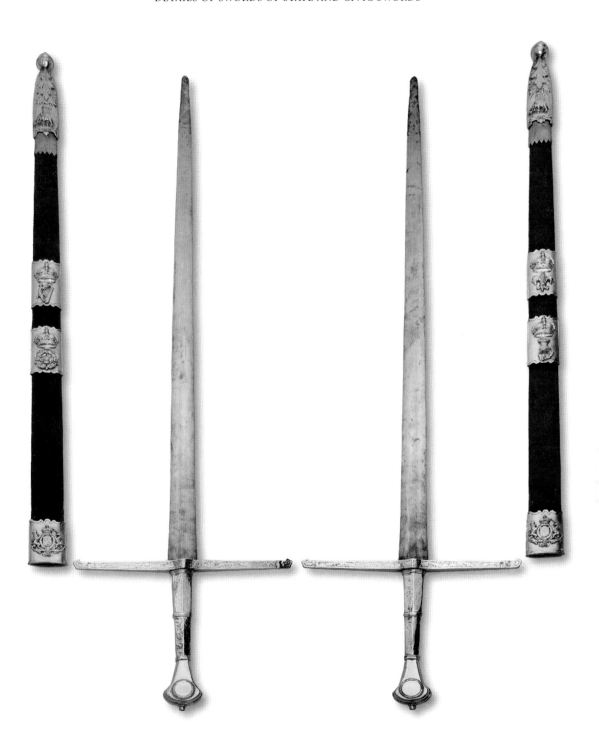

The City of Coventry Sword of State – *c.* 1430

Sword

The fifteenth-century blade of the current sword is in good condition, with an armourer's mark on a trefoil in a broad, 19in-long fuller. The tip is now pitted and a little eroded over the first 5in. The hilt is silver-gilt. The quillons are box-shaped, straight, engraved with leaf-work and turn up slightly at the ends. The grip is a tube of flattened hexagonal section with medial and end bands; on one side are engraved the words 'Civitas Coventre' (City of Coventry) and foliage, with an elephant and castle; on the other side, 'Domine Salvu fac Regem' (God save the King) and leaf-work, with figures of Our Lady and Child and a saint. The edges also bore an inscription (now illegible). The pommel is pear-shaped and somewhat flattened, with circular discs on each face, now plain and obviously modern, with the edges chased with foliage. There is a small chased tang button. The sword, blade and hilt, dates from about 1430.

Scabbard

The scabbard is covered with scarlet velvet with four silver-gilt lockets, which bear in relief the following: (1) the chape, which has, on both sides, the arms of the city, with acanthus leaves – previously it ended in an orb and cross, but the cross is now broken off; (2) a crowned harp on one side and a crowned fleur-de-lis on the other; (3) a crowned rose on one side and a thistle on the other; and (4) the mouth-locket with the royal arms, probably of Charles II, within the Garter and crowned, on both sides. The mounts on the scabbard only date from the Restoration. The velvet on the section nearest the hilt is now rather worn and is in need of attention. The portion of the scabbard under the chape appears to have been replaced. The new piece of velvet covering is rather crudely stitched on and a new end to the scabbard can be felt through it. It may be that the damage to the tip of the blade is of the same period. An old plain brass mount is partly hidden under the newer chape – perhaps an earlier mount.

The Sword Hilt – c. 1461–83

Length of sword	Unknown	Weight of sword	Unknown
Length of blade	2in – 0.520m – Double-edged	Width of blade	1⅝in – 0.041m
Length of hilt	8¾in – 0.222m – One-handed	Width of guard	7⅛in – 0.181m

Sword

The hilt and part of the blade of a sword of Coventry was found on a scrap heap in London some years ago and is now part of the Burrell Collection in the Glasgow Museum.

Guy Laking, who at the time owned this hilt, wrote:

A most interesting sword that has only recently come to light, a hilt of robust proportions, that may yet reveal its history, is worthy of examination; for from the heraldic evidence

The City of Coventry Sword Hilt – *c.* 1461–83
(CSG CIC Glasgow Museums Collection)

which it furnishes it must at one time have been the hilt of one of the civic swords
of Coventry. The medium is latten, formerly gilt, decorated with delicately engraved
York roses alternating with Edward IV's badge of the sun in splendour. The quillons
are straight, the extreme ends curling *upwards*. The pommel is roughly heart-shaped
in outline. It has inset on either side engraved silver plaques that have at one time been
enamelled respectively with the arms of Coventry and those of England. These are so
placed that only when the sword is held point upwards are they seen in the correct
position. Its proportions are certainly those of the fighting sword of the time; but the
rather soft hilt medium of gilded latten lends additional weight to the theory of its
having been made for purposes of ceremony. We may therefore consider that this hilt
is from one of the two swords that disappeared from Coventry after 1704; although
neither the sword to which this hilt belonged nor the one now at Coventry could have
been the sword which in 1384 Richard II ordered to be carried behind the mayor of
the town, both being of XV century date, and not of the period of that monarch …
and that the hilt may have been made in 1471 for a sword replacing the one which
Edward IV took away; but it may be that this hilt belongs to a sword made about 1481
to replace the 1430 sword stolen during the riots in that year, which was not recovered
for some months later.[16]

147

The description above fails to mention that the cross-guard has écussons, that the quillons are pointed at the ends, that the grip is of ivory and ends with a small raised collar next to the pommel, the edges of which bear traces of scroll-work, and that a small tang button rests in the cleave of the heart.

Scabbard

There is no scabbard.

Cap of Maintenance

In the accounts are various references to 'the velvet hatt and hatt of mayntenaunce', from which we learn that, as in the City of London, there was a hat for summer and another for winter wear. In 1606, the cap of maintenance (presumably the fur one) was lost – a new hat was made in 1615. A new summer velvet hat was made in 1623. The summer 'velvet hatt' was almost certainly crimson but is now rather faded. It has a broad brim which, oddly, is split on each side; this is possibly to allow for heads of differing sizes. The crown is dome-shaped with a central circular flat button which secures a fringe of short gilt tassels. The diameter of the brim is 16in, while the brim itself is 4in wide. The crown is 6in high. There are two gilt cords with tassels to secure the hat. The present winter fur cap dates only from Queen Victoria's visit to Coventry in 1858 and is of thick dark grey mink fur, with a black velvet crown, with a gold cord round the side fastened up with a gold loop; from this, the cord is continued to the shoulder and ends in two gold tassels. The hat is 8in wide at the headband, 6½in high and 11in wide at the crown.

Today, unusually, the sword-bearer wears a grey legal wig instead of either of the caps.

The city has a Guild of Freemen. Annually, in May, they hold a freeman's service which includes the lord mayor. On this occasion, the sword is still borne before the lord mayor, but is carried by a freeman wearing the summer cap of maintenance and a black robe. The mace-bearer, another freeman, wears the winter fur hat and a black robe.

Uniform

A black academic gown with black velvet tufts and facings and white lace cuffs is worn over a dark suit, white shirt, white jabot, black shoes and white cotton gloves.

Lincoln

Prerogative

There is no formal charter or other record for the city to have a sword borne before the mayor. It is said that the oldest sword was given to the city by Richard II, when he visited the city in 1386, at which time he conferred upon the mayor, John Sutton, the privilege of having a sword carried before him on all civic occasions and processions.

Lincoln has four swords.

The Sword of State – pre-1367

Length of sword	4ft 3¾in – 1.314m	Weight of sword	5lb 8oz – 2.495kg
Length of blade	3ft 5⅛in – 1.044m – Double-edged	Width of blade	2⅜in – 0.060m
Length of hilt	10⅝in – 0.270m – Two-handed	Width of guard	13⅛in – 0.333m
Length of scabbard	3ft 5⅞in – 1.063m	Weight of scabbard	2lb 3oz – 0.991kg

Sword

This sword, known as the Richard II sword, has a Solingen blade with the armourer's marks, a wolf and the orb and cross. The hilt is original. There is no quillon block. The quillons, which are covered with silver, with the remains of a gilded decoration, have a slight deflection upward at the terminations. Along the top edge is inscribed 'IHESVS EST AMOR MEVS' (Jesus is my love), and on the other 'A DEO ET REGE' (For God and King), which were added in 1595. The grip is bound with silver wire. The pommel is a circular flattened disc of silver, with a secondary small raised disc on each side, encircled by a hollow groove. The groove is engraved with rays, similar to those pounced on the monumental effigy of Richard II, and on the small discs are the royal arms, France ancient and England quarterly, of Edward III, between two ostrich feathers. The edge of the pommel is engraved with roses and fleurs-de-lis. The hilt was substituted in 1734 but the original was restored in 1902. Although it is believed that the sword was presented in 1386, the royal arms are those of Edward III and ceased to be used after 1367. It is therefore probable that the sword was actually made at least nineteen years prior to the date of acquisition.

Scabbard

The current modern scabbard was designed by Sir William St John Hope and dated 1902. It is covered with crimson velvet with a stripe of silver-gilt scrolling along each side, and six silver (white) harts and four other silver-gilt mounts, each edged with small fleur-de-lis. These are: (1) the chape, which has leaf-work (O) and pea pods (R); (2) a white hart (O), with the reverse bare; (3) a white hart (O), the reverse being bare:

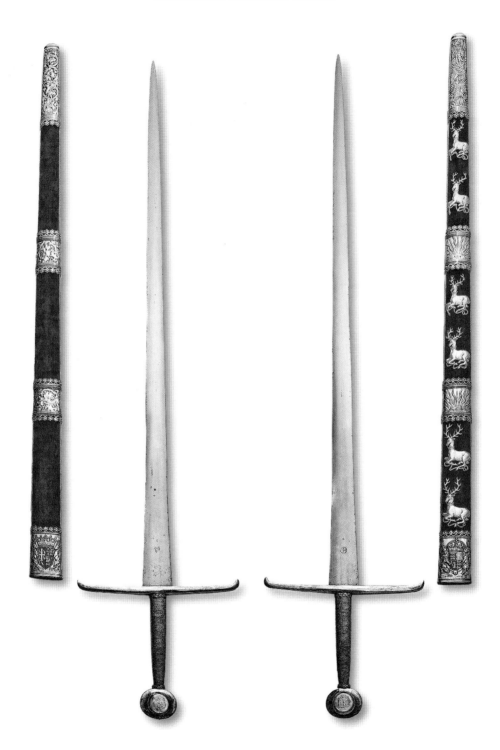

The City of Lincoln Sword of State – pre-1367

(4) a broad band with a sunburst (O) and leaf-work (R); (5) a white hart (O), with the reverse bare; (6) a white hart (O), the reverse bare; (7) a broad band with a sunburst (O) and leaf-work (R); (8) a white hart (O), the reverse being bare; (9) a white hart (O), with the reverse bare; and (10) the mouth-locket with the royal arms, England, Scotland and Ireland quarterly, those of Edward VII (1902), within the Garter and crowned, with supporters but no motto (O), and the royal arms, France ancient and England quarterly impaled with the ancient seal of Edward the Confessor and crowned with no Garter but with the stag supporters of Richard II (R). The previous scabbard is now on the fourth George II sword that was assembled in 1902.

The Mourning or Lent Sword – c. 1486

Length of sword	3ft 8⅝in – 1.133m	Weight of sword	4lb 9½oz – 2.082kg
Length of blade	2ft 11⅜in – 0.899m – Double-edged	Width of blade	2⅛in – 0.054m
Length of hilt	9¼in – 0.235m – Two-handed	Width of guard	11½in – 0.292m
Length of scabbard	3ft 2¼in – 0.972m	Weight of scabbard	1lb 2½oz – 0.516kg

Sword

This sword, known as the Henry VII sword, was presented to the city by Henry VII in 1487 when he visited the cathedral to give thanks for the victory at Bosworth and at East Stoke, where his forces had just killed John de la Pole, Earl of Lincoln, who had supported Lambert Simnel's Yorkist rebellion. This sword is another fine ancient example, of fifteenth-century date, and complete with its original blade, which is seemingly of English manufacture. The hilt is silver-gilt. There is no quillon block. The quillons are square in shape and curve gently upwards, with rounded and deflected terminations, and damascened with a gilded scroll pattern. The grip is wire-bound with Turk's head knots at either end. The pommel is pear-shaped and octagonally facetted, with fleurs-de-lis and other leaf-work on all faces.

It is only carried if a mayor dies in office. It was carried last for the funeral of Councillor Frank Wright in 1983 – for the first time in 150 years.

Scabbard

The current scabbard is covered with black velvet with gold lace down each side and two silver-gilt lockets. The obverse is embroidered with crowns, roses and fleurs-de-lis and the initials 'C.L.' (*Civitas Lincolnia*), and has a diapered pattern on the reverse. The velvet is now quite worn and the stitching needs attention. The chape is plain, while the mouth-locket is inscribed 'Thomas Kent Mayor 1685' on the obverse and 'Anno Domini 1685' on the reverse.

The City of Lincoln Mourning or Lent Sword – *c.* 1486

The City of Lincoln Charles I Sword – *c.* 1642

The Charles I Sword – *c.* 1642

Length of sword	3ft 8in – 1.118m	Weight of sword	1lb 4oz – 0.568kg
Length of blade	2ft 9⅝in – 0.854m – Double-edged	Width of blade	1⅜in – 0.035m
Length of hilt	10⅜in – 0.263m – Two-handed	Width of guard	No hilt
Length of scabbard	3ft 2in – 0.965m	Weight of Scabbard	1lb 1oz – 0.480kg

Sword

This blade, probably presented by Charles I during his visit in 1642, has no hilt. The length of the hilt above is judged by the length of the tang (see the diagram at the beginning of this chapter). It was made in Solingen and shows a cross, orb and a wolf on each side of the blade. There is an inscription in the fuller on each side. The edges are worn, making it uncertain; it is thought to be a Latin text, 'For justice I have fallen on', but this is speculative.

Scabbard

The scabbard is covered with purple velvet with gold lace down each side and two silver-gilt lockets. The obverse is embroidered with crowns, roses and fleurs-de-lis and the initials 'C.L.' (*Civitas Lincolnia*), and has a diapered pattern on the reverse. The velvet is now very worn and the stitching needs serious attention. Both the chape and mouth-locket are plain. The embroidery on this scabbard is an exact copy of the one described above and it appears they were made at the same time – the differences being the colour of the velvet and the lack of an inscription.

The George II Sword – pre-1734

Length of sword	4ft 2in – 1.270m	Weight of sword	4lb 10½oz – 2.111kg
Length of blade	3ft 0¾in – 0.933m – Double-edged	Width of blade	1¾in – 0.045m
Length of hilt	13¼in – 0.336m – Two-handed	Width of guard	11⅞in – 0.302m
Length of scabbard	3ft 6⅛in – 1.070m	Weight of scabbard	1lb 14¼oz – 0.857kg

Sword

This sword was assembled in about 1902 from the discarded 'second' hilt of the Sword of State and another blade. The blade was made in Solingen, with the mark of the wolf and the orb and the cross, is older than the hilt and is probably seventeenth-century. The hilt, which was made in 1734 to replace the original on the Sword of State, is silver-gilt. The quillon block has the royal arms of George II, within the Garter and crowned, with supporters on the obverse and the arms of Lincoln on the reverse. The quillons are flat and straight, with ornate terminals, and have engraved '*IHESVS EST AMOR*

MEVS' (Jesus is my love) on the obverse and '*A DEO ET REGE*' (For God and King) on the reverse. The grip is slightly oval. The almost spherical pommel is engraved with the city arms, with the later addition of 'JOHN KENT MAYOR 1777' around the arms, on the obverse, and 'CITY OF LINCOLN. JOHN KENT MAYOR 1734' on the reverse. The edge of the pommel is inscribed 'JOHN BECKE Esqre MAYOR A.D.1760'. There is a small tang button. The metalwork also bears the London hallmarks for 1745–46, and the maker's mark, NY with pallet over. It was used as the Lent/Mourning Sword but now the Henry VII sword is used.

Scabbard

This scabbard is very clearly the previous scabbard for the Richard II sword, which was replaced in 1902. It is covered with crimson velvet, with silver-gilt locket and chape, and embroidered with devices similar to the second and third swords. The chape is inscribed on the obverse 'Regalia restored Peter Platts Dickenson Mayor 1877', the reverse is plain. The embroidery consists of: (1) a rose; (2) the initials 'P P D'; (3) some foliage; (4) a portcullis; (5) a harp; (6) a crown; (7) a rose; (8) a thistle; (9) the Lincoln arms; (10) the letters 'C L'; (11) a crown; (12) the royal arms of Queen Victoria; and (13) '1877'. Many of these devices are raised with padding. The reverse of the scabbard is covered in the same diapered pattern stitching as on the previously mentioned scabbards, and again is in need of attention. This leads to the conclusion that all three of these embroidered scabbards were restored at the same time, as indicated by the inscription on the chape. When new, they must have been very beautiful and vibrant with colour. The mouth-locket is inscribed on the obverse with 'Regilt and new scabbard, ROBT. FEATHERBY MAYOR 1818', and on the reverse 'Regalia restored, A D 1845, JOHN STEVENSON, ESQ^re MAYOR'.

Cap of Maintenance

The city's first cap was purchased in 1534. Today four caps of maintenance in the 'Tudor hat' style are held, and all are virtually identical. The earliest held is a broad-brimmed hat of crimson velvet, embroidered, and with the inscription 'The City of Lincoln John Kent Mayor 1734'. A second hat bears the inscription 'The City of Lincoln M Sewell Mayor 1814'.

The practice of wearing the hat was abandoned with the local government reforms of 1835, but was restored in 1937 when a new hat of similar design was purchased for the coronation of George VI with the inscription 'George VI Rex 1937 City of Lincoln'. This third hat was worn until 2006.

The fourth hat held, and currently in use, was donated by the current mayor's officer and a former city sheriff with help from other local benefactors in 2006 to mark 800 years of the mayoralty in Lincoln. It has a wide brim and a flat crown and is cover with embroidered crimson velvet. The hat weighs 3lb 5¼oz (1.51kg). It is not perfectly circular and so the brim measures at its widest 19½in (0.495m) in diameter and the brim

The City of Lincoln George II Sword – pre-1734

is 5½in (0.14m) wide. The crown is 5¾in (0.146m) high and 10½in (0.268m) across, and is embroidered with a large rose and other foliage. The hat has long cords ending in tassels, like a cardinal's hat. The inscription around the crown reads 'ELIZABETH II (Royal Arms) REGINA 2006 CITY OF (City Arms) LINCOLN'.

Uniform

The sword-bearer wears a dark bottle green morning-coat edged with gold braid and with gold piping and white lace cuffs, with a red waistcoat, matching green breeches with gold braid, white shirt with white jabot, white wool stockings, black court shoes with silver buckles and white cotton gloves.

The Victoria and Albert Museum Scabbard

One additional scabbard of Lincoln is held by the Victoria and Albert Museum in London. It is thought to be of the seventeenth century and is believed to be the original. A Mr Robert Hillingford, a well-known collector of arms and armoury, acquired the scabbard, but it is not known how or when. The scabbard was subsequently sold by his housekeeper without authority and Mr Hillingford was fortunate in buying the items back. Mr Hillingford left the scabbard to his grandson, Dr Cecil C. Harrison. In his will dated 1924, Dr Harrrison left the scabbard to the city.

The wooden scabbard is covered with very faded crimson velvet that is embroidered on the obverse in yellow (probably original silver-gilt thread) with roses, fleurs-de-lis and the initials 'CL'. On the reverse, the embroidery is of trellis pattern which is now completely worn away. There were probably two silver-gilt mounts; however, the chape is now missing, as are the first several inches. The mouth-locket is inscribed on the obverse 'Thomas Kent, Mayor 1685' and on the reverse 'Anno Domini 1685'. The current length is 2ft 7in, but comparing the pattern on the other two 'identical' scabbards, it appears that some 6 or 7in are missing. This would mean that the scabbard used to be approximately 3ft 2in long.

There can be little doubt that the scabbards currently on the Henry VII and Charles I blades are replacements for this scabbard. However, there is no distinguishing feature to date either of them. They are virtually the same length, with identical embroidered patterns, and this original scabbard has a similar pattern, which is incomplete. Measurement indicates that if complete and with a chape this scabbard would be of similar length to the newer pair (3ft 2¼in and 3ft 2in respectively). By length, therefore, the original could have fitted either the Henry VII blade – (2ft 11¾in and late fifteenth-century), the Charles I blade (2ft 9⅝in and mid-seventeenth-century) or the blade just described (3ft 0¾in and seventeenth-century).

Guy Laking, in chapter XVIII of his *Record of European Armour and Arms* of 1920–22,[16] described the scabbard thus:

Its chape mount is lost, but the locket mount is in position engraved on one side as, on the copy, with the name Thomas Kent, Mayor, and on the other the date Anno Domini 1685. Although from the design of this chape [should have read 'mouth-locket'] it might appear to be almost of Elizabethan times, with the inscription added later, there is a maker's mark upon it, the letters G. S. within a shield, which being a well known, though unidentified mark, of late seventeenth century date, precludes any possibility of the scabbard being earlier than the latter part of that century.

The original 1924 V&A file records that the scabbard was offered as '17th century scabbard of one of the state swords of the City of Lincoln, of crimson velvet'. However, a note by another V&A curator in 1924 describes it as for 'one of the State Swords of the city of Lincoln (known as the Henry VII sword)'. Yet in the same year, a note by C.A. Barley, also of the V&A, suggests that 'I have examined [this scabbard] with Mr. Trendell and we arrived at the conclusion that the embroidered velvet sheath is of late 16C date: the silver-gilt locket dated 1685 takes the place of an older mount, the impression of which still shows on the velvet'.

Thus we have a conundrum. If of late sixteenth-century vintage, it will fit only one blade but could not be the original, being about 100 years newer. If of late seventeenth-century vintage, it will fit all three blades and could just be the original scabbard of either of the two later swords. If the argument about the earlier mount impression is correct, then the scabbard was probably made for the Henry VII blade, but it is, most certainly, not the original as claimed.

The City of York Sword-Bearer
(Photo by *The Press*, York)

York

Prerogative

Francis Drake, in his *Eboracum* of 1736, says that on the occasion of the visit of Richard II to York in 1388: 'It was at this time that our own records speak King Richard took his sword from his side and gave it to be born [sic] before William de Selby as first Lord Mayor of York.' By charter dated May 1396, Richard II granted and confirmed to the citizens of York and their successors for ever:

> that the mayor of the said city and his successors who shall have been, according to circumstances, may be carried and may cause to be carried their sword, given to them by us, or another sword of any kind pleasing to them, outside our presence and that of our heirs, in their presence, with the point upwards, in the presence of as such of other magnates and lords of the Kingdom of England who belong to us by blood line, and as of any others whomsoever in any way whatever.

The city records show that Selby's successor appointed two officers, one to serve the mayor, the other to carry the sword. A sword-bearer has been appointed since 1389.

Drake describes 'four swords as belonging to the lord-mayor, during his office':

> The first of the swords and the largest was a gift of the Emperor Sigismund, father-in-law to King Richard II: it is seldom born [sic] but on Christmas-day and St. Maurice. Another given by King Richard II, from his side, from whence the title of lord accrued to our chief magistrate. This is the least among them, but the greatest in value for the reason above. A third is that of Sir Martin Bowes, Lord-Mayor of London, which is the most beautiful, and is born [sic] every Sunday and other principal days before the lord-mayor. The fourth was formerly made use of every time the lord-mayor went abroad or stirred from home.

The second and fourth of these swords have now disappeared; no one seems to know when or whither. They were in existence down to 1796.

The city currently has two remaining swords.

The Sigismund Sword – *c.* 1416

Length of sword	4ft 4in – 1.321m	Weight of sword	8lb 9oz – 3.887kg
Length of blade	3ft 3⅛in – 0.993m – Double-edged	Width of blade	2¾in – 0.070m
Length of hilt	12⅞in – 0.327m – 1½-handed	Width of guard	13in – 0.330m
Length of scabbard	3ft 4¾in – 1.035m	Weight of scabbard	1lb 5¾oz – 0.611kg

Sword

This fine sword is of exceptional interest, as being the one hung up, according to custom, over the stall in St George's Chapel, Windsor, of Sigismund, King of Hungary and Bohemia and Holy Roman Emperor, on his election as a Knight of the Garter in May 1416. He was a contemporary and close friend of Henry V. On the emperor's death in 1437, it was offered up as usual at the mass for his soul, and then became the pre-requisite of the Dean and Canons of Windsor. According to a contemporary record in the city archive, it was given by the Dean of Windsor to one of the canons, master Henry Hanslap, who was also a canon of Howden and rector of Middleton near Pickering in Yorkshire, and a native of York itself. Hanslap presented it to the city on 5 May 1439, to be carried before every successive mayor. Detailed accounts of this sword, and of the lost one given by Richard II, are held by the city and contain two interesting facts. First, that the scabbard to the sword was originally ornamented with 'red scorpions worked in silk', instead of the existing silver-gilt dragons; secondly, that the sword given by Richard II was considered too precious for ordinary use, another sword having been bought at the cost of the city for everyday wear. Today the sword is carried sheathed before the lord mayor on ceremonial occasions and on royal visits.

The Sword of State, and the older and larger of the two swords, is an exceedingly fine example of the early part of the fifteenth century. The tapering blade is of diamond section. The lower 17½in of the blade is blued, and damascened with the royal arms, France modern and England quarterly, probably of Henry IV, though the fleur-de-lis and lions are in the wrong quarters, on the obverse; and those of the city on the reverse. Below these and just above the cross-guard on both sides is engraved '*SIGISMVNDI . IMPERAT . DAT . MC . EB . 1439*' (Emperor Sigismund . ??? . ?? . York 1439) and '*ORNAT . HENRI . MAY . MAIOR 1586*'. The armourer's mark is a Lombardic 'H'. The hilt is of gilt latten. The cross-guard is hexagonal, straight, with the quillons tapering towards the ends where they are slightly bent toward the point. In 1895, the wooden grip was covered in red velvet. It was later bound in wire and was rebound in silver wire in 2010. The grip is encircled just below the cross-guard by a massive lobed ring with characteristic Elizabethan fringe on each side (one piece is missing), all of silver-gilt and dating from 1586. The pommel is pear-shaped and faceted with eight sides, with the tang end hammered into the pommel end.

Scabbard

The scabbard is covered with crimson velvet, which is badly worn for the last 13in on the reverse and somewhat worn on the obverse – this appears to have been worn away when holding the scabbard to insert the blade. It has strips of gold lace down both edges, now somewhat worn, a silver-gilt chape, six splendid dragons on one side only (the device of the knightly Society of the Dragon – founded by the Holy Roman Emperor Sigismund in 1408) and a mouth-locket, all made in 1586. The mounts are: (1) the plain chape

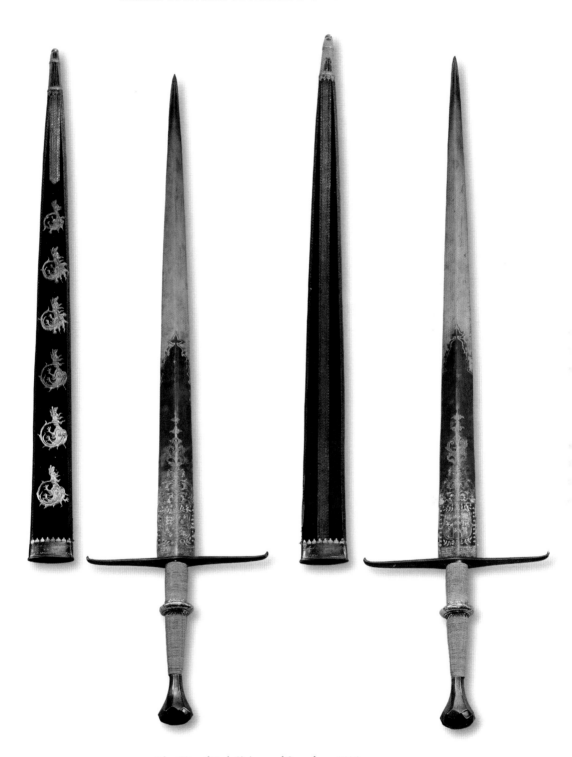

The City of York Sigismund Sword – *c.* 1416

with an Elizabethan edge, which has, on the obverse a galloon of gold lace between it and the first mount, while on the reverse the galloon extends to the mouth-locket; (2) a dragon measuring 2¾in in length; (3) a dragon measuring 3in in length; (4) a dragon measuring 3in in length; (5) a dragon measuring 3½in in length; (6) a dragon measuring 3½in in length; (7) a dragon measuring 3in in length; and (8) the mouth locket, which is inscribed 'This sword was repaired and new gilt AD 1781 HEN MYRES ESQ Ld MAYOR' (O) and 'This sword was repaired and new gilt AD 1872 WILLM WALKER ESQ^{RE} LD MAYOR' (R) . The scabbard was certainly re-covered in 1580. In 1586, it was redecorated and it appears that the original 'red scorpions worked in silk' were replaced by the current six silver-gilt dragons – the three large ones are identical, the two medium-sized identical but slightly different from the three large ones, whilst the smallest is slightly different again. The scabbard was much re-gilded in 1605. A new scabbard was made in 1648 and it appears that all the mounts were transferred.

The Bowes Sword – 1545

Length of sword	4ft 0⅛in – 1.222m	Weight of sword	4lb 6¼oz – 1.991kg
Length of blade	3ft 0⅝in – 0.930m – Double-edged	Width of blade	2in – 0.051m
Length of hilt	11½in – 0.292m – Two-handed	Width of guard	13½in – 0.343m
Length of scabbard	3ft 2¾in – 0.984m	Weight of scabbard	1lb 1¼oz – 0.486kg

Sword

The blade of this sword is blued for the lower 32in of its length and has makers' marks of X and D on the obverse. Along the obverse is engraved 'SYR MARTYN BOWES KNYGHT BORNE WITHIN THIS CITIE OF YORKE AND MAIOR OF THE CITIE OF LONDON 1545 FOR A REMEMBRANCE', and on the reverse is 'GAVE THIS SWORDE TO THE MAIOR AND COMMVNALTIE OF THIS SAID HONORABLE CITIE'. The hilt is silver-gilt. The cross-guard is further ornamented on one side with three large imitation jewels, in the middle and at the ends (one is missing). The quillon block is engraved with three semi-precious stones on the obverse and strap-work and foliage on both sides. The quillons of rectangular section are straight with lozenge-shaped ends, and are engraved with scroll-work. The grip is wrapped with silver wire, now very loose, over a wooden handle. The pommel is formed of a flattened circular disc of crystal, which is quite loose, with four straps of silver-gilt and another around the centre (one section is now missing). The tang button is in the form of a fleur-de-lis.

Sir Martin Bowes was a famous London goldsmith. He was born in the York parish of St Cuthbert. When he heard the church was to be closed, he wrote to the city asking them to reconsider. When they did, he wrote to thank them in 1549 and presented a sword. The letter which accompanied the gift of the sword is held in the city archives. He died in 1566 and was buried in London. The sword is believed to have been 'carried

The City of York Bowes Sword – 1545

away by some officer of the Court of King James I during that monarch's visit to the city in the year 1603 and that it was not recovered without much delay and difficulty'. Today the sword is carried sheathed before the lord mayor to council meetings and placed on brackets behind the lord mayor's chair in the council chamber.

Scabbard

The sheath was originally covered with crimson velvet, garnished with stones and pearls set upon silver-gilt. It is currently covered with crimson velvet, edged with gold lace, and bears four silver-gilt mounts. Both sides are identical. The mounts are: (1) the chape, which has a small finial and on the upper half has a handsomely wrought panel, on which are a pair of bows connected by an interlaced knot, and on the lower half a painted shield of the city arms (missing on one side and very faded on the other) covered by a circular plate of crystal, both now very scratched and opaque; (2) and (3) lockets, each engraved with leaf-work, and set with five large clear crystals (several now damaged) – from portraits of past mayors it appears that the stones were once red (rubies or garnets?) and green (emeralds?) and probably changed within the period of 1738 and 1787; (4) there is no mouth-locket – a simple throat-locket protects the scabbard.

Cap of Maintenance

City historians are convinced that the gift of the cap or hat coincided with the gift of the sword by Richard II in 1388, and he stipulated that it should not be taken off before God or king. A new hat was purchased in 1445. The next recorded purchase of 'new mace, scabbard and cap' was in 1580, and this hat, made by Peter Wilkinson, hatter, and costing 40s, is still held in a sealed case, though, not surprisingly it is in a somewhat dilapidated condition. It is in the Tudor felt hat style 'in Crymsyn velvet' with a 'goulde edge', 'goulde band' and 'goulde tassell' in the crown, and was used until 1914. The current style is unique. The previous hat, given by George V in 1915 in the fifth year of his reign to Lord Mayor John Bowes Morrell, is said to have been made from the coronation robes of George V. The maker was Anderson & Son, hatters, of York. It was restored in 1985 by the Victoria and Albert Museum. It was replaced by a brand-new hat, which was presented by the sovereign on Maundy Thursday in 2012. It is the same style as that of 1915, with a hard, slightly domed crown and a brim looped up at the sides and back, thus forming a peak at the front. It is covered in crimson velvet trimmed with ermine, and embroidered with the royal arms of Elizabeth II, within the Garter and crowned, with supporters and motto.

Uniform

A typical eighteenth-century design of tail-coat, tights, shoes with silver buckles and a dress sword was discontinued in 1947. Today a black frock-coat with a black flash and a chain of office with badge, black trousers, black waistcoat, white shirt with white bow tie, black shoes and white cotton gloves are worn.

Newcastle upon Tyne

Prerogative

The privilege of having a sword borne before the mayor was conferred upon the town by Richard II, by letters patent dated 25 January 1391 as follows:

> Richard, by the grace of God, King of England and France and Lord of Ireland, to all those to whom the present letters shall come, greeting. Know ye that in our considering the esteem in which the town of Newcastle upon Tyne of our especial grace have granted to our beloved William Bishopdale, now mayor of the same town, for as long as he himself shall have been mayor and all those who in the future shall be mayors of the aforementioned town that they may have one sword carried before them. Which sword we have indeed consented to give for the aforementioned reason. In testimony of which matter we have caused these letters of ours to become patent. With I myself as witness at Westminster on 25th day of January in the fourteenth year of our reign.

The city has two swords. The Sword of State is carried behind the mace.

The Sword of State – *c.* 1460

Length of sword	3ft 10¾in – 1.187m	Weight of sword	3lb 7¼oz – 1.564kg
Length of blade	2ft 9¾in – 0.857m – Double-edged	Width of blade	1⅝in – 0.041m
Length of hilt	13in – 0.330m – Two-handed	Width of guard	10¾in – 0.273m
Length of scabbard	3ft 1⅛in – 0.943m	Weight of scabbard	11½oz – 0.327kg

Sword

This sword appears to date from *c.* 1460 and is a fine example of a state sword of the middle of the fifteenth century. The blade, which may be the original, is without fullers or ridges, and has near the hilt, on both sides, the Solingen or Passau wolf mark. The hilt is that of the original sword, and is steel-plated with silver-gilt. The quillon block has pointed écussons and has three deep grooves on each side, not unlike the Chester sword, chased with trophies, etc., apparently a late sixteenth-century restoration. The long flat quillons curve slightly upwards with a sharp curl at the ends and are chased, with a running leaf pattern on either side of the central ridge. The grip is covered with crimson red velvet, well-worn but serviceable, bound with gilt wire. The pommel is 5in long, of lozenge form, with a deep central groove on each side. Both sides are chased with spirited leaf-work, and the groove with a slight running scroll. At the top of the pommel is a small foliated cap, the result of a repair, and through carelessness in putting together the pieces of the hilt the band next to the pommel has been reversed, and its supposed

The City of Newcastle upon Tyne Sword of State – *c.* 1460

loss made good in common base metal. There is a small tang button with the end of the tang hammered into it.

Scabbard

The scabbard is covered in crimson velvet edged with gold lace along each edge and ornamented with four handsomely chased silver-gilt lockets, of a date *c.* 1760; the velvet is now in need of attention. The mounts, wrought in *repoussé* but not hallmarked, are: (1) the chape, which has a figure of a Triton with a trident, astride a dolphin and with leaf-work (O), and a blank cartouche (R); (2) a locket with a ship in full sail on one side (O), and a blank cartouche (R); (3) an ornate cartouche with the three castles of Newcastle (O) and arabesque scrolls, etc. (R); and (4) the mouth-locket, which has a deep cleavage for the écussons, and has, under a tent, the royal arms, probably of George III, within the Garter, and crowned, with supporters and motto on the obverse and a trophy of arms on the reverse.

The Second Sword – *c.* 1791

Length of sword	4ft 5½in – 1.359m	Weight of sword	4lb 10¼oz – 2.103kg
Length of blade	3ft 4⅛in – 1.020m – Double-edged	Width of blade	1⅝in – 0.041m
Length of hilt	13⅜in – 0.340m – Two-handed	Width of guard	10½in – 0.267m
Length of scabbard	3ft 5in – 1.041m	Weight of scabbard	11½oz – 0.327kg

Sword

The second sword is a good example of the type produced at the end of the eighteenth century. The blade has no obvious marks. The hilt is gilt. The quillon block, which is essentially diamond-shaped, is unusual in that the shoulders of the blade end in a plate against which the scabbard sits. The plate is joined to the block with a narrow neck. The block bears on the obverse the city arms, with crest, supporters and motto, in relief, and on the reverse, very unusually, a winter cap of maintenance and crossed mace and staff. The quillons curve like a dolphin and are decorated with leaf-work. The grip is covered with much worn crimson velvet but bound with a spiral wire, probably gilt originally. It has a lozenge-shaped pommel wrought in relief, with a ship with furled sails on the obverse and a figure of Justice with sword and scales on the reverse. The sides are decorated with leaf-work. The pommel screws onto the tang and there is a tiny hammered tang nut.

Scabbard

The scabbard is covered with crimson velvet, which is very worn and torn in places, with four handsomely wrought silver-gilt mounts. These are: (1) the chape, which has scallop shells and leaf-work on each side; (2) and (3), lockets with leaf-work similar but not

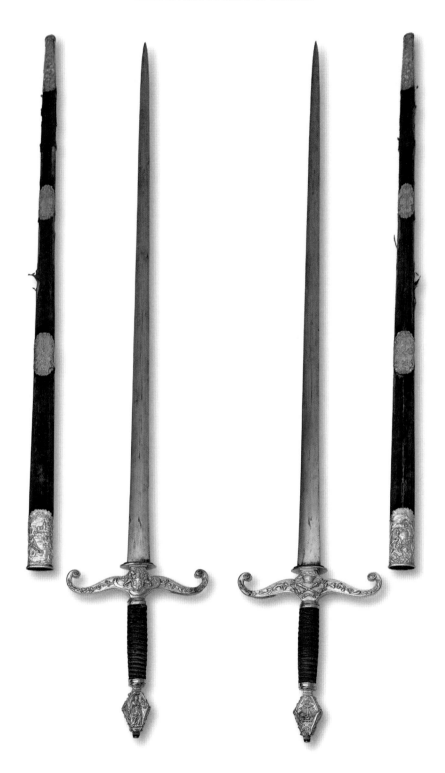

The City of Newcastle upon Tyne Second Sword – *c.* 1791

identical on each side; and (4) the mouth-locket, which has, in relief, a ship in harbour with two castles on shore and barrels, an anchor and a flag on the obverse, with scallops and leaf-work on the reverse. In the centre of this is an almost obliterated inscription which appears to be 'J. Bland' the maker. A James Bland was made free of the Goldsmiths' Company of London in 1791.

Cap of Maintenance

The fur cap of maintenance is of the same type as that worn by the sword-bearer of the City of London, and is in fact the type of hat worn at the time when Richard II granted to the mayor of Newcastle the right to have a sword borne before him. It is of light grey squirrel fur with a firm crown of crimson velvet, gold braid round the head band, and has long pendant gold cords ending in tassels.

Uniform

A knee-length black frock-coat with stiff high collar and epaulettes, with gold lace on the collar, epaulettes and wrists, and 'stay-bright' buttons, over matching black trousers with gold side stripe and black shoes. A crimson cummerbund is worn, as are white cotton gloves.

The City of Newcastle upon Tyne Sword-Bearer (Photo by Steve Brock)

Chester

Prerogative

In 1354, the mayor was one of the king's escheators, and as such was entitled to have sword borne before him. However, the sword is said by Ormorod to be the one presented to the city by Richard II in 1394. He stated that 'in September 1394, King Richard II was entertained at Chester. He was accompanied by the Duke of Gloucester and other nobles, and was met by the mayor and escorted into the city in procession. On this occasion the Sword of State was presented by the King to the city.' The sword is not mentioned in Richard II's charter to the city, nor are the shape and the mounts of the existing sword of so early a date.

Thomas Hughes, FSA, writing in 1872, mentions one Hugh Dutton as sword-bearer in 1489, and that the city sword was carried before Henry VII on his visit to Chester in 1494.

The first charter which mentions the sword is that of Henry VII, dated 6 April 1506, which provides that 'the mayor of the said city and his successors for the time being may have *their sword which we gave them* or any other, as may please them, borne before them out of our presence, and may cause it to be borne before them with the *point upright* in the presence as well of other nobles and lords of our realm of England who are related to us in the line of consanguinity and of any others whomsoever, as in any manner whatsoever'.

From the above, it is quite clear that a sword was given to the city by Henry VII before 1494, and there is little doubt it is the one preserved, with a new scabbard and mounts added in 1668, the hilt and pommel being of course original.

Writing in 1894, Canon Rupert Morris suggests that 'the present Sword of State is possibly fifteenth or early sixteenth century'. The sword held ties in with this comment and the dates of 1489, 1494 and 1506 mentioned above, and indicates that the current sword must have been acquired between Henry VII's accession in 1485 and 1494 when he visited.

When the grant of arms was made to the city in 1580, it was natural that the significance of the sword should form some part of it, and this was affected by the crest of the city being declared to be 'a sword with the point erect'.

In 1617, on the occasion of the visit of James I to the city, 'the mayor delivered the city's sword to the king, who gave it to the mayor again. And the same was borne before the king by the mayor, being on horseback. And the sword of estate was borne by the right honourable William, Earl of Derby, chief chamberlain of the county palatine of Chester.'

The Sword of State – *c.* 1490

Length of sword	3ft 11¾in – 1.213m	Weight of sword	4lb 1½oz – 1.858kg
Length of blade	3ft 1⅝in – 0.956m – Double-edged	Width of blade	1⅞in – 0.048m
Length of hilt	10⅛in – 0.257m – Two-handed	Width of guard	13¼in – 0.336m
Length of scabbard	3ft 3in – 0.991m	Weight of scabbard	13½oz – 0.381kg

Sword

The sword, which bears no date, has a steel blade with three fullers and bears the orb and cross-maker's mark and traces of decoration for about 11in from the hilt. The first 3in of the blade at the point show signs of severe damage and have at some stage been filed down. Due to repeated cleaning, some elements are now illegible; shields and other decorations are obscured by what appears to be another electroplating. However, there are clear traces in the fullers of garbs and swords, thus indicating the city arms on each side of the blade, though not at the same level, with chasing below. There are no royal arms but there is a shield, possibly of royal arms, on either side at the diagonal, but both appear to have been defaced, perhaps during the Commonwealth. The hilt is silver-gilt. The quillon block has a small pointed écusson and the quillons curve upwards; each end has on one side a lion's head, on the other a garb. The grip is covered with shagreen, has ferrules at each end with longitudinal metal strips, and terminates in a lozenge-shaped pommel which is elaborately worked and what appears to be a head – a nose, eye, eyebrow and what might be an ear and some hair are visible. The pommel is loose. The tang end is flat. The sword corresponds to other swords of about that period.

Scabbard

The scabbard is of cedar wood covered with crimson velvet, and edged with gold lace along each side. The bottom section is now worn and much darker, probably as a result of continual handling. There are ten silver-gilt mounts on each side. These are: (1) the chape, edged with fleurs-de-lis inscribed 'Patlⁿ Ellames Esqʳ Mayor 1781' above the city arms on the obverse and a blank cartouche on the reverse; (2) a small locket inscribed 'Robt Morry/Wm Wilson – Treasurers 1669' on the obverse, the reverse a plain diamond-shaped locket; (3) a broad band crowned above an inscription 'John Thomason Esqᵉ Mayor Peace proclaimed May the 12 1713', with fleurs-de-lis below on the obverse, the reverse being plain; (4) a plain diamond-shaped locket on each side; (5) a broad band edged with fleurs-de-lis inscribed 'John Minshult Esqʳ Mayor 1711' on the obverse, the reverse plain; (6) a plain diamond-shaped locket on each side; (7) a broad band edged with fleurs-de-lis inscribed 'Edward Oulton Esqʳ Mayor 1687' on the obverse, the reverse being plain; (8) a plain diamond-shaped locket on both sides; (9) the locket bears the arms then borne by the city – a sword between three garbs, attached to a circular band, on the obverse, and on the reverse, below the narrow band, a shield inscribed 'Carried

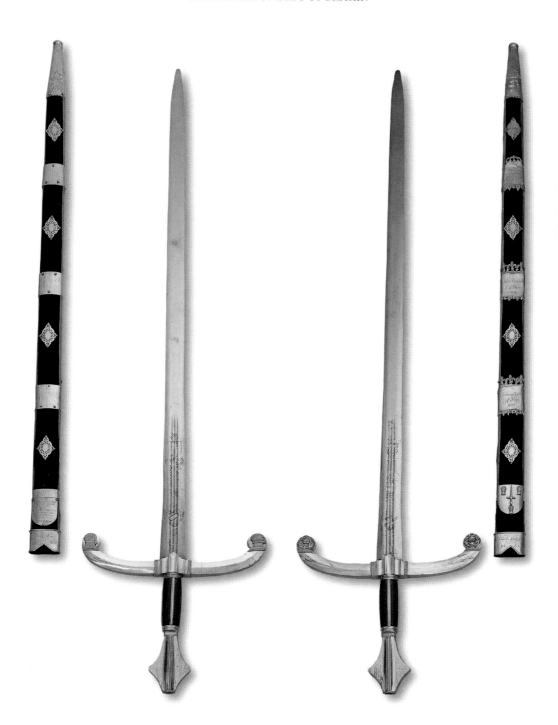

The City of Chester Sword of State – *c.* 1490

as the Sword of State at CAERNARVON CASTLE 13 July 1911 before KING GEORGE V and QUEEN MARY at the Investiture of the PRINCE OF WALES Earl of Chester – D L Hewitt Mayor'; and (10) the mouth-locket is inscribed on the obverse 'Charles Earle of' and on the reverse 'Derbye Maior'. '1668' is below on each side and is cut out for the protecting écussons on both sides. The scabbard itself is not cut out.

Cap of Maintenance
There is no cap of maintenance; the sword-bearer wears a bi-corn, fore and aft, with small metal links instead of a flash.

Uniform
The sword-bearer wears a deep rust-coloured morning-coat with matching breeches, a buff waistcoat with matching large and small metal buttons, white shirt and jabot, black wool stockings, black shoes and white cotton gloves.

The City of Chester Sword-Bearer.

Dublin

Prerogative

In March 1403, Henry IV granted letters patent to Dublin. These stated:

> The King, to all to whom etc., Greeting. May you know that by our special grace we have granted and given licence on behalf of ourselves and our heirs in perpetuity to our beloved and faithful liegemen in greater townland of and to the Community of our City Dublin in our land of Ireland, and to their heirs and successors in perpetuity that the mayor of the said City who now is in office may have and the mayors succeeding him of the same City as long as they exist may in perpetuity have and be able to have a certain gilded sword to carry in their presence in our honour and in that of our heirs and our faithful liegemen of the aforesaid City in the same manner and form as our Mayor of our City of London has a sword of this kind to carry in his own presence.

The ostensible reason for the grant was to do honour to an important city but, given the situation in the English lordship at the time, we may reasonably speculate that the real reason was what would now be called a public relations exercise designed to help to improve the relationship between Dublin and the English Crown. In 1399, Henry IV, on deposing Richard II, inherited the Irish problem that Richard had been trying to solve immediately before. Royal authority was effective only in parts of the south and east, and the population of the rest of the country operated as if it barely existed. Following a delegation of Anglo-Irish in June 1401, Henry appointed his second son, Thomas of Lancaster, as his lieutenant in Ireland. After two years of great difficulty and dwindling funds, Thomas handed over to a deputy in November 1403 and returned to England.

The first mention of a sword-bearer was in 1481.

Today Dublin has two swords. In 1821, one of the swords was used by George IV to confer knighthoods on the recorder and two sheriffs.

Nearly all the information about these swords has been gleaned from *The Dublin Swords*[4] and by inspection.

The Great Sword – *c.* 1390–99

Length of sword	4ft 6⅝in – 1.387m	Weight of sword	7lb 12oz – 3.518kg
Length of blade	3ft 7¼in – 1.099m – Double-edged	Width of blade	2¾in – 0.690m
Length of hilt	11⅜in – 0.289m – Two-handed	Width of guard	16¾in – 0.425m
Length of scabbard	3ft 7⅝in – 1.107m	Weight of scabbard	3lb 2oz – 1.419kg

Sword

This sword was made originally for Henry Bolingbroke during the 1390s and was used by him before becoming Henry IV in 1399. It is probable that much of the work on the sword was by Herman van Cleve of London, his personal goldsmith. It is believed that the Great Sword was a gift from the king himself, probably in 1409 or 1410. The sword is part of a permanent display in the City Hall but is still processed on special occasions.

The steel blade is tapering and straight, of flattened hollow diamond section. About 4in from the point it narrows rather suddenly, and the point itself is formed as a flattened isosceles triangle; both features are probably alterations to a blade that originally tapered evenly to a sharp point. Two now indecipherable makers' marks are visible. There is some chipping on the edges. The cross-guard is of iron encased in thick silver-gilt. The long, slender, straight quillons are of rectangular section, tapering to the pointed up-turned tips. Fitted over the centre is a silver chappe, formed of a thin plate cut in silhouette to form two back-to-back lobes, like solid addorsed 'D's, pierced centrally and threaded over the tang of the blade between the grip and the cross, with the lobes bent upwards to right angles to form a semicircular flap over each face of the base of the blade; the edge is scalloped below a narrow, raised, rounded moulding. It would originally have been cut from a single sheet, but it has at some time been broken along the straight edges of the lobes, where they are bent over, and repaired by adding a central soldered strip of new silver. The side of the cross bears traces of longitudinal herringbone foliage on a central stem, while each lobe is engraved with oak foliage above a scroll with a central pucker separating the words 'Souereyne Souereyne' in Gothic miniscules (this motto was used by Henry). The grip, possibly of wood, is covered in a thick silver-gilt sheet. It tapers from the cross-guard to the pommel and is divided approximately in half by a prominent rounded moulding, above which it is of stiff diamond section, and below of flattened diamond section, almost oval. At each end is a narrow raised moulding, at the top single and at the bottom triple. There are longitudinal bands of scrolling stems bearing quatrefoil flowers with slightly pointed petals (probably forget-me-nots – an emblem oft used by Henry), set alternately with diagonal bands of 'S'-shaped scrolling-tendrils. The large inverted-plummet-shaped iron pommel is encased in thick silver-gilt sheet and is of octagonal section with a flat moulding round the grip end corresponding to a moulding round the edge of the domed top. The decoration on the pommel is particularly badly rubbed, but its broad outlines and some of the details can be made out. It is confined to the faces between the two horizontal mouldings, which themselves bear faint traces of an open cable pattern, and comprises, on the two faces in line respectively with the centre of each face of the blade, a large vertical ostrich feather (used by Henry as Earl of Derby), quill to the cross and set at intervals with diagonal bands containing traces of a pattern or writing; on the remaining faces are variously oak leaves and trails of flowers, as on the chappe and the grip. The domed top of the pommel, above the upper moulding, bears no sign of decoration. It has a large acorn-shaped tang button of silver made separately, which is the only part of this sword that is not original.

Scabbard

The scabbard, made in the 1690s, is made of wood covered with crimson velvet, now somewhat rubbed, and with eight silver-gilt mounts – all are viewed point down, except the chape. There are two V-sectioned edging-bands with their own inner edges scalloped. The mounts are: (1) the chape, which has a quadruple raised moulding along the upper edge and a round tip. It is slightly too small for the scabbard and must come from the missing scabbard of the King's sword. It is chased on each face with the arms of Dublin under a cherub's head supporting a basket of fruit. This decoration, in contrast to everything else on the sword and scabbard, is the right way up when the point is upwards; (2) a narrow band carrying in the centre of each face a baroque cartouche, rather roughly cast and chased in low relief with a crowned Irish harp; (3) a narrow band carrying in the centre of each face a baroque cartouche, rather roughly cast and chased in low relief with the Stuart royal arms; (4) a narrow band carrying in the centre on each face a baroque cartouche, rather roughly cast and chased in low relief with a crowned Tudor rose between the initials 'CR' and within an oval pearled frame; (5) a mount comprising two crossed Garters (of the Order of the Garter), one in the centre of each face, linked at the sides by a narrow hinge and pin attachment. They are cast and chased in relief and frame shields of the arms of William III surmounted by his monogram, a letter 'W' flanked by a pair of addorsed 'R's; (6) a narrow band carrying in the centre of each face a baroque cartouche, rather roughly cast and chased in low relief with a crowned Tudor rose between the initials 'CR' and within an oval pearled frame; (7) a locket in the form of a buckled Garter with its free end looped under and over and then back under itself, and originally hanging down but now lacking the pendent portion. It carries a fixed ring on each side for a belt attachment, and each of its edges is bordered by a narrow raised moulding followed on its inner side by a twisted wire. The three simulated eyelets to take the tongue of the buckle are fitted with large applied washers, of which two original ones are sexfoil: the third, a later replacement, forms the head of a split-pin and is octfoil. Engraved on the part of the Garter across the obverse of the scabbard, between two pairs of parallel lines, is a running design of a scrolling stem carrying quatrefoil flowers, as on the hilt, and the word 'souereyne' in gothic miniscules, the last letter covered by the later washer; and (8) the deep mouth-locket has its upper edge bordered by a multiple raised moulding and its lower wedge scalloped.

Some of the mounts are from the original scabbard, the remainder from after the Restoration.

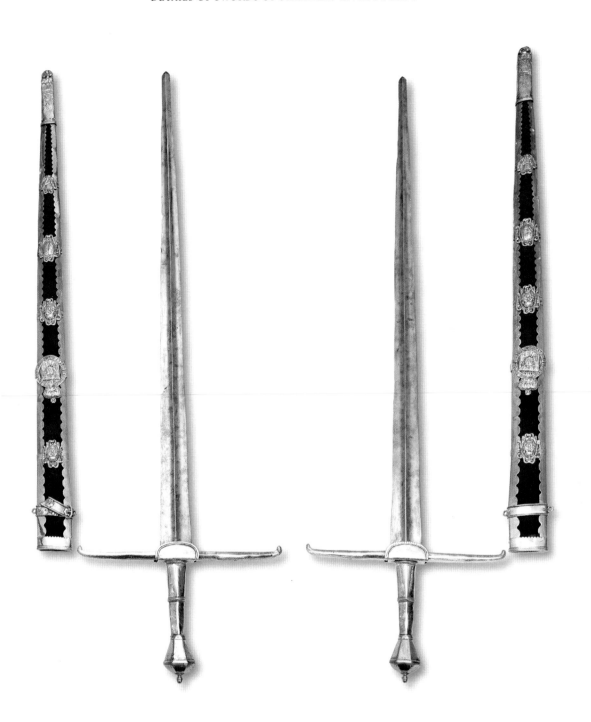

The City of Dublin Sword of State – *c.* 1390–99

The King's or City Sword – sixteenth century

Length of sword	3ft 8⅝in – 1.140m	Weight of sword	3lb 10oz – 1.645kg
Length of blade	2ft 11¼in – 0.895m – Double-edged	Width of blade	1⅝in – 0.041m
Length of hilt	9⅝in – 0.245m – Two-handed	Width of guard	7½in – 0.190m

Sword

The sixteenth-century steel blade, although with minor rust damage, is in good condition. It is straight, tapering and of flattened diamond section, and of rather ordinary quality. The cross-guard is very unusual. It is strongly arched and made in flattened rectangular section with lobe-shaped tips, drawn down in the centre to form an extension (modern escutcheon) of a rounded shield shape over each face of the base of the blade. Engraved on one escutcheon is a shaped shield bearing the coat of arms of Dublin, while on the other is chased a chrysanthemum-like flower. It is decorated with running acanthus-like foliage, chased in shallow bas-relief. The silver-gilt grip, from 1608, is of oval section, tapering slightly from cross-guard to pommel, and with a plain flat moulding at each end. It is decorated with a band of acanthus foliage encircling the bottom of the grip: this last overlaps the engraved decoration and so may be a later addition. Originally, it bore the royal arms, possibly of James I. The thick, hollow silver-gilt pommel is circular, flattened on top, of oblong section slightly chamfered on each face, supported on a concave moulding, and with a separate small rounded tang button made of copper (probably a late replacement). On one face of the pommel is a rococo shield with the coat of arms of Dublin, on the other is a crowned harp; both are on discs inlaid flush with the surface and with the edge marked by an engraved line. The foliage on the pommel involves scallop-shaped shells, while on each side at the top is an acanthus leaf in low relief. The current pommel may well have been made by John Doyle in 1649, but the discs are more likely from about 1660–61.

The original hilt of this sword is by the Dublin goldsmith James Bee, who was later elected as mayor but died before taking office. However, the grip was replaced in 1649 by John Doyle when the Commonwealth required all royal symbols to be removed from such objects. All decorations are viewed point down.

The sword is no longer used and is on display in the museum.

Scabbard

The scabbard does not survive but it is probable that the chape and some of the other mounts on the scabbard of the Great Sword originally belonged to this one.

Cap of Maintenance

There is no cap of maintenance. The sword-bearer wears the black military-style peaked cap of the Dublin Fire Brigade.

Uniform

The sword-bearer is a member of the Dublin Fire Brigade and wears a navy single-breasted uniform with silver buttons, a light blue shirt with navy blue tie, a white belt and white cotton gloves.

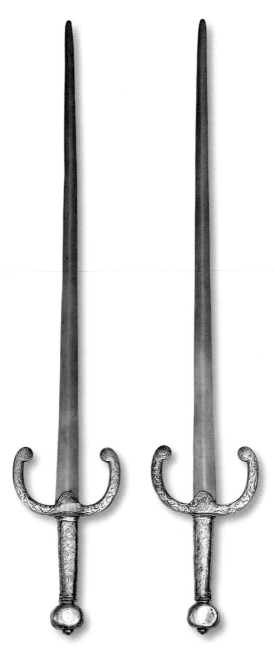

The City of Dublin King's or City Sword – sixteenth century

Norwich

Prerogative

The right to have a sword borne before the mayor was conferred upon the city by Henry IV in 1404 with the power 'to elect a Mayor and Sheriffs yearly, who should have a sword carried before them with point erect in the presence of all nobles, whether of royal blood or no, the King and his heirs only excepted, and also maces adorned with the King's arms'.

Whether the city actually possessed a sword given by the king is uncertain, as the existing one is of a much later date. From records held, it is evident that in 1545 there were two swords belonging to the corporation: the 'best sword' with a 'crymsyn scaberd' (for ordinary occasions) and a 'purpyll scabard' (used probably in times of mourning); and a 'worser sword'. It is probable that one of these swords was contemporary with the charter of 1404–05.

It may be noted that when Elizabeth I visited the city in 1578, the mayor resigned to her the sword, which he described in his address as 'this regalia of our preferment and favour, which the most merciful Prince Henry IV granted to us on the fifth year of his reign, with the mayor, aldermen and others'.

The mourning scabbard and second sword have since been lost. The city now has two swords, though one is a presentational item.

The Sword of State – c. 1545

Length of sword	4ft 1in – 1.245m	Weight of sword	4lb 2oz – 1.871kg
Length of blade	2ft 10⅝in – 0.879m – Double-edged	Width of blade	2in – 0.051m
Length of hilt	14¼in – 0.362m – Two-handed	Width of guard	13½in – 0.343m
Length of scabbard	3ft 0⅛in – 0.917m	Weight of scabbard	1lb 1oz – 0.481kg

Sword

The current sword has a blade which is probably of sixteenth-century date and of Spanish workmanship. The fuller is inscribed for 9in with 'SEBASTIAN' on one side and 'HERNANTEZ' on the other, the name of a famous Toledo smith, but it was probably made in Solingen where smiths regularly put their name on their own blades. On the quillon block is engraved on one side 'Ex Dono Honorabil: | Fraternitatis Sti: | Georgij in Norwico | Anno Dom 1705' (A gift from the Honourable Company of St George in Norwich) and on the other side are the royal arms of Queen Anne, within the Garter and crowned, with supporters and motto. Each of the flat quillons is decorated with acanthus leaves, is larger at the end and terminates in a cross formed of three fleurs-de-lis. The grip is wrapped with silver wire. The large pear-shaped pommel which is currently quite

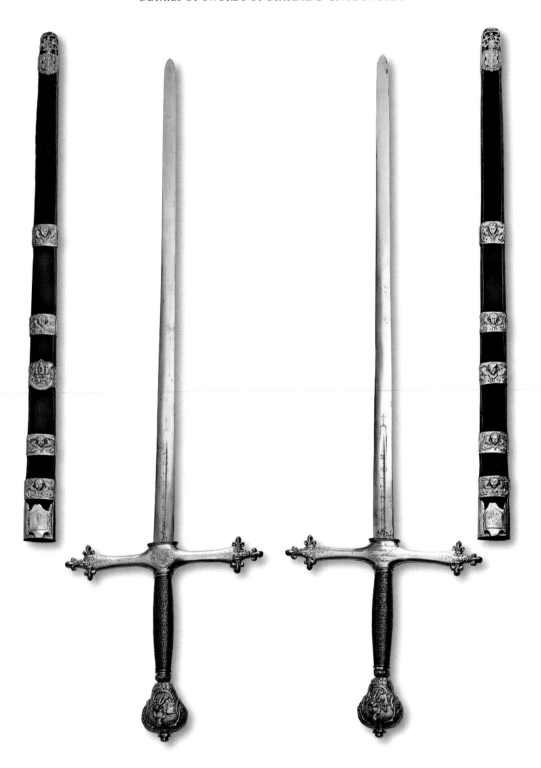

The City of Norwich Sword of State – *c.* 1545

loose is slightly flattened with acanthus leaves on each edge, and wrought in relief with the figure of Justice with sword and scales on one side and of Prudence with a book and globe on the other, and is on upside down. The tang nut is obscured by a small cap.

Scabbard

The scabbard is covered with crimson velvet with rather dilapidated gold lace galloon down each edge and with seven silver-gilt mounts. These consist of: (1) the chape, which has the royal arms of the Tudor sovereigns, probably that of Henry VIII, within the Garter and crowned, with supporters and motto, on each side; (2) a cherub's head on each side; (3) a cherub's head on each side; (4) a shield of the city arms on one side and another cherub's head on the other, (5) a cherub's head on each side; (6) a cherub's head on each side; and (7) the mouth-locket with the royal arms of the Stuart sovereigns, probably Charles II, within the Garter and crowned, with supporters and motto, on both sides, though one may have been made later. The mouth-locket should be viewed point down.

The cherub mounts are very unevenly spaced and have slipped over the years. The cherubs all have different faces or expressions. All the mounts except the chape appear to belong to the reign of Charles II (1660–85). The chape is probably that made for the scabbard in 1545, which ties in with the sixteenth-century blade, and is viewed point up, as are the cherubs (in 1895 the cherubs were viewed point down). A new scabbard was ordered from Mr Samuel Harmer in 1735 and the metal mounts were sent to Mr Roe in London for inclusion. The bill for the new scabbard and cleaning the blade amounted to 25s.

The following entry appears in the minute books of the St George's Company: 'St George's Assembly, 18 Dec. 1704. The Committee for this Company are desired to provide a new blade & scabbard for the Mayor's sword usually borne before him & a new scabbard for the mourning sword such as they think most fit.'

The sixteenth-century blade and the Henry VIII chape indicate that the original sword is probably one of those mentioned in 1545. The wire-bound grip is a feature on swords of all ages. A civic portrait of an unknown mayor, c. 1680, quite clearly shows a very similar sword with the quillons ending with distinctive but unusual fleurs-de-lis (though a touch of artistic licence is included). The pommel is almost identical to five other pommels dating from 1677 to 1684. The scabbard mounts appear to belong to the reign of Charles II. With two parts of the sword and the scabbard dating from the sixteenth century, and several others from the seventeenth century, it is evident that the sword and scabbard are considerably older than its presentation date. It may well be that the sword said to be donated in 1705 was a refashioned and refurbished edition of the self same older sword. The only direct evidence of any new work done by the St George Company is the inscription and the arms of Queen Anne (1702–07) on the quillon block.

Cap of Maintenance

Originally there would have been two caps of maintenance, a tall winter one of fur and a flatter one of velvet for summer. It was customary for the sword-bearer to wear a hat on some occasions and on others a cap of maintenance. In 1473, two entries appear in the accounts – 'a newe bever hatte for ye Swerdberer' and a new 'hatte of pure grey, and for a newe hatte of calabor, to the Swordberer'. It may be that 'calabor' is 'calibre' and refers to the 'bever hatte'. In the 1680 mayor's portrait referred to above, there are two caps of maintenance – one obviously of fur and the other of the velvet type. There is a record of a charge in 1694 for a 'Ffurre Capp & Case, for the sword-bearer' priced at £8 12s. There is no further mention of a fur cap. A red velvet hat was purchased in 1765. In 1832, the sword-bearer wore a flat broad hat of crimson velvet ornamented with gold lace, and on particular occasions he wore a fur cap (of maintenance). A coloured lithograph of 1850 shows the sword-bearer wearing a summer 'silk' cap with a winter fur cap on a table beside him. In 1895, he wore a flat broad-brimmed hat of red velvet, with pendant cords and tassels of comparatively modern date. Neither of these two caps can be found 115 years later.

Today there is no cap of maintenance; the sword-bearer wears a top hat with gold lace galloon around the base of the crown in place of the hat band.

Uniform

In 1832, the sword-bearer wore a black silk gown. The 1850 lithograph shows a heavily brocaded black silk gown with tufts. Today he wears a black frock-coat, a red waistcoat, black trousers, white shirt, black bow tie, black shoes and white cotton gloves.

The City of Norwich Sword-Bearer

Kingston upon Hull

Prerogative

The privilege of having a sword borne erect before him within the town and liberty and precinct of the same was conferred on the mayor of Kingston upon Hull by letters patent of Henry VI, granted on 2 July 1440, within two months of the charter of incorporation. The same charter authorises the mayor and aldermen to wear livery gowns like those worn by the mayor and aldermen of London, and appointed the mayor as escheator. No time was lost in buying the Sword of State, the charges of which are given among the 'Costages of the Chartere'. It is clear that the sword was mounted in silver-gilt, and furnished with three 'shethis'. Of these, one was covered with a cloth of gold, for state occasions; the second with blue velvet, for ordinary use; and the third with black velvet, for use in times of mourning or great solemnity. The blue and the cloth of gold sheaths had silver-gilt chapes, but the third sheath had a chape of less precious metal.

Local tradition and history alike assert that the Sword of State was given to the town by Henry VIII on the occasion of his visit in 1541; but the evidence of the corporation records (the chamberlain's accounts of 1450–51 mention 'a mayor's sword'), and of the sword itself, show that it was originally made to order in 1440. Two Garters preserved with other insignia, of plain crimson and black velvet respectively, with silver-gilt mounts, not improbably once formed part of the girdle of the sword. One has a beautifully designed buckle and pendant of fifteenth-century work. The other has a plain modern buckle which is attached to a Tudor hinge, and an ancient pendant with three coronets in relief. The modern buckle probably dates from 1797, when one was purchased.

From 1835 to 1851, the sword and other items of insignia were locked away in the town hall before being 'exhumed, cleaned and again restored to use'.

The city has two swords, though one is a non-bearing-sword.

The Sword of State – 1440

Length of sword	3ft 8in – 1.118m	Weight of sword	3lb 4½oz – 1.485kg
Length of blade	2ft 9½ in – 0.851m – Double-edged	Width of blade	1½in – 0.038m
Length of hilt	10½in – 0.267m – Two-handed	Width of guard	11¾in – 0.298m
Length of scabbard	2ft 11½in – 0.902m	Weight of scabbard	2lb 3¼oz – 0.999kg

Sword

The current sword, although it has lost its original blade and been otherwise altered, still retains some interesting portions of the sword made in 1440. The blade, which appears to be late eighteenth-century and not in keeping with the hilt, has the lower 12in blued

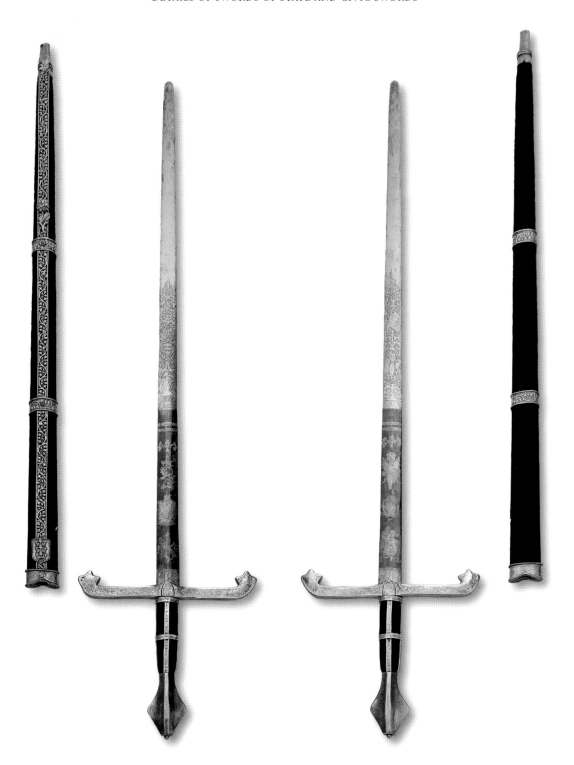

The City of Kingston upon Hull Sword of State – 1440

and bears, on both sides, various devices, all executed in a style redolent of the late eighteenth century. On the obverse, it bears the town arms, the figure of Hope with wings and an anchor, some leaf-work, the royal arms – error-strewn and very poorly executed – probably of George III, within the Garter and crowned, with supporters and motto (however, the half-quarter of Scotland is omitted) and the maker's name, 'WOOLEY & Co', which was in being from 1790 to 1797. On the reverse, it bears a trophy of arms, the royal arms of George I, another trophy of arms with 'GR' twice, the town arms and the figure of Britannia. The hilt is silver-gilt and of several dates. The cross-guard is, without doubt, that of the sword of 1440. The quillon block has a small écusson and has, on the obverse, a shield of the royal arms, France modern and England quarterly, as borne by five English sovereigns but probably of Henry VI given the date of manufacture, and on the reverse, a shield of the town arms. The quillons are rectangular in section and are decorated throughout with an engraved scroll of leaf-work. They are turned up at the ends and spread out. The grip is covered in blue velvet, over which are four longitudinal and two transverse reeded bands. The pommel is lozenge-shaped with central ridge, but is quite plain, and apparently of more recent date. There is a very small tang button.

Scabbard

A new scabbard was ordered in 1776 and another in 1882. In 1895, it was covered in red velvet. In about 1934, it was re-covered. In 1955, as a result of a report that the old 1882 scabbard had deteriorated sufficiently to crack a silver mount, the council accepted the gift of a new metal sheath. Mappin and Webb of Sheffield were commissioned to re-cover it, and repair and transfer the gilt mounts from the old sheath.

Today the scabbard is covered with dark blue velvet, with six silver-gilt mounts. Along the obverse of the sheath, from chape to mouth-locket, is affixed a beautiful longitudinal band of silver-gilt, ¾in wide, wrought with a running pattern of vine leaves and grapes of pierced work in high relief. The mounts are: (1) the chape, encircled by a reeded band, with, in high relief, a dimidiated Tudor rose and pomegranate, the badge of Queen Katherine of Aragon and her daughter Queen Mary (O), and a small sunburst (R); (2) a stemmed rose; (3) an unpierced reeded band with vines and grapes and a period screw (O); (4) an unpierced reeded band with vines and grapes and a period screw (O); (5) a shield of the town arms in high relief (O); and (6) the mouth-locket, which is slightly concave, has cabled edges, engraved on the obverse with roses and acorns, and with a silver-gilt slipped rose, modelled in full relief held by an extremely modern self-tapping galvanised screw; and the date 1613 divided by a small shield with the initials 'I L M' for John Lister, mayor, on the reverse. These beautiful mounts of the sheath are of the fifteenth century, and probably formed part of the decorations of the sword made in 1440.

In 1895, there still existed a second much-battered scabbard once covered in black velvet, with plain gilt metal chape, which was formerly used with one or other of the swords on occasions of mourning. It had for many years been the usage on occasions of state mourning to enclose the sword and mace within black crepe. In 1955, the Guildhall Sub-Committee examined the desirability of again providing a black velvet mourning scabbard with simple silver or silver-gilt mounts but, despite receiving two alternative designs, the matter was deferred. This scabbard has since disappeared.

Cap of Maintenance

A cap of badger skin was in persistent use in Tudor times. A new cap of maintenance was ordered in 1776, and the following year £4 10*s* was paid for 'a Velvet Lac'd Hatt Tassil and Case'; this was clearly not a high fur 'winter' hat, so presumably was a 'summer' hat. In 1806 or 1810, sums were expended for repairing the sword-bearer's hat, for crimson velvet to cover the same and for 2¼ yards of gold 2in Granby lace, and gold fringe. However, when the use of the cap was discontinued in 1835, the position of sword-bearer was also discontinued and the sword borne by the senior beadle. In 1866, 'the Cap of Maintenance of velvet' was mentioned, but between then and 1895 it disappeared. At the end of 1893, Sir William St John Hope visited the Hull and East Riding Antiquarian Society and adversely commented on the decision to discontinue the wearing of the cap. This resulted in a change of heart, and in June 1895 the then mayor, Alderman

The City of Kingston upon Hull Sword-Bearer

Richardson, resurrected the tradition with the presentation of a new fur cap of maintenance, 'similar to the one worn by the sword-bearer of the Corporation of the City of London', of sable with a sable crown lined with red velvet. This cap was replaced in 2007 and is now preserved in a display case. The latest cap is of synthetic black sable fur. It is 6½in high and 11in wide at the crown.[17]

Uniform

There is no record of what the sword-bearers wore in earlier times. But in the nineteenth and early twentieth centuries, the beadles wore knee breeches, apparently of velvet, with tail coats and silk hats. The sword-bearer, after 1895, when carrying the sword, wore this livery with the cap of maintenance, and a black tasselled gown following the usage of London, but of cloth instead of silk.

Today the day-to-day wear is a double-breasted suit of royal blue Melton cloth, with three gold wrist stripes (the mace-bearer has two stripes and the chauffeur has one stripe).

When carrying the sword, the sword-bearer wears a traditional black gown with tufts over a royal blue tail-coat, piped with red, with velvet and silver braided collar, silver braided and buttoned cuffs and silver armorial buttons. The trousers are similarly piped and worn with white shirt, with a black bow tie, black shoes and white cotton gloves.

King's Lynn

Prerogative

The privilege to bear a sword was granted personally by Henry VI in 1446 but later rescinded. When Henry VI visited Lynn in 1446, Thomas Salisbury, the mayor, petitioned the king to permit his successors to have a sword carried before them. The king granted the mayor's request but, despite several indisputable records conforming this, the Bishop of Norwich objected. Despite a strong campaign and the mayor being summoned to London, the king found for the bishop and the grant was annulled in November 1446.

It was not until 1524 that the right was returned. The first charter of definite incorporation was granted by Henry VIII on 27 June 1524. It said 'that in all places within the borough the mayor for the time being may have a sheathed sword borne before him by a Sword-bearer to be elected for that purpose by the Mayor and aldermen or the greater part of them'.

However there are several references to a sword before this. According to William Taylor, writing in *The Antiquities of King's Lynn, Norfolk* in 1844: 'It is known that a sword has been carried before the mayors of Lynn from the time of King Henry III.' In 1389–90, there was '2*s* 5*d* paid for a scabbard to the Sword of the Mayor with goldsmith's work for the same'. The sword was carried before the bishop when in Lynn and behind his vassal the mayor.

The ascription of the gift of the sword to King John, as well as the statement that he took the sword from his own side, is certainly not correct as regards the present sword. The story about the inscription has changed over the years due to misquotes. Charles R. Beard, writing in *The Connoisseur* in 1941, states:

> Edmund Gibson, in the Additions to his edition of William Camden's *Britannia* (1695) gives the following account of what occurred – 'I found a loose paper of Sir Henry Spelman's, dated Sept 15, 1630 to this purpose; That he was then assur'd by Mr. Tho. Kenet, Town clerk of Len, that one John Cooke the Sword-bearer about 50 years before, came to Mr. Ivory, the School-master, and desir'd him, because one side of the hilt of the town sword was plain, and without any inscription, that he would direct how to engrave upon it, that King John gave that Sword to the town. Whereupon he caused the said Thomas Kenet, being then his scholar, to write these words: "Ensis hic donum fvit Regis Johannis a svo ipsivs latere datvm" after which the Sword-bearer carry'd the writing to one Cooke a goldsmith, and caus'd him to engrave it.'

Thomas Cooke, goldsmith, became a freeman of Lynn in 1579–80.

Beard is also of the opinion that the sword is a century older than had been previously thought. He believed:

[T]he stout tapering quillons of rectangular section and the facetted plummet-shaped pommel can be duplicated on a score of brasses of the reign of Henry V and no other period … the heavy hexagonal sectioned blade is no less characteristic of the era. To my mind there can be no question that this is the old Mayor's sword of Bishop's Lynn concerning which there was such a to-do in 1446. The silver overlaying and the inscription of 1528–29 were presumably added in that year to commemorate Henry VIII's charter of 1524. Thereafter followed Ivory's inscription in or around 1580, while the grip seems to have been bound in the seventeenth century.

The date attributed to this sword is therefore based upon this detailed research.

The Sword of State – *c.* 1446

Length of sword	3ft 11⅛in – 1.197m	Weight of sword	5lb 4oz – 2.378kg
Length of blade	2ft 11in – 0.889m – Double-edged	Width of blade	2in – 0.051m
Length of hilt	12⅛in – 0.308m – Two-handed	Width of guard	14⅜in – 0.365m
Length of scabbard	3ft 0in – 0.914m	Weight of scabbard	2lb 5½oz – 1.060kg

Sword

The sword is beautiful example of its class in the early fifteenth century. The blade, which is in very good condition, is probably of Solingen manufacture and has the armourer's marks of a crozier and an orb and moon in two places on each side. The iron hilt is silver-gilt. There is no quillon block. The rectangular quillons are straight throughout, though tapering, and end simply. Each side is inscribed throughout its length. On one side is *'ENSIS HIC DONVM FVIT REGIS JOHANNIS A SVO IPSIVS LATERE DATVM'* (This sword was the gift of King John, given of he himself from his side). On the other side is *'VIVAT REX HENRICVS OCTAVVS ANNO REGNI SVO 20'* (Long live King Henry VIII in the twentieth year of his reign [1528–29]). The tapering grip is covered with silver-gilt wire. The octagonal scent-stopper-shaped pommel is beautifully wrought in identical panels chased with foliage and ends with a screw tang nut of recent origin. It is somewhat difficult to reconcile the King John statement with the date given on the sword, viz. 20 Henry VIII, as the inscriptions on both sides of the quillons are clearly contemporary.

Scabbard

Taylor also states that Richard Clark, mayor in 1583, 'during his mayoralty gave a new scabbard of crimson velvet for the corporation sword, trimmed with silver, and double gilt, with the queen's and town-arms engraved thereon'. And that in 1650 'the King's Arms was ordered to be removed from the scabbard of the sword, and the state's arms put thereon'. The present five mounts of the sword appear to date from the Restoration, when they doubtless replaced the state's arms and other non-legal emblems. A Hall

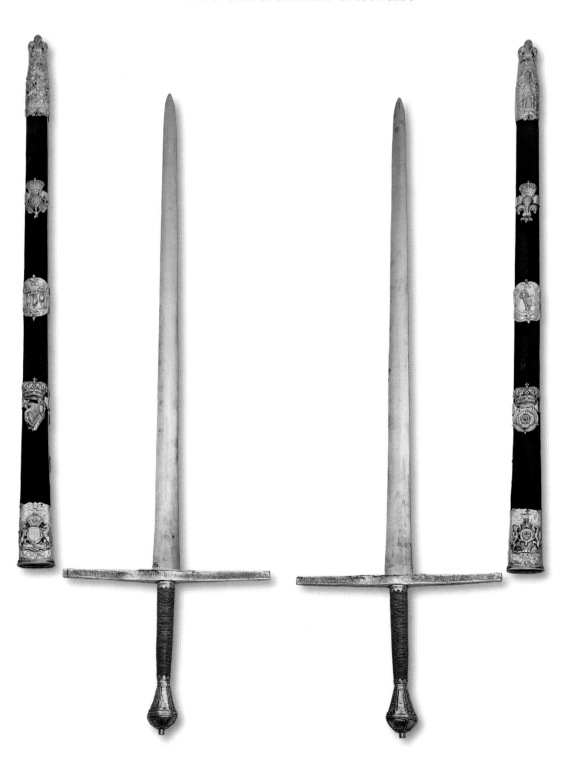

The King's Lynn Sword of State – *c.* 1446

book entry of 28 January 1661 states: 'It is this day ordered that the old scabbard with the garnishes thereupon having the States Armes be taken out of the Treasury and sent to London in order for the makeing of a new scabbard with the King's arms on the new garnishes and that Mr Mayor be pleases to take upon him the care and trouble of accomplishing and that the charges thereof be borne by this house'. The silver-gilt mounts were reused in 1771, when a new scabbard was ordered. The scabbard was subsequently re-covered.

The King's Lynn Sword-Bearer

The scabbard today is covered with crimson velvet with five silver-gilt mounts, with a galloon of gold lace down each side which is now in need of some repair. They are: (1) the chape, which terminates in a fleur-de-lis, has a king riding over prostrate foes on the obverse and a figure of a king in armour, believed to be Charles I, brandishing a sword, on the reverse; (2) a crowned thistle on the obverse and a crowned fleur-de-lis on the reverse; (3) the arms of Lynn on the obverse and a shield with a pelican in its piety on the reverse; (4) a crowned harp on the obverse and a crowned rose on the reverse; and (5) the mouth-locket, which has the royal arms of the Tudor sovereigns, probably Henry VIII, within the Garter and crowned, with dragon and greyhound supporters, on the reverse, and the royal arms of the Stuart sovereigns, probably of Charles II, within the Garter and crowned, with supporters, on the reverse. These Tudor arms were used by five different sovereigns but this is almost certainly a reproduction of those of Henry VIII, given the date on the quillons of 1528–29 in the comment above, and applied to the new scabbard in 1661.

Cap of Maintenance

There is no cap of maintenance. No record has been found of the use of either the traditional winter fur or summer velvet caps of maintenance. The sword-bearer wears a black bi-corn (side to side) with broad gold lace galloon, with embossed button centrally on the front.

Uniform

The sword-bearer wears a black superfine robe with gold piping round the collar and on the sleeves, with frilly white lace cuffs attached to half-sleeves, white jabot, white shirt, black trousers, black shoes and white cotton gloves.

Waterford

Prerogative

In 1461, Waterford council had to enact special legislation in order to persuade members of the merchant oligarchy to 'accept the office of mayor and not absent themselves from the mayoral elections'. Recent attacks on the city by two strong families had shown that the office of mayor had few perks, especially as the mayor was expected to lead the city's army against the enemy when under attack.

The new king, Edward IV, was aware of this and sought to strengthen the position of the mayor. He decided to court the support of Waterford and in 1461 he reduced the rent owed to him and granted a charter that decreed that the city should *have* 'a sword with an adjoined scabbard, borne before the mayor by a sergeant within the city and when the occasion arises to be borne before the king', i.e. in the event of a visit from the monarch; it also mentioned 'as in Bristol'.

A new civic ceremony was initiated in 1481, when 'all the council shall proceed from the chapel to the Guildhall with the sword-bearer holding aloft the civic sword and when there to elect a mayor and bailiffs for the year following'.

Today Waterford has two swords, both of which are on display in the new museum together with the cap of maintenance. The last time the Sword of State (Henry VIII) was processed was at a ceremony in Dublin in 1998.

Much of the information contained in this section has been extracted from *Waterford Treasures* by Eamonn McEneaney and Rosemary Ryan.[10]

The Edward IV Sword – 1461

Length of sword	3ft 7⅝in – 1.108m	Weight of sword	2lb 5¾oz – 1.073kg
Length of blade	2ft 10⅞in – 0.887m – Double-edged	Width of blade	1⅛in – 0.029m
Length of hilt	8¾in – 0.221m – Two-handed	Width of guard	12½in – 0.316m
Length of scabbard	2ft 11in – 0.889m	Weight of scabbard	11oz – 0.311kg

Sword

The steel is narrow, tapers and is quite sharp. The surface is rather mottled but in quite good condition. There are some indecipherable marks on each side that may be makers' marks. The steel cross-guard is one piece. It is narrow and plain, swelling in both planes to simple champhered ends. It is extremely loose. The baluster-shaped grip is clad in silver, with a collar at each end, and is undecorated. There is an extra sleeve at the mid-point with scalloped edges. The steel pommel is hexagonal and roughly diamond-shaped. There is a circular sunken part on each main face – the insets are long gone.

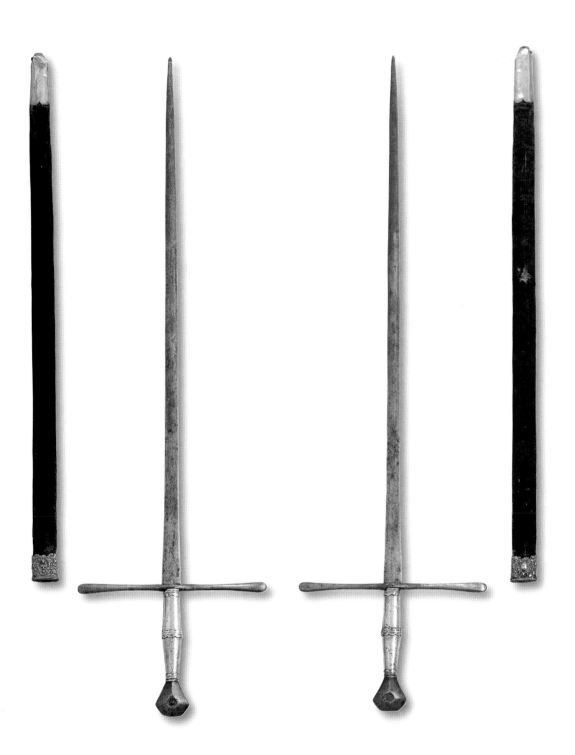

The City of Waterford Edward IV Sword – 1461

There is no tang button so it could be screwed on or it may be that the sunken areas in fact cover some form of dowel holding the pommel in place.

Scabbard

The leather scabbard is almost certainly original and very flexible but the black velvet covering is relatively modern. There is a silver chape and mouth-locket. The chape is plain and extremely battered. The mouth-locket has on the obverse two semi-clad female figures on either side of another slightly larger figure. On the reverse are two similar semi-clad female figures either side of a face. This could be the face of the king (a frequent practice) but it is too worn to be identified. The female figures have similar poses.

   Given the black covering, it may well be that this was the city's mourning sword in years gone by.

The Henry VIII Sword – 1536

Length of sword	4ft 9⅝in – 1.464m	Weight of sword	5lb 5½oz – 2.421kg
Length of blade	3ft 8½in – 1.130m – Double-edged	Width of blade	1⅛in – 0.028m
Length of hilt	13⅛in–0.334m – Two-handed	Width of guard	18¼in – 0.465m
Length of scabbard	3ft 8⅜in – 1.126m	Weight of scabbard	1lb 2¾oz – 0.534kg

Sword

The sword was the gift, along with a cap of maintenance, of Henry VIII in 1536, as a reward for loyalty at the time of a rebellion in 1534. The king sent a letter with the sword and cap saying that the sword was 'to be borne before the mayor from time to time within our said city'. The sword is an extremely fine example of the art of the sixteenth-century European cutler. The steel blade is quite narrow, tapers, is quite sharp, is flexible and in fair condition. There are no obvious makers' marks. There is a 10½in ricasso ending in a set of hooks. However, these are unusual in that they are right-angled triangles with one side affixed to the blade, a flat edge to the point and the angled side has a scalloped edge. The hooks are 4½in wide and 5¼in from the cross-guard. It is one of three swords included in the book with hooks. There are two 9in fullers on each side right at the edge of the ricasso. The cross-guard is of tubular brass with scoured rings on each quillon and ends in tiered finials, which may be later alterations. There is a second rather superfluous sleeve on each tube which may have been added to give extra strength. There is an écusson. The cross-guard is very loose. The baluster-shaped grip is copper covered with silver. It is made up of three sections. The top section has a collar at the top and is openwork with twelve boxes on the reverse, six tear drops on the obverse and three diamonds on each side. The central section has a collar at each end, an inscription 'VOP' above the Green Man motif on the obverse and an inscription 'MMD' above the Green Man motif in between a bird and what appears to be a

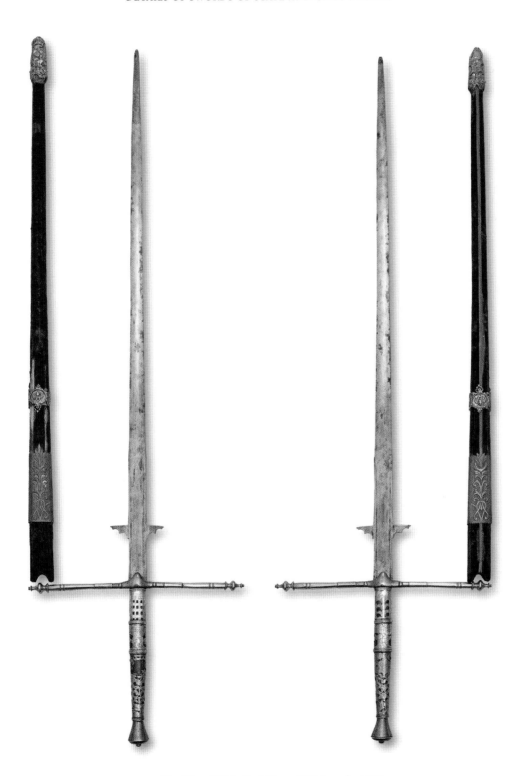

The City of Waterford Henry VIII Sword – 1536

knot of cloth on the reverse. The bottom section has, on the obverse, the royal arms, probably of Henry VIII – (oddly viewed point down – everything else is viewed point up). The reverse is badly damaged, with several parts missing. It ends with a collar. A decoration of stylised plant ornamentation covers many of the gaps on each section. The steel pommel is pear-shaped, with a slightly domed end and a small tang nut.

Scabbard

The wooden scabbard is covered in crimson velvet with a gold lace galloon along one face. Of the three mounts, the silver-gilt chape has the royal arms, viewed point down, on the obverse and the Tudor rose on the reverse. The edges are crimped. A central silver-gilt locket bears a cherub within an oval on each face. Unusually, the end of the scabbard is cut back some 4¾in on each side to pass over the hooks. Just above this point, to prevent splitting, is a brass mouth-locket chased with leaf-work.

Cap of Maintenance

A fine summer cap of maintenance is held and it is displayed in the new museum. It was a gift of Henry VIII in 1536 and is believed to be the oldest surviving cap of this type. It is made of red velvet, embroidered with Tudor roses and marguerites and was probably made at the royal court. The velvet was possibly produced in Lucca, Italy. The red rose was the symbol of the Tudor dynasty. The marguerites are motifs often repeated in Tudor decoration and on clothing associated with Henry VIII. The symbolism is important as the marguerite represents Margaret Beaufort, Henry's grandmother. A strip of baleen, supporting the crown of the cap, has been confirmed to be that of a whale, and carbon dating has shown that it is the same age as the cap. This is one of the oldest caps in Europe and it is the only piece of Henry VIII's wardrobe to survive.

Today, there being no sword-bearer, the cap of maintenance remains on display in the museum.

Uniform

No sword-bearer means no uniform.

Drogheda

Prerogative

Drogheda was granted the privilege of having a sword borne before the mayor in 1469 by the Irish Parliament in recognition of the city's services against the native Irish, and especially to John O'Reilly for services to the English Crown, confirmed by letters patent in July 1469 and *inspeximus* of Edward IV of February 1470. The actual wording mentions 'the mayor for the time being might wear a sword as the mayor of London did'.[18]

It is worth noting that the mayor was created the King's Escheator in 1413 – this allowed him to have a sword borne before him, as in Bristol.

No record exists of any original sword.

The Sword of State – mid-seventeenth century

Length of sword	3ft 6⅞in – 1.090m	Weight of sword	2lb 8¾oz – 1.158kg
Length of blade	2ft 8¾in – 0.832m – Double-edged	Width of blade	1⅝in – 0.041m
Length of hilt	10⅛in – 0.257m – Two-handed	Width of guard	11⅜in – 0.289m
Length of scabbard	2ft 8⅞in – 0.835m	Weight of scabbard	1lb 1¼oz – 0.489kg

Sword

The steel blade is in fair condition. There is a shallow fuller for 9in with a running wolf mark and a cross in a circle mark. There is one other mark. The hilt is silver-gilt. The cross-guard has a simple quillon block onto which the quillons are welded/braised. The block is chased with two vaguely star-shaped images – one on top of the other. The quillons are very thin and sweep up in strong curves terminating in circular ends. They are a little out of alignment due to the thinness. They are somewhat crudely chased with a foliage design with scrolls. The wooden grip is covered with leather. The pommel is a largish hollow flat disc made of silver-gilt plates, now rather battered. On one face is incised the crest of the town; the other face is badly scratched, and bears the odd initial (ancient graffiti?). The bottom of the disc has been repaired with a dark brown substance around the tang nut. There is a small tang nut into which the tang end is hammered.

The sword is no longer processed but is on display in the city museum.

Scabbard

The leather scabbard is covered in cloth and bound with seven silver-gilt mounts. These are all plain on one side. The decorations are: (1) the chape, which is holed at the tip, is chased with leaf-work, and bears the letters 'C R' indicating *Carolus Rex* (King Charles); (2) a crowned rose; (3) the royal arms of the Stuarts within the Garter, and crowned; (4) the same; (5) the same but larger; (6) a crowned rose; and (7) the mouth-locket, which is

The Drogheda Sword of State – mid-seventeenth century

slightly damaged, also chased with leaf-work. There is evidence of gilding. The scabbard is viewed point down.

A sword is said to have been given by William III in 1690 shortly after the Battle of the Boyne, but it was not the sword used personally by the king. However, it seems to have been made earlier than the reign of William. No part of the sword appears to be as early as the fifteenth century. The quillons and pommel are similar in style to the Dublin King's Sword (mid-seventeenth century?) and the Clonmel sword (1656). The chape, two Tudor roses and mouth-locket indicate sixteenth century and may have been from the scabbard of a sword obtained soon after the grant. The three clasps with the royal arms would put it between 1603 and 1688.

It may well be that this is one of the swords from the royal armoury and passed on at a later date.

The sword was last processed in 1920.

Cap of Maintenance

There is no record of a cap of maintenance.

Uniform

There is no sword-bearer and therefore no uniform.

Hereford

Prerogative

An entry in a mayor's inventory in October 1475 lists 'two swords of the said lord the King', thus indicating that the city had been granted the right to bear a sword before that date. It is believed that around 1528 Henry VIII presented a sword to the city during a visit. The sword is said to have connections to the Battle of Mortimer's Cross in 1461, after which Owen Tudor, one of his ancestors, was beheaded in the city. On 26 October 1597, there is record of 'three swords called the Quenes swords with theire scabbardes to the said three swordes belonginge & the three chapes of silver guilte for the said three swordes wayinge ?? ownces and two bands of silver guilt maide for the said swords wayinge ?? ownces. And the said James Boile hathe deliv'ed to the said Walter Hurdman one case of tymber guilded to put the said swords in four maces of silver'. Certainly in the Municipal Corporations Act of 1835 there is mention of a sword-bearer.

Hereford has two swords.

The Mourning Sword – late fifteenth century

Length of sword	3ft 5⅛in – 1.044m	**Weight of sword**	2lb 14¾oz – 1.324kg
Length of blade	2ft 7⅜in – 0.797m – Double-edged	**Width of blade**	1⅝in – 0.041m
Length of hilt	9¾in – 0.248m – Two-handed	**Width of guard**	7½in – 0.190m
Length of scabbard	2ft 7¾in – 0.806m	**Weight of scabbard**	6oz – 0.168kg

Sword

The 'steel' sword or 'King's steel' is believed to have been presented by Henry VIII around 1528, although there is nothing to substantiate this claim. The blade appears to be Elizabethan. The cross-guard and pommel styles of this sword appear to be of late fifteenth-century date. It is called the 'steel sword' from the hilt being supposed to be of that metal; it is actually, however, of bronze or latten, with traces of the original gilding. The blade, which has a 16½in fuller, is not original, but may be Elizabethan. The quillons are flat with an écusson and terminate in curved and pointed ends. On one side of the quillons is engraved 'Maior Civitatis Herefordie'. The other side has a guilloche pattern. The grip is of ebony, with a silver-gilt scalloped and beaded band at each end, and is also of Elizabethan date. The pommel, which should be viewed point down, is heart-shaped, with, on one face, a shield of the royal arms, France modern and England quarterly, possibly of Edward IV (1461–70 and 1470–83), and on the other a shield of the old city arms. Both these shields have the spandrels filled with a rose and foliage, and were originally enamelled; slight traces of the colouring remain. The rounded edges of the pommel also have a guilloche pattern. There is a simple chased tang button. At one

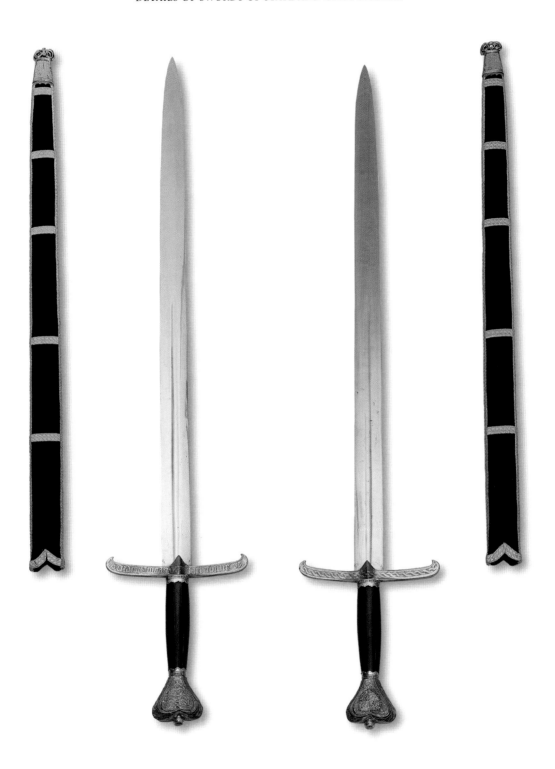

The City of Hereford Mourning Sword – fifteenth century

stage the pommel and hilt were japanned black, thus obscuring much of the detail and workmanship; however, they were re-gilded at the end of the nineteenth century. The sword is only carried in the event of the death of the reigning monarch or mayor during his year of office.

Scabbard

The scabbard is covered with black velvet with gold lace along each edge and one silver-gilt mount. This is (1) the chape, which is slightly off-centre, of Elizabethan date ending in scroll-work, and engraved with a shield of the royal arms, France modern and England quarterly, probably of Edward IV, on one side, and with the city arms on the other side. Five gold lace bands, (2), (3), (4), (5) and (6), are spaced along the scabbard; and (7) is another gold lace band but made to conform to a cut-out at the mouth of the scabbard to accommodate the écusson of the hilt. In 1895, it was stated that 'the mouth-locket was added in 1889'. Today there is no mouth-locket.

The cross-guard and pommel are remarkably similar in style to the Coventry hilt.

The Sword of State – 1677

Length of sword	4ft 2⅜in – 1.280m	Weight of sword	4lb 2½oz – 1.883kg
Length of blade	3ft 0⅞in – 0.937 – Double-edged	Width of blade	1½in – 0.038m
Length of hilt	13½in – 0.343m – Two-handed	Width of guard	12in – 0.305m
Length of scabbard	3ft 2¼in – 0.972m	Weight of scabbard	1lb 5¾oz – 0.614kg

Sword

The 'silver' sword is of remarkably fine character and in very good condition. The blade has, on each side, three fullers, two short and narrow and one long and wide. The latter fuller, extending about 9½in from the cross-guard with gilt damascened work, now much obliterated, has the date '1677' and, roughly cut, the letters 'S A H A G V M'. There is a thin brass collar to protect the hilt. The hilt is silver. The recurved quillons, in *repoussé*, have a rose in the centre, are richly foliated, start with acanthus leaves and bear a rose in the middle on either side. Each quillon terminates with a lion's head on each side. The grip is of bold spiral form anti-clockwise with a band and wire. The pommel is pear-shaped and has in *repoussé*, on one face, a seated figure of Justice with sword and scales and, on the other, of Law with book and three seals. The sides are decorated with acanthus leaves. There is a tang button in the form of an acorn decorated with fleur-de-lis. This sword was given to the city in 1677 by Paul Foley, Esq., MP for, and afterwards auditor of, Hereford and later Speaker of the House of Commons.

Elsewhere it is recorded as the gift of the Duke of Beaufort in 1682, but the date on the blade contradicts this.

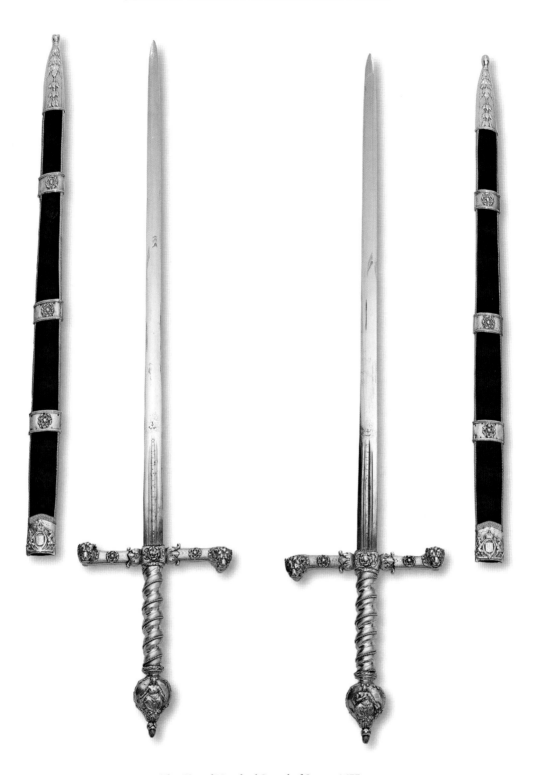

The City of Hereford Sword of State – 1677

Scabbard

The scabbard is of crimson velvet with gold lace along each edge and along the edge of the mouth-locket and five silver-gilt mounts in *repoussé*. These are: (1) the chape, which should be viewed point down, has a spherical finial and acanthus foliage on each face; (2), (3), and (4) are bands with Tudor roses on each side; and (5) the mouth-locket, which has, on each side, the royal arms, probably of Charles II, within the Garter and crowned, with supporters and motto. The silver work is not hallmarked.

Cap of Maintenance

A bill of 1535 for the making a cap of maintenance 'that the sworde berer werith' is preserved. This summer hat of black velvet had given way by 1554 to another of purple velvet, but in 1579 there were 'twoo velvet hatte the one of blacke velvet the other of redde velvet'. An additional red one was afterwards made, and in the indenture of 1596 are 'three velvet hatte the one blacke velvet and thother two of redd velvet and one Case or box to putt the said hatt in'. By 1600, one of the red hats had disappeared and a second

hat was laid aside, for the indenture has 'two velvet hatte' altered to 'one velvet hat', and the words 'the one blacke and the other redde' are struck out. The subsequent history of the hat has yet to be made out from the city accounts. No record has been found of a winter fur cap, but today the sword-bearer wears a winter cap of maintenance of mink fur with a burgundy velvet crown, the purchase date of which is unknown.

Uniform

The sword-bearer wears a black morning-coat with gold braid edging and epaulettes, red collar and cuffs and other gold braid embellishment, a red waistcoat, black trousers with a gold stripe, white shirt and white bow tie, black shoes and white cotton gloves.

The City of Hereford Sword-Bearer

Gloucester

Prerogative

The right to have a sword carried before the mayor is specially conferred upon the city of Gloucester by the charter of Richard III, dated of 2 September 1483:

> [A]nd the same mayor and his successors of the said town appearing, according to circumstances, as long as they shall be in the office of mayor of that town, may have a sword carried in their presence within the same town and the freedoms of the same town in the same manner and nature as is used in other cities and towns within our Kingdom of England.

No mention is, however, made of the officer who shall carry the sword until the charter of Charles I, in 1626–27, when leave is given to appoint 'a sword-bearer who shall carry before the mayor a sword with a coloured sheath bearing our arms and those of the city aforesaid, of otherwise adorned'.

Three swords were mentioned in the inventory of 1637–38. The third sword had a figure of Elizabeth I and 'E.R.1574' and the city arms, as they then were, upon it. This sword could not be found in 1895 and all trace of it seems to be lost.

The city has two swords and three scabbards.

The Mourning Sword – *c.* 1483

Length of sword	3ft 6in – 1.066m	Weight of sword	1lb 7oz – 0.651kg
Length of blade	2ft 11⅛in – 0.892m – Double-edged	Width of blade	1¾in – 0.045m
Length of hilt	6⅞in – 0.178m – One-handed	Width of guard	8in – 0.203m
Length of scabbard	3ft 1⅛in – 0.943m	Weight of scabbard	10oz – 0.279kg

Sword

This sword, now known as the 'mourning' sword, is probably the sword provided in accordance with Richard III's charter. The tapered blade is of Solingen or Passau manufacture with the running wolf mark – not now obvious, and probably of late sixteenth-century date. The narrow 12½in fuller has the letters 'L I D E T E D III' punched on one side and 'O D ? I D II I I T' on the other. The cross-guard is in three pieces; the centre, which has a small écusson on each side, is chased. The two extensions, which appear to be of late sixteenth-century date, are riveted on and consist of a slightly curved main stem with a smaller stem branching off towards the point. One of these branches is missing. The whole cross-guard is of poor workmanship and is very wobbly. The leather grip, which is japanned, has a broad, well-chased ferrule by the

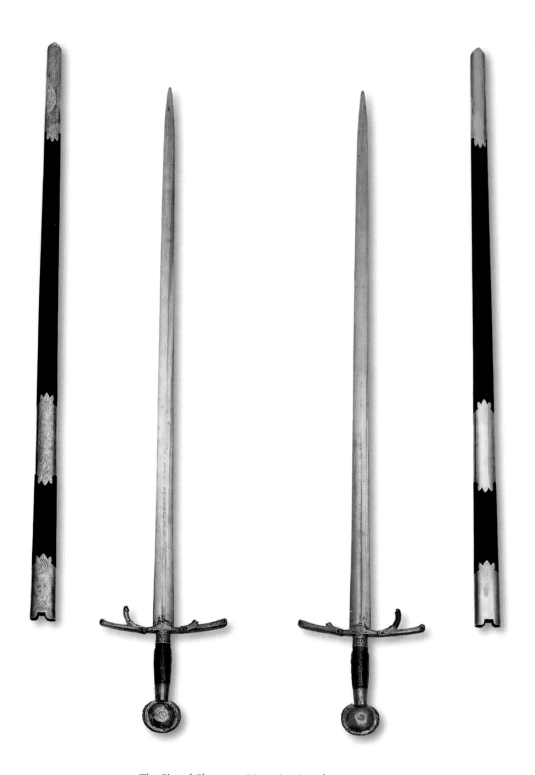

The City of Gloucester Mourning Sword – *c.* 1483

cross-guard and a totally different one next to the pommel. The disc-shaped pommel is probably original and has a raised dome on each side which is chased with a rose and other foliage round the rim. The grip and pommel are loose. The tang end is hammered into the pommel. An entry in the chamberlain's accounts from 1676 to 1677 mentions 'mending the swords'. In 1895, the whole hilt was painted black, which concealed any workmanship, but now only the grip is painted.

Scabbard

A new scabbard was presented by the RAF in 1943. It is covered with black velvet with three silver mounts. These are: (1) the chape, which is chased with a floral pattern (O) and is plain (R); (2) the central locket bears a rose and other floral devices (O) and is plain (R); and (3) the mouth-locket is chased and bears the city arms (O) and is plain (R) with a square cut-out. There is no record of the previous scabbard; however, it is possible that the other scabbard was merely re-covered and the older mounts re-applied.

The Sword of State – c. 1627

Length of sword	4ft 0⅛in – 1.222m	Weight of sword	2lb 1¾oz – 0.958kg
Length of blade	3ft 1⅝in – 0.956m – Double-edged	Width of blade	1¾in – 0.044m
Length of hilt	10½in – 0.267m – 1½-handed	Width of guard	11⅜in – 0.289m
Length of scabbard	3ft 4½in – 1.029m	Weight of scabbard	3lb 6¼oz – 1.539kg

Sword

This sword is a very fine example of its kind. When the city first became possessed of it is uncertain: it is usually stated to have been procured in 1660 during the mayoralty of Toby Jordan, but a very interesting discovery, confirmed by entries in the city accounts and minute books, enables us to assign its date with some degree of certainty to the reign of Charles I, and probably to the beginning of 1627, when a new and important charter was granted.

At the west end of the south side of the nave of the cathedral church of Gloucester is an alabaster monument, painted and gilt, to Alderman John Jones, mayor in 1597, 1618 and 1625, who died in 1630. This monument, which is said to have been erected in the alderman's lifetime, has in front a full-sized representation of the city Sword of State. It has a flattened circular gilt pommel with the royal arms within the Garter and crowned, with supporters; the grip is shown as covered with gilt wire, and the cross-guard is ornamented with a large scallop shell. The sword is laid on its edge so that only one quillon could be shown, and this is broken off. The scabbard is painted red, with a gold band along the edges, and is divided into three sections by gilt bands carved in relief. The uppermost band bears the figure of Justice; the second, an equestrian figure of the king; the third, a half-effigy of the king; and the chape, a draped

female figure. Between each of the bands are two roses and two fleurs-de-lis placed
alternately. The chape ends in a crown. This sculptured figure of the sword is especially
worthy of notice, not only because it shows us one side of the sword in its original state,
which has since been considered altered, but because we are enabled to trace the extent
and date of the alterations.

The blade, of oval section, is of Solingen make with the wolf mark inlaid with gold,
and has a short ricasso. The quillon block, which has écussons, bears a large scallop
shell in relief on each side. The quillons are straight, chased and widen towards the
ends, which bear a small scallop shell on each side and a small finial. The baluster
grip, the only part of the sword which appears to be of a later date than 1627, had
a raised middle part common in hand-and-a-half swords, and is covered with silver
wire with a simple band at each end. The pommel is flat and circular and bears on the
obverse a medallion of the royal arms, of Charles II, within the Garter and crowned, with
supporters, similar to, if not identical with, those shown on the Jones monument; and on
the reverse, a medallion of the city arms of 1652. Each side has a grotesque and foliage.
There is a small tang button.

Scabbard

The scabbard is covered with crimson velvet with a gold lace galloon along each edge (now
detached on each side just above the mouth-locket) and four main and nine minor silver-
gilt mounts. They are: (1) the chape, which has, on the obverse, a figure of Fame blowing
a trumpet and a fully armed female figure on the reverse. The chape terminates in a cross
set on a finial; (2) a crowned thistle on each side; (3) a crowned fleur-de-lis on each side;
(4) a crowned harp on each side; (5) a locket with, in relief, a cartouche of the city arms
below on the obverse, and the royal arms, of Charles II, within the Garter, and crowned,
with supporters, in a circle between an oak tree above and an ornate cartouche with the city
arms, on the reverse; (6) a crowned rose on each side; (7) a crowned fleur-de-lis on each
side; (8) a crowned thistle on each side; (9) a locket with the king riding over fallen foes on
the obverse, and the king erect and in armour, and brandishing his sword, on the reverse;
(10) a crowned rose on each side; (11) a crowned fleur-de-lis (O) and a crowned harp (R);
(12) a crowned harp (O) and a crowned fleur-de-lis (R); and (13) the mouth-locket, which
has a figure of Justice with sword and scales under a grotesque under a cherub's head on
the obverse, and on the reverse, under a cherub's head, the inscription 'Gloucester | Toby
Jordan *Esqr Maior* | *Anno Regni Regis Car* 2d XII | *Anno Domi* 1660'; originally this bore
another inscription, subsequently erased. The mouth-locket has a small cut-out.

From the accounts etc., we learn that in 1652 the sword was sent to London to be
altered, i.e. stripped of all emblems of royalty, the work being executed by Alderman
Viner, a noted London goldsmith. As may be seen, however, by comparing the sword
with the monument, the original hilt and the figure of Justice on the scabbard were
not done away with. In 1660, the sword was again sent to London, and altered to the

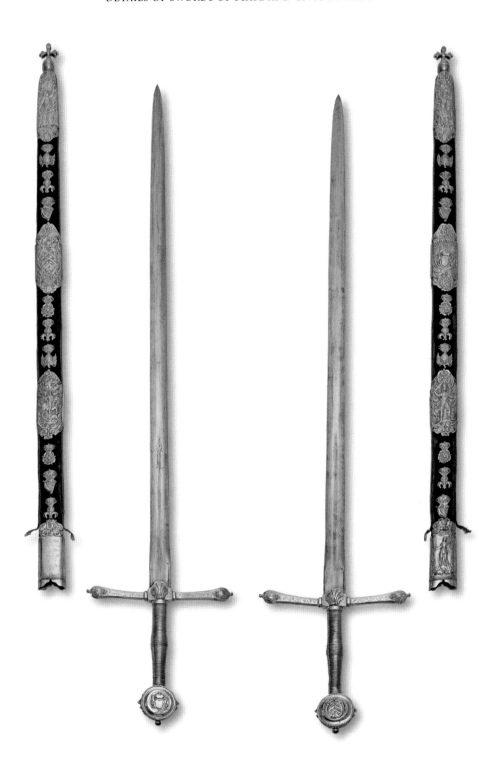

The City of Gloucester Sword of State – *c.* 1627

condition in which we now see it by Mr Cuthbert, a goldsmith in Cheapside. The workmanship of the new bands is very inferior to that with the figure of Justice.

Mourning Scabbard

A second, older scabbard is held. It is covered in black velvet, with three, much-worn, black silk embroidered mounts, and must have been extremely elegant in its day. These are: (1) the chape, which has on both sides a floral device worked with the date '1677' (the tip is now threadbare); (2) the central lockets, which have floral devices; and (3) the mouth-locket, which has on one side the city arms, on the other a crowned rose. This scabbard, which is 3ft 4in long and weighs 12oz, is of a similar size to that of the Sword of State and was almost certainly the mourning scabbard for the Sword of State. This scabbard is remarkably similar to three in Lincoln and one at the Victoria and Albert Museum.

Cap of Maintenance

From the chamberlain's accounts of 1558–59 there is mention of the purchase of 'ffelte to make a hat for the swirdebez of the seid citie', and in 1628–29 '2 gould buttons for the swordbearers hatt of mayntaynance' were purchased. From this it is clear that at one time there were as usual two hats, the one of beaver for winter wear, the other cap of maintenance, probably of velvet, with gold buttons, etc., for summer wear. A new cap was bought in 1659–60, probably to replace one done away with during the Commonwealth period. An old 'royal' cap with a red velvet crown and ermine band, and the previous fur cap held in 1895, have now been lost.

A new cap of maintenance, with cushion, was presented to the city by a former mayor, Councillor W.L. Edwards, on 27 September 1933 and is worn today. It is of sable fur, with a rolled rim 3in deep and extending 1½in all round beyond the cap itself. The cap is 7½in high and has a sunken crown of crimson velvet 2½in from the top.

Uniform

The sword-bearer wears a plain burgundy coloured superfine robe with black velvet collar and trimmings on cuffs and hem, over a dark navy suit with council badges, with white shirt, dark navy council tie, black shoes and white cotton gloves.

The City of Gloucester Sword-Bearer

Exeter

Prerogative

According to a sixteenth-century manuscript source, Henry VII, on his visit to the city in October 1497 after the unsuccessful siege by Perkin Warbeck, 'to encourage the mayor and citizens to be myndefull of their duties and to continue dutyfull and obedient subgects hensforth as tofore they had donne: he toke his sword which he then wore about his mydle & gave it to the mayere together with a hatte of mayntenaunce to be borne before him and his successors as it is used in the Citie of London'. The date of the grant, but not the personal gift of a sword by the king, is confirmed by entries in the accounts of the city recorder for 1497–98 for the purchase of a sword and hat in London.[4]

Richard Izacke, writing in 1731, stated that the sword, together with the cap of maintenance, was given to the city by Henry VII on his visit to the city on 7 October 1497, after his victory over the followers of the so-called Perkin Warbeck, when:

[H]e heartily thanked the citizens for their faithful and valiant service done against the Rebels, promised them the fullness of his favour, and (for an addition of honour to the said city) gave them a Sword taken from his own side and also a Cap of Maintenance, commanding that for the future in all publick places within the said City, the same Sword should be borne before the Mayor as formerly, as for the like purpose his noble predecessor King Edward the fourth (1461–83) had done, and said Cap to be worn accordingly, whereupon a Sword-bearer was elected and sworn to attend that Office.

The sword-bearer was Laurence Prous and his salary was 20s per year.

Izacke also states that another sword is said to have been given to the city by Edward IV on the occasion of his visit in 1470, 'to be carried before the mayor (on all public occasions) in all publick places, within the said city'. However, no record has been found to substantiate this claim nor any sword or part thereof.

The city currently has four swords, though two are presentational items.

The Sword of State – c. 1497

Length of sword	4ft 0¾in – 1.238m	Weight of sword	3lb 4oz – 1.471kg
Length of blade	3ft 1½in – 0.953m – Double-edged	Width of blade	1½in – 0.038m
Length of hilt	11¼in – 0.286m – Two-handed	Width of guard	9⅜in – 0.238m
Length of scabbard	3ft 8½in – 1.130m	Weight of scabbard	4lb 10oz – 2.095kg

The City of Exeter Sword of State – *c.* 1497

Sword

The sword has a tapered steel blade of diamond section. The hilt is silver-gilt, now somewhat worn. The quillon block has, on each face, a very pointed écusson with a shield bearing a crowned fleur-de-lis between the initials 'I' and 'R'. The straight quillons have a guilloche pattern terminating in roundels with a Tudor rose on each side. The wooden grip has a Turk's head ferrule at each end and is covered with a spiral band interspersed with silver-gilt wire. The pommel is pear-shaped and flattened, bearing on one side an inserted gold coin bearing a shield of the royal arms of James I (1603–25) between the initials 'I' and 'R', on the other an inserted gold medallion with the city arms. The sides are chased with foliage and have a raised cable embellishment. The gilt is rather worn. The tang button is quite large, ornate and chased with foliage. The inclusion of the Stuart arms twice on the pommel and the initials on the quillon block are curious, as there is no obvious reference to this period unless a new hilt was added then.

Scabbard

A wooden scabbard was added in 1556. According to Izacke, 'a suitable scabbard for the Sword of Justice usually carried before the Mayor' was obtained in 1634. The old scabbard, which was replaced in 2010, is covered with crimson velvet, embroidered throughout its length with silver-gilt thread in the form of a repetitive palm tree pattern and a multitude of spangles over a diapered background with a gold lace galloon along each edge, and across below the chape and above the mouth-locket. It has two silver-gilt mounts. These are: (1) the chape, which is adorned with *repoussé* work of the bust of a young woman below a basket of flowers on each side, and has its point fixed within the circle of a royal crown about 6in high and 4in across, and wrought in silver-gilt; and (2) the mouth-locket, which has in relief, on the obverse, the royal arms of the Tudor sovereigns – possibly Queen Mary – within the Garter and crowned, with supporters and motto, and on the reverse the arms of the city (unfortunately the three towers have the centre one forward instead of at the back). The scabbard remains on display.

In 2010, a new scabbard was made of perspex and then covered in embroidered crimson velvet. A newly cast mouth-locket and a chape were then added. This is identical to its predecessor above and is described in some detail under the manufacture of scabbards given earlier in the second chapter.

The Mourning Sword – *c.* 1577–78

Length of sword	3ft 10½in – 1.181m	**Weight of sword**	4lb 14¾oz – 2.230kg
Length of blade	3ft 0⅝in – 0.930m – Double-edged	**Width of blade**	1⅞in – 0.048m
Length of hilt	9⅞in – 0.251m – Two-handed	**Width of guard**	8¼in – 0.210m
Length of scabbard	3ft 1in – 0.940m	**Weight of scabbard**	9oz – 0.255kg

Sword

The steel blade of this sword, which has a maker's mark on one side, is the only part of the original to be preserved. The hilt is of bronze. The quillon block is a rude casting with the middle section having an écusson with a diamond on each face with a central raised cable vertically. The top and bottom faces of the quillons are patterned with ringlets terminating in blunt serpents' heads and necks. The grip, which is bored, was covered with black cloth, but is now just plain wood with a ferrule at each end. The globular pommel is gadrooned. The tang is crudely hammered into the pommel. The bronze parts of the hilt, which was at one time japanned black, have now been cleaned. The present hilt is said to date from the Restoration, when the sword was put into mourning to be borne in public on the anniversary of the death of Charles I the martyr. Since the disuse of the service for that day in the Book of Common Prayer, the sword has ceased to be so employed. It is possible that the hilt is of the sixteenth century.

The sword is carried on occasions of public mourning and other solemn occasions wrapped in crêpe, the last being the memorial service to Sir Winston Churchill in Exeter Cathedral in 1964.

Scabbard

The scabbard is said to date from the Restoration and in 1895 had a base metal chape and no mouth-locket. Today this scabbard is a sorry item. The wood is now split and flaking and is held together with card on the inside and a piece of modern black crêpe on the outside. It has no strength and no mounts. It is utterly unfit for purpose and in dire need of replacement.

Cap of Maintenance

The cap of maintenance given by Henry VII is of black felt and is still preserved inside the crimson velvet cover made for it in 1634 at a cost of £21. This low-crowned hat has a broad flat brim embroidered in silver-gilt thread and spangles, with a somewhat similar pattern of palms to the sword scabbard. Round the crown of the hat is worked a bold jewelled circlet of Maltese crosses and fleurs-de-lis, in the manner of a coronet, and on the top is an excellent and vigorous representation of the armorial insignia of the city with supporters and motto. The underside of the brim is also embroidered. The diameter of the crown is 12in; the diameter of the brim 16½in; the width of the brim 4in; and the height of the crown 5¼in. It weights just over 3lb. Dr Oliver, in his description of the swords and cap of maintenance, records 'that William Birdall, being discharged from his office of sword-bearer on 24th March, 1641–2, with a pension of 10*l*, his successor, Robert Bletchinden, found neither cap or sword; for on 26th July 1642, it appears that Mr. Sheriff White brought into this House the blade of a new sword, and on information that the late sword-bearer had converted the old cap of maintenance to his own use, it was ordered that his pension be denied until he make satisfaction for

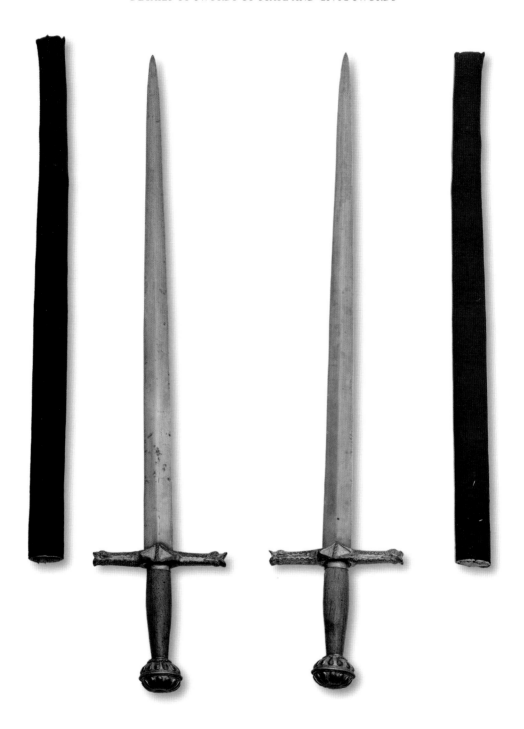

The City of Exeter Mourning Sword – *c.* 1577–78

The City of Exeter Cap of Maintenance
Bearer (Photo by Rob Jinman)

The City of Exeter Sword-Bearer (Photo by
Rob Jinman)

the same.' Dr Oliver also records an order dated 13 May 1624, 'to provide a new hat for the sword-bearer, either at London or elsewhere, of a comely fashion as it is now used in London or Bristow'. 'On 6th January 1651–52, another hat was ordered for the sword-bearer to be by him worn at such time chiefly as he waits on Mr. Mayor, and not otherwise. Another hat and a satin doublet were voted on 22nd December 1668. On 9th March 1685–86, the Receiver was ordered by the Council to procure a beaver hat for Mr. Sword-bearer, and therein to lay out the sum of 4*l*, or thereabout.' It is evident therefore that, as at London, Kingston upon Hull and elsewhere, the sword-bearer had a fur cap or hat for winter as well as the ancient cap of maintenance. There is now no trace of the winter fur hat.

The crimson velvet hat was renovated in 1766 but has not been worn since 1917, and has been borne before the mayor on a cushion due to its fragility. A new hat identical to that described above was made in 2010. Details of its manufacture are given in chapter 5.

Today the sword-bearer wears a black 'Tudor hat' with a green and white band (the Tudor colours and those of the city) around the crown and with a badge above the left ear. The hat is much smaller than the cap of maintenance. The diameter of the crown is 8¾in; the diameter of the brim 12¾in; the width of the brim 2⅜in; and the height of the crown 4¾in. It weighs only 15oz.

Uniform

The sword-bearer wears a plain black superfine robe trimmed with black velvet collar and with velvet trimming on cuffs and hem, over a dark suit with white shirt, black tie, black shoes and white cotton gloves. A slender chain of office is worn round the neck.

The cap-bearer is identically attired.

Carmarthen

Prerogative

In the 1546 charter of Henry VIII, it was ordered that, in addition to two sergeants-at-mace, there should be 'a sword-bearer of the said mayor, who shall freely and lawfully carry the sword before the said mayor, in manner as is accustomed to be done in our city of London'. Carmarthen is the only town or city in Wales with this privilege. This charter was confirmed by James II in 1686 and by George III in 1764. For many years the sword and maces were borne by members of the Borough Police Force.

It is said that the original sword was of 'jewel encrusted Castilian steel'. In 1633, the 'common chest' of the corporation contained 'one sword and two scabbards, three velvett hats' – one for the sword-bearer and two for the mace-bearers. In *J&H* in 1895, the sword was 'about 4ft and 7¼lbs'. In a description in 1937, it was 4ft 6in and 7lb 4oz. Clearly, this is not the same sword as described below, at 4ft ½in and 6lb 12⅛oz. The scabbard is only ⅝in longer than the blade, so the 1937 comment could be a misprint with a '6' instead of a '0'. However, the discrepancy in the weight between 1895/1937 and 2013 cannot be accounted for.

In time of war, the sword is unsheathed and remains so until peace is declared, as at Bury St Edmunds and Great Yarmouth. This policy dates from the Battle of Waterloo (1815) and included the Crimean War (1854–56) and the Great War (1914–18). When entering a church, the sword is reversed to form a cross.

The Sword of State – *c.* 1680

Length of sword	4ft 0½in – 1.232m	**Weight of sword**	5lb 7oz – 2.467kg
Length of blade	2ft 10⅝in – 0.879m – Double-edged	**Width of blade**	1¾in – 0.045m
Length of hilt	13⅞in – 0.352m – Two-handed	**Width of guard**	12⅜in – 0.314m
Length of scabbard	2ft 11¼in – 0.895m	**Weight of scabbard**	1lb 5¾oz – 0.611kg

Sword

On both sides of the blade are three fullers, each about 9in long. The central wide one is engraved with the marks and name of 'ANDREA FERARA' of Toledo (one of which is rather worn) together with other armourer's marks. The two narrow ones are each marked 'xxx – xx – xxx'. The blade has evidence of previous rusting but is still in quite good condition. The hilt is of brass. The quillon block has a heraldic rose on each side. The quillons are decorated with acanthus leaves and spirally fluted, and terminate with a lion's head on each side. The grip is similarly spirally fluted. The large pear-shaped brass pommel has, on one side, a male figure, in alto-relievo, of Justice with sword and scales. On the other side is a male figure of Law with orb and a scroll, with four seals

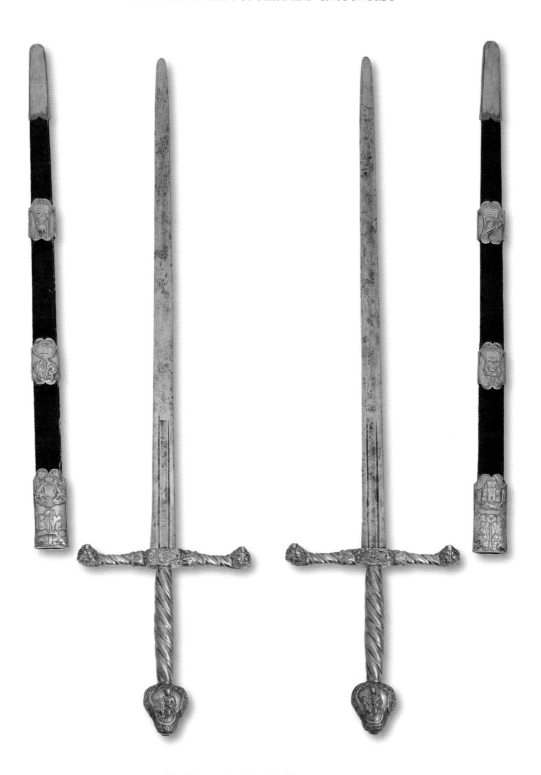

The Carmarthen Sword of State – *c.* 1680

pendant. The sides of the pommel are decorated with fruit and acanthus leaves. There is a small, flat tang button. The hilt is of the same type, and probably by the same maker, as the Swords of State at Hereford, Thetford, Bury St Edmunds and Great Yarmouth – all dating *c.* 1677–84. At one stage both the pommel and the quillons were reversed, but now only the quillons are the wrong way up.

Scabbard

The old wooden scabbard is covered with red velvet and has four silver-gilt mounts. These are: (1) the chape, which is plain on both sides; (2) a locket, which has a crowned thistle (O) and a crowned harp (R); (3) a locket, which has a crowned fleur-de-lis (O) and a crowned rose (R); and (4) the mouth-locket, which has the royal arms, probably of Charles II, within the Garter and crowned, with supporters, and acanthus leaves below, on the obverse; and the arms of Carmarthen with a ribbon underneath inscribed '*Ex Dono Ricardis Birtt. Armigeri*' (The gift of Richard Birtt, swordbearer), and acanthus leaves below, on the reverse. The mayor in 1564 was one Robert Birtt, who would have been of the same family as the donor of the sword. The velvet is now quite worn. In 1895, there was no mention of a chape. Given the lack of decoration on the current one, it is probable that a new chape has been added since then. The edges of the three 'original' lockets are crimped along each edge, which is very uncommon and perhaps indicates that they are from an earlier scabbard.

Cap of Maintenance

No record has been found of the old caps of maintenance. Today the sword-bearer wears a black tri-corn trimmed with a broad band of gold lace and a gold flash on the right side.

Uniform

The sword-bearer wears a deep blue superfine robe with a wide cape type collar trimmed with two broad red stripes with a 'gold' clasp, worn over a dark suit with dark blue shirt, sombre tie, black shoes and white cotton gloves.

Thetford

Prerogative

The charter of Elizabeth I in 1573 stated that: 'The mayor may have a sword born before him and he shall chose his sword-bearer, and two serjeants, who may bear two silver maces before him, and do all things as the serjeants … in London do, every serjeant being to be sworn to the faithful performance of his office.' The fact that there is over a century between the charter and the presentation of the current sword indicates that there must have been a previous sword. However, no evidence exists of such a sword.

The Sword of State – 1678

Length of sword	4ft 3⅜in – 1.305m	Weight of sword	5lb 7½oz – 2.479kg
Length of blade	3ft 1¾in – 0.959m – Double-edged	Width of blade	1¾in – 0.045m
Length of hilt	13⅝in – 0.346m – Two-handed	Width of guard	12¾in – 0.324m
Length of scabbard	3ft 3in – 0.991m	Weight of scabbard	1lb 6¾oz – 0.644kg

Sword

The sword is of remarkable elegance. The blade, made in Solingen, is engraved on the ricasso and chased with scrolls of foliage for just over 13in, and has five armourer's marks; a crowned 3 and a crescent enclosing a pellet on both sides and the running wolf mark on one side only. There is a very long fuller. The hilt is of silver-gilt. The quillon block projects slightly with a scrolled edge, but it cannot be considered a protecting plate. It has, on the obverse, a cartouche inscribed '*In usum Majoris et Burgensium antiqui Burgi de* THETFORD. D.D. JOSEPHUS WILLIAMSON Esq.: *Aur: Sac: Reg: Mati a Consiliis intimis et Primarius Secretarius Status* A. D. 1678' (for the use of the mayor and burgesses in the ancient borough of Thetford – Joseph Williamson Esq.?. .?. His Majesty's Special Counsellor and First Secretary); and on the reverse, the donor's arms. The recurved quillons start with acanthus leaves, have a small rose midway on each side and terminate in boldly modelled double lions' heads. The grip is spirally fluted. The large, slightly flattened, pear-shaped pommel bears, in high relief, on the obverse, a seated figure of Justice with sword and scales, and on the reverse, a figure of Law with hand on heart and a scroll with three seals. The sides have acanthus leaves and it ends in a small tang button obscured by four small leaves. The hilt is by the same maker as the hilts of the Swords of State of Hereford, Carmarthen, Bury St Edmunds and Great Yarmouth. The inscription is identical to that on the town's Great Mace.

The Thetford Sword of State – 1678

Scabbard

The scabbard is covered with crimson velvet edged with gold lace, which is now discoloured and extremely worn with parts missing, and has four silver-gilt mounts. These are: (1) the chape, which is 6½in long and ends in an acorn finial, has, on either side, the royal cipher of Charles II of two 'C's interlaced and crowned; (2) a locket, which has a crowned rose on one side and a crowned fleur-de-lis on the other; (3) a locket, which has a crowned harp on one side and a crowned thistle on the other; and (4) the 5⅝in long mouth-locket, which is a little battered, has the royal arms of the Stuart sovereigns, probably of Charles II, within the Garter and crowned, with supporters and motto on one side, and a representation of the Thetford common seal and acanthus leaves on the other. The scabbard and mounts appear to have been manufactured in 1678 at the same time as the Great Mace.

Cap of Maintenance

The cap of maintenance is a black velvet Tudor bonnet with a gilt cord and tassels. A gilt badge, now rather worn and without colour, is worn above the right ear.

Uniform

A black academic robe with large square collar is worn over a dark suit with white shirt and sombre tie, black shoes and white cotton gloves.

Limerick

Prerogative

In 1575, a charter to the city of Limerick by Elizabeth I stated:

> [A]s a token of more honourable esteem, for us, our heirs and successors, to our said liege subjects, the present mayor, bailiffs and citizens of the said city, and their successors that the mayor of the city aforesaid, for the time being, in all places within the walls of the said city and suburbs thereof, shall and may have a sword with fit scabbard, and adorned with our ensign, to be carried before the mayor who now is, and before all other mayors for the time being, in all places within the walls of the aforesaid city, and within the suburbs and the liberties of the same: and we will that the sword bearer be adorned with a notable hat, commonly called a 'hat of maintenance', when and where they shall think fit, for the reasons aforesaid.

The sword is no longer used and is on display in the museum.

The Sword of State – c. 1575

Length of sword	4ft 4⅛in – 1.324m	Weight of sword	4lb 1oz – 1.843kg
Length of blade	3ft 7½in – 1.105m – Double-edged	Width of blade	1¾in – 0.043m
Length of hilt	8½in – 0.217m – Two-handed	Width of guard	15⅜in – 0.390m

Sword

The steel blade is quite sharp and flexible but has no fuller and bears no marks. The hilt is of iron. The cross-guard, which appears to have been cast, is flat and widens towards the pointed tips, which curve towards the sword point. It is decorated with a criss-cross pattern with raised Tudor roses along each side. There is a fleur-de-lis emblem on the block area (viewed point down). On each end there is a flat grotesque with hair in the shape of ram's horns. The top and bottom edges are plain. There is no longer a grip, merely the rough tang. This means that the cross-guard has no support and can be moved at will. The iron pommel is globular in shape with a Tudor rose on a garland of leaves on each face. They are similar but not the same. On each side is a full-faced grotesque, again with hair in the form of a ram's horns. The tang end is hammered flat into the pommel.

Scabbard

No scabbard exists.

Cap of maintenance

There is no cap of maintenance, nor is there a sword-bearer.

Uniform

No sword-bearer means no uniform.

The City of Limerick Sword of State – *c.* 1575

Clonmel

Prerogative

In 1608, the charter of Incorporation from James I granted Clonmel the privilege to have a sword borne before the mayor: 'We give and grant unto ye said Mayor and Bayliffs, Ffreeburgesses and Commonality of the said Town or Borrough and their successors, full power and authority to name, elect and constitute one Sword-bearer and three Sergeants-at-mace within the Borrough aforesaid.'

The current sword was presented to the city in 1656 by Sir Thomas Standley.

The Sword of State – 1656

Length of sword	3ft 11¼in – 1.200m	Weight of sword	3lb 1¼oz – 1.396kg
Length of blade	2ft 10⅜in – 0.874m – Double-edged	Width of blade	2in – 0.050m
Length of hilt	12⅞in – 0.326m – Two-handed	Width of guard	13⅞in – 0.351m
Length of scabbard	3ft 0¾in – 0.933m	Weight of scabbard	10oz – 0.286kg

Sword

The blade, which is quite broad for much of its length, has a 1⁹⁄₁₆in ricasso and is of Spanish manufacture. It bears on one face the word 'Jesu' and on the other 'Maria', together with the marks of the Toledo fabric, a cross and anchor. All these marks are now indecipherable due to rusting of the blade. It is quite sharp and flexible. The cross-guard is very loose and can be moved 1in. The decoration is quite crude and not symmetric. The block has an acorn and leaves on each side. The quillons are flat – broad to start, then narrowing and widening, ending in circular ends with acorns inscribed. A leaf pattern is used along the quillons, and is a segment with upturned points. It is rudely chased with oak leaf ornament, acorns being placed at the centre and extremities. The top edge is hatched. One end has been broken at some stage and has been reattached. The grip is formed of fine silver wire wound closely round a core. The wire is loose and unbound at one end. The circular pommel is 2in in diameter. The obverse face of the pommel bears the arms of the town; on a bridge of three arches in fess, masoned, a deer and hound courant, in base a stream fluent with three fishes: the motto 'Fidelis in eternum'. On the reverse are the Standley arms; on a bend three stags' heads caboshed on the sinister canton a vallary crown of three points. An inscription in cursive hand is carried around the shield 'Ex dono x Thoniex Standlyx1656'. The sides have a laddered pattern of leaves.

The Clonmel Sword of State – 1656

Scabbard

The very old leather scabbard is covered with crimson velvet with a chape about 4in long which is almost contemporary with the handle. The chasing is even cruder than at the grip. At the extremity on each side, a rough crown is punched between with a crude 'C.R.'. The rest of the chape is engraved with a rose and marigold design and has a scalloped edge. There is no mouth-locket or other adornment.

Both the sword and scabbard are rather dilapidated and are in need of serious attention. They used to be on display in the town hall but have recently been moved to the County Museum. The sword is used for ceremonial occasions, particularly for civic receptions, when it is displayed in the council chamber.

The above information is taken from *Corporation of Clonmel – Record of the Insignia (Standing Order no.82)*.

Cap of Maintenance

The sword-bearer is bare headed. There is no record of any cap of maintenance.

Uniform

The Town Sergeant, who is the sword-bearer, wears a robe, similar to that of the Town Clerk, over a dark suit, white shirt and dark tie, black shoes and white cotton gloves.

Canterbury

Prerogative

The right to have a sword borne before the mayor was conferred upon the city by James I, who ordained, in his charter of 8 December 1608:

[A]nd furthermore we wish and through these presents on behalf of our noble heirs and successors grant to the aforementioned mayor etc, that the aforementioned and his successors for the rest for all time have, and may have, and have the power to have within the aforementioned city a sword-bearer who shall be, and shall be called the sword-bearer of the aforementioned city. He indeed shall be officially called the sword-bearer of the aforementioned city and shall be nominated, chosen and appointed by the mayor of the aforementioned city for the time he holds office and from time to time attendant on and around the mayor of the same city for the time of his office. He indeed shall be officially called the sword-bearer, shall carry and bear, and have the power to carry and bear a sheathed sword or blade anywhere within the afore-mentioned city, its boundaries, freedoms, and surrounding area, in the presence of the mayor of the said city.

A sword–bearer was first appointed in 1608–09, at a salary of £10 per annum.

The city has two swords.

The Sword of State – 1608

Length of sword	4ft 0½in – 1.232m	Weight of sword	4lb 1¼oz – 1.848kg
Length of blade	3ft 2⅝in – 0.981m – Double-edged	Width of blade	1¾in – 0.045m
Length of hilt	10⅜in – 0.263m – Two-handed	Width of guard	15in – 0.381m
Length of scabbard	3ft 4¾in – 1.035m	Weight of scabbard	15oz – 0.424kg

Sword

This fine and original sword is now in indifferent condition, but retains considerable traces of its original beauty. The blade, which is blued for 19½in, has a single broad but quite short fuller and bears, on the obverse, the Solingen mark of the wolf, and in gold letters, the inscription 'THIS SWRDE, WAS GRAVNTED BY OVR GRATIOVS SOVERAIGNE LORD KINGE IEAMES TO THIS CITTY OF CANTERBVRY AND TO THOMAS PARAMOUR ESQVIRE BEINGE THEN MAYOR OF THE SAME CITTY TO BE BORNE BEFORE HIM AND ALL OTHERS THAT SHALL SVCCEEDE HIM', with the royal arms of James I, within the Garter and crowned, with supporters, crest and lion in colour above the cross-guard. On the reverse it bears the letters 'I V S T I T I A' above a figure of Justice with sword and scales above a circle, in which is a small orb atop the word 'CANTERBERY'. There follows a quaint rendering of the law of Moses: 'YEE SHALL NOT DOE VNIVSTLY IN IVDGMENT IN LYNE IN WAIGHT OR IN MEASVRE YOV SHAL HAVE IVST BALLANCE TREWE WAIGTES A TREWE EPHAH AND A TREWE HIN. 19 LEVITICVS:VEAR 35.36'. Below this is a maker's mark of an orb, with city arms in colour above the cross-guard. The hilt is iron. The quillon block, which has an écusson on each side, retains portions of a design wrought in silver with a boss on each side of this on each face, and probably once enamelled. The quillons are straight, slightly spreading out towards the ends, which are flat and cut off obliquely, one up and one down; they are inlaid with silver threads enclosing two oblong and one oval spaces with gilded fleur-de-lis patterns. Connecting them together are two smaller spaces on each side, each of which has a small boss within it. Traces of gilding remain. The grip, which tapers slightly, is covered with a silver casing richly engraved above a floriated pattern of roses, thistles, etc., a shield of the city arms (O) and a shield of the royal Stuart arms, surmounted by a crown, between the initials 'C R' (R). The grip could, therefore, be an addition made before or after the Restoration. The pommel is disc-shaped and flattened, with the same designs on its faces and sides as on the cross-guard. There are four small bosses on each face. The tang end is hammered into the base of the pommel.

The cost of the sword was entered in the accounts of 1607–08:

> The chardges and expenses laid out for the procuringe of our newe charters granted unto us by our most gracious Lord the Kings Matie. that now is, and for the confyrma-tion of all our oulde charters, liberties, and letter patents, heretofore had and granted, and for the swords, all maner of waies, as by the particulars therof may appere amount-ith to the sum of 379*l*. 13*s*. Wheras (the above written statement) doth not shew what the swerd cost by ytself. ... The seid sworde and skabert engraving and enamelinge therof by ytself cost the sum of X1i VIs, which was thought fytt to be so particularlie declared that in tymes to come the price of that memorable ensigne of honor and justice myght always be remembered [this was, of course, £10 6*s*].

Scabbard

In the accounts for 1643–44 is a payment 'for a new scabbard and for trymmyng the city sword'; and in 1659–60, on the Restoration, a payment 'for making a new scabbard and cleaning the city sword'. The current scabbard is covered with light crimson velvet with a gold lace galloon down the centre of one side and five gilt iron mounts – the gilt is now much rubbed off. All the mounts appear to be Italian, perhaps Florentine, work. They are the same on each side. These are: (1) the chape, which bears an oval cartouche, with a boss on each side of this on each face, which retains portions of a design wrought in silver, and was probably once enamelled and inlaid with silver threads, near the point on

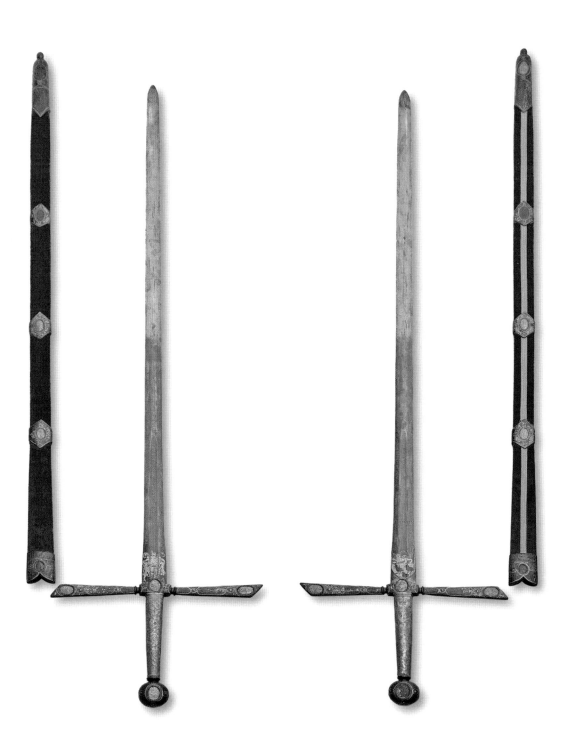

The City of Canterbury Sword of State – 1608

each side. There is a small finial; (2) a locket on each side attached to a band; (3) a similar locket; (4) a similar locket; and (5) the rather short mouth-locket, with a cut-out, with a similar design. The similarity of the scabbard mounts to the designs on the cross-guard and pommel indicate that they are all of the same era. The velvet on the section nearest the mouth is now rather worn.

The Vision Sword – 1988

Length of sword	4ft 3in – 1.295m	Weight of sword	5lb 9½oz – 2.540kg
Length of blade	3ft 3¼in – 0.997m – Double-edged	Width of blade	1⅝in – 0.041m
Length of hilt	11¾in – 0.298m – Two-handed	Width of guard	12¾in – 0.324m
Length of scabbard	3ft 4¼in – 1.023m	Weight of scabbard	1lb 13oz – 0.820kg

Sword

A new 'Vision' Sword was commissioned in 1988 when Elizabeth II granted the title 'Lord Mayor' to the City of Canterbury. The blade, which has a 3in ricasso, bears one of the usual Wilkinson etching patterns. On the obverse is etched the inscription 'The privilege of bearing a sword before the Mayor of Canterbury was granted by King James I. This sword continues the privilege and commemorates the grant by our Sovereign Lady Queen Elizabeth II of the style and title of Lord Mayor of Canterbury, during the mayoralty of Thomas Steele, Esquire, Justice of the Peace, 13 July 1988', and next to the hilt the royal cipher. On the reverse are the 'by royal appointment' arms and the Wilkinson logo. The hilt is gilt. The quillon block has, on the obverse, an enamelled shield of the city arms – a lion passant above three black choughs (crows): the reverse is plain. The quillons are box-shaped but narrower on the upper edge and taper at the ends, which are slightly curved and chisel-ended. The tapered grip is spirally bound with gilt wire. The pommel is of a flattened lozenge shape and plain. There are a few rust spots on the blade which need attention.

Scabbard

The scabbard is covered in brown leather with five brass mounts with enamelled crests. These are: (1) the simple, almost square-ended chape bearing the badge of the Canterbury Cross; (2) a simple band bearing an enamelled arms of the university; (3) a simple band bearing the badge of the Queen's Regiment; (4) a simple band bearing the enamelled arms of the Archbishop's See – the Primate of All England; and (5) the mouth-locket bearing the Tudor rose. The backs of all the mounts are plain. The leather near the chape needs some attention.

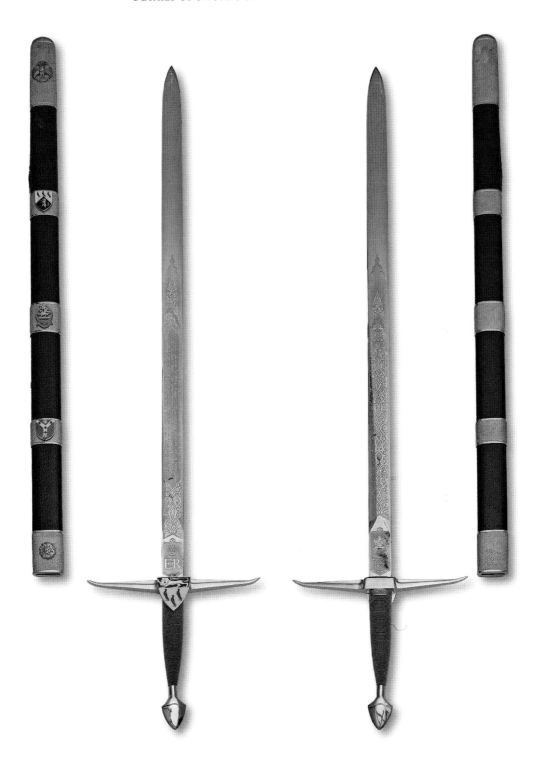

The City of Canterbury Vision Sword – 1988

The City of Canterbury Sword-Bearer (Photo by Robert Berry)

Cap of Maintenance

There is no cap of maintenance. The sword-bearer is normally provided by a local military unit and naturally wears a peaked uniform cap.

Uniform

Military uniform is worn, sometimes with white cotton gloves.

Kilkenny

Prerogative

In 1609 it was the turn of Kilkenny to be made a city and to be granted by James I the privilege to have a sword borne before the mayor and to appoint a sword-bearer:

[A]nd further we do will and ordain, and by these presents for us, our heirs and successors, we do grant to the said mayor and citizens of the said city, and their successors that the mayor of the said city for the time being and his successors may and shall be able, as long as he or they shall happen to continue in the office of mayor of the said city, to have a sword carried before him or them within the said city and county of the said city, as they will pleasure, in such manner and form as is used in any other city or cities before any other mayor or mayors within the said kingdom of Ireland.

In procession, the sword-bearer and mace-bearer flank the mayor. The mace-bearer, on the left, bears the mace upright in his left hand. The sword-bearer, on the right, bears the sword upright in his right hand in the manner of a military sword on parade.

The sword is processed on a regular basis.

The Sword of State – c. 1609

Length of sword	3ft 8⅜in – 1.126m	Weight of sword	3lb 4½oz – 1.488kg
Length of blade	2ft 10⅜in – 0.874m – Double-edged	Width of blade	1¾in – 0.046m
Length of hilt	9⅞in – 0.251m – Two-handed	Width of guard	12½in – 0.319m
Length of scabbard	3ft 0⅛in – 0.918m	Weight of scabbard	1lb 5½oz – 0.605kg

Sword

The steel blade has a 2in ricasso and a 9¹³⁄₁₆ fuller. The blade narrows at the end of the ricasso. There appears to be some inscription in the fuller on each face but it is now indecipherable ('ANDREA FERARA'?). The hilt is silver-gilt. At the centre of the cross-guard, that has flowers and leaf-work, there is an écusson. The quillons are straight and narrow, widening at the ends and terminating in offset points. The faces of each are chased with leaf-work. The grip narrows from the cross-guard to the pommel. Each face is divided into four segments. The border of each is a raised ladder of leaves with superimposed roses, shamrocks and thistles, as are the bands at the top, middle and bottom of the grip. In each of the upper four segments is an incised figure, a grotesque with the body of an animal or a fish and a vaguely human face crowned with a very spiky crown. The four lower panels are chased with leaf-work. The pommel is oval and flat. Each face has similar leaf-work as already mentioned. The inner edge is scalloped.

Each side has incised leaf-work and a small button. There is a simple tang nut it appears to be screwed on but may be a very delicate hammering of the tang end.

Scabbard

The wooden scabbard is covered in red leather with six silver mounts and is richly decorated. The mounts are: (1) the chape, which has a small finial and crowned Tudor roses on each face with chased leaf-work. There is what appears to be a later addition of a small cap made of leaves, perhaps to cover previous damage; (2) (3) and (4) are banded mounts with a plate bearing grotesque lions' heads on each face – these are similar but not the same – and all are surrounded with leaf-work; (5) has on the obverse a plate bearing the royal arms of the Stuarts, probably James I, within the Garter, crowned with helm, supporters and motto. On the reverse, the plate bears the arms of the city with a cannon underneath; and (6) the mouth-locket, which has on the obverse an inscription 'The sword and mace repaired, Barry Colles Esq., mayor 1743', and on the obverse 'The charter school endowed, linen manufacture introduced 174(3)' – the end is cut out for the écusson. There are side galloons of brass between the fifth locket and the mouth-locket.

Cap of Maintenance

There is no record of a cap of maintenance. The sword-bearer wears a military-style navy blue peaked cap with gold braid round the cap.

Uniform

The sword-bearer wears a navy blue uniform with a light blue shirt, navy blue council tie, black shoes and white gloves.

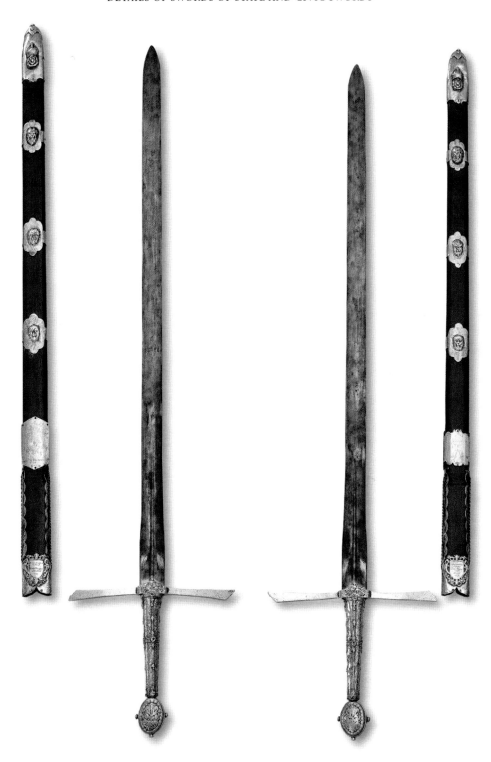

The City of Kilkenny Sword of State – 1609

Edinburgh

Prerogative

Authority to bear, along with the mace, a civic sword before the Provost was granted by James I (James VI of Scotland) in a charter of 1609, which states: 'His Majesty willed and granted that in all time comeing the Provost of the said burgh of Edinburgh, and his successors, shall have the privilege of bearing and carrying before them, when passing through their streets, a sword, sheathed in velvet, of such kind and as oft, as is used to be carried before the Mayor of London'. No gift of a sword accompanied this charter. The information in this paragraph and those below have been extracted from the proceedings of the Society of the High Constables of Edinburgh.[9]

In March 1627, Charles I presented a sword and a gown to the Provost, David Aikinhead, with the words: 'Trustie and weilbelovit, We greet you weill … We have sent yow a token of Oure favour, a Sword and a gowne to be worne by your Proveist, at such times and in such manner as was appointed by our late deare Father.'

For some years after the mace and sword were in the possession of the city, they appear to have been regularly used on all civic occasions; the practice had apparently fallen into desuetude prior to 1657, for in that year it was resuscitated by an act and deed of the Corporation: 'And that the mace and sword be likwayis provyded to be caried befoir the Provest and Baillies as formerlie'.

On no portion of the scabbard does any hallmark appear; and although it is probable that the sword was mounted in London, in the absence of a hallmark this cannot be definitely established. It will be noted that it is only on those portions of the mounting that have been renewed by the Scottish goldsmith that the national and civic emblems appear, and although the sword bears the date 1627, when it was presented, it is possible that it was not specifically made for presentation to the City of Edinburgh; it is also likely that these additions were added purposefully afterwards with the view of making it more appropriate.

The Sword of State – 1627

Length of sword	4ft 1¼in – 1.251m	Weight of sword	4lb 6½oz – 1.999kg
Length of blade	3ft 0⅛in – 0.917m – Double-edged	Width of blade	1¾in – 0.044m
Length of hilt	13⅛in – 0.333m – Two-handed	Width of guard	12⅜in – 0.314m
Length of scabbard	3ft 0¾in – 0.933m	Weight of scabbard	1lb 0oz – 0.450kg

Sword

The sword is elaborately mounted. The blade, which is tapered and round at the point, has a 2½in ricasso. The 11in nearest the hilt are richly decorated on both sides with an

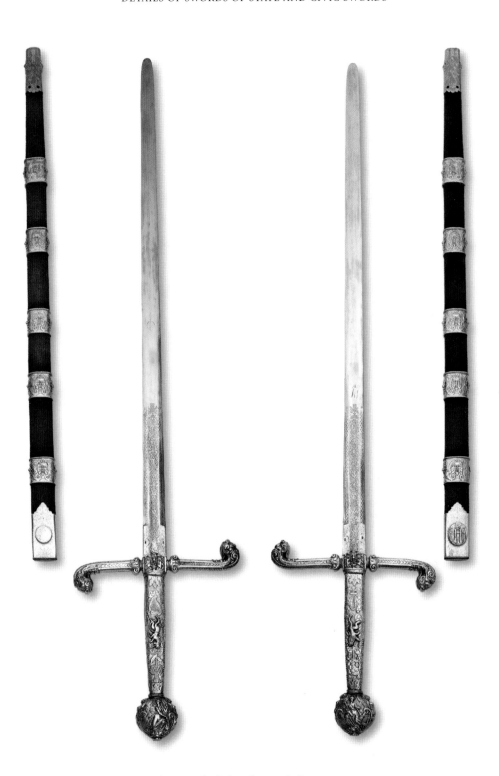

The City of Edinburgh Sword of State – 1627

etched pattern, partly filled in with gold, and bears a thistle and the date 1627 at the top. The hilt is silver-gilt. The quillon block has a very short protecting plate on each side and bears on both sides in relief a rose and a grotesque with a worn nose. The re-curved quillons are chased and terminate at each end with a scroll, enriched with a grotesque head; there is a small crack along one top edge. The grip is decorated on one side with a thistle, a unicorn rampant in relief and a harp, flat chased, and on the other side a rose, a lion rampant and a fleur-de-lis, while each of the flat edges bears a view of Edinburgh Castle, with two thistles above and two below with acanthus leaves. The globular but slightly flattened pommel is decorated in *repoussé* and resting on festoons, and bears on the obverse a figure of Glory bearing a branch and on the reverse the figure of Fame with two trumpets. Each edge bears a winged female figure without arms, possibly Terpsichore and Venus. All these decorations are viewed point up, while the grip is point down. The grip, it may also be noted, is of different workmanship from the rest of the hilt, and is evidently an addition by a Scottish craftsman. Surprisingly, there are no royal arms.

The City of Edinburgh Sword-Bearer

Scabbard

The wooden scabbard is covered with deep crimson velvet with seven silver-gilt mounts. These are: (1) the chape, which has a flat tip and is decorated with scrollwork and the figures of two nymphs, executed by flat chasing, and two grotesques on each edge, on both sides; (2) (3) (4) (5) and (6) have an embossed grotesque mask, surrounded by scrolls, on each side; and (7) the mouth-locket, which bears on one side a coronation medal of Charles I, and a representation of Edinburgh castle on a raised disc on the other, with a chevron pattern down each edge. The mouth-locket and chape are of different workmanship from the masks, and are, like the grip of the handle, of Scottish manufacture. The five masks are alike in pattern but differ individually. They are slightly larger nearer the hilt. The mouth-locket is slightly damaged, while the velvet is rather worn in the lower section and split on one edge – this appears to be the result of the sword being longer than the arm of the person drawing the sword, which forces the point off-line. There are no hallmarks.

Cap of Maintenance

There is no cap of maintenance. The sword-bearer is bareheaded.

Uniform

The sword-bearer wears a black tail-coat embellished with red collar and city-badged buttons, a matching red waistcoat, a white shirt and white bow tie, black trousers, black shoes and white cotton gloves.

Galway

Prerogative

Following a petition to King James I in person, letters signed by the Privy Council of England, with royal assent, were transmitted to the Lord Lieutenant of Ireland, in pursuance of which, by charter dated 18 December 1610, all former privileges were confirmed and Galway was 'henceforth and for ever to be called the county of the town of Galway' and the corporation was 'empowered to have and use several ensigns and ornaments for the honour and dignity of the town; and the mayor, for the time being, to have a sword borne before him, as a mark of the very great eminence of the office of mayor of the town and the authority thereto belonging'. It also granted the right of appointing a sword-bearer.

Much of the information below has been gleaned from *The Galway Sword and Mace* by G.A. Hayes-McCoy.[19] The corporation was abolished in 1841. It appears that the sword and mace were presented to the then mayor, Edmond Blake, as compensation for his loss of office (his claim for monetary award was rejected). In 1901, they were referred to as 'carefully preserved by the surviving members of the family of the last mayor of Galway'. Blake died in 1805 and the sword and mace passed into the hands of his daughter, Miss Anne Blake. The sword and mace were included in the 1908 Galway exhibition.

Subsequently, Miss Blake sold the items to a Louis Wine, an art dealer in Dublin. The municipal corporation of Galway had been restored in 1937. It petitioned for the sword and mace to be returned and even supported a suggestion that they be given to the National Museum of Ireland. However, despite considerable opposition, the sword and mace were sold in 1938 by Christies in Dublin to the celebrated American publisher William Randolph Hearst – whose mother's family came from Galway. Shortly before his death in 1951, Mr Hearst expressed the wish that the sword and mace be returned to the City of Galway.

In early 1960, the Hearst Foundation sought to return the sword and mace. There followed an unseemly wrangle between the city council and the Irish Parliament over who should travel to New York to receive the sword and mace. So it was not until 27 October 1960 that his widow, on behalf of the Hearst Foundation, actually presented them to Cllr James Reddington, the 88-year-old mayor of Galway, at a ceremony in the City Hall, New York, in the presence of the mayor of New York, with the words: 'I now formally on behalf of the Hearst Foundation present these historic heirlooms to you, Mr Lord Mayor, with our best wishes for the happiness and prosperity of the city and citizens of Galway'. On the return to Ireland, for some inexplicable reason the Taoiseach (Prime Minister of Ireland) then formally handed the sword and mace to the mayor of Galway (who had already received them in New York). There was also heated debate in November 1960, in the Dáil, the Irish Parliament, effectively over precedence.

The sword is still used about five times a year but is normally kept on display in the City Museum.

The Sword of State – *c.* 1610

Length of sword	4ft 6½in – 1.383m	Weight of sword	5lb 6¾oz – 2.455kg
Length of blade	3ft 2¾in – 0.985 – Double-edged	Width of blade	2¼in – 0.057m
Length of hilt	15¾in – 0.398m – Two-handed	Width of guard	15⅞in – 0. 408m
Length of scabbard	3ft 4¼in – 1.023m	Weight of scabbard	1lb 1¾oz – 0.500kg

Sword

By style this was a fighting sword. On one side of the steel blade there are three makers' marks and two on the other. These marks indicate that the blade is of German manufacture and almost certainly sixteenth-century. The ricasso is 3in long, with two short grooves and a central 10½in fuller on each side. The hilt is of silver. The quillon block has a small écusson. The quillons, which at some point have been broken off and replaced, curve upwards and have swollen and flattened terminals. They are tubular and are of elliptical section, flattening towards the terminals. They are ornamented with raised elliptical bosses and chased bands linked together in a most effective pattern. There are two silversmiths' marks. The grip is clad in silver and has a different design, an all-over fish scale pattern with a central reeded band. This covering appears to be later than the quillons and pommel, and may be a replacement for a wire-bound grip. The pommel is of flattened oval shape and is decorated with the same strap and boss pattern as the quillons, and with a pattern of conventional foliage at the top and bottom. There can be little doubt it was made at the same time as the quillons by the same craftsman. It is now a little battered. The screwed tang nut is now pressed into the base of the pommel.

Scabbard

The scabbard is a mighty object. It is of wood and covered with crimson velvet, with four silver mounts added at differing times. These mounts are: (1) the chape, which is chased with foliage at the top and has incised hatching marks near the bottom. A rose is incised on each side. There is an inscription that has been deliberately obliterated in parts but can be assessed to read 'PETER STVBERS, MAJOR 1655'. Stubbers was a notorious Cromwellian colonel who became a ruthless tyrant. Two additional inscriptions, one on each face are, 'JOHN SHAW ESQ[R] MAYOR 1755' (O) and 'PAT BLAKE ESQ[R] Mayor 1756' (R); (2) this large ornamental fitting bears the royal cipher 'WM' (for William and Mary). It is composed of two rectangular plates, one on each face and above each a domed plate. Each plate has a reeded border. The royal monogram is formed within semi-circular reeded bars. This fitting is inscribed on either face. The inscription in the domed portion of the plate on one face (R) reads '*GULIELMUS & MARIA D G ANG SCO FRAN & HIBER REX & REGINA*' (and on the plate below) '*LEGES & LIBERTATES PRIVILEGIA & POSSESSIONES, VITAM (VITAQUE POTIOREM) RELIGIONEM PURAM & PRIMAEVAM FELICISSIME RESTAURARUNT STRENUE DEFENDUNT INSIGNITER ORNANT. THO REVET MAYOR 1692*' (William and Mary, by the grace of God, King and Queen of England, Scotland, France and Ireland: of law and liberty, privileges and possessions, of life, and – what is more than life – pure and primeval religion, the happy restores, the strenuous defenders, the conspicuous adorners). The back was originally blank. It now bears the inscription (in the domed portion) 'CROASDAILE SHAW ESQ MAYOR 1746 & 1759'. On the rectangle below is 'CHA. REVETT SEN^R MAYOR 1727 CHA REVETT HIS SON MYOR 1761 PAT^K BLAKE OF DRUM ESQ MAYOR 1771' (O). On this side is also a makers' mark 'BF', thought to be Bartholomew Fallon, a Galway silversmith who died in 1722; (3) this mount is in the form of a rectangular plate, with reeded borders at top and bottom, placed flat against the scabbard and a framework with a rectangular opening in the centre, backing it on the other side of the scabbard. The plate is inscribed '1830 Lt COLONEL JOHN BLAKE OF FURBOUGH, FIRST R. CATHOLIC MAYOR OF GALWAY SINCE 1688 EDMOND BLAKE ESQ^R HIS SON MAYOR AND D^Y MAYOR FROM 1831 TO 1841 AND LAST MAYOR OF GALWAY'. It has Dublin hallmarks. This fitting was added in 1876 while the sword was in the possession of Edmond Blake; and (4) the mouth-locket, which bears on one face (O) a fine rendering of the arms of Galway with two floral sprigs, one of a rose and the other a thistle issuing from a common stem (a Stuart device alluding to the union of the English and Scottish Crowns in 1603), on the other face (R) is the inscription '*REX GREX LEX ET ECCLESIA RESTAVRATI ANNO DOMINI* 1660 JOHN MORGAN MAYOR' (King, People, Law and Church restored in the year of the lord 1660). The side are engraved with a diamond pattern.

The chape and mouth-locket appear to be original and made at the same time as the quillons and pommel, with the inscription added at the relevant dates – 1655, 1660, 1755 and 1756.

The scabbard is beginning to show signs of ageing and the velvet covering is now rather worn. Conservators had recommended that the sword remain in the scabbard to prevent any further deterioration. This changed in September 2012, when conservation work was authorised on the scabbard. When the scabbard was removed, the blade was found to have a considerable amount of rust damage, particularly to the bottom foot of the blade, which would have been prevented had the blade been extracted and checked on a regular basis.

Many other authorities have replaced old scabbards. If the scabbard is deemed to be so precious, a much better solution would be to have a new scabbard made, as has been done in Exeter, with copies of the mounts. A simpler solution would be to have a new

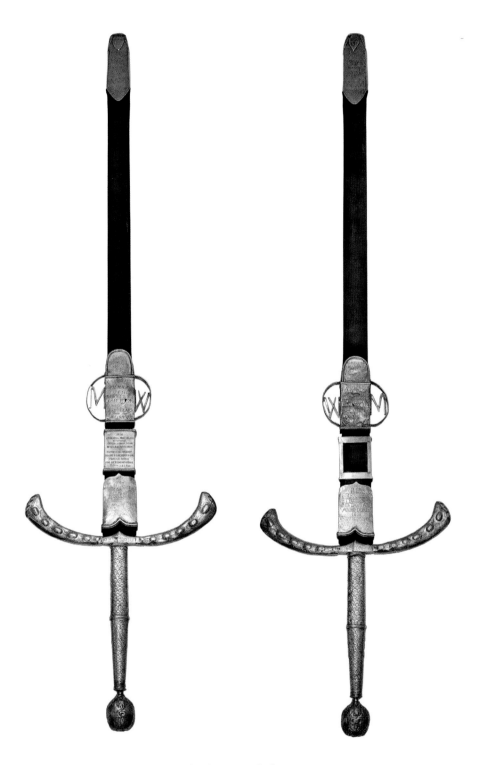

The City of Galway Sword of State – *c.* 1610

scabbard made, cover it in velvet and then transfer the mounts from the old to the new, as has been done in a considerable number of cases. The old scabbard could then be placed on permanent display in the museum and so escape further perceived damage.

Cap of Maintenance

There is no record of a cap of maintenance. Today the sword-bearer is always a member of the Galway Fire Brigade and wears a peaked uniform cap.

Uniform

The sword-bearer wears a navy blue single-breasted Galway Fire Brigade uniform with light blue shirt, black tie, black shoes and white cotton gloves.

The City of Galway Sword-Bearer

Derry

Prerogative

In 1613, a royal charter by James I granted the city the privilege to have a sword and a sword-bearer:

> And further we will, and by these presents, for us, our heirs and successors, do grant
> to the aforesaid Mayor and Commonality and Citizens of the city of Londonderry
> aforesaid, and their successors for ever, and from henceforth, shall and may have within
> the city of Londonderry aforesaid, one Sword-Bearer who shall be and shall be named
> the Sword-Bearer of the city aforesaid, which said officer called the Sword-Bearer of
> the city aforesaid, shall be named, elected and appointed by the Mayor and Aldermen,
> of the city aforesaid, for the time being, and from time to time shall be attendant upon
> the Mayor, of the city aforesaid, for the time being, which said officer called the Sword-
> bearer, shall and may carry and bear everywhere within the city aforesaid, the limits,
> liberties and precincts of the same, one sword sheathed before the Mayor of the city.

Derry is the ancient name of the city, but this same charter from James I formally changed the name to Londonderry. While this remains the official and legal name, the city is now known by its original name.

The city has two swords, both kept on display in the museum.

O'Doherty's Sword – c. 1603–08

Length of sword	3ft 10½in – 1.182m	Weight of sword	2lb 8¼oz – 1.130kg
Length of blade	3ft 1⅜in – 0.950 – Double-edged	Width of blade	1⅝in – 0.041m
Length of hilt	9⅛in– 0.232m – Two-handed	Width of guard	12⅞in – 0.327m
Length of scabbard	3ft 1⅞in – 0.962m	Weight of scabbard	13oz – 0.366kg

Sword

The sword is believed to have belonged to Sir Cathair O'Doherty, who was killed in 1608. The steel blade has a single very broad fuller, about ¾in wide and 13¾in long. The blade tapers and is quite sharp. There is some old rust damage around the tip and a few more recent areas on both faces. There is also one quite long 4¼in scratch about 7⅛in from the tip – it may be a flaw. There is one simple maker's mark on the reverse. The cross-guard is brass. The quillon block has an écusson and floral decoration on both faces, including a thistle and a rose – indicating the union of Scotland with England in 1603. The quillons are narrow and have recurring patterns of thistles, roses and other flowers. They widen at the ends and terminate in oblique cut pointed tips. One has been

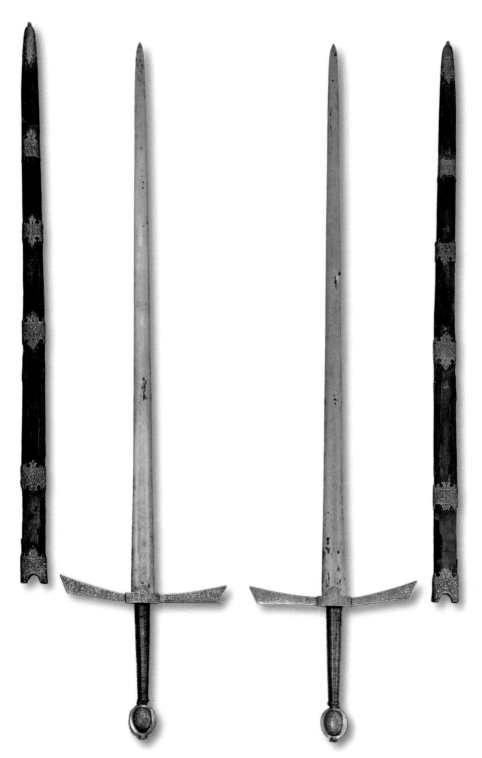

The City of Derry O'Doherty's Sword – *c.* 160308

broken off in the past and has been reattached with a fillet held in place by three rivets on each side. The joint now has play in it and the quillons are not at right angles to the blade. The grip is bound in silver wire that is in reasonable condition. There is a Turk's head knot at the bottom, but that from the top is missing. The pommel is a flat ovoid with each face raised. On one face is the raised name 'LON DON DRE RE'. The other face has the same pattern of flowers as elsewhere. There is a small tang nut and the tang end is hammered – however, the nut is damaged.

Scabbard

The wooden, probably original, scabbard has seen better days – it is now quite dilapidated. The covering appears to be velvet but there is very little left; however, there are galloons down each edge, probably gold, and just one short section is missing. There are six unevenly spaced brass mounts. All are similar with floral designs – the rose and thistle are again prominent with patterned edges and larger nearer the hilt. Only one is now whole; each of the others is missing portions. The chape has a small finial, while the mouth-locket is cut-out for the écusson.

The Sword of State – 1616

Length of sword	3ft 10⅞in – 1.190m	Weight of sword	3lb 1¾oz – 1.410kg
Length of blade	3ft 0⅞in – 0.937 – Double-edged	Width of blade	1¾in – 0.045m
Length of hilt	10in – 0.253m – Two-handed	Width of guard	10in – 0.254m
Length of scabbard	3ft 1¼in – 0.946m	Weight of scabbard	12½oz – 0.354kg

Sword

The sword was a gift in 1616 from The Honourable The Irish Society, who were the promoters of the Londonderry plantation.

The steel blade is flexible, quite sharp and in good condition. It has a 2⅜in ricasso and a quite broad 7¼in long fuller that has the word 'ANDREA' on one side and 'FERARA' on the other. Below the name on each face is what appears to be the number '117S'. The ricasso is scored along each edge on each face and along the length of the fuller. There are three + marks and another maker's mark on each side. The steel cross-guard is one simple piece with an écusson, narrow in section, and widens at the ends, which both curl back on themselves on the 'FERARA' side of the blade. The quillons are short and not quite square. The grip is bound in gilt-wire and is still in very good condition. There is a Turk's head knot at each end. The pommel is wheel-shaped with a raised disc on each face. There are no marks on either of the faces or on the sides. There is a hammered tang end.

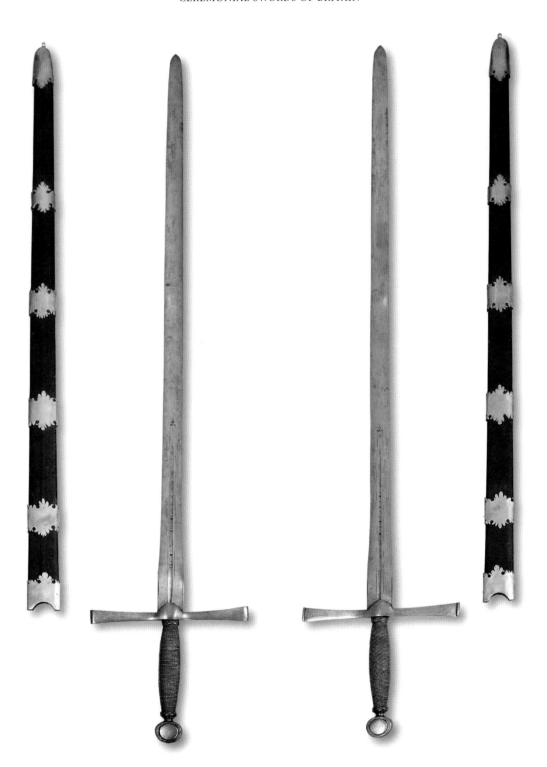

The City of Derry Sword of State – 1616

Scabbard

The wooden scabbard is covered in black leather that is relatively recent – the stitching is down one face. There are six evenly spaced brass mounts. All are plain, somewhat crudely cut and similar, with the same floral edges, and get larger nearer the hilt – some have minor damage. The chape has a small finial and the mouth-locket is cut out for the écusson.

Cap of maintenance

There is no record of any cap of maintenance.

Uniform

There is no sword-bearer and therefore no uniform.

Worcester

Prerogative

In 1622, James I confirmed all previous charters. By the charter, the mayor, aldermen and citizens were empowered to have a sword-bearer and 'one sword in the sheath, and in comeliness and beauty as it shall please the mayor for the time being, which might be carried wherever it hath been customary in times past for the maces to be borne before the bailiff'.

The same charter grants leave to appoint four sergeants-at-mace, who 'shall bear maces silvered and gilded, and with the sign and arms graven and decked of this our realm of England'.

The charter also provides for the proper carrying of the sword and maces before the king, his heirs and successor, the sword in its sheath, the maces borne by four aldermen. Before any other member of the royal family, the maces alone are to be borne before the mayor and three of the aldermen.

The city has three swords.

The Old Sword – sixteenth century

Length of sword	4ft 1in – 1.245m	Weight of sword	3lb 4¼oz – 1.481kg
Length of blade	3ft 2½in – 0.978m – Double-edged	Width of blade	1¾in – 0.045m
Length of hilt	10½in – 0.267m – Two-handed	Width of guard	12⅛in – 0.308m

Sword

This sword was held in the city solicitor's office for many years. The blade is of diamond section and is not in good condition. The quillon block is a simple collar between the shoulders of the blade and the grip. The attached quillons, which are plain, are of oval section and terminate in slightly wheel-shaped flat ends with a raised border with a small stud in the centre of each face. The grip is of plain polished wood with ferrules at each end. The pommel is of similar design to the quillon ends, but is slightly flattened and has two raised rings round the stud. There is a simple tang button. For its age it is in a reasonable state of repair. There was no mention of this sword in 1895.

Scabbard

The scabbard is missing.

The City Of Worcester Old Sword – sixteenth century

The City of Worcester Mourning or Poll Sword – sixteenth century

The Mourning or Poll Sword – sixteenth century

Length of sword	4ft 0in – 1.219m	Weight of sword	3lb 9½oz – 1.627kg
Length of blade	3ft 0⅛in – 0.917m – Double-edged	Width of blade	2in – 0.051m
Length of hilt	11¾in – 0.298m – Two-handed	Width of guard	13¾in – 0.349m

Sword

This sword is of sixteenth-century origin and is not in good condition. The blade, which is somewhat pitted, has three short fullers and a 2½in ricasso. The iron cross-guard is flat with small écussons and the quillons swell out at the ends and terminate in a tiny button. The grip is of plain dark wood; the leather binding found in 1895 has disappeared. The iron pommel is mushroom-shaped. There is a small end button. The metalwork, which was japanned in 1895, is now mostly worn away. Unused since 1895, today the sword stands in a corner and is in a poor state of repair. There is no marking.

Scabbard

In 1895, the sheath was covered in black velvet with a shield of arms, a fess between three pears. The metalwork was japanned black. Today the scabbard is missing.

The Sword of State – 1655

Length of sword	4ft 5¾in – 1.365m	Weight of sword	7lb 0¼oz – 3.183kg
Length of blade	3ft 2⅛in – 0.968m – Double-edged	Width of blade	2in – 0.051m
Length of hilt	15¼in – 0.388m – Two-handed	Width of guard	16¾in – 0.425m
Length of scabbard	3ft 3⅛in – 0.994m	Weight of scabbard	2lb 6oz – 1.076kg

Sword

The first sword apparently disappeared at the time of the Battle of Worcester (1651). A 'silver' sword was presented to the city by Nathaniel Harding in 1655, but only the blade of this sword remains today. The date of the blade was identified when the sword and scabbard were restored by Wilkinson Sword in 1996. The blade, which is blued, chased and has traces of gilding, bears the armourer's name 'PETER ENGLISH' and his mark, a king's head crowned in profile to the left, in the 10½in fuller on each face. It also bears, on a band next to the hilt, the royal arms, of William III, within the Garter and crowned with supporters (however, these would appear to have been added later) on one side, and those of the city on the other. The silver-gilt hilt appears to date from this same period of 1694–1702. The quillon block has, on each side, the royal arms, of William III, within the Garter. The quillons are highly ornamented with what appears to be a small figure of Justice with sword and scales at each end of each quillon and on each face – eight in total. These figures have a small cornucopia between them and

The City of Worcester Sword of State – 1655

the whole is chased with oak leaves and acorns and ends with a tiny button. The grip is bound with silver wire with several differing strands and a ferrule chased with roses, fruit, oak leaves and acorns at the hilt end, and a rope ferrule at the other. The globular but somewhat flattened pommel has on either face the city arms in relief with acanthus leaves and fruit, though one bears a lion's head and the other what appears to be a bull's head. There is a small tang button.

Scabbard

The scabbard is covered with deep crimson velvet, with a gold lace galloon along both edges, and nine silver-gilt mounts, which are almost identical on each side. These are: (1) the chape, which bears the city arms surmounted by a figure of Justice with sword and scales; (2) the figure of Justice with sword and scales; (3) the figure of Justice with sword and scales; (4) the royal arms of William III, within the Garter and crowned, with supporters and motto; (5) the city arms; (6) the city arms; (7) the letters 'G R' in monogram,

The City of Worcester Sword-Bearer

and below 'Saml¹ Taylor Esq. Mayor 1752' on one side, and 'J. Saunders Sheriff 1752' on the other; (8) the royal arms of William III, within the Garter and crowned, with supporters and motto; and (9) the mouth-locket, which has the city arms with acanthus leaves beside – unfortunately the locket has, at some stage, been removed and is now in upside down . The only mark is that of the maker, 'F H'. The engraving of the royal arms of William III on the scabbard mounts indicate a period between 1694 and 1702. All the mounts are original except (7), which was added later, probably replacing an original mount. The scabbard is in good condition.

Cap of Maintenance

The cap of maintenance is of the winter hat design but made of beige felt without a brim. The hat is 7¼in (0.184m) tall, with a headband diameter of 8½in (0.219m) and crown diameter of 11⅜in (0.290m). There is red and gold braid round the top. It has two long braided cords with solid tassels hanging down. It has three white ostrich feathers similar to the Garter feathers.

Uniform

A black academic robe is worn over a beige tail-coat with wide cuffs and white lace extensions, matching waistcoat and breeches, white stock, white calf-length wool stockings, black shoes with silver buckles and white cotton gloves.

In a couple of 1905 photographs, the sword-bearer is shown wearing a tail-coat and top hat; however, a painting hanging in the Guildhall, dated 1767, shows the then sword-bearer wearing an identical costume to the one worn today.

Kendal

Prerogative

By the charter of Charles I in 1636, the mayor was empowered that 'a sword-bearer shall carry and bear our sword and that of our heirs and successors anywhere within the said borough and the surrounding area of the same, in the presence of the mayor of the aforementioned borough for his time in office'. This privilege was confirmed by the charter of Charles II in 1684.

The Sword of State – *c.* 1660

Length of sword	3ft 10⅜in – 1.178m	Weight of sword	3lb 3¾oz–1.465kg
Length of blade	3ft 0⅛in – 0.917m – Double-edged	Width of blade	1¾in – 0.045m
Length of hilt	10⅛in – 0.257m – Two-handed	Width of guard	10¼in – 0.260m
Length of scabbard	3ft 2in – 0.965m	Weight of scabbard	8¼oz – 0.235kg

Sword

The sword is believed to be of the time of Charles II, if not later. The blade bears a maker's mark on each side and is in good condition, but narrows close to the hilt. The hilt is of silver. The quillon block has small semi-circular écussons and bears, on the obverse, the shield of the royal arms, probably of Charles II, and on the reverse the arms of Kendal. The quillons are square cut but thin and plain, but widen towards the ends, terminating with a wedge-shaped insert with leaf-work, and end with an added button. The grip is covered with black velvet. The pommel is flat and is essentially triangular, being shaped rather like an arrow-head, and matches the ends of the quillons with leaf-work, but bears the engraved head of the king (?) in profile wearing a laurel wreath on the insert on each side. There is a prominent tang button.

Scabbard

The scabbard is covered with black velvet, which is normally used only with mourning swords, and has three silver-gilt mounts. These are: (1) the chape, which has an engraved head of the king (?) in profile, set in an oblique shield, on each side; (2) the central locket, which has a cut out 'K K' for Kirkbie Kendal surrounded with some leaf-work on the obverse and a floral pattern of the reverse; and (3) the pointed mouth-locket, which is cut out to receive the quillon block and has a simple pattern along the edge of the cut-out on each side, but is otherwise plain. For some unknown reason the central locket is on upside down.

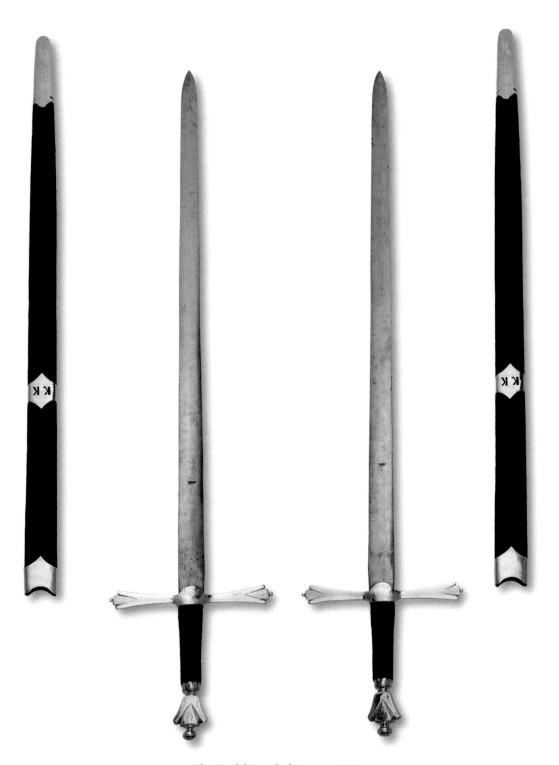

The Kendal Sword of State – *c.* 1660

Cap of Maintenance

There is no cap of maintenance. A military-style peaked cap of Kendal Green is worn and has a copy of the town's arms as its cap-badge.

Uniform

The sword-bearer wears a suit of Kendal Green with a badge on each sleeve of the town's arms, a white shirt with green tie, black shoes and white cotton gloves.

Carlisle

Prerogative

The 1637 charter of Charles I renewed former charters and granted that:

[T]here shall be in the aforementioned city, four other officers, that is to say, one officer who shall be and shall be called our sword-bearer in the presence of the mayor of the city aforesaid and three other officers who shall be and shall be called sergeants-at-mace ... and in the same offices the sword-bearer and sergeants-at-mace shall continue during the good pleasure of the same mayor ... that as well the aforesaid sword-bearer shall carry and bear the sword of us, our heirs and successors ... everywhere within the said city of Carlisle the limits and liberties of the same before the mayor of the city aforesaid for the time being.

Very unusually, and incorrectly, it is carried at the slope despite it being two-handed.

The Sword of State – 1509

Length of sword	3ft 8⅞in – 1.140m	Weight of sword	2lb 10oz – 1.192kg
Length of blade	3ft 0in – 0.914m – Double-edged	Width of blade	1½ in – 0.038m
Length of hilt	8⅞in – 0.226m – Two-handed	Width of guard	12⅛in – 0.308m
Length of scabbard	3ft 0⅞in – 0.937m	Weight of scabbard	13oz – 0.367kg

Sword

The Italian blade, made in Milan, is probably the oldest part of this sword. The cutting edges cease at the short ricasso, which is narrower and has a short wide fuller. The blade has two small fullers above on each side, bearing on the obverse the words 'MAIL LAND' and on the reverse 'ANNO 1509'. It also has the Solingen wolf mark on the obverse. The hilt is gilt. There is no quillon block, merely a raised section of the quillons, which are straight, chased and square-shaped, but thinning towards the ends and splaying at the ends. The grip, which was covered with black velvet in 1895, is now covered with ivory with a spiral gilt wire securing it and a ferrule bearing the same pattern as the quillons. The pommel, which is essentially triangular, is slightly flattened, chased on the edges and currently is loose. There is a small tang button. The sword was purchased in London in 1535–36 and the accounts record 'item for a sword of honour for ye citie £4. 13. 0'.

Scabbard

The scabbard, which was covered with black velvet in 1895, today is covered with purple velvet, with a galloon of gold lace from chape to mouth-locket on the reverse.

The City of Carlisle Sword of State – 1509

The velvet is well-worn on the lower section and along the edges. There are three gilt mounts: (1) the chape, which is viewed point down, is decorated with leaf-work and an Elizabethan fringe on each side; (2) the centre locket, which is viewed either way, is chased and bears the letter 'S' cut through the metal on one side, the other side having leaf-work; and (3) the mouth-locket, which is viewed point up, is decorated with the old and new arms of the city without supporters on the obverse with the city motto 'Be just and fear not', the reverse being plain, and both sides end with an Elizabethan fringe. There has been much speculation as to the meaning of the letter 'S', but no satisfactory solution has been found.

Cap of Maintenance

There is no cap of maintenance. Nowadays, a military-style peaked cap with a badge bearing the city crest is worn.

Uniform

The sword-bearer wears a black single-breasted military-style suit, with silver buttons, white shirt and black tie, black shoes and white cotton gloves.

Shrewsbury

Prerogative

By the charter of Charles I in 1638. it is provided:

> [T]hat the mayor, aldermen, and burgesses may appoint a sword-bearer to attend upon the mayor, who shall carry and bear before him a sheathed sword in all places where maces have in the past been accustomed to be borne before the bailiffs, but the said sword is not to be borne erect in any church or chapel consecrated to the honour and worship of God.

In accordance with the terms of the charter, it was in 1638 forthwith 'ordered that a sword be provided for the sword-bearer on the town's charge against the day the mayor is to be sworn'. The cost of the sword was £9 2s. Whether the sword was destroyed, mis-placed or hopelessly defaced under the Commonwealth does not appear, but in 1669, a new large sword was ordered to be bought, to be carried before the mayor on public days.

The town has two swords.

The Old Sword – 1638

Length of sword	4ft 3¼in – 1.302m	Weight of sword	3lb 15¾oz – 1.803kg
Length of blade	3ft 5in – 1.041m – Double-edged	Width of blade	1⅝in – 0.041m
Length of hilt	10¼in – 0.260m – Two-handed	Width of guard	10⅜in – 0.263m

Sword

This sword, which at one time was housed in the museum, is now displayed in the mayor's parlour. The steel blade bears traces of gilding on the 4½in ricasso, and on it are engraved the royal arms, probably of Charles I, within the Garter and crowned, and a rose and other leaf-work on the obverse, and the town arms on the other. The hilt is also of steel with traces of gilding. The square silver-gilt quillons, which are not embellished, widen towards the ends and the scrolled tips curve towards the blade. The wooden grip tapers and is bound with cord at either end. The brass pommel, which should be viewed point down, is best described as triangular. It is slightly wedge- or bell-shaped and has six facets – the main two with lions' heads, the remainder chased – with shoulders top and bottom and a button finial. It is believed that the sword dates from about 1560–80; however, given the engraved royal arms, it may well be that the sword was ordered and made in 1638.

Scabbard

The scabbard is missing.

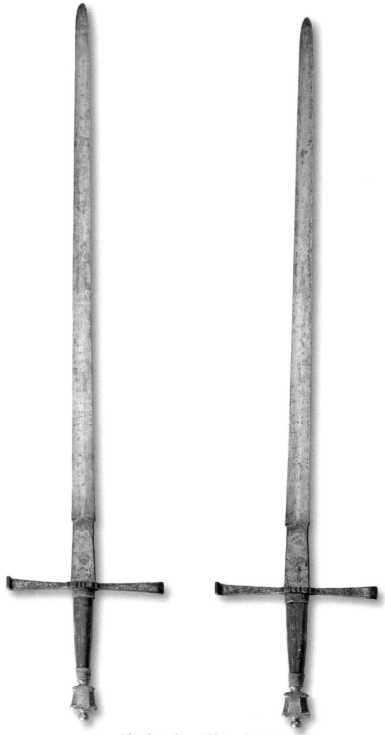

The Shrewsbury Old Sword – 1638

The Sword of State – 1669

Length of sword	4ft 4in – 1.321m	Weight of sword	4lb 7¾oz – 2.033kg
Length of blade	3ft 2in – 0.965m – Double-edged	Width of blade	1¾in – 0.044m
Length of hilt	14in – 0.356m – Two-handed	Width of guard	12½in – 0.318m
Length of scabbard	3ft 2¼in – 0.972m	Weight of scabbard	15¼oz – 0.432kg

Sword

This sword cost £34 2s. The highly polished steel blade, of which the bottom 4in is gilt, is partly chased with acorns, cherub's heads on each side one smiling, one not, with the date 1669 and initials 'R B'; and bears the armourer's name 'IOHANNIS HARTCOPP', twice on each side in the 12in fuller, with his own mark, a globe surmounted with a triple cross twice on each side, and the Passau or Solingen wolf mark once on each side. The hilt is silver-gilt and richly chased, and evidently the work of the same maker as the London 'Sunday' and Appleby swords, which it closely resembles. The quillon block has the royal arms of Charles II within the Garter and crowned, and within a border of fleurs-de-lis, on the obverse, and the arms of the town on the reverse. The handsome quillons are chased with oak leaves and acorns on each side and hatching on the top and the bottom, with two trumpets on each side. The ends turn up and terminate with a single upturned lion's head with a grotesque in the mane facing backwards (possibly a bull or a pig). The grip, which tapers very slightly, has a ferrule at each end and is covered in double rope wire within a spiral channel, and is bound at one end with sticky tape. This needs attention. The pommel, which is globular, is wrought in *repoussé* with a figure of Justice with sword and scales on the obverse, and the figure of Fame with two trumpets on the reverse. There is a cherub on each side. The tang nut is segmented and chased but has been dropped and is missing two segments, and the whole nut is askew. The sword was repaired and newly gilt in 1820.

The fact that this sword can be positively dated to 1669 is very helpful in dating the London Sword of State and Appleby civic sword, as all three have identical hilts.

Scabbard

The scabbard was covered with crimson velvet in 1895. Today it is covered with blue velvet with five silver-gilt mounts. Each side is identical except for a galloon of gold lace running from chape to mouth-locket on one side only. The beautifully wrought mounts are: (1) the chape, which bears a semi-naked female figure with wings with a grotesque above and a leopard's head below, and a cornucopia in each lower corner and a rose in each upper corner, on each side, is tipped with an acorn finial; (2) this locket bears a leopard's head on each side; (3) this locket bears a cherub's head and wings on each side; (4) this locket bears a leopard's head on each side; and (5) the

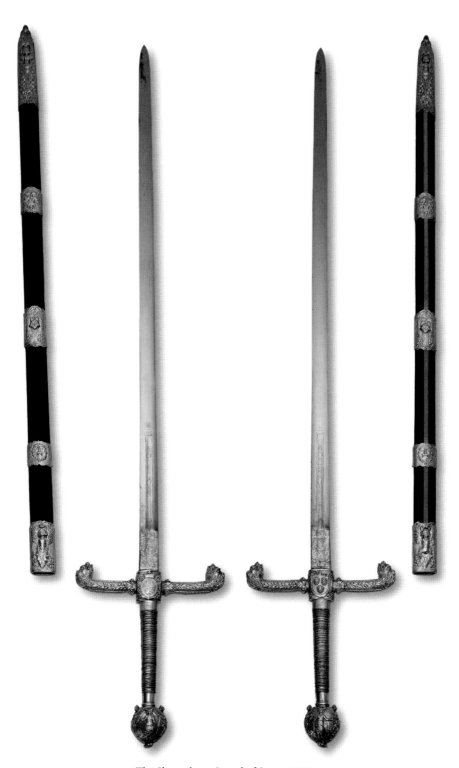

The Shrewsbury Sword of State – 1669

mouth-locket bears acanthus leaves and a figure of a semi-naked female with wings, fruit and a grotesque above on each side. All the leopard heads are similar but not identical.

Cap of Maintenance

There is no cap of maintenance. The sword-bearer wears a black tri-corn with a gold braid border and gold flash.

Uniform

The sword-bearer wears a black superfine robe with gold piping and facings over a black suit, white shirt with wing collar and black bow tie, black shoes and white cotton gloves.

Wigan

Prerogative

A key charter from Charles II in May 1662 stated: '[A]nd is granted as a special token of our favour for the town's "fidelity to us and our Most Dear Father constantly manifested throughout that late infamous revolt of the subjects of the realm", the right to bear a ceremonial sword inscribed with the royal arms before the mayor'. The sword was the gift of the king and it is said that he presented it to the then mayor, Sir Roger Bradshaigh.

The Sword of State – c. 1662

Length of sword	4ft 3in – 1.295m	Weight of sword	3lb 14½oz – 1.770kg
Length of blade	3ft 2¼in – 0.972m – Double-edged	Width of blade	1¾in – 0.044m
Length of hilt	12¾in – 0.324m – Two-handed	Width of guard	13⅛in – 0.333m
Length of scabbard	3ft 5⅛in – 1.044m	Weight of scabbard	1lb 1½oz – 0.495kg

Sword

This steel sword is in very good condition. The long, tapered steel blade has no distinguishing marks. The hilt is steel. The quillon block is simple while the quillons, which slightly increase in width towards the extremities, are terminated by similar small circular bosses with a small raised stud on each side. The grip, which has been re-covered with crimson velvet fairly recently, starts with a gilt ferrule, has a gold lace galloon down each side and tapers to a much smaller gilt ferrule. The pommel is plain, flat and circular with a raised boss on each side and ends with a brass tang button.

Scabbard

The scabbard is covered with crimson velvet with a gold lace galloon down each edge from chape to mouth-locket – one section is a little loose – and three mounts. These are: (1) a very long steel chape has two sets of incised rings round it but is otherwise plain on each side and ending in a brass cap and a small finial; (2) the central gilt locket, which should be viewed point down, has on the obverse the royal arms of Charles II, within the Garter and crowned, with supporters and motto, and on the reverse a shield with helm, crest of a hart, and mantling, the arms of Bradshaigh quartering Hoghton and Ashton, surrounded by leaf-work; and (3) the 4½in steel mouth-locket is plain with one set of incised rings on each side.

Cap of Maintenance

There is no cap of maintenance; the sword-bearer wears a top hat with a gold lace galloon round the base of the crown.

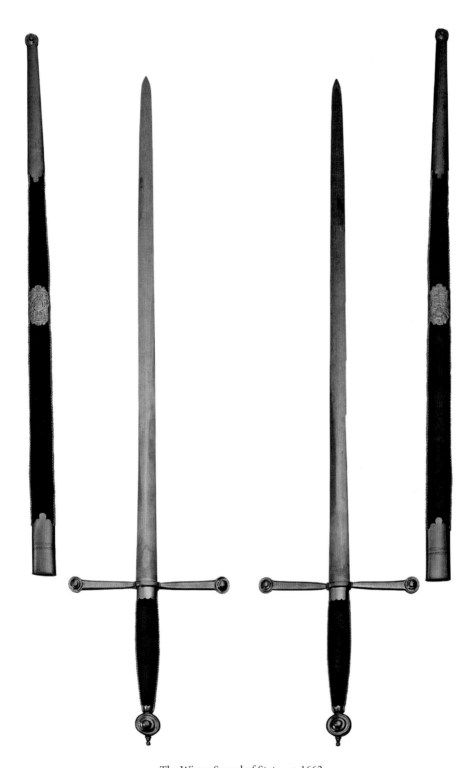

The Wigan Sword of State – *c.* 1662

Uniform

A black full-length cloak trimmed with scarlet with a very wide collar bearing the Wigan arms, two on the front and a larger one on the back, over a dark suit with white shirt, dark corporate tie, black shoes and white cotton gloves.

Appleby

Prerogative

There is no Royal charter or other authority for bearing this sword. The donor of the sword is believed to have been John Dalston. Today there is no actual evidence of this.

John Dalston, who was one of the Members of Parliament for Appleby from 1661 to 1679 and died in 1692, is the most likely donor given the comment about the 1895 inscription below. Another possible donor could have been Sir John Dalston (2nd Baronet), who was High Sheriff in 1661 and died in 1711, but he does not really fit the bill. A third John Dalston was mayor of the town from 1701 to 1703 but it is unlikely that he was the donor due to the dates.

The first recorded appointment of a sword-bearer was in 1709.

The Civic Sword – *c.* 1670

Length of sword	4ft 0¼in – 1.225m	Weight of sword	6lb 7¾oz – 2.940kg
Length of blade	2ft 11½in – 0.902m – Double edged	Width of blade	1¾in – 0.045m
Length of hilt	12¾in – 0.324m – Two handed	Width of guard	12¾in – 0.324m
Length of scabbard	3ft 0⅝in – 0.930m	Weight of scabbard	13½oz – 0.382kg

Sword

The sword is virtually identical to that at Shrewsbury and at London (Sunday), and very similar to several other swords. In 1895, the blade was described as bearing on the obverse the arms of the donor, with the inscription '*Ex dono Iohis Dalston Ar: Unuis Burgensis in Parliamento pro Burgo de Appleby*'. Today there is little left of the arms and no inscription is visible – there is an unidentifiable mark. There is another unidentifiable mark on the reverse. The blade is, unusually, quite sharp. The hilt is silver-gilt. The quillon-block has on the obverse the royal arms, probably of Charles II, within the Garter and crowned, but without supporters or motto, set within an oblique shield with fleurs-de-lis all around, and on the reverse the town arms with scroll-work. The quillons are covered with oak leaf-work with acorns, with hash marks along each edge, and turn up at the ends with a single upturned lion's head with a grotesque in the mane pointing backwards (possibly a bull or a pig). One now screws on and has a badly fitting base-metal washer. The grip is bound with silver-gilt wire, which is need of attention, over red velvet; on one end is a Turk's head knot while the other has a crude piece of velvet. The pommel, which is globular, is loose and has, wrought in *repoussé* with flattened faces, the figure of Justice with sword and scales on the obverse, and the figure of Fame with two trumpets on the reverse. On each edge is a cherub. There is a small, screwed-on tang button.

Scabbard

The leather scabbard, believed to be the original, is very flexible and is covered with crimson velvet with a thin gold lace galloon down the reverse from chape to mouth-locket. It has four gilt-brass mounts: (1) the chape, which has a harp surmounting a crowned lion passant guardant on the obverse and an angel on the reverse, with a flower-like finial; (2) this locket has a lion passant guardant on the obverse and a harp on the reverse; (3) this locket has a crowned rose on the obverse and a harp on the reverse; and (4) the mouth-locket, which is 4¾in long, has the same inscription as the blade with a grotesque above on the obverse, and a lion passant guardant with a grotesque above on the other. There are no hallmarks on the mounts. Mounts (2) and (3) have been put on upside down.

The hilt of this sword is identical to the Swords of State in London and Shrewsbury, making it slightly older than was previously thought.

Cap of Maintenance

There is no cap of maintenance. The sword-bearer wears a black tri-corn.

Uniform

An unadorned black academic robe is worn over a dark suit, white shirt, black tie, black shoes and white cotton gloves.

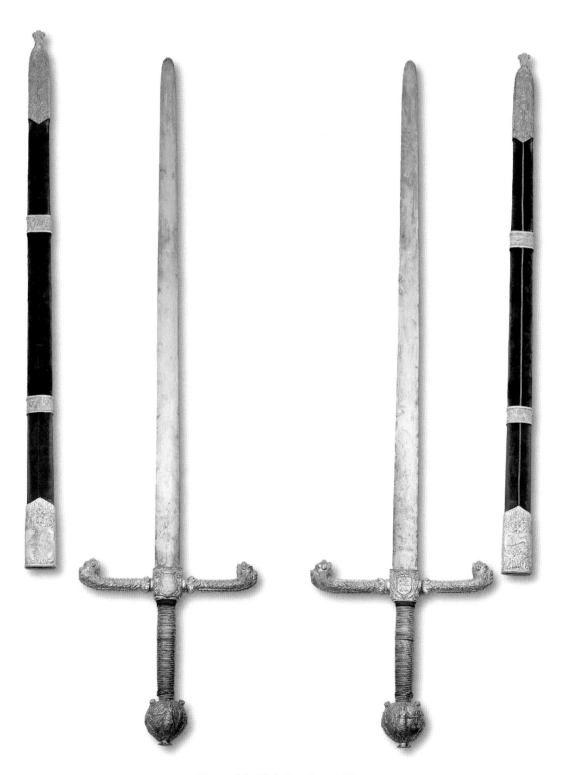

The Appleby Civic Sword – *c.* 1670

Hertford

Prerogative

A charter from Charles II in November 1680 said:

> [T]hat from henceforth for ever there may be and shall be in the borough aforesaid two officers who shall be called Serjeants-at-Mace … and that the said Serjeants-at-Mace shall bear and carry as well as the sword, the mace of gold or silver engraven and adorned with our arms everywhere within the borough aforesaid the liberties, bounds and precincts thereof before the mayor of the borough aforesaid for the time being.

Among the corporation muniments, in the *Gift Book* is the entry: 'Sir Charles Caesar of Bennington Place in this County, Knight, being chosen one of the Burgesses to sitt in Parliament for this Borough about the year 1678 did afterwards give One hundred pounds towards the renewing of the Charter and purchasing of a sword and Sundry other things for the good and credit of this Corporation.'

The Sword of State – 1680

Length of sword	3ft 9¼in – 1.149m	Weight of sword	2lb 10oz – 1.192kg
Length of blade	3ft 0⅛in – 0.917m – Double-edged	Width of blade	1½in – 0.038m
Length of hilt	9⅛in – 0.232m – Two-handed	Width of guard	13¼in – 0.336m
Length of scabbard	3ft 1¼in – 0.946m	Weight of scabbard	1lb 0½oz – 0.468kg

Sword

The sword has a double-fullered blade with the maker's mark 'ANDREA FERARA' in each fuller. The 2½in ricasso is gilt and chased with scrolls. The hilt is silver-gilt. The quillon block extends over the last ½in of the blade and has on one side the royal arms of the Stuart sovereigns, probably of Charles II, within the Garter and crowned, with supporters, and on the other those of the Duchy of Lancaster. The quillons are adorned with shields, scroll-work, etc., and terminate in oval bosses with lions' heads in relief. The grip has a spirally ornamented covering of metal. The pommel is globular and slightly ovoid. The flattened sides have, in *alto relievo*, on one side the arms of the borough and on the other a head in profile, surrounded by a trophy of arms. There are in all eight marks of the maker, 'I H' in a shield, one on each side of the pommel and three on each edge of each side of the quillons.

The Hertford Sword of State – 1680

Scabbard

The scabbard is covered with crimson velvet with five silver-gilt mounts. These are: (1) the chape, which has a figure of Justice with sword and scales, and leaf-work on each side, and a button finial; (2) a locket with the arms of the Duchy of Lancaster on each side; (3) a locket bearing the royal arms of the Stuart sovereigns, probably Charles II, within the Garter and crowned, with supporters on each side; (4) a locket bearing the arms of the borough on each side; and (5) the mouth-locket bearing the donor's arms and crest, and the inscription '*Ex dono Caroli Cesar Militis* 1680' on each side.

Cap of Maintenance

The fur cap of maintenance is of sable with a black velvet crown.

Uniform

The sword-bearer wears a dark blue robe, trimmed with gold, over a dark suit, with white shirt and tie, black shoes and white cotton gloves.

Bury St Edmunds

Prerogative

In 1606, James I granted a charter of incorporation which empowered the corporation to elect an alderman (mayor) and two officers to carry maces before the alderman. In early 1684, Charles II withdrew the 1606 charter. However, on 3 July 1684, a new charter by Charles II reconstituted the corporation with a mayor, aldermen, etc., and it is presumed that this authorised the bearing of a sword before the mayor. Unfortunately, there is no proof of this as this charter was recalled by James II in 1687. Yet proof exists in a lateral sense in that the corporation minute book has two records. On 2 October 1684, it is recorded 'that thanks were given to Sir Thomas Hervey Kt. for the gift of the sword', who had presented the sword 'upon His Majesty creating a Mayor town'. On 29 December of the same year, the minute book records 'that the mayor shall have the sword and maces carried before him on such days as the maces were formally carried before the alderman'.

As with Great Yarmouth and Carmarthen, the tradition of unsheathing the sword on the declaration of war is followed.

Very unusually, and incorrectly, it is carried at the slope despite it being two-handed.

The Sword of State – *c.* 1684

Length of sword	4ft 3⅝in – 1.311m	**Weight of sword**	4lb 10oz – 2.098kg
Length of blade	3ft 0⅞in – 0.937m – Double-edged	**Width of blade**	1⅝in – 0.041m
Length of hilt	14¾in – 0.375m – Two-handed	**Width of guard**	13⅛in – 0.333m
Length of scabbard	3ft 1¾in – 0.959m	**Weight of scabbard**	2lb 0oz – 0.907kg

Sword

The sword has a poor, slightly pitted blade with a double fuller along the whole length and etched trophies on each side at the base. The large hilt is silver-gilt. The quillon block has a rose on each side. Each quillon starts with *repoussé* leaf-work, is then spirally twisted and ends in a double lion's head. The grip is spirally twisted and identical in design to the Swords of State of Carmarthen, Thetford and Great Yarmouth. The large pommel is pear-shaped and slightly flattened, with the figure of Justice with sword and scales on one side, and of Law holding a scroll with four pendant seals believed to represent the first four charters of the town (1608, 1608, 1617 and 1664) on the other. On each edge is a cornucopia. The tang button is partly hidden within a spray of four small leaves.

The Bury St Edmunds Sword of State – *c.* 1684

Scabbard

The wooden scabbard is covered with crimson velvet with four silver-gilt mounts. These are: (1) the chape, which is long and chased with acanthus leaf-work and crowned roses on each side, and ends in a small crown; (2) a locket with the town arms on each side; (3) a locket with a crowned rose chased on each side; and (4) the mouth-locket, which is 6⅝in long and chased with acanthus leaves, and bears on each side the royal arms of the Stuart sovereigns, probably of Charles II, within the Garter and crowned, with supporters. There are no hallmarks.

Cap of Maintenance

There is no cap of maintenance: the sword-bearer wears a top hat with a gold lace galloon around the base of the crown, as does the mace-bearer.

Uniform

The sword-bearer wear a black wool frock-coat with red collar, black trousers, white shirt, white tie, black shoes and white cotton gloves.

Great Yarmouth

Prerogative

By the charter of Charles II in 1684, the office of mayor was instituted and the mayor was entitled to have a sword in a scabbard carried before him, everywhere within the borough and the liberties thereof. The sword was adopted at this time. When the charter was abrogated by James II, the sword was placed in the 'hutch' or chest, and there remained until the charter of Queen Anne in 1703 again authorised the election of a mayor and appointed a sword-bearer, who was empowered to carry a sword in a scabbard before the mayor and his deputy, everywhere in the borough etc. Until 1738, the sword was carried by the water bailiff, but in that year the marshal of the admiralty court was appointed to that duty with an allowance of £1 13s 4d per annum for a gown.

It is an ancient and invariable custom at Yarmouth whenever war is declared, between England and any other power, to unsheathe the sword and let it remain naked until peace is declared, when it is again placed in the scabbard. This tradition was followed in 1739 for the war against Spain and again for the Crimean War (1853–56). Carmarthen and Bury St Edmunds follow a similar tradition.

The Sword of State – c. 1684

Length of sword	4ft 4⅜in – 1.330m	Weight of sword	5lb 1oz – 2.292kg
Length of blade	3ft 1½in – 0.953m – Double-edged	Width of blade	1⅞in – 0.048m
Length of hilt	14¾in – 0.375m – Two-handed	Width of guard	13in – 0.330m
Length of scabbard	3ft 2¾in – 0.983m	Weight of scabbard	2lb 2¼oz – 0.974kg

Sword

This sword, or Sword of Justice as it is known, has a double fuller blade chased on each side for some 4½in from the hilt. The hilt is silver-gilt. The quillon block has a large rose on each side. The quillons are straight, start with leaf-work followed by a narrow band and terminate with double lions' heads. The grip is spirally fluted. The large pear-shaped pommel is slightly flattened. It bears in high relief on one side a figure of Justice with sword and scales, and on the other a figure of Law with book and three seals. It has leaf-work around the base and ends in a pointed finial nut which has been crushed and now points to one side.

Scabbard

The wooden scabbard is covered with crimson velvet with four silver-gilt mounts and a gold lace galloon down one face. These are: (1) the chape, which has a crowned rose and acanthus leaves on each side; (2) a locket with the Yarmouth arms on each side;

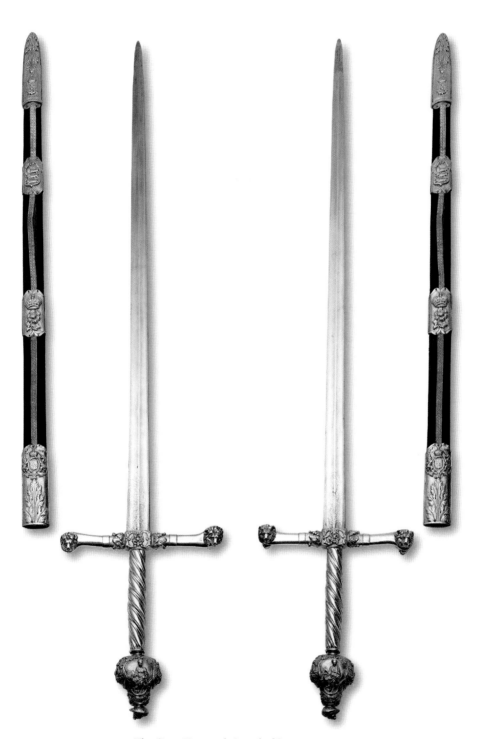

The Great Yarmouth Sword of State – *c.* 1684

(3) a locket with a rose slipped and crowned on each side; and (4) the long and massive mouth-locket has, besides rich foliage, the royal arms of the Stuart sovereigns, probably Charles II, within the Garter and crowned, with supporters, on each side.

Cap of Maintenance

There is no cap of maintenance. The sword-bearer wears a black top hat with a gold galloon round the base of the crown.

Uniform

A black academic robe with gold facings is worn over a black suit, with white shirt, black tie, black shoes and white cotton gloves.

Lichfield

Prerogative

In 1686, a charter from James II granted the city the privilege of bearing a sword before the mayor on all occasions. The sword was donated by George Legge, created Baron Dartmouth in 1682, who was recorder of Lichfield in 1686 and gave the sword that year.

An entry in the records in 1657, shows 6*s* was paid 'to Mr. William Lamb, for a sword for the Bailiffs seat'. Another sword 'of much plainer character' was bought in 1690, when 4*s* was paid 'for a sword, to set up in St. Mary's church between the mace rests'. Neither of these swords can now be traced.

The Sword of State – 1686

Length of sword	4ft 4⅜in – 1.330m	Weight of sword	4lb 8oz – 2.042kg
Length of blade	3ft 3½in – 1.003m – Double-edged	Width of blade	2in – 0.051m
Length of hilt	12⅞in – 0.327m – Two-handed	Width of guard	15½in – 0.393m
Length of scabbard	3ft 4¼in – 1.023m	Weight of scabbard	2lb 4¼oz – 1.027kg

Sword

The sword is of great beauty and is in quite good condition. The blade is blued for the first 20in and gilt, with, on the obverse, the royal arms, probably of James II, within the Garter and crowned; the armourer's mark of three kings' heads; a lion holding a flag with the cross of St George in one quarter and a unicorn holding a flag of St Andrew; a figure of Justice with sword and scales, and various leaf-work. On the reverse are the royal arms, probably of Charles II, within the Garter and crowned, the armourer's mark of three kings' heads, a mace and sceptre in saltire, oak leaves and acorns, and crossed cornucopia. The hilt and mountings, being silver-gilt, are richly decorated in high relief. On each side of the quillon block is the king's bust in profile, between his initials 'J' and 'R'. The quillons are straight with a ferrule and acanthus leaves at each end, two cherubs' heads on each side and elaborate chasing with foliage, and terminate with a lion's head on each side of each end. The grip, which is bound with silver-gilt wire, is straight with a Turk's head knot ferrule at each end. The spherical and slightly ovoid pommel is chased and bears the royal profile with the initials 'J' and 'R' on either side.

Scabbard

The metal scabbard is covered with deep crimson velvet with a gold lace galloon along the length on the obverse and five silver-gilt mounts. These are: (1) the chape, which bears a figure of Justice with sword and scales on each side and has a small finial; (2) this locket bears the royal arms of James II, within the Garter and crowned, with supporters,

The City of Lichfield Sword of State – 1686

on each side; (3) this locket bears the arms of the donor on each side; (4) this locket bears the city arms chased with various weapons, axes, swords and a mace on each side; and (5) the mouth-locket bears a mace and sceptre in saltire surmounted by a royal crown on each side. The hallmarks are of London 1685–86 and the maker 'W C'. The velvet on the last section near the hilt is worn.

The Second Sword – c. 1840

Length of sword	Not applicable	Weight of blade	1lb 7¾oz – 0.676kg
Length of blade	3ft 2⅛in – 0.969m – Double-edged	Width of blade	2in – 0.051m
Length of hilt	None	Width of guard	None

Sword

This blade is of a similar length to the other sword but the tang is foreshortened to 2½in with two holes in it. This is presumably to attach a handle to, though it would lack any strength so would be a display item only. The blade is blued for the first 22½in and is

The City of Lichfield Sword-Bearer.

289

heavily decorated. On the obverse are the makers' names 'WOOLEY and SARGANT'; an enormous trophy of arms including pikes, helmets, a crown and an oblique royal arms within the Garter, a Roman legion standard, trumpets, maces, quivers of arrows, three flags (one Union) and a banner; the city arms; a sword and mace in saltire (on one side); a dove below a crown; and a figure of Justice with sword and scales. On the reverse are: a large urn surrounded with chasing; a muscular man with a spiked mace and a standing figure of Britannia; St George slaying the dragon; the city arms; a sword and mace in saltire (upright); an eagle with '*Dieu et Mon Droit*' supporting unicorn passant supporting a slipped royal arms, of the period from 1837 onward, within the Garter and crowned; a seated Britannia with a trumpet behind; and a small trophy of arms with a rose. The inclusion of such a modern royal arms indicates that this blade is neither that of 1657 nor 1690 mentioned above. The makers existed, in one guise or another, between 1815 and at least 1850, which ties in with the royal arms. There is no hilt.

Scabbard
There is no scabbard.

Cap of Maintenance
There is no cap of maintenance: the sword-bearer wears a tri-corn trimmed with silver braid around the edge of the brim and with a silver flash above the right ear.

Uniform
A scarlet double-breasted frock-coat, with folded cuffs with buttons and white linen inserts and a large badge bearing the arms of Lichfield, black breeches above black buttoned gaiters, with a white jabot, black shoes and white cotton gloves.

The City of Lichfield Second Sword – *c.* 1840

Liverpool

Prerogative

The right of having a sword borne before the mayor was conferred upon the town by the charter of William III in 1695 in the clause:

> And furthermore we wish and through the presents for ourselves, our heirs and successors have granted to the mayor, bailiffs and burgesses of the aforementioned town and to their successors that the mayor, bailiffs and burgesses of the aforementioned town and their successors for the rest in all future time may have and shall have a sword, and full power and authority for bearing the sword in this way in front of the mayor of the aforementioned town for the time of his office … one upright man … shall be and is the bearer of the sword of the said town.

In 1895, the city had three swords, though two were presentational swords. Today it has only two swords.

No trace can now be found of the Norris sword. This was formerly displayed in the council chamber with the other insignia, having a tablet bearing the following inscription: 'This Sword of State carried before His Excellency Sir Wm Norris of Speke in his Embassy to the Great Mogul was given as a memorial of his respect to this Corporation Anno Domini 1702 – John Cockshott Mayor.' Sir William Norris was Member of Parliament for Liverpool from 1695 to 1701. He was sent to India in 1699 and was given a sword by Aurangzeb, the Mogul. He died at sea on the way home in 1702. The sword had a leather sheath with a silver chape. It is thought it might have been stolen along with other items when the Guildhall was closed between 1900 and 1906.

The Sword of State – 1764

Length of sword	4ft 2¾in – 1.289m	Weight of sword	3lb 8oz – 1.589kg
Length of blade	3ft 1¾in – 0.959m – Double-edged	Width of blade	1¾in – 0.045m
Length of hilt	13in – 0.331m – Two-handed	Width of guard	10¼in – 0.260m
Length of scabbard	3ft 5¾in – 1.060m	Weight of scabbard	15½oz – 0.442kg

Sword

This sword was purchased in 1764. The blade is somewhat pitted and bears no maker's mark. The handsome hilt is silver-gilt. The quillon block is chased and bears, on the obverse, the royal crown, with a mace and sceptre in saltire. On the reverse is a liver bird. The quillons are slightly curved and terminate in single lions' heads. The grip

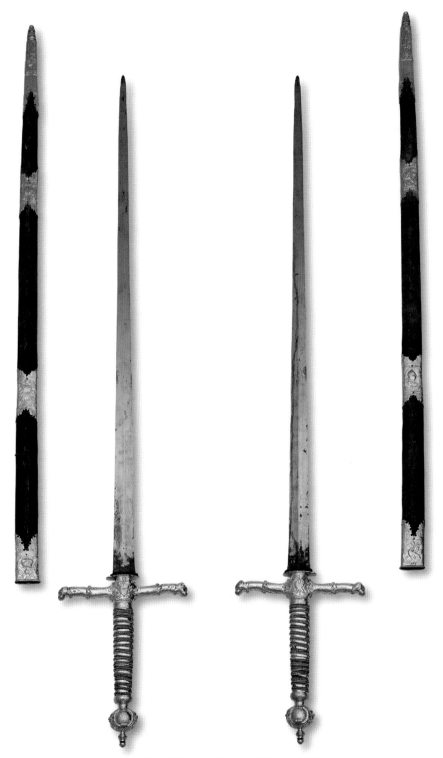

The City of Liverpool Sword of State – 1764

is bound with triple stranded wire but is in serious need of attention. The flattened, circular pommel is chased with the inscription 'Geo Campbell Esq. Mayor Anno 1764' on the obverse and a bear (?) on the reverse. On each side of the pommel is a grotesque. There is an extended tang button. While the blade, pommel and button are firm, the cross-guard and grip are loose. There are London hallmarks for 1763–64. There was some rust on the blade just above the quillon block, obviously caused by lack of drying after being carried in rain.

Scabbard

The scabbard is covered with purple velvet and four silver-gilt mounts. In 1895, there were narrow strips of engrailed silver-gilt guarding each edge – today these are missing. The velvet covering is worn and damaged and in need of attention. The mounts, which are all chased, are: (1) the chape, which bears a cornucopia on the obverse and two broad leaves on the reverse; (2) this locket has two trumpets in saltire and drums on the obverse, and a lion rampant regardant on the reverse; (3) this locket has a crown upon a sword and sceptre in saltire on the obverse, and an embossed portrait of George III on the reverse; and (4) the mouth-locket has a sword and sceptre in saltire, with a crown above on the obverse and the liver bird on the reverse.

Cap of Maintenance

There is no cap of maintenance. Despite old photographs showing insignia-bearers wearing headdress, today the sword-bearer is bareheaded.

Uniform

The sword-bearer wears a black superfine academic-style robe trimmed with gold, over a black morning-jacket, pin-striped trousers and black waistcoat, with white shirt and dark tie, black shoes and white cotton gloves.

Carrickfergus

Prerogative

There is no Royal charter or other authority for this bearing-sword. It was presented, together with a mace, to the Corporation of Carrickfergus in 1712 by Robert Gardner, who was a member of a prosperous merchant family and is recorded as a 'Colonel' and as an 'Armourer of London'.

As a sword-bearer is recorded well before the presentation date, it must be assumed that there was a previous sword, later lost, stolen or destroyed, probably in one of the battles of the seventeenth century against James II.

Although previously borne in procession, it has not been used for many years and is now displayed in the town museum.

The Civic Sword – 1712

Length of sword	4ft 2in – 1.270m	Weight of sword	4lb 6oz – 1.985kg
Length of blade	3ft 0in – 0.915m – Double-edged	Width of blade	2in – 0.051m
Length of hilt	14in – 0.356m – Two-handed	Width of guard	13¼in – 0.336m
Length of scabbard	3ft 1in – 0.940m	Weight of scabbard	9oz – 0.259kg

Sword

This civic sword has a fine straight tapered blade of Sheffield steel of diamond section. At the base of the blade there are engraved markings. The hilt is of silver-gilt. The quillon-block is much broader than the quillons and bears, on both faces, the royal arms of Queen Anne, within the Garter, crowned with supporters and motto on one face. The letter 'A' is in the upper corner of the block and the letter 'R' in the other corner. The straight quillons are very elaborate and bear the mark of Thomas Vicaridge, the silver-hilt-maker and cutler of St Bride's, London. Nearest the block is a ridged wheel device, next, in *alto relievo*, is a floral base of acanthus leaves, the main square sectioned bar ornamented and chased with leaf-work with scroll-work borders. The ends are some-what bulbous with a small lion's mask against a matted background on each face, and terminate with a grotesque on each end – a small end nut acting as the nose. The cross-guard is hallmarked. The wooden grip tapers and is bound with silver ribbon with a double strand of silver twisted wire superimposed. There is a Turk's head knot collet at each end. The pommel is globular with, on both faces, the royal arms of Queen Anne, within the Garter, crowned with supporters and motto on one face. On one side are the arms of the town around with the inscription '*SIGILLUM COMITATUS VILLAE DE CRAGFERGUS*'. On the other side is another coat of arms round which is an inscription in Latin indicating that the sword and the mace were the gifts of Robert Gardner in 1712

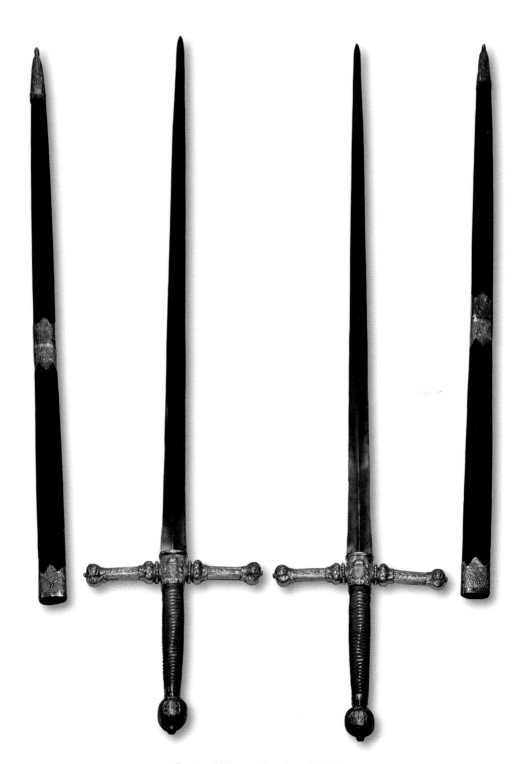

The Carrickfergus Civic Sword – 1712

in honour of his native town. The top edge is in the form of a cup, which covers the bottom Turk's head knot of the grip with an engraved collar. The tang button is dome-shaped and segmented and the tang end is hammered flat very neatly.

Scabbard

The wooden scabbard is covered with crimson velvet with three silver-gilt mounts. These are: (1) the chape, which is viewed point down, is chased with flowers and leaf-work. There is a small grotesque on each face. The edge is zigzag with leaf-work. There is a dome-shaped finial; (2) the central locket is actually two lockets back to back, which are viewed point up. The lower one is a smaller mirror image of the mouth-locket on each face including the small grotesque. The upper half is of the same basic pattern but the edge is similar but of simpler design. It bears on the obverse the royal arms of Queen Anne, within the Garter, crowned with supporters and motto side, and on the reverse the arms of the town; (3) the mouth-locket, which is viewed point down, has the same design as the chape, including the small grotesque on each face. The upper edge is more ornate with swirls of leaves.

Cap of Maintenance

There is no cap of maintenance as there is no longer a sword-bearer.

Uniform

None.

Southampton

Prerogative

There is no Royal charter or other authority for this bearing-sword. Nor is there any record of when or how it was obtained. The sheathed sword is on display in the mayor's suite.

The Civic Sword – sixteenth century

Length of sword	5ft 9in – 1.752m	**Weight of sword**	7lb 8½oz – 3.416kg
Length of blade	4ft 2½in – 1.283m – Double-edged	**Width of blade**	2in – 0.051m
Length of hilt	18½in – 0.470m – Two-handed	**Width of guard**	17¼in – 0.438m
Length of scabbard	3ft 10½in – 1.181m	**Weight of scabbard**	1lb 10oz – 0.733kg

Sword

This extremely long sword is first mentioned in 1801 as follows, 'the sword of state is very ancient and curious. It is one of the vast two-handed weapons of our ancestors, with very fine blade'.[20] The sword is of somewhat rough workmanship and of the form in use among the Swiss infantry in the sixteenth century. The narrow blade, which is in good condition given its length, has a 6½in ricasso with protecting 'hooks' about 5in from the cross-guard. It has been painted with gold paint over a number of older coats, which are now very damaged and uneven. The hilt is of iron. The whole guard is very loose. The quillon block has a *pas-d'âne*. The quillons have traces of gilt, are long with small scrolls halfway along and terminate in scrolled tips which curve towards the blade. The grip is of bored oak and is plain except for an incised collar halfway along. There is a simple brass ferrule at either end, once japanned black but now much worn away. The pommel is quite large and mushroom-shaped; it is circular and flat with a segmented edge. The end of the tang end is hammered into the pommel.

Scabbard

The scabbard, restored in 1877, is of brown leather with three brass mounts; however, the leather is now gone except for those pieces under the mounts. These are: (1) the long 11¼in chape, which has a square end with a finial and is cut out at the other end, is plain on both sides except for a chased line; (2) the central locket, which bears on the obverse the inscription 'THIS ANCIENT SWORD THE PROPERTY OF THE BOROUGH OF SOUTHAMPTON WAS RESTORED AND RENOVATED BY A L McCALMONT ESQ JP MAYOR 1877–78'. The reverse bears the arms of the city; and (3) the long 8½in mouth-locket, which is plain and similar in design to the chape but with cut-outs on each side to close over the blade hooks. These are now somewhat damaged from being driven on too hard.

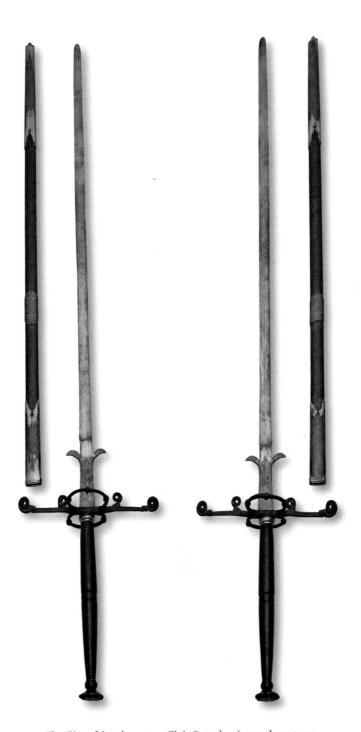

The City of Southampton Civic Sword – sixteenth century

Cap of Maintenance

There is no cap of maintenance as there is no sword-bearer.

Uniform

None.

Royal Wootton Bassett

Prerogative

There is no Royal charter or other authority for this bearing-sword. The town claims to have been part of the Honour (i.e. lands owned directly by the king) of Wallingford from the time of Alfred the Great and therefore to have the right to bear a sword, but there is no formal authority. The sword was presented to the town by one of their Members of Parliament, John Attersol, in 1812. It is believed to have cost 100 guineas.

The prefix 'Royal' was officially bestowed on the town on 16 October 2011 by the Princess Royal, who delivered letters patent on behalf of the Queen in recognition of the spontaneous respect accorded by the townspeople to the corteges of coffins bearing servicemen killed in Afghanistan which were repatriated through the town.

The Civic Sword – c. 1812

Length of sword	3ft 8¾in – 1.137m	Weight of sword	4lb 2oz – 1.871kg
Length of blade	2ft 10⅛in – 0.867m – Double-edged	Width of blade	2in – 0.051m
Length of hilt	10¼in – 0.260m – Two-handed	Width of guard	9⅛in – 0.232m
Length of scabbard	2ft 10¾in – 0.883m	Weight of scabbard	9¾oz – 0.275kg

Sword

The sword is a handsome weapon of good work for its period. The blade is quite plain. The hilt is gilt-brass. The quillon block has engraved leaf-work in an oval cartouche on each side. The quillons are short, broad but narrowing in the middle, and are well engraved with acanthus leaf-work. The tapering grip has a ferrule with a chevron pattern and is of ivory carved spirally and bound with silver wire. The bottom ferrule is part of the pommel, which is spherical, ends with a large flanged button and again is covered in leaf-work. Both sides are identical. The tang end is poor, uneven, rusty and hammered into the pommel.

Scabbard

The scabbard is covered with very worn and faded red velvet and has gold lace along each edge, with two slender bands marking thirds of the whole. It has four gilt-brass mounts. These are: (1) the chape, which is engraved with leaf-work on both sides; (2) this locket is engraved with leaf-work on both sides; (3) this locket bears the arms of James Kibblewhite Esq., MP for the borough in 1812, on the obverse, and leaf-work on the reverse; and (4) the mouth-locket, which has the borough arms on the obverse, and the arms of the donor, John Attersol, Esq., MP for the borough in 1812, on the reverse. Mounts (3) and (4) are bordered with acanthus leaf-work. Although the sword bears

The Royal Wootton Bassett Civic Sword – *c.* 1812

the arms of both representatives in Parliament, it was the gift of Mr Attersol only, while Mr Kibblewhite presented the borough with the mayor's and aldermen's robes.

Cap of Maintenance

There is no cap of maintenance: the sword-bearer wears a black tri-corn trimmed with gold braid but no flash and a single large white ostrich feather.

Uniform

The sword-bearer wears a maroon frock-coat with gold galloons around the collar, along the coat edges and around the cuffs. The buttonholes are also of gold braid. Gilt buttons adorn the facings and cuffs. The coat is worn with a maroon waistcoat, white shirt, white jabot, maroon breeches, black shoes with silver buckles and white cotton gloves.

Derby

Prerogative

There is no Royal charter or other authority for this bearing-sword. The sword was presented to the city in 1870 by the then mayor, Thomas Evans, who felt the previous wooden sword was inappropriate.

There is a spurious story about the sword being used by Queen Victoria in 1891 to confer a knighthood upon the then mayor, Alfred Seale Haslam, on platform one of Derby station just before she departed, and that she nicked his ear as the sword was so heavy. He was indeed knighted, but the sword used was that of her Equerry-in-Waiting and the venue was the retiring room, not the platform. This can be seen in a photo with description in a book of the visit held in the mayor's office.

It is processed at the annual mayor-making ceremony but, uniquely, is carried *behind* the mayor.

The Civic Sword – *c.* 1870

Length of sword	4ft 2½in – 1.283m	**Weight of sword**	6lb 2oz – 2.787kg
Length of blade	3ft 1⅝in – 0.955m – Double-edged	**Width of blade**	1¾in – 0.044m
Length of hilt	12⅞in – 0.327m – Two-handed	**Width of guard**	13¼in – 0.336m
Length of scabbard	3ft 6⅝in – 1.082m	**Weight of scabbard**	2lb 2oz – 0.965kg

Sword

This unremarkable sword, like most of the civic swords, is quite long and heavy. In the short fuller on one side of the blade are the words 'BOROUGH of DERBY. T. W. EVANS, Esqʳᵉ. MAYOR MAY 5TH, 1870'. There is a small ricasso and on one side almost hidden by the protecting plate is inscribed 'GEORGE ROBINSON Maker Birmingham'. The hilt is electro-gilt. The quillon block has protecting plate on each side and has a shield of the borough arms on each side. The massive flat quillons are richly decorated with *repoussé* leaf-work, splay out at the ends and curve slightly. The thickness is fairly normal and they are 1in deep at the block but 3½in at the ends. The grip is flat and narrow in the middle but quite wide at each end, and similarly decorated. The pommel is merely the curved end of the elaborate grip and ends in a small finial tang nut. Apart from the arms, the hilt is identical to that at Ipswich.

Scabbard

The scabbard is covered with purple velvet, which is much worn and split at one point, and has a gold lace galloon down the centre on one side only. There are three richly foliated gilt mounts. These are: (1) the exceptionally long chape with a horseshoe guard;

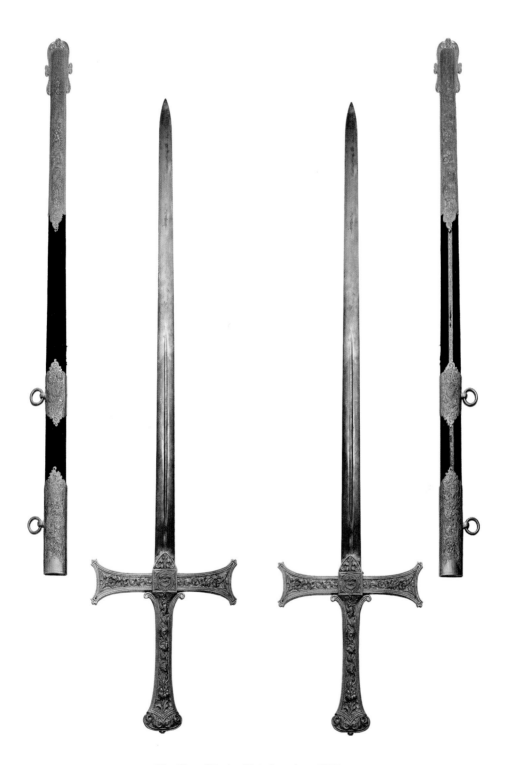

The City of Derby Civic Sword – *c.* 1870

(2) a central locket with a ring attached; and (3) a very long mouth-locket (18½in) with a ring attached and a blank cartouche on each side under the protecting plate. The rings appear to be merely decorative, as it would be very awkward to carry the sheathed sword from a baldric and virtually impossible to draw the sword.

Cap of Maintenance
There is no cap of maintenance as there is no permanent sword-bearer.

Uniform
There is no uniform; the civic attendant wears a dark suit, white shirt with Corporation tie, black shoes and white cotton gloves.

Ipswich

Prerogative

There is no Royal charter or other authority for this bearing-sword. The sword was presented to the city in 1887 by the then mayor, Edward Packard Jnr.

It is usual for the council to request that a member of one of the local cadet forces carry the sword. The council have found that they need to insist that the cadet is physically quite large due to the size and weight of the sword and scabbard.

The Civic Sword – *c.* 1887

Length of sword	4ft 8⅞in – 1.445m	Weight of sword	7lb 13½oz – 3.560kg
Length of blade	3ft 8in – 1.117m – Double-edged	Width of blade	2½in – 0.063m
Length of hilt	12⅞in – 0.327m – Two-handed	Width of guard	13in – 0.330m
Length of scabbard	3ft 8⅝in – 1.133m	Weight of scabbard	1lb 5oz – 0.594kg

Sword

The sword is etched over the lower half of its length with leaf-work. On one side, within a tree, is inscribed 'Presented by E Packard Jʳ Mayor 1887', and below that is inscribed 'In commemoration of the Queen's Jubilee'. On the other side is the royal cipher of 'VR' crowned, and below that the borough arms. There is a short ricasso with on one side the name of the maker, 'Freeman and Son, Fenchurch, London', and on the other a Star of David. Both are obscured by a protecting plate. The hilt is electro-gilt. The quillon block has on one side the borough arms, and on the other a small and somewhat battered shield shape but without identification. The massive flat quillons are richly decorated with *repoussé* leaf-work, splay at the ends and, unusually, curve slightly. The thickness is fairly normal and they are 1in deep at the block but 3½in deep at the ends. The grip is flat and narrow in the middle but quite wide at each end, and is similarly decorated. The pommel is merely the curved end of the elaborate grip and ends in a small finial tang nut. Apart from the arms, the hilt is identical to that at Derby, indicating the same maker.

Scabbard

The wooden scabbard is covered with very deep crimson, possibly purple, velvet with two electro-gilt mounts. The chape is 7½in long but plain on both sides. The mouth-locket is 7½in long and again plain, though rather battered, at the mouth itself. The scabbard is straight but bowed, having spent many years upright but leaning in a cupboard.

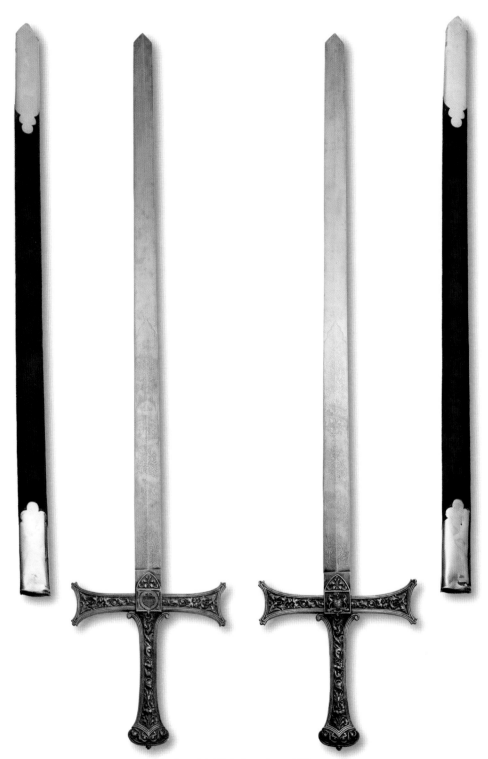

The Ipswich Civic Sword – *c.* 1887

Cap of Maintenance

There is no cap of maintenance as the sword-bearer is usually a local military cadet.

Uniform

Military uniform is worn with white cotton gloves.

Warrington

Prerogative

There is no Royal charter or other authority for this bearing-sword. The sword was presented to the town in 1897 by Henry Thornton to mark Queen Victoria's Diamond Jubilee.

The Civic Sword – 1897

Length of sword	3ft 9⅝in – 1.159m	Weight of sword	2lb 12¾oz – 1.271kg
Length of blade	2ft 10¼in – 0.870m – Double-edged	Width of blade	1¾in – 0.045m
Length of hilt	11⅜in – 0.289m – Two-handed	Width of guard	9⅛in – 0.232m
Length of scabbard	2ft 11¼in – 0.895m	Weight of scabbard	1lb 3¼oz – 0.545kg

Sword

This quite elegant sword was made by Elkington and Co. Ltd of Birmingham. The blade, which is in very good condition, is electroplated steel, with elaborate ornamental etching for 22½in. The fuller on each side is etched with foliage. This includes, on the obverse, a lion, a garb, a crossed fasces and mace, three castles, a rose, the emblems of Lancashire, Cheshire and the Boteler family, the royal arms of Queen Victoria etc., an inscription on either side of the fuller 'PRESENTED TO THE BOROUGH OF WARRINGTON BY HENRY THORNTON ESQUIRE OF "FEARNHEAD" WARRINGTON and IN COMMEMORATION OF THE 60th YEAR OF QUEEN VICTORIA'S REIGN JUNE 20th 1897', a unicorn rampant and a shield of six lions rampant, both part of the borough arms, and the motto '*DEUS DAT INCREMENTUM*'. On the reverse are a garb, an inscription '*ANNO DECIMO VICTORIA REGINA*', crossed flags, a pair of globes (?), a pair of roses, a pair of garbs, a pair of roses, a pair of lions rampant, a pair of larger roses and the royal arms, of Queen Victoria, within the Garter and crowned, with supporters and motto. The hilt is silver-gilt. The quillon block has a prominent lion's head on each side surrounded by roses and foliage. The quillons are square, curve upwards and terminate with a single lion's head which, unusually, faces inward. Two sides are chased with foliage and roses and the other two with oak leaves and acorns. The grip is covered in deep crimson velvet and bound with a single silver-gilt wire, now very loose. The pommel resembles a somewhat squashed sphere with, around the edge, four lions rampant in relief. There is a small segmented tang button.

Scabbard

The scabbard is covered with deep crimson velvet, with a silver-gilt strip down each edge and thirteen silver-gilt mounts. These are: (1) the chape, which is 6¾in long and has

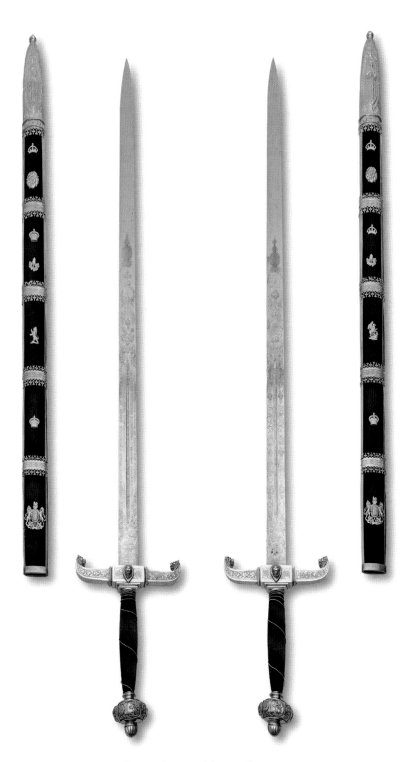

The Warrington Civic Sword – 1897

on the obverse a figure of Justice with sword and scales, ringed with foliage, and on the reverse a cartouche bearing a fasces. The borders are edged with fleur-de-lis; (2) a crown; (3) a rose; (4) a plain band; (5) a crown; (6) an acorn; (7) a plain band; (8) St George slaying the dragon (O) and a lion rampant (R); (9) a plain band; (10) a crown; (11) a plain band; (12) the royal arms of Queen Victoria, within the Garter and crowned, with supporters; and (13) a very short mouth-locket of just a ½in band. Mounts (2) to (7) and (9) to (13) are the same on both sides.

Cap of Maintenance

There is no cap of maintenance. The sword-bearer wears a tri-corn, trimmed with gold lace.

Uniform

The sword-bearer wears a dark blue robe with a collar edged with gold braid, with the borough arms over the left breast and another large one at the back, over a dark suit with white shirt, white jabot, black shoes and white cotton gloves.

Bath

Prerogative

There is no Royal charter or other authority for this bearing-sword. In 1900, the city was loaned an ancient sword dated 1523, said to have been found in the roof of a barn at Oriel Lodge, just outside Bath. The owners of the estate on which it had been found, Oriel College, Oxford, demanded its return; today it hangs in the college refectory. Robert Edmund Dickinson, who had been mayor in 1900, but was by then Member of Parliament for Bath, commissioned Wilkinson Sword to make a replica. He presented it to the city in 1902. It was presented on what was to have been the coronation day of Edward VII, but he was sick and crowned on a later day.

The sword is borne, incorrectly, unsheathed. An attempt was made by a recent mayor to have the scabbard refurbished/replaced, but it came to naught.

The Civic (Bladud) Sword – 1902

Length of sword	5ft 3⅞in – 1.622m	Weight of sword	7lb 5¾oz – 3.337kg
Length of blade	3ft 10½in – 1.181m – Double-edged	Width of blade	1¾in – 0.044m
Length of hilt	17⅜in – 0.441m – Two-handed	Width of guard	18½in – 0.470m
Length of scabbard	3ft 6⅛in – 1.069m	Weight of scabbard	1lb 5¼oz – 0.602kg

Sword

This very long sword, which is an exact replica of the original, has a fairly sharp etched blade, somewhat worn by cleaning. The shallow diamond-sectioned blade, which has a 7in ricasso with four striations on each side, with 4½in-wide hooks, has, on the obverse, a shield with three wavy lines across it and a 'P' to the left and a 'D' to the right. Below this is stamped the date 1523 (once over-stamped to read 1423), and is inscribed on the ricasso below with 'TO THE CORPORATION OF BATH THE GIFT OF ROBERT EDMUND DICKINSON, MP, MAYOR OF BATH 1899–1900 ON CORONATION DAY 1902'. On the reverse, there is a much-worn panel of leaf and scrollwork, and the letters 'P ? N A ? ? ? O ? P A R ? N A' (perhaps the original maker's name?), and below on the ricasso is inscribed 'THIS SWORD IS A REPRODUCTION OF THE CIVIC SWORD KNOWN AS THE BLADUD SWORD ORIGINALLY BELONGING TO THE CITY OF BATH BUT NOW DEPOSITED IN ORIEL COLLEGE, OXFORD', and below it 'MADE BY WILKINSON, PALL MALL, LONDON'. The iron cross-guard, which is rather loose, is simple with a large (7⅝in-wide) *pas-d'âne* of two concentric circles, the inner one ending with scrolls, with a capsule shape on the outside edge of each ring. The straight, octagonal quillons flair slightly near the ends and terminate with a similar capsule shape with a small finial. The grip is of wood covered with leather, which has then been ribbed

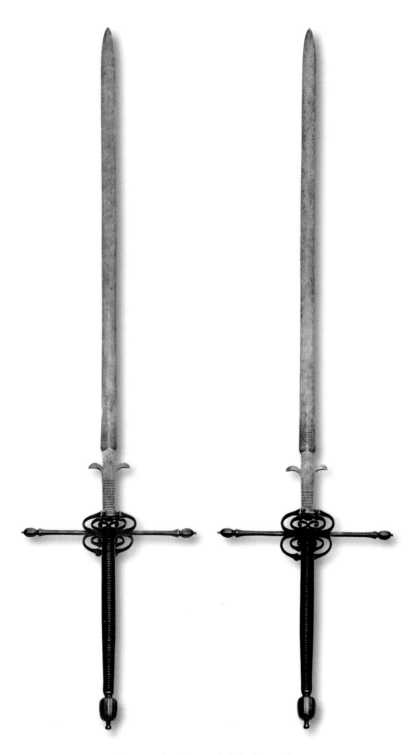

The City of Bath Civic (Bladud) Sword – 1902

(now a little worn). The pommel is essentially globular but with a flattened top and bottom. The side has fourteen facets and flattish bevelled ends. The tang nut is shaped like a top and is slightly rusty. For many years the two inscriptions were hidden by black wire in an attempt to conceal the fact that the sword was a reproduction.

Scabbard

The scabbard is covered in much-worn black leather with two metal mounts, a chape and a mouth-locket. Both are plain, basic and need replacement, as does the leather.

Cap of Maintenance

Although not entitled to one, the cap of maintenance is in the winter style and of sable. There is no crown and the sides are free-standing.

Uniform

A green serge beggar's costume, similar to a 'Robin Hood' tunic, is worn, with scalloped sleeves with deep red lining and embellishment and a large embroidered badge of the city arms on the left sleeve, with a chain drooped round the shoulders and secured with deep red bows. The costume is worn over black velvet breeches, black stockings, black shoes with silver buckles and brown leather gloves.

Durham

Prerogative

For some eighteen years between 1895 and 1913, Durham appears to have borne a civic sword before the mayor without any royal authority.

However, in answer to a Prayer to the King, on 3 May 1913, George V granted 'the privilege of bearing within the confines of the said City a sword ornamented with the royal arms which should be borne before the Mayor erect and sheathed and that the bearer of the sword might be attired in an appropriate cap or hat to which no special name of significance should be attributed'. The Earl of Durham presented a Sword of State to the city in 1913 to commemorate his being elected mayor of the city.

The city has two swords.

The Civic Sword – 1895

Length of sword	3ft 11⅜in – 1.203m	Weight of sword	3lb 3¼oz – 1.454kg
Length of blade	3ft 3⅛in – 0.994m – Double-edged	Width of blade	2⅛in – 0.054m
Length of hilt	8¼in – 0.210m – Two-handed	Width of guard	7⅞in – 0.200m
Length of scabbard	3ft 3¼in – 0.997m	Weight of scabbard	14oz – 0.394kg

Sword

This sword is of modern manufacture. The blade is in extremely good condition and is etched for the first 8in. It bears the inscription 'Edward Jepson MD Mayor 1895 – DURHAM CORPORATION' above a shield with the city cross set between '18' and '95' on the obverse, and 'F. Barnes & Co London' on the reverse. The rather short quillons are chased with foliage, taper toward the ends and terminate in leaf-shaped bosses. The quillon block has a protecting plate over the scabbard on each side. The grip is wire-bound and the pommel is small and pear-shaped with flattened sides, and is chased with foliage. It has a small tang button. The sword should be viewed point down.

Scabbard

The scabbard is covered with black leather with two brass mounts: the chape (1) is simple and decorated with leaf-work on the obverse, while the reverse is plain; (2) the mouth-locket, which is 6½in long, bears the inscription 'Edward Jepson MD Mayor 1895 – DURHAM CORPORATION' above a shield with the city cross set between '18' and '95' on the obverse, while the reverse is plain. The scabbard should be viewed point down.

The City of Durham Civic Sword – 1895

The Sword of State – 1913

Length of sword	4ft 1⅜in – 1.254m	Weight of sword	5lb 1¼oz – 2.305kg
Length of blade	3ft 0⅜in – 0.924m – Double-edged	Width of blade	1½in – 0.038m
Length of hilt	13in – 0.330m – Two-handed	Width of guard	13½in – 0.343m
Length of scabbard	3ft 2in – 0.966m	Weight of scabbard	1lb 11oz – 0.763kg

Sword

The blade of this beautiful sword is decorated for the first 25in. On the obverse, the fuller bears the inscription 'PRESENTED TO THE MAYOR AND CORPORATION OF THE CITY OF DURHAM BY JOHN GEORGE THIRD EARL OF DURHAM KG 1913'. Above this are three simple shields, being representations of the arms of the Earl of Durham, the County of Durham and the City of Durham. On the ricasso is etched the name of the maker 'HENRY WILKINSON PALL MALL LONDON'. The reverse is decorated with scrolls, leaf-work and other patterns, and ends with a Star of David and a fleur-de-lis between each point. The square hilt is silver-gilt. The raised quillon block bears the royal arms of George V, within the Garter and crowned, with supporters and motto on the obverse, and a rose on the reverse. The square quillons are box-shaped, straight and decorated in relief with two roses on top and bottom on each quillon and three roses on each side of each quillon. They terminate in foliated, bulbous ends with a rose in relief on each. The grip is bound with gilt wire. The pommel is pear-shaped with four slightly proud shoulders and is decorated with acanthus leaves. There is a small tang button. This sword should also be viewed point down.

Scabbard

The scabbard is covered with purple velvet, the colour of the old Palatine of Durham, with five silver-gilt mounts and a gold lace galloon from chape to mouth-locket on the reverse. These are: (1) the chape, which is 7⅝in long, chased with foliage on each side and is topped with a button finial; (2) this locket bears the enamelled arms of the Earl of Durham (O) and a rose (R); (3) this locket bears the enamelled arms of the County of Durham (O) and a rose (R); (4) this locket bears the enamelled arms of the City of Durham (O) and a rose (R); and (5) the mouth-locket, which is chased with foliage on each side, ends with a raised ring round the throat. Again the scabbard should be viewed point down.

The top part of the scabbard is free of mounts, while the lower part bears three. This is most unusual, as all other scabbards viewed have mounts equidistant from each other. It is extremely probable that these three mounts were originally symmetrically spaced between the chape and mouth-locket and have slid down, without correction, over the years. It is recommended that they be restored to their original positions.

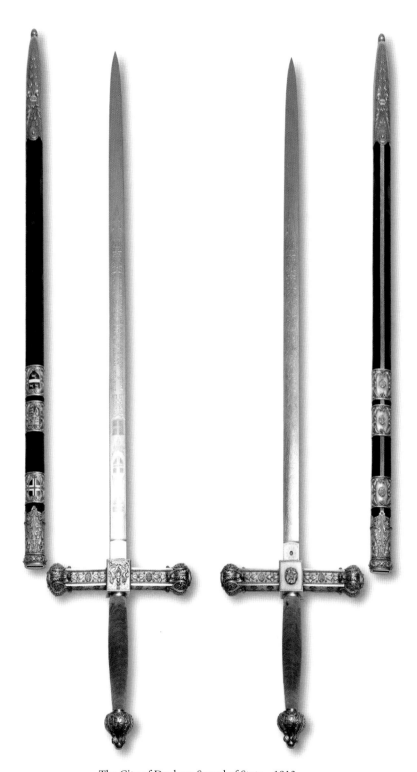

The City of Durham Sword of State – 1913

Cap of Maintenance

There is no cap of maintenance. The sword-bearer wears a black velvet 'Tudor bonnet' that is in keeping with the sentiments of the grant.

Uniform

The sword-bearer wears a black academic robe trimmed with gold over a dark suit with white shirt, blue corporation tie, black shoes and white cotton gloves.

Stratford upon Avon

Prerogative

There is no Royal charter or other authority for this bearing-sword. The sword comes from a well-known group of swords dating from the late fifteenth and early sixteenth century. The closest known parallel to it is the sword preserved with other Drake relics at Buckland Abbey, Devon. Swords of similar design are also to be found in the Tower of London. This example was possibly acquired and first used as 'stage-property' in the pageant play, or riding, of St George and the Dragon produced annually in pre-Reformation times. It is said to have been borne before the High Bailiffs of Stratford upon Avon in 'early years' before the incorporation of the borough by Edward VI in 1553. Its use on civic occasions was revived on Shakespeare Sunday, 30 April 1916. By 1977, the sword and scabbard had deteriorated badly and the council asked the Royal Engineers to undertake a complete refurbishment.

The Civic Sword – c. 1470–1500

Length of sword	4ft 10⅞in – 1.495m	Weight of sword	5lb 7oz – 2.465kg
Length of blade	3ft 5½in – 1.054m – Double-edged	Width of blade	1⅝in – 0.041m
Length of hilt	17⅜in – 0.441m – Two-handed	Width of guard	16⅝in – 0.423m
Length of scabbard	3ft 5½in – 1.054m	Weight of scabbard	15oz – 0.428kg

Sword

This large sword has a tapering steel blade, which has rather battered edges towards the point. The plain hilt is of iron. The quillon block is simple, while the quillons are narrow, circular and terminate with small bosses. The hollow grip is of metal with a tan leather covering. The pommel is spherical and plain. The tang end is flat.

Scabbard

The tan-coloured leather scabbard has two brass mounts. These are: (1) the chape, which is short and plain but badly damaged at the tip where the blade pokes through; and (2) the mouth-locket, which is plain. A comment in the local history of the sword states, 'the brass mount from the mouth of the scabbard, and the brass strips which connected it with the middle locket have been missing for many years.' The sword is very tight in the scabbard which is very whippy rather than the usual stiff type and appears to be quite modern which might explain the loss of the middle locket. The stitching on the reverse needs attention.

The Stratford upon Avon Civic Sword – *c.* 1470–1500

Cap of Maintenance

There is no cap of maintenance, the sword-bearer being a member of the local yeomanry.

Uniform

Military uniform with white cotton gloves.

Winchester

Prerogative

There is no Royal charter or other authority for this bearing-sword. The sword was presented to the city in 1957 by a former mayor, Vera Dilys Neate, and her husband, Councillor Eric Neate, to mark their silver wedding in 1956. It is not processed but is displayed sheathed on special occasions.

The Civic Sword – 1957

Length of sword	3ft 7⅛in – 1.096m	Weight of sword	3lb 13¾oz – 1.751kg
Length of blade	2ft 8¼in – 0.819m – Double-edged	Width of blade	1⅞in – 0.047m
Length of hilt	11⅛in – 0.282m – Two-handed	Width of guard	9½in – 0.241m
Length of scabbard	2ft 9½in – 0.851m	Weight of scabbard	2lb 1oz – 0.929kg

Sword

The sword was designed by A.G. Styles and manufactured by Garrard & Co. Ltd, the Crown Jewellers. The blade is of finely tempered steel, now rather marked, with a 1½in ricasso. The obverse is etched along the blade with the inscription 'The gift of Eric and Dilys Neate to the City of Winchester * 8th August 1956'. The hilt is richly gilt and is of sturdy proportions. The quillon block has slight écussons over a recessed socket. The quillons, which have a flat lower side and a curved upper edge, curve towards the point and taper towards the ends, that turn up and terminate in a square section with small lion mask on each end. The grip is formed with alternating plain bands and a double-twisted wire. The globular pommel is slightly ovoid and has raised enamelled shields, pressed into shallow recesses on each face of the pommel, showing the full arms of the city on top of a sunburst surrounded by leaf garlands on each face. The sides are smooth. There is a small tang nut. The sword should be viewed point down.

Scabbard

The scabbard is covered with red leather with fifteen silver-gilt mounts and a silver-gilt band along each edge. Each side is identical. These are: (1) the mouth-locket, which fits into a socket in the hilt, and is chased and features the central section of the city arms; (2) this is an elongated star; (3) the shape of this locket is defined by the four 'W's repeated upon a cross form and including sprigs of rose leaves, and bears the Dragon or Wyvern of Wessex within the Hampshire Rose; (4) this locket bears the badge of The Royal Hampshire Regiment; (5) the shape of this locket is defined by the four 'W's repeated upon a cross form and including sprigs of rose leaves, and bears the 'lion passant guardant Or' – the lion of England; (6) an elongated star; (7) the shape is defined

The City of Winchester Civic Sword – 1957

by the four 'W's repeated upon a cross form and including sprigs of rose leaves, and bears the arms of the See with the Bishop's mitre; (8) this locket bears the badge of The King's Royal Rifle Corps; (9) the shape of this locket is defined by the four 'W's repeated upon a cross form and including sprigs of rose leaves, and bears the triple-turreted castle of the city arms, derived from Eleanor of Castile and used on the silver seal of the city granted by Edward I; (10) this locket is an elongated star; (11) the shape of this locket is defined by the four 'W's repeated upon a cross form and including sprigs of rose leaves, and bears the two 'E's indicative of the reigns of Elizabeth I and Elizabeth II; (12) this locket bears the badge of The Rifle Brigade; (13) the shape of this locket is defined by the four 'W's repeated upon a cross form and including sprigs of rose leaves, and bears the arms of Winchester College; (14) this locket is an elongated star; and (15) the chape, which bears the figure of King Alfred holding aloft a sword – point down – and holding a shield while standing upon symbolic references to his work – the scales of justice, the book of learning and the anchor, symbolising the creation by him of the navy. Immediately about this figure and along the edges are sprigs of rose leaves. There is no finial. The four 'W's are set in a wavy border and get smaller nearer the chape. The scabbard needs to be viewed point down.

Cap of Maintenance

There is no cap of maintenance as there is no sword-bearer.

Uniform

None.

Dewsbury

Prerogative

There is no Royal charter or other authority for this bearing-sword. The sword was presented to the mayor by John Long, a former mace-bearer, in about 1972; however, there is no record of provenance. In the 1974 local government reorganisation, Dewsbury became part of Kirklees Metropolitan Borough Council. Kirklees (based in Huddersfield) retained the office of mayor, while Dewsbury lost its entitlement to have a mayor. Today the sheathed sword languishes in a small cabinet in the old mayor's office in the Town Hall and is not processed.

The Civic Sword – unknown

Length of sword	4ft 2⅝in – 1.286m	Weight of sword	3lb 7¼oz – 1.537kg
Length of blade	3ft 0⅛in – 0.917m – Double-edged	Width of blade	2in – 0.051m
Length of hilt	14½in – 0.368m – Two-handed	Width of guard	11¼in – 0.286m
Length of scabbard	3ft 0⅞in – 0.937m	Weight of scabbard	1lb 2¾oz – 0.531kg

Sword

This unremarkable sword has a simple tapering blade which is slightly discoloured but without embellishment. The brass cross-guard has an oblong centre, is flat and tapers a little towards the ends, which curve slightly upward. The grip is bound with galvanised (?) wire. The brass pommel is spherical and segmented. There is no tang button or sign of one, but perhaps a screw fitting. It bears no marks.

Scabbard

The wooden, tapered and box-shaped scabbard appears to have been homemade. It is covered with red velvet which has been glued on and is now coming loose. There are no proper mounts. Black and gold lace galloons in a double zigzag pattern are glued along each edge and are also used to replace the usual metal chape and mouth-locket. Two embroidered badges – one of crossed maces, the insignia of the Guild of Mace-bearers, and the other of the town arms – are sewn onto one side of the covering; the other side is blank.

Cap of Maintenance

There is no cap of maintenance as there is no sword-bearer.

Uniform

None.

The Dewsbury Civic Sword – Unknown

Leeds

Prerogative

There is no Royal charter or other authority for this bearing sword. The sword was presented to the city in 2003 by the Trustees of the Royal Armouries Museum.

It is not processed but is displayed sheathed in the City Hall.

The Civic Sword – 2003

Length of sword	4ft 9⅞in – 1.467m	Weight of sword	5lb 9¼oz – 2.531kg
Length of blade	3ft 9⅛in – 1.146m – Double-edged	Width of blade	2⅝in – 0.067m
Length of hilt	12¾in – 0.324m – Two-handed	Width of guard	11⅜in – 0.289m
Length of scabbard	3ft 10in – 1.168m	Weight of scabbard	1lb 12½oz – 0.810kg

Sword

The civic sword was designed by John Waller, the then head of Interpretation at the Royal Armouries. It has a large plain diamond-shaped, unadorned but very shiny blade from India and was totally custom-built by John Truscott, the 'gunmaker' at the Royal Armouries. The decorative elements are all closely connected with the full arms of Leeds. The hilt is gilt. The quillon block has small écussons and bears three raised mullets on each side. The square quillons rise slightly and the terminals were cast in the form of crowned owls (the supporters in the arms) on each side on each end. The grip is made of two pieces of black ebonite with a gilt band around the centre, engraved with the words *'PRO REGE ET LEGE'* ('For King and Law') from the Leeds arms. The gilt pear-drop-shaped pommel, cast in bronze and gilded, is decorated with the lamb suspended on both sides (the 'dead' sheep or fleece motif). The sword should be viewed point down.

Scabbard

The scabbard is covered with royal blue leather, with four silver-gilt decorative clasps. These are: (1) the mouth-locket, which is cut out, bears the city arms, including the supporting owls; (2) this locket bears the inscription 'THE LEEDS SWORD PRESENTED TO THE LORD MAYOR OF LEEDS COUNCILLOR BRYAN NORTH AND THE CORPORATION OF THE CITY OF LEEDS BY THE TRUSTEES OF THE ROYAL ARMOURIES … IN COMMEMORATION OF THE CLOSE TIES BETWEEN THE CITY OF LEEDS AND THE ROYAL ARMOURIES MUSEUM ST. GEORGES DAY 23RD APRIL 2003'; (3) this locket bears St George and the Dragon, in recognition of the day of presentation; and (4) the chape, which is plain. The reverse of the mounts is plain. The scabbard needs to be viewed point down.

The City of Leeds Civic Sword – 2003

Cap of Maintenance

There is no cap of maintenance as there is no sword-bearer.

Uniform

None.

APPENDIX 1

KINGS AND QUEENS

Towns and cities given, or believed to have been given, Royal charters or gifted swords by the sovereign are shown in red, by the Lord Protector in blue, or by another in green.

Monarch	Years	Duration	Towns and Cities
The House of Wessex (restored)			
Edward II (The Confessor)	1042–1066	23 years	
Harold II (Godwinesson)	1066	10 months	
Edgar (The Atheling) (proclaimed but not crowned)	1066	2 months	
The House of Normandy			
William I (The Conqueror)	1066–1087	20 years	
William II (Rufus)	1087–1100	12 years	
Henry I	1100–1135	35 years	
Stephen	1135–1154	18 years	
The House of Plantagenet			
Henry II	1154–1189	34 years	
Richard I (The Lionheart)	1189–1199	9 years	
John	1199–1216	17 years	
Henry III	1216–1272	56 years	
Edward I (Longshanks)	1272–1307	34 years	
Edward II	1307–1327	19 years	
Edward III	1327–1377	50 years	London (pre-1387), Bristol (1373)

Monarch	Years	Duration	Towns and Cities
Richard II	1377–1399	22 years	Coventry (pre-1384), Lincoln (1386), York (1388), Newcastle upon Tyne (1391), Calais (1392), Chester (1394)
The House of Lancaster			
Henry IV	1399–1413	13 years	Dublin (1403), Norwich (1404)
Henry V	1413–1422	9 years	
Henry VI	1422–1461	39 years	Kingston upon Hull (1440), King's Lynn (1446), Oxford (pre-1446)
The House of York			
Edward IV	1461–1470	9 years	Waterford (1461), Drogheda (1468)
House of Lancaster (restored)			
Henry VI	1470–1471	9 months	
House of York (restored)			
Edward IV	1471–1483	12 years	Hereford (pre-1475)
Edward V	1483	2 months	
Richard III	1483–1485	2 years	Gloucester (1483)
The House of Tudor			
Henry VII	1485–1509	23 years	Exeter (1497)
Henry VIII	1509–1547	37 years	Carmarthen (1546)
Edward VI	1547–1553	6 years	
Jane	1553	14 days	
Mary	1553–1558	5 years	
Elizabeth I	1558–1603	44 years	Thetford (1573), Limerick (1575)

Monarch	Years	Duration	Towns and Cities
The House of Stuart			
James I	1603–1625	22 years	Clonmel (1608), Canterbury (1608), Kilkenny (1609), Edinburgh (1609), Galway (1610), Londonderry (1613), Worcester (1622)
Charles I	1625–1649	23 years	Kendal (1636), Carlisle (1637), Shrewsbury (1638)
The Commonwealth			
Rump Parliament	1649–1653	4 years	
Nominated Assembly	1653	5 months	
Oliver Cromwell	1653–1658	5 years	Salisbury (1656)
Richard Cromwell	1658–1659	8 months	
The House of Stuart (restored)			
Charles II	1660–1685	24 years	Wigan (1662), Appleby (1670), Hertford (1680), Bury St Edmunds (1684), Great Yarmouth (1684)
James II	1685–1688	3 years	Lichfield (1686)
William & Mary	1689–1702 (Mary 1689–1694 only)	13 years	Liverpool (1695)
Anne	1702–1714	12 years	Carrickfergus (1712)
The House of Hanover			
George I	1714–1727	12 years	
George II	1727–1760	33 years	
George III	1760–1820	59 years	Southampton (1801?), Wootton Bassett (1812)
George IV	1820–1830	10 years	
William IV	1830–1837	7 years	

Monarch	Years	Duration	Towns and Cities
Victoria	1837–1901	63 years	Derby (1870), Ipswich (1877), Warrington (1897)
The House of Saxe-Coburg			
Edward VII	1901–1910	9 years	Bath (1902)
The House of Windsor			
George V	1910–1936	25 years	Durham (1913), Stratford upon Avon (1916)
Edward VIII	1936	10 months	
George VI	1936–1952	15 years	
Elizabeth II	1952-		Winchester (1959), Dewsbury (1972), Leeds (2003)

APPENDIX 2

SUMMARY AND COMPARISON OF SWORDS BY AGE AND OTHER CRITERIA

CITY/TOWN	AGE OF SWORD OR OLDEST PART	AUTHORITY – CHARTER OR GIFT DATE	ROYAL ARMS ON SWORD	ROYAL ARMS ON SCABBARD	SCABBARD COVERING	ÉCUSSON	HANDS	EDGES
Fourteenth Century								
St George's Chapel, Windsor	14th C	N/A					2	2
Westminster Abbey	14th C	N/A					2	2
City of Bristol 1 – Mourning	Pre-1367	1373	Edw III	Edw III	Black velvet		2	2
City of Lincoln 1 – State	Pre-1367	1386	Edw III	Rich II/Edw VI	Crimson velvet		2	2
City of Dublin 1 – State	1390	1403		Stuart/Will III	Crimson velvet	Yes	2	2
City of Bristol 2 – Pearl	Pre-1399	1373	Rich II	EIIR cipher	Crimson velvet		2	2
Fifteenth Century								
City of York 1 – Sigismund	1416	1388	Hen IV		Crimson velvet		2	2
Manx 1 – State	1417 or 1422	1417			Black leather	Yes	2	2
Tower of London 1	Early 15th C	N/A					2	2
Tower of London 2	Early 15th C	N/A					2	2
City of Coventry 1 – State	c. 1430	Pre-1384		Cha II	Crimson velvet		2	2
City of Kingston upon Hull 1 – State	1440	1440	Hen VI/Geo III		Blue velvet	Yes	2	2
Kings Lynn	c. 1446	1446	Hen VIII scrip	Cha II/Hen VIII	Crimson velvet		2	2

CITY/TOWN	AGE OF SWORD OR OLDEST PART	AUTHORITY – CHARTER OR GIFT DATE	ROYAL ARMS ON SWORD	ROYAL ARMS ON SCABBARD	SCABBARD COVERING	ÉCUSSON	HANDS	EDGES
City of Newcastle upon Tyne 1 – State	c. 1460	1391		Geo III	Crimson velvet	Yes	2	2
City of Waterford 1 – Edward IV	1461	1461			Black velvet		2	2
City of Coventry 2 – Museum	1461–83	Pre-1384			No scabbard	Yes	2	2
Stratford upon Avon	c. 1470–1500	None			Tan leather		2	2
City of Gloucester 1 – Mourning	c. 1483	1483			Black velvet	Yes	2	2
City of Lincoln 2 – Mourning	c. 1486	1386			Black velvet		2	2
City of Chester	c. 1490	1394			Crimson velvet		2	2
City of Exeter 1 – State	c. 1497	1497	Jam I	Mary	Crimson velvet	Yes	2	2
City of Bristol 3 – Lent	c. 1499	1373	Hen VII	Hen VII	Black velvet		2	2
City of Hereford 1 – Mourning	Late 15th C	Pre-1475	Edw IV	Edw IV	Black velvet	Yes	2	2
Sixteenth Century								
City of Dublin 2 – Kings or City	16th C	1461			No scabbard	Yes	2	2
City of Worcester 1 – Old	16th C	1622			No scabbard	Yes	2	2

CITY/TOWN	AGE OF SWORD OR OLDEST PART	AUTHORITY – CHARTER OR GIFT DATE	ROYAL ARMS ON SWORD	ROYAL ARMS ON SCABBARD	SCABBARD COVERING	ECUSSON	HANDS	EDGES
City of Worcester 2 – Mourning	16th C	1622			No scabbard		2	2
City of Southampton	16th C	None			Brown leather		2	2
Scotland	1507	N/A			Crimson velvet		2	2
City of Carlisle	1509	1637			Purple velvet		2	2
City of Waterford 2 – State	1536	1461	Hen VIII		Crimson velvet	Yes	2	2
City of York 2 – Bowes	1545	1388			Crimson velvet		2	2
City of Norwich – State	1545	1404	Anne	Hen VIII/Cha IIx2	Crimson velvet		2	2
City of London 1 – Pearl	1554?	Pre-1373			Crimson velvet		2	2
City of London 2 – Old Bailey	1563?	Pre-1373	Geo IV	Geo (I, II or III)	Crimson velvet		2	2
City of Limerick	1575	1575			No scabbard	Yes	2	2
City of Exeter 2 – Mourning	c. 1577–78	1497			Black crepe	Yes	2	2
Seventeenth Century								
City of Derry 1 – O'Doherty	Pre-1608	1613			Crimson velvet	Yes	2	2

CITY/TOWN	AGE OF SWORD OR OLDEST PART	AUTHORITY – CHARTER OR GIFT DATE	ROYAL ARMS ON SWORD	ROYAL ARMS ON SCABBARD	SCABBARD COVERING	ÉCUSSON	HANDS	EDGES
City of Canterbury 1 – State	1608	1608	Jam I		Crimson velvet	Yes	2	2
City of Kilkenny	1609	1609		Jam I	Red leather	Yes	2	2
City of Galway	1610	1610		WM cipher	Crimson velvet	Yes	2	2
City of London 3 – Mourning	1615 or 1623	Pre-1373			Black velvet		2	2
City of Derry 2 – State	1616	1613			Crimson velvet	Yes	2	2
Royal 1 – Mercy or Curtana	1626?	N/A			Crimson velvet	Yes	1	2
Royal 2 – Spiritual Justice	1626?	N/A			Crimson velvet	Yes	1	2
Royal 3 – Temporal Justice	1626?	N/A			Crimson velvet	Yes	1	2
City of Edinburgh	1627	1609	Cha I medal		Crimson velvet		2	2
City of Gloucester 2 – State	c. 1627	1483	Cha II	Cha II	Crimson velvet	Yes	2	2
Shrewsbury 1 – Old	1638	1638	Cha I		No scabbard		2	2
City of Lincoln 3 – Charles III	c. 1642	1386			Purple velvet		2	2

CITY/TOWN	AGE OF SWORD OR OLDEST PART	AUTHORITY – CHARTER OR GIFT DATE	ROYAL ARMS ON SWORD	ROYAL ARMS ON SCABBARD	SCABBARD COVERING	ÉCUSSON	HANDS	EDGES
City of Worcester 3 – State	1655	1622	Will III x 2	Will III + 'GR'	Crimson velvet		2	2
City of Clonmel	1656	1608			Crimson velvet		2	?
City of Drogheda	Mid-17th C	1468		Stuart	Crimson velvet		2	2
Kendal	c. 1660	1636	Cha II		Black velvet	Yes	2	2
Royal 4 – Irish	c. 1660–61	N/A	Will III	Geo (I, II or III)	Crimson velvet		2	2
Wigan	c. 1662	1662		Cha II	Crimson velvet		2	2
Shrewsbury 2 – State	1669	1638	Cha II		Blue velvet		2	2
City of London 4 – State (Sunday)	c. 1670	Pre-1373	Geo IV/Cha II	Geo IV/Cha II	Crimson velvet		2	2
Appleby	c. 1670	None	Cha II		Crimson velvet		2	2
City of Hereford 2 – State	1677	Pre-1475		Cha II x 2	Crimson velvet		2	2
Thetford	1678	1573		Cha II + cipher	Crimson velvet		2	2
Royal 5 – Great	1678	N/A		Will III	Crimson velvet		2	2
Carmarthen	c. 1680	1546		Cha II	Red velvet		2	2
Hertford	c. 1680	1680	Cha II	Cha II	Crimson velvet		2	2
Bury St Edmunds	c. 1684	1684		Cha II	Crimson velvet		2	2
Great Yarmouth	c. 1684	1684		Cha II	Crimson velvet		2	2

CITY/TOWN	AGE OF SWORD OR OLDEST PART	AUTHORITY – CHARTER OR GIFT DATE	ROYAL ARMS ON SWORD	ROYAL ARMS ON SCABBARD	SCABBARD COVERING	ECUSSON	HANDS	EDGES
City of Lichfield 1 – State	1686	1686	Jam II	Jam II x 2	Crimson velvet		2	2
Eighteenth Century								
Manx 2 – Atholl	1704 or 1724	1417			Blue velvet		2	2
Carrickfergus	1712	1712	Anne	Anne	Crimson velvet		2	2
City of Lincoln 4 – George III	1734	1386	Geo II	Vic	Crimson velvet		2	2
City of Bristol 4 – State	1752	1373		Geo II	Crimson velvet		2	2
City of Liverpool 1 – State	1764	1695		Geo III (portrait)	Purple velvet		2	2
City of Newcastle upon Tyne 2 – Second	c. 1791	1391			Crimson velvet		2	2
Nineteenth Century								
Royal Wootton Bassett	c. 1812	None			Red velvet		2	2
Royal 6 – Offering (Jewelled)	1820	N/A	Geo IV		Gold/jewelled		1	2
City of London 5 – Justice Room	c. 1830	Pre-1373		Vic	Crimson velvet		2	2
City of Lichfield 2 – St Mary's	c. 1840	1686	Vic		No scabbard		(2)	2

CITY/TOWN	AGE OF SWORD OR OLDEST PART	AUTHORITY – CHARTER OR GIFT DATE	ROYAL ARMS ON SWORD	ROYAL ARMS ON SCABBARD	SCABBARD COVERING	ÉCUSSON	HANDS	EDGES
City of Derby	c. 1870	None			Purple velvet		2	2
Ipswich	c. 1887	None	Vic cipher		Crimson velvet		2	2
City of Durham 1 – Old	1895	1913			Black leather		2	2
Warrington	1897	None	Vic	Vic	Crimson velvet		2	2
Twentieth Century								
City of Bath	1902	None			Black leather		2	2
City of Durham 2 – State	1913	1913	Geo V		Purple velvet		2	2
City of Winchester	1957	None			Red leather	Yes	2	2
City of London 6 – Travelling	1962	Pre-1373	Eliz II	Eliz II	Crimson velvet		2	2
Dewsbury	c. 1972	None			Red velvet		2	2
City of Canterbury 2 – Vision	1988	1608	EIIR cipher		Brown leather		2	2
Twenty-first Century								
City of Leeds	2003	None			Blue leather	Yes	2	2

SUMMARY AND COMPARISON OF SWORDS BY MEASUREMENT (IMPERIAL)

CITY/TOWN	LENGTH SWORD	BLADE	HILT	SCABBARD	WIDTH BLADE	CROSS	WEIGHT SWORD	SCABBARD	LENGTH TOTAL[1]	WEIGHT TOTAL[2]
Royal – Tower of London 1	7ft 7in	5ft 5in	26in	Nil	3⅛in	24½in	14lb 6oz	Nil	7ft 8in[4]	14lb 6oz[5]
Royal – Tower of London 2	7ft 5in	5ft 6in	23in	Nil	3in	23¼in	14lb 3oz	Nil	7ft 6in[4]	14lb 4oz[5]
Royal – Westminster Abbey	7ft 3in	5ft 4in	23in	Nil	3½in	24½in	18lb 0oz	Nil	7ft 4in[4]	18lb 0oz[5]
Royal – St George's Chapel, Windsor	6ft 8¼in	5ft 4in	16¼in	Nil	2¼in	16in	9lb 12½oz	Nil	6ft 9¼in[4]	9lb 12½oz[5]
City of Southampton	5ft 9in	4ft 2½in	18½in	3ft 10½in[3]	2in	17¼in	7lb 8½oz	1lb 10oz	5ft 10½in[3]	9lb 2½oz
City of Bath	5ft 3⅞in	3ft 10½in	17⅜in	3ft 6⅛in[3]	1¾in	18½in	7lb 5¾oz	1lb 5¼oz	5ft 4⅜in[3]	8lb 11oz
Stratford upon Avon	4ft 10⅞in	3ft 5½in	17⅜in	3ft 5½in	1⅝in	16⅝in	5lb 7oz	0lb 15oz	4ft 10⅞in	6lb 6oz
City of Leeds	4ft 9⅞in	3ft 9⅛in	12¾in	3ft 10in	2⅝in	11⅜in	5lb 9¼oz	1lb 12½oz	4ft 10¾in	7lb 5½oz
City of Waterford 2 – Henry VIII	4ft 9⅝in	3ft 8½in	13⅛in	3ft 8⅜in	1⅛in	18¼in	5lb 5½oz	1lb 2¾oz	4ft 9½in	6lb 8¼oz
Ipswich	4ft 8⅞in	3ft 8in	12⅞in	3ft 8⅝in	2½in	13in	7lb 13½oz	1lb 5oz	4ft 9½in	9lb 3½oz
City of Bristol 4 – State	4ft 8in	3ft 5⅜in	15in	4ft 2 ¾in	4¼in	17⅛in	11lb 6oz	10lb 0oz	5ft 5¾in	21lb 6oz
City of Dublin 1 – Great	4ft 6⅝in	3ft 7¼in	11⅜in	3ft 7⅝in	2¾in	16¾in	7lb 12oz	3lb 2oz	4ft 7in	10lb 14oz
City of Galway	4ft 6½in	3ft 2¾in	15¾in	3ft 4¼in	2¼in	15⅞in	5lb 6¾oz	1lb 1¾	4ft 8in	6lb 8½oz
Scotland	4ft 6¼in	3ft 3in	15¼in	4ft 2⅜in	1¾in	17¼in	6lb 0oz	5lb 0oz	5ft 5⅝in	11lb 0oz
City of Worcester 3 – State	4ft 5¾in	3ft 2⅛in	15¼in	3ft 3⅛in	2in	16¾in	7lb 0¼oz	2lb 6oz	4ft 6⅜in	9lb 6oz
City of Newcastle upon Tyne 2 – Second	4ft 5½in	3ft 4⅛in	13⅜in	3ft 5in	1⅝in	10½in	4lb 10¼oz	0lb 11½oz	4ft 6⅜in	5lb 5¾oz
City of Lichfield 1 – State	4ft 4⅜in	3ft 3½in	12⅞in	3ft 4¼in	2in	15½in	4lb 8oz	2lb 4¼oz	4ft 5⅛in	6lb 12¼oz
Great Yarmouth	4ft 4⅜in	3ft 1½in	14¾in	3ft 2¾in	1⅞in	13in	5lb 1oz	2lb 2¼oz	4ft 5½in	7lb 3¼oz
Limerick	4ft 4⅛in	3ft 7½in	8½in	Nil	1¾in	15⅜in	4lb 1oz	Nil	4ft 5⅛in[4]	4lb 1oz[5]
City of York 1 – Sigismund	4ft 4in	3ft 3⅛in	12⅞in	3ft 4¾in	2¾in	13in	8lb 9oz	1lb 5¾oz	4ft 5⅝in	9lb 14½oz
Shrewsbury 2 – State	4ft 4in	3ft 2in	14in	3ft 2¼in	1¾in	12½in	4lb 7¾oz	0lb 15¼oz	4ft 4¼in	5lb 7oz
City of London 6 – Travelling	4ft 3¾in	3ft 2⅝in	12¾in	3ft 4in	1⅝in	12¼in	4lb 0oz	2lb 3¾oz	4ft 4¾in	6lb 3¾oz

CITY/TOWN	LENGTH SWORD	BLADE	HILT	SCABBARD	WIDTH BLADE	CROSS	WEIGHT SWORD	SCABBARD	LENGTH TOTAL[1]	WEIGHT TOTAL[2]
City of Lincoln 1 – State	4ft 3¾in	3ft 5⅛in	10⅝in	3ft 5⅞in	2⅜in	13⅛in	5lb 8oz	2lb 3oz	4ft 4½in	7lb 11oz
Bury St Edmunds	4ft 3⅝in	3ft 0⅞in	14¾in	3ft 1¾in	1⅝in	13⅛in	4lb 10oz	2lb 0oz	4ft 4½in	6lb 10oz
Thetford	4ft 3⅜in	3ft 1¾in	13⅝in	3ft 3in	1¾in	12¾in	5lb 7½oz	1lb 6½oz	4ft 4⅝in	6lb 14oz
Shrewsbury 1 – Old	4ft 3¼in	3ft 5in	10¼in	Nil	1⅝in	10⅜in	3lb 15¾oz	Nil	4ft 4¼in[4]	3lb 15½oz[5]
City of Lichfield 2 – St Mary's	4ft 3⅛in[6]	3ft 2⅛in	13in[6]	Nil	2in	Nil	1lb 7¾oz[6]	Nil	4ft 4⅛in[4]	1lb 7¾oz[5]
City of Canterbury 2 – Vision	4ft 3in	3ft 3¼in	11¾in	3ft 4¼in	1⅝in	12¾in	5lb 9½oz	1lb 13oz	4ft 4in	7lb 6½oz
Wigan	4ft 3in	3ft 2¼in	12¾in	3ft 5⅛in	1¾in	13⅛in	3lb 14½oz	1lb 1½oz	4ft 5⅞in	5lb 0oz
Royal 4 – Irish	4ft 2⅞in	3ft 2½in	12⅜in	3ft 3½in	2¼in	12⅛in	6lb 9¼oz	1lb 4¾oz	4ft 3⅞in	7lb 14oz
City of Liverpool 1 – State	4ft 2¾in	3ft 1¾in	13in	3ft 5¾in	1¾in	10¼in	3lb 8oz	0lb 15½oz	4ft 6¾in	4lb 7½oz
Dewsbury	4ft 2⅝in	3ft 0⅛in	14½in	3ft 0⅞in	2in	11¼in	3lb 6¼oz	1lb 2¾oz	4ft 3⅜in	4lb 8¾oz
City of Derby	4ft 2½in	3ft 1⅝in	12⅞in	3ft 6⅝in	1¾in	13¼in	6lb 2oz	2lb 2oz	4ft 7½in	8lb 4oz
City of London 3 – Mourning	4ft 2⅜in	3ft 2⅜in	12in	3ft 3¼in	1⅞in	11¼in	3lb 12oz	0lb 10oz	4ft 3¼in	4lb 6oz
City of Hereford 2 – State	4ft 2⅜in	3ft 0⅞in	13½in	3ft 2¼in	1½in	12in	4lb 2½oz	1lb 5½oz	4ft 3¾in	5lb 8oz
City of London 4 – State (Sunday)	4ft 2¼in	3ft 1½in	12¾in	3ft 3in	1⅝in	12¾in	5lb 1¼oz	1lb 14½oz	4ft 3¾in	6lb 15¾oz
City of Lincoln 4 – George II	4ft 2in	3ft 0¾in	13¼in	3ft 6⅛in	1¾in	11⅞in	4lb 10½oz	1lb 14¼oz	4ft 7⅜in	6lb 8½oz
Carrickfergus	4ft 2in	3ft 0in	14in	3ft 1in	2in	13¼in	4lb 6oz	0lb 9oz	4ft 2in	4lb 15oz
City of Coventry 1 – State	4ft 1⅞in	3ft 2⅛in	11¾in	3ft 3¼in	2in	15in	4lb 6¼oz	2lb 6oz	4ft 3in	6lb 12¼oz
City of Durham 2 – State	4ft 1⅜in	3ft 0⅜in	13in	3ft 2in	1½in	13½in	5lb 1¼oz	1lb 11oz	4ft 3in	6lb 12½oz
City of Bristol 3 – Lent	4ft 1¼in	3ft 3⅞in	9¾in	3ft 10in	2in	11in	4lb 3½oz	4lb 2¼oz	4ft 7¾in	8lb 5¾oz
City of Edinburgh	4ft 1¼in	3ft 0⅛in	13⅛in	3ft 0¾in	1¾in	12⅜in	4lb 6½oz	1lb 0oz	4ft 1⅞in	5lb 6½oz
City of Worcester 1 – Old	4ft 1in	3ft 2½in	10½in	Nil	1¾in	12⅛in	3lb 4¼oz	Nil	4ft 2in[4]	3lb 4¼oz[5]
City of Norwich	4ft 1in	2ft 10⅝in	14¼in	3ft 0⅛in	2in	13½in	4lb 2oz	1lb 1oz	4ft 2⅜in	5lb 3oz
City of Exeter 1 – State	4ft 0¾in	3ft 1½in	11¼in	3ft 8½in	1½"	9⅜in	3lb 4oz	4lb 10oz	4ft 7¾in	7lb 14oz
City of Canterbury 1 – State	4ft 0½in	3ft 2⅝in	10⅜in	3ft 4¾in	1¾in	15in	4lb 1¼oz	0lb 15oz	4ft 3⅛in	5lb 0¼oz

CITY/TOWN	LENGTH				WIDTH		WEIGHT		LENGTH	WEIGHT
	SWORD	BLADE	HILT	SCABBARD	BLADE	CROSS	SWORD	SCABBARD	TOTAL[1]	TOTAL[2]
City of Bristol 2 – Pearl	4ft 0½in	3ft 0in	12½in	3ft 2⅝in	1½in	12⅝in	4lb 5¼oz	1lb 2oz	4ft 3⅛in	5lb 7oz
Carmarthen	4ft 0½in	2ft 10⅝in	13⅞in	2ft 11¼in	1¾in	12⅜in	5lb 7oz	1lb 5½oz	4ft 1¼in	6lb 12½oz
Appleby	4ft 0¼in	2ft 11½in	12¾in	3ft 0⅝in	1¾in	12¾in	6lb 7¾oz	0lb 13½oz	4ft 1⅜in	7lb 5½oz
City of Gloucester 2 – State	4ft 0⅛in	3ft 1⅝in	10½in	3ft 4½in	1¾in	11⅜in	2lb 1¾oz	3lb 6¼oz	4ft 3in	5lb 8oz
City of York 2 – Bowes	4ft 0⅛in	3ft 0⅝in	11½in	3ft 2¾in	2in	13½in	4lb 6¼oz	1lb 1¼oz	4ft 2¼in	5lb 7oz
City of Worcester 2 – Mourning	4ft 0in	3ft 0⅛in	11¾in	Nil	2in	13¾in	3lb 9½oz	Nil	4ft 1in[4]	3lb 9½oz[5]
City of Chester	3ft 11¾in	3ft 1⅝in	10⅛in	3ft 3in	1⅞in	13¼in	4lb 1½oz	0lb 13½oz	4ft 1⅛in	4lb 15oz
Royal 5 – Great	3ft 11¾in	2ft 11¾in	12in	3ft 2in	1⅝in	12⅝in	5lb 11oz	2lb 5¼oz	4ft 2in	8lb 0¼oz
City of Durham 1 – Old	3ft 11⅜in	3ft 3⅛in	8¼in	3ft 3¼in	2⅛in	7⅞in	3lb 3¼oz	0lb 14oz	3ft 11½in	4lb 1¼oz
City of Bristol 1 – Mourning	3ft 11¼in	3ft 2⅝in	8⅝in	3ft 3½in	2⅛in	14⅛in	5lb 1½oz	2lb 10oz	4ft 0⅛in	7lb 11½oz
Clonmel	3ft 11¼in	2ft 10⅜in	12⅞in	3ft 0¾in	2in	13⅞in	3lb 1¼oz	0lb 10oz	4ft 1⅝in	3lb 11¼oz
Kings Lynn	3ft 11⅛in	2ft 11in	12⅛in	3ft 0in	2in	14⅜in	5lb 4oz	2lb 5½oz	4ft 0⅛in	7lb 9½oz
City of Derry 2 – State	3ft 10⅞in	3ft 0⅞in	10in	3ft 1¼in	1¾in	10in	3lb 1¾oz	0lb 12½oz	3ft 11¼in	3lb 14¼oz
City of London 1 – Pearl	3ft 10¾in	3ft 0in	10¾in	3ft 1⅜in	1¾in	11⅞in	4lb 6¾oz	1lb 13oz	4ft 0⅛in	6lb 3¾oz
City of Newcastle upon Tyne 1 – State	3ft 10¾in	2ft 9¾in	13in	3ft 1⅛in	1⅝in	10¾in	3lb 7¼oz	0lb 11½oz	4ft 2⅛in	4lb 2¾oz
City of London 2 – Old Bailey	3ft 10⅝in	2ft 11¾in	11¼in	3ft 1⅜in	1⅝in	8½in	3lb 6¾oz	1lb 0¾oz	4ft 0⅝in	4lb 7¼oz
City of Derry 1 – O'Doherty	3ft 10½in	3ft 1⅜in	9⅛in	3ft 1⅞in	1⅝in	12⅞in	2lb 8¼oz	0lb 13oz	3ft 11in	3lb 5oz
City of Exeter 2 – Mourning	3ft 10½in	3ft 0⅝in	9⅞in	3ft 1in	1⅞in	8¼in	4lb 14¾oz	0lb 9oz	3ft 10⅞in	5lb 7¾oz
Kendal	3ft 10⅜in	3ft 0⅛in	10⅛in	3ft 2in	1¾in	10¼in	3lb 3¾oz	0lb 8¼oz	4ft 0⅛in	3lb 12oz
Royal 1 – Spiritual Justice	3ft 10in	3ft 3¼in	6¾in	3ft 4¼in	1in	7in	2lb 6¼oz	0lb 11oz	3ft 11in	3lb 1oz
City of London 5 – Justice Room	3ft 9¾in	2ft 9⅝in	11¾in	3ft 5¼in	1½in	11⅝in	4lb 13oz	1lb 8oz	4ft 5in	6lb 5oz

CITY/TOWN	LENGTH SWORD	BLADE	HILT	SCABBARD	WIDTH BLADE	CROSS	WEIGHT SWORD	SCABBARD	LENGTH TOTAL[1]	WEIGHT TOTAL[2]
City of Coventry 2 – Museum	3ft 9⅝in[8]	3ft 0in[8]	8¾in	3ft 1in[8]	1⅝in	7⅛in	NK	Nil	3ft 10⅝in[8]	NK
Warrington	3ft 9⅝in	2ft 10¼in	11⅜in	2ft 11¼in	1¾in	9⅛in	2lb 12¾oz	1lb 3¼oz	3ft 10⅞in	4lb 0oz
Hertford	3ft 9¼in	3ft 0⅛in	9⅛in	3ft 1¼in	1½in	13¼in	2lb 10oz	1lb 0½oz	3ft 10½in	3lb 10½oz
Royal 2 – Temporal Justice	3ft 9in	3ft 3in	6in	3ft 4in	1½in	8⅛in	2lb 5½oz	0lb 11oz	3ft 10in	3lb 0½oz
City of Carlisle	3ft 8⅞in	3ft 0⅛in	8⅞in	3ft 0⅞in	1½in	12⅛in	2lb 10oz	0lb 13oz	3ft 9¾in	3lb 7oz
City of Dublin 2 – King's/ City	3ft 8⅞in	2ft 11¼in	9⅝in	Nil	1⅝in	7½in	3lb 10oz	Nil	3ft 9⅞in[4]	3lb 10oz[5]
Royal Wootton Bassett	3ft 8¾in	2ft 10⅛in	10¼in	2ft 10¾in	2in	9⅛in	4lb 2oz	0lb 9¾oz	3ft 9in	4lb 11¾oz
City of Lincoln 2 – Mourning	3ft 8⅝in	2ft 11⅜in	9¼in	3ft 2¼in	2⅛in	11½in	4lb 9½oz	1lb 2½oz	3ft 11½in	5lb 12oz
Kilkenny	3ft 8⅜in	2ft 10⅜in	9⅞in	3ft 0⅛in	1¾in	12½in	3lb 4½oz	1lb 5½oz	3ft 10in	4lb 10oz
City of Lincoln 3 – Charles I	3ft 8in	2ft 9⅝in	10⅜in	3ft 2in	1⅜in	Nil	1lb 4oz[7]	1lb 1oz	4ft 0⅜in	2lb 5oz
City of Kingston upon Hull 1 – State	3ft 8in	2ft 9½in	10½in	2ft 11½in	1½in	11¾in	3lb 4½oz	2lb 3¼oz	3ft 10in	5lb 7½oz
City of Waterford 1 – Edward IV	3ft 7⅝in	2ft 10⅞in	8¾in	2ft 11in	1⅛in	12½in	2lb 5¾oz	0lb 11oz	3ft 7¾in	3lb 0¾oz
Manx 2 – Atholl	3ft 7½in	2ft 9½in	10in	2ft 11⅛in	1⅝in	8½in	2lb 6oz	0lb 9¼oz	3ft 9⅛in	2lb 15¼oz
City of Winchester	3ft 7⅛in	2ft 8¼in	11⅛in	2ft 9½in	1⅞in	9½in	3lb 13¾oz	2lb 1oz	3ft 8⅝in	5lb 14¾oz
Drogheda	3ft 6⅞in	2ft 8¾in	10⅛in	2ft 8⅞in	1⅝in	11⅜in	2lb 8¾oz	1lb 1¼oz	3ft 7in	3lb 10oz
Manx 1 – State	3ft 6in	2ft 5⅝in	12⅜in	2ft 5½in	1⅝in	11⅝in	2lb 8¾oz	0lb 10oz	3ft 6⅞in	3lb 2¾oz
City of Gloucester 1 – Mourning	3ft 6in	2ft 11⅛in	6⅞in	3ft 1⅛in	1¾in	8in	1lb 7oz	0lb 10oz	3ft 8in	2lb 1oz
City of Hereford 1 – Mourning	3ft 5⅛in	2ft 7⅜in	9¾in	2ft 7¾in	1⅝in	7½in	2lb 14¾oz	0lb 6oz	3ft 5½in	3lb 4¾oz
Royal 6 – Offering (Jewelled)	3ft 2⅝in	2ft 7⅝in	7in	2ft 8⅝in	1⅛in	5⅞in	1lb 8oz	2lb 13oz	3ft 3⅝in	4lb 5oz

| CITY/TOWN | LENGTH | | | | WIDTH | | WEIGHT | | | LENGTH | WEIGHT |
	SWORD	BLADE	HILT	SCABBARD	BLADE	CROSS	SWORD	SCABBARD		TOTAL[1]	TOTAL[2]
Royal 3 – Mercy or Curtana	3ft 2in	2ft 7¼in	6¾in	2ft 9¼in	1in	7½in	2lb 10oz	0lb 11¼oz		3ft 4in	3lb 5¼oz

1 Total length is generally the length of hilt plus the length of scabbard.

2 Total weight is the weight of sword plus the weight of scabbard.

3 Southampton and Bath have short scabbards due to the 'hooks'.

4 Where no scabbard exists the blade length plus 1in inch has been used to approximate the total length.

5 Sword only.

6 Blade only – no tang so no hilt.

7 Blade only – tang but no hilt.

8 Hilt only – all other measurements are estimates.

APPENDIX 4

SUMMARY AND COMPARISON OF SWORDS BY MEASUREMENT (METRIC)

CITY/TOWN	LENGTH SWORD	BLADE	HILT	SCABBARD	WIDTH BLADE	CROSS	WEIGHT SWORD	SCABBARD	LENGTH TOTAL[1]	WEIGHT TOTAL[2]
Royal – Tower 1	2.312m	1.651m	0.661m	Nil	0.081m	0.626m	6.501kg	Nil	2.338m[4]	6.501kg[5]
Royal – Tower 2	2.257m	1.676m	0.584m	Nil	0.076m	0.590m	6.435kg	Nil	2.283m[4]	6.435kg[5]
Royal – Westminster Abbey	2.210m	1.625m	0.584m	Nil	0.089m	0.622m	8.166kg	Nil	2.236m[4]	8.166kg[5]
Royal – St George's Chapel, Windsor	2.033m	1.625m	0.416m	Nil	0.057m	0.410m	4.430kg	Nil	2.059m[4]	4.430kg[5]
City of Southampton	1.752m	1.283m	0.470m	1.181m[3]	0.051m	0.438m	3.416kg	0.733kg	1.785m[3]	4.149kg
City of Bath	1.622m	1.181m	0.441m	1.069m[3]	0.044m	0.470m	3.337kg	0.602kg	1.635m[3]	3.139kg
Stratford upon Avon	1.495m	1.054m	0.441m	1.054m	0.041m	0.423m	2.465kg	0.428kg	1.495m	2.873kg
City of Leeds	1.467m	1.146m	0.324m	1.168m	0.067m	0.289m	2.531kg	0.810kg	1.492m	3.341kg
City of Waterford 2 – Henry VIII	1.464m	1.130m	0.334m	1.126m	0.028m	0.465m	2.421kg	0.534kg	1.460m	2.955kg
Ipswich	1.445m	1.117m	0.327m	1.133m	0.063m	0.330m	3.560kg	0.594kg	1.460m	4.154kg
City of Bristol 4 – State	1.422m	1.051m	0.381m	1.289m	0.108m	0.435m	5.158kg	4.536kg	1.670m	9.694kg
City of Dublin 1 – Great	1.387m	1.099m	0.289m	1.107m	0.069m	0.425m	3.518kg	1.419kg	1.400m	4.937kg
Galway	1.383m	0.985m	0.398m	1.023m	0.057m	0.408m	2.455kg	0.500kg	1.421m	2.955kg
Scotland	1.378m	0.991m	0.387m	1.280m	0.044m	0.438m	2.722kg	2.268kg	1.667m	4.988kg
City of Worcester 3 – State	1.365m	0.968m	0.388m	0.994m	0.051m	0.425m	3.183kg	1.076kg	1.382m	4.259kg
City of Newcastle upon Tyne 2 – Second	1.359m	1.020m	0.340m	1.041m	0.041m	0.267m	2.103kg	0.327kg	1.381m	2.430kg
City of Lichfield 1 – State	1.330m	1.003m	0.327m	1.023m	0.051m	0.393m	2.042kg	1.027kg	1.350m	3.069kg
Great Yarmouth	1.330m	0.953m	0.375m	0.983m	0.048m	0.330m	2.292kg	0.974kg	1.359m	3.266kg
Limerick	1.324m	1.105m	0.217m	Nil	0.043m	0.390m	1.843kg	Nil	1.350m[4]	1.843kg[5]
City of York 1 – Sigismund	1.321m	0.993m	0.327m	1.035m	0.070m	0.330m	3.887kg	0.611kg	1.362m	4.498kg
Shrewsbury 2 – State	1.321m	0.965m	0.356m	0.972m	0.044m	0.318m	2.033kg	0.432kg	1.328m	2.465kg
City of London 6 – Travelling	1.315m	0.981m	0.323m	1.016m	0.041m	0.311m	1.816kg	1.012kg	1.340m	2.828kg
City of Lincoln 1 – State	1.314m	1.044m	0.270m	1.063m	0.060m	0.333m	2.495kg	0.991kg	1.334m	3.486kg
Bury St Edmunds	1.311m	0.937m	0.375m	0.959m	0.041m	0.333m	2.098kg	0.907kg	1.334m	3.000kg

SUMMARY AND COMPARISON OF SWORDS BY MEASUREMENT (METRIC)

CITY/TOWN	LENGTH				WIDTH		WEIGHT		LENGTH TOTAL[1]	WEIGHT TOTAL[2]
	SWORD	BLADE	HILT	SCABBARD	BLADE	CROSS	SWORD	SCABBARD		
Thetford	1.305m	0.959m	0.346m	0.991m	0.045m	0.324m	2.479kg	0.644kg	1.337m	3.123kg
Shrewsbury 1 – Old	1.302m	1.041m	0.260m	Nil	0.041m	0.263m	1.803kg	Nil	1.327m[4]	1.803kg[5]
City of Lichfield 2 – St Mary's	1.299m[6]	0.969m	0.330m[6]	Nil	0.051m	Nil	0.676kg[6]	Nil	1.324m[4]	0.676kg[5]
City of Canterbury 2 – Vision	1.295m	0.997m	0.298m	1.023m	0.041m	0.324m	2.540kg	0.820kg	1.321m	3.360kg
Wigan	1.295m	0.972m	0.324m	1.044m	0.044m	0.333m	1.770kg	0.495kg	1.368m	2.265kg
Royal 4 – Irish	1.292m	0.978m	0.314m	1.003m	0.056m	0.308m	2.985kg	0.590kg	1.344m	3.575kg
City of Liverpool 1 – State	1.289m	0.959m	0.331m	1.060m	0.045m	0.260m	1.589kg	0.442kg	1.391m	2.031kg
Dewsbury	1.286m	0.917m	0.368m	0.937m	0.051m	0.286m	1.537kg	0.531kg	1.305m	2.088kg
City of Derby	1.283m	0.955m	0.327m	1.082m	0.044m	0.336m	2.787kg	0.965kg	1.409m	3.752kg
City of London 3 – Mourning	1.280m	0.975m	0.305m	0.997m	0.048m	0.286m	1.700kg	0.284kg	1.302m	1.984kg
City of Hereford 2 – State	1.280m	0.937m	0.343m	0.972m	0.038m	0.305m	1.883kg	0.614kg	1.315m	2.497kg
City of London 4 – State (Sunday)	1.276m	0.952m	0.324m	0.991m	0.041m	0.324m	2.302kg	0.866kg	1.314m	3.168kg
City of Lincoln 4 – George II	1.270m	0.933m	0.336m	1.070m	0.045m	0.302m	2.111kg	0.857kg	1.406m	2.968kg
Carrickfergus	1.270m	0.915m	0.356m	0.940m	0.051m	0.336m	1.985kg	0.259kg	1.295m	2.244kg
City of Coventry 1 – State	1.267m	0.968m	0.298m	0.997m	0.051m	0.381m	1.994kg	1.076kg	1.295m	3.070kg
City of Durham 2 – State	1.254m	0.924m	0.330m	0.966m	0.038m	0.343m	2.305kg	0.763kg	1.296m	3.068kg
City of Bristol 3 – Lent	1.251m	1.013m	0.248m	1.169m	0.051m	0.279m	1.915kg	1.877kg	1.417m	3.792kg
City of Edinburgh	1.251m	0.917m	0.333m	0.933m	0.044m	0.314m	1.999kg	0.450kg	1.266m	2.449kg
City of Worcester 1 – Old	1.245m	0.978m	0.267m	Nil	0.045m	0.308m	1.481kg	Nil	1.270m[4]	1.481kg[5]
City of Norwich	1.245m	0.879m	0.362m	0.917m	0.051m	0.343m	1.871kg	0.481kg	1.279m	2.352kg
City of Exeter 1 – State	1.238m	0.953m	0.286m	1.130m	0.038m	0.238m	1.471kg	2.095kg	1.416m	3.566kg
City of Canterbury 1 – State	1.232m	0.981m	0.263m	1.035m	0.045m	0.381m	1.848kg	0.424kg	1.299m	2.272kg
City of Bristol 2 – Pearl	1.232m	0.914m	0.318m	0.981m	0.038m	0.321m	1.962kg	0.505kg	1.299m	2.467kg
Carmarthen	1.232m	0.879m	0.352m	0.895m	0.045m	0.314m	2.467kg	0.611kg	1.251m	3.078kg
Appleby	1.225m	0.902m	0.324m	0.930m	0.045m	0.324m	2.940kg	0.382kg	1.254m	3.322kg

CITY/TOWN	LENGTH				WIDTH		WEIGHT		LENGTH TOTAL[1]	WEIGHT TOTAL[2]
	SWORD	BLADE	HILT	SCABBARD	BLADE	CROSS	SWORD	SCABBARD		
City of Gloucester 2 – State	1.222m	0.956m	0.267m	1.029m	0.044m	0.289m	0.958kg	1.539kg	1.296m	2.497kg
City of York 2 – Bowes	1.222m	0.930m	0.292m	0.984m	0.051m	0.343m	1.991kg	0.486kg	1.276m	2.477kg
City of Worcester 2 – Mourning	1.219m	0.917m	0.298m	Nil	0.051m	0.349m	1.627kg	Nil	1.245m[4]	1.627kg[5]
City of Chester	1.213m	0.956m	0.257m	0.991m	0.048m	0.336m	1.858kg	0.381kg	1.248m	2.239kg
Royal 5 – Great	1.213m	0.908m	0.305m	0.965m	0.041m	0.321m	2.581kg	1.057kg	1.270m	3.638kg
City of Durham 1 – Old	1.203m	0.994m	0.210m	0.997m	0.054m	0.200m	1.454kg	0.394kg	1.210m	1.848kg
City of Bristol 1 – Mourning	1.200m	0.981m	0.219m	1.003m	0.054m	0.359m	2.314kg	1.190kg	1.222m	3.504kg
Clonmel	1.200m	0.874m	0.326m	0.933m	0.050m	0.351m	1.396kg	0.286kg	1.259m	1.682kg
Kings Lynn	1.197m	0.889m	0.308m	0.914m	0.051m	0.365m	2.378kg	1.060kg	1.222m	3.438kg
City of Derry 2 – State	1.190m	0.937m	0.253m	0.946m	0.045m	0.254m	1.410kg	0.354kg	1.199m	1.764kg
City of London 1 – Pearl	1.187m	0.914m	0.273m	0.949m	0.044m	0.303m	2.007kg	0.819kg	1.222m	2.826kg
City of Newcastle upon Tyne 1 – State	1.187m	0.857m	0.330m	0.943m	0.041m	0.273m	1.564kg	0.327kg	1.273m	1.891kg
City of London 2 – Old Bailey	1.184m	0.908m	0.286m	0.949m	0.041m	0.216m	1.548kg	0.477kg	1.235m	2.025kg
City of Derry 1 – O'Doherty	1.182m	0.950m	0.232m	0.962m	0.041m	0.327m	1.130kg	0.366kg	1.194m	1.496kg
City of Exeter 2 – Mourning	1.181m	0.930m	0.251m	0.940m	0.048m	0.210m	2.230kg	0.255kg	1.191m	2.480kg
Kendal	1.178m	0.917m	0.257m	0.965m	0.045m	0.260m	1.465kg	0.235kg	1.222m	1.700kg
Royal 1 – Spiritual Justice	1.168m	0.996m	0.171m	1.022m	0.025m	0.177m	1.080kg	0.312kg	1.193m	1.392kg
City of London 5 – Justice Room	1.163m	0.854m	0.298m	1.048m	0.038m	0.295m	2.185kg	0.678kg	1.346m	2.863kg
City of Coventry 2 – Museum	1.159m[8]	0.914m[8]	0.222m	0.940m[8]	0.041m	0.181m	NK	Nil	1.184m[8]	NK
Warrington	1.159m	0.870m	0.289m	0.895m	0.045m	0.232m	1.271kg	0.545kg	1.184m	1.816kg
Hertford	1.149m	0.917m	0.232m	0.946m	0.038m	0.336m	1.192kg	0.468kg	1.178m	1.660kg
Royal 2 – Temporal Justice	1.143m	0.991m	0.152m	1.016m	0.039m	0.205m	1.060kg	0.314kg	1.168m	1.374kg
City of Carlisle	1.140m	0.914m	0.226m	0.937m	0.038m	0.308m	1.192kg	0.367kg	1.166m	1.559kg
City of Dublin 2 – King's/City	1.140m	0.895m	0.245m	Nil	0.041m	0.190m	1.645kg	Nil	1.160m[4]	1.645kg[5]
Royal Wootton Bassett	1.137m	0.867m	0.260m	0.883m	0.051m	0.232m	1.871kg	0.275kg	1.143m	2.146kg

CITY/TOWN	LENGTH				WIDTH		WEIGHT		LENGTH TOTAL[1]	WEIGHT TOTAL[2]
	SWORD	BLADE	HILT	SCABBARD	BLADE	CROSS	SWORD	SCABBARD		
City of Lincoln 2 – Mourning	1.133m	0.899m	0.235m	0.972m	0.054m	0.292m	2.082kg	0.516kg	1.207m	2.598kg
Kilkenny	1.126m	0.874m	0.251m	0.918m	0.046m	0.319m	1.488kg	0.605kg	1.169m	2.093kg
City of Lincoln 3 – Charles I	1.118m	0.854m	0.263m	0.965m	0.035m	Nil	0.568kg[7]	0.480kg	1.228m	1.048kg
City of Kingston upon Hull 1 – State	1.118m	0.851m	0.267m	0.902m	0.038m	0.298m	1.485kg	0.999kg	1.169m	2.484kg
City of Waterford 1 – Edward IV	1.108m	0.887m	0.221m	0.889m	0.029m	0.316m	1.073kg	0.311kg	1.110m	1.384kg
Manx 2 – Atholl	1.105m	0.851m	0.254m	0.892m	0.041m	0.216m	1.074kg	0.265kg	1.146m	1.339kg
City of Winchester	1.096m	0.819m	0.282m	0.851m	0.047m	0.241m	1.751kg	0.929kg	1.133m	2.680kg
Drogheda	1.090m	0.832m	0.257m	0.835m	0.041m	0.289m	1.158kg	0.489kg	1.092m	1.647kg
Manx 1 – State	1.067m	0.753m	0.314m	0.749m	0.041m	0.295m	1.158kg	0.286kg	1.063m	1.444kg
City of Gloucester 1 – Mourning	1.066m	0.892m	0.178m	0.943m	0.045m	0.203m	0.651kg	0.279kg	1.121m	0.930kg
City of Hereford 1 – Mourning	1.044m	0.797m	0.248m	0.806m	0.041m	0.190m	1.324kg	0.168kg	1.054m	1.492kg
Royal 6 – Offering (Jewelled)	0.981m	0.803m	0.178m	0.828m	0.029m	0.146m	0.680kg	1.278kg	1.007m	1.958kg
Royal 3 – Mercy or Curtana	0.965m	0.794m	0.171m	0.844m	0.025m	0.190m	1.190kg	0.318kg	1.015m	1.508kg

1 Total length is generally the length of hilt plus the length of scabbard in metres.

2 Total weight is the weight of sword plus the weight of scabbard.

3 Southampton and Bath have short scabbards due to the 'hooks'.

4 Where no scabbard exists the blade length plus 0.026m has been used to approximate the total length.

5 Sword only.

6 Blade only – no tang so no hilt.

7 Blade only – tang but no hilt.

8 Hilt only – all other measurements are estimates.

APPENDIX 5

ENGLISH RULE IN IRELAND IN THE FIFTEENTH AND SIXTEENTH CENTURIES

Until 1167, Ireland was divided into a number of minor kingdoms. However, in that year, the first Normans landed in Ireland, followed by many more. In order to prevent a Norman takeover, Henry II of England landed with a large fleet at Waterford in 1171, becoming the first English king to set foot on Irish soil. Henry awarded his Irish territories to his son, John, with the title 'Lord of Ireland'. When John unexpectedly became King John, the 'Lordship of Ireland' fell directly under the English Crown. John visited in 1185 and 1210.

The Black Death arrived in Ireland in 1348. Because most of the English and Norman inhabitants of Ireland lived in towns and villages, the plague hit them much harder than it did the native Irish, who lived in more dispersed rural settlements. After it had passed, the Gaelic Irish language and customs came to dominate the country again. The English-controlled territory shrank back to a fortified area on the east coast around Dublin (the Pale), and the king had little real authority outside Dublin (beyond the Pale).

Towards the end of the fifteenth century, English authority in Ireland had all but disappeared. England's attentions were diverted by the Wars of the Roses. The Lordship of Ireland lay in the hands of the powerful Fitzgerald Earl of Kildare, who dominated the country by military force and alliances with lords and clans around Ireland. Around the country, local Gaelic and Gaelicised lords expanded their powers at the expense of the English government in Dublin, but the power of the Dublin government was seriously curtailed by the introduction of Poynings' Law in 1494, which put the Irish Parliament under the control of the Westminster Parliament.

In the sixteenth century, the Fitzgerald dynasty of Kildare, who were by then effectively the rulers of Ireland, had become very unreliable allies of the Tudor monarchs. Having put down a Fitzgerald-led rebellion against the Crown in 1536; Henry VIII resolved to bring Ireland under English government control so the island would not become a base for future rebellion or foreign invasions against England. In 1541, Henry upgraded Ireland from a lordship to a full kingdom. He was proclaimed King of Ireland at a meeting of the Irish Parliament that year. With the institutions of government in place, the next step was to extend the control of the English kingdom of Ireland over all its claimed territory. This took some sixty years, with various English administrations in the process either negotiating or fighting with the independent Irish or Old English lords.

The re-conquest was completed during the reigns of Elizabeth I and James I, after several extremely brutal conflicts. From this point the English authorities in Dublin established real control over Ireland for the first time, bringing a centralised government to the entire island and successfully disarming the native lordships. However, the English were not successful in converting the Catholic Irish to the Protestant religion, and the brutal methods used by Crown authority heightened the resentment of English rule.

From the mid-sixteenth and into the early seventeenth century, Crown governments carried out a policy of land confiscation and colonisation in the form of plantations. Scottish and English Protestants were sent as colonists to the provinces of Munster and Ulster and elsewhere. These Protestant settlers replaced Irish Catholic landowners, who were removed from their lands. It was effectively completed by 1603, when James VI of Scotland, in the Act of Union, inherited the English and Irish thrones, and the harp was added to the royal arms. An uneasy rule continued despite many wars and rebellions, much a result of differences between Catholics and Protestants.

In 1801, the English, Irish and Scottish Parliaments enacted another Act of Union, creating the United Kingdom of Great Britain and Ireland. This continued, despite persistent unrest, until Home Rule, the Easter Rising and the War of Independence resulted in the creation of the Irish Free State in 1921 – Northern Ireland elected to remain part of the United Kingdom. The Republic of Ireland was created in 1937.

This short history of the fifteenth, sixteenth and early seventeenth centuries is necessary to cover the period between 1403 and 1613, when eight towns and cities in Ireland were granted royal charters, giving them the right to bear a Sword of State before the mayor. It seems that they were granted to encourage their support when English influence was low.

It is fascinating that this right, bestowed by English sovereigns, has continued in a number of Irish cities despite the change in constitutional status, and demonstrates that tradition sometimes overcomes politics!

APPENDIX 6

CEREMONIAL SWORDS IN FREEMASONRY

It would be neglectful not to mention the place of ceremonial swords in Masonic ritual, as there are a considerable number of such swords – though of differing sizes and uses.

The Grand Lodge of England is the oldest in the world and was formed in 1717. The Grand Lodge of Scotland was formed in 1725 and the Grand Lodge of Ireland in 1736. The United Grand Lodge of England (UGLE) was formed in 1813 as a result of the amalgamation of two English Grand Lodges. The UGLE has three swords, all held in Freemasons' Hall in London and borne sheathed.

The sword borne before the Most Worshipful Grand Master is the Sword of State of the United Grand Lodge of England. It is 44⅝in (1.134m) long, double-edged and two-handed. The blade is straight. The silver-gilt cross-guard is straight and of cubed section. The grip is silver and spirally bound with a pair of silver wires. The pommel is a silver-gilt orb. Both the quillon block and pommel bear Masonic symbols. The scabbard is covered in dark blue velvet edged with gold lace, and a silver-gilt chape, a quite long central mount and a mouth-locket. Between these are two embroidered mounts bearing arms. The blade is reputed to have been lying across the body of Gustav Adolphus, King of Sweden, killed at the Battle of Lützen in 1632. It was brought back to England and restored. It was presented to the UGLE by Thomas, 8th Duke of Norfolk, to mark his year in office as 13th Grand Master of the Grand Lodge in 1730.

The second sword is the Sword of State of the Grand Chapter of England. It is 44½in (1.132m) long and is double-edged and two-handed. The straight blade has wavy edges. The cross-guard is gilt, with the quillons in the form of serpents grasping the block with their mouths. The grip is spirally bound with copper wire. The pommel is a gilded orb. Each face is engraved. There is a very long tang button. The scabbard is covered in crimson velvet with gold galloons, and with a very long gilt chape and mouth-locket and two other mounts.

The third sword is the Sword of State of the Grand Chapter of England and of the Antients Grand Lodge. This is 46⅜in (1.179m) long, two-handed and double-edged.

The blade is straight and wavy-edged. The silver-gilt cross-guard has quillons in the form of serpents grasping the block in their mouths. The grip is sharkskin spirally wound with gold wire. The silver-gilt pommel is an orb with designs on each face. The scabbard is covered in crimson velvet with gilt chape, a mouth-locket and two intermediate mounts.

The next level down is that of Provincial Grand Lodges – essentially conforming to the counties of England, Wales, the Isle of Man and the Channel Islands. There are forty-seven of these lodges. Each provincial Grand Lodge has a Provincial Grand Sword-bearer, appointed along with the other Provincial Officers. The Provincial Grand Master is preceded by his sword-bearer into every meeting. The uniform of a Grand Sword-Bearer is the normal dress of a mason with the appropriate apron, plus a jewel or badge with crossed swords on a collar.

At the elections in a Provincial Grand Lodge, the sword is borne by the outgoing sword-bearer; the newly elected sword-bearer carries the sword on the next occasion. Each Provincial Grand Lodge has a ceremonial sword, normally a two-handed, double-edged bearing sword, borne sheathed. They vary in style and length – in Wiltshire, the provincial sword is 41⅝in (1.056m) long, two-handed and double-edged. It is very simple and modern, with a straight square section quillons, wire-bound grip and a pommel with designs on each face. The scabbard is covered in blue leather with a chape with an emblem and a simple mouth-locket.

The Provincial sword is used at installation ceremonies at lodges. A number of officials enter in turn and take up specific positions until finally the sword, borne by the Provincial Sword-Bearer, precedes the Provincial Grand Master. The sword is then placed in a cradle for the ceremony.

All masons belong to a lodge. Each lodge annually elects a Worshipful Master (the President). Other officers elected by the lodge or appointed by the Master are a Senior Warden and a Junior Warden (the Vice Presidents), a Secretary, a Treasurer and a Tyler. The Tyler sits outside the entrance to the lodge room, guarding while the lodge is in session, with sword in hand. There are over 8,000 lodges in the UGLE, which means there are some 8,000 Tyler's swords; these are generally smaller swords, often ex-military ones.

APPENDIX 7

NON-BEARING SWORDS

Bearing-swords are designed and made to be borne before a person of dignity. Only those bearing-swords included in the insignia of towns and cities have been included in the main body of the book.

Just nine presentational non-bearing swords are featured in this appendix. In 1895, *J&H* included details of the second sword at Kingston upon Hull and a sword at Crewe. They were both included in an annex listing all the bearing-swords discovered in the insignia of corporations. *J&H* commented, in a simple line at the end of that annex, that in six other towns and cities 'there are other swords, of different kinds, at Southampton, Lichfield, Liverpool, Wenlock, Rochester and Preston'. The bearing-swords at Southampton and Lichfield have been included in the description in the sixth chapter. The sword at Liverpool, which from a picture of the hilt was definitely a bearing-sword, has since been lost.

Naval swords held at Norwich, Liverpool and Exeter and a new(ish) sabre at Exeter are now included.

These nine swords form no part of the general discussion but are included because they either are part of the insignia of a town or city mentioned in the main body of the book, or have been mentioned historically. There is no royal charter or other authority for having these non-bearing swords.

They are listed in order of the age of each sword. They are: the second short sword at Kingston upon Hull – *c.* 1636; the small sword at Much Wenlock 1757; the Spanish Admiral's sword at Norwich – *c.* 1790; the Nelson sword at Liverpool – 1801; the Nelson sword at Exeter – 1805; the Addison sword at Preston – 1845; the Foord sword at Rochester – 1868–69; the short sword at Crewe – *c.* 1877; and the Buller sabre at Exeter – 1901.

It should be noted that all these swords are small, one-handed, and as all are side arms they are all described point down. None except Preston have any civic function.

Although the three coronation swords, the Swords of Spiritual Justice and of Temporal Justice and the Curtana, and the Sword of Offering are all one-handed, they are carried with two hands.

It must be presumed that there are other swords in civic collections up and down the country. They may be part of the corporate insignia or be in museum collections.

While, no doubt, of interest to sword collectors and buffs, they are not included for obvious reasons.

Kingston upon Hull – The Second Sword – *c.* 1636

Length of sword	3ft 0¼in – 0.921m	Weight of sword	2lb 3oz – 0.993kg
Length of blade	2ft 6¼in – 0.768 – Double-edged	Width of blade	1⅜in – 0.035m
Length of hilt	6in – 0.152m – One-handed	Width of guard	7⅛in – 0.181m
Length of scabbard	2ft 7⅞in – 0.809m	Weight of scabbard	7¼oz – 0.205kg

Sword

This sword has an ancient blade with double fuller, originally covered near the hilt with engraving: all this, however, is now nearly ground down. The hilt is silver-gilt. The pommel is a simple sphere. The grip is covered with black leather with silver-gilt straps of poor quality. There is no quillon block. The straight plain quillons are oblong in section but bend backwards at the ends.

Neither the accounts nor the minutes contain any reference to the sword about the dated named. Despite inventory records of the sword in 1674, 1679, 1694 and subsequent dates to 1837 as including two swords, the supposition that it was given by Charles I in 1639 appears to be without foundation. This sword had apparently a velvet belt, which was renewed in 1777, but has since disappeared. The grip of the sword was repaired by the Tower armouries in 1961.

Scabbard

The present scabbard is covered in crimson velvet with two much-worn silver-gilt mounts. These are: (1) the mouth-locket, which is plain; and (2) the chape, which has, in high relief, on one side a crowned rose and on the other a crowned thistle with the date '1636' and ends in a small finial. The chape is of far better quality than the mouth-locket, which is very ordinary. There are no hallmarks.

Much Wenlock The Sword – *c.* 1757

Length of sword	3ft 6½in – 1.080m	Weight of sword	1lb 11¼oz – 0.773kg
Length of blade	2ft 8in – 0.812m – Single-edged	Width of blade	1¼in – 0.032m
Length of hilt	10½in – 0.267m – One-handed	Width of guard	5⅞in – 0.146m
Length of scabbard	2ft 8¾in – 0.832m	Weight of scabbard	11oz – 0.310kg

Sword

This sword, thought to be from the mid-seventeenth century, has been described as a German 'flamberg'. This is incorrect, as a 'flamberg' means flame-edged, i.e. has wavy edges to the blade. It is a 'small sword', possibly of the middle of the eighteenth century, which fits with the type of sword and the inscription on the scabbard. The blade bears 'S H O I L ? V' on the obverse and 'B R I D G' on the reverse. It narrows close to the guard. The cross-guard is rather crude and simple. It is a hollowed shell with a scalloped edge and is attached to two very short quillons, which are forged to the tang and terminate with elaborate screwed caps. It is ornamented with chasing and engraving. The grip tapers and is bound with wire. There is a Turk's head knot collar at each end. The pommel is small, egg-shaped and twisted. There is a small tang button. The metalwork is all bronze, painted black and decorated with gold paint.

Scabbard

The scabbard is of black leather, cracked near the chape, with three bronze mounts. These are: (1) the mouth-locket, which is 4½in long with a frog on the obverse; (2) a brass band about 8in from the point is inscribed on the obverse '*Deus Rex Lex A* xxx G2 *Ris*' (God King Law in the 30 year of the reign of George II) (1756–57), and on the reverse 'Jno Smitheman, Ball: Wm Hayward, Recordr. Ao Dm 1757'; and (3) the horse-shoe chape, which is 8½in long.

Except from the general age and the inscription on the scabbard, there no record of when or how this sword was obtained. It is displayed, on brackets, in front of the town's coat of arms and is therefore not processed.

Norwich – The Spanish Admiral's Sword – *c.* 1797

Length of sword	2ft 4in – 0.711m	Weight of sword	Not weighed
Length of blade	1ft 10in – 0.569m – Single-edged	Width of blade	1½in – 0.038m
Length of hilt	6in – 0.152m – One-handed	Width of guard	2¾in – 0.070m
Length of scabbard	2ft 0in – 0.610m	Weight of scabbard	Not weighed

Sword

On losing the Battle of Cape St Vincent in 1797, the sword of the wounded Spanish admiral, Don Francisco Xavier Winthuysen, of the *San Josef*, was surrendered to Commodore Horatio Nelson. Nelson's action resulted in him being promoted to Rear Admiral and made a Knight of the Order of the Bath. He later presented the sword to the city. The blade is slightly curved, as expected as a naval cutlass, but it has rusted away near the tip and is now very badly corroded and somewhat fragile; for this reason it has not been inspected close-up and has not been weighed. Unusually for a naval sword, it has a cross-guard rather than a basket hilt. The hilt is of silver and mother of pearl. The quillon block is relatively large. Again unusually, the quillons turn towards the handle at the ends and are extremely short with rounded ends. The grip is of inlaid mother of pearl attached to the broad tang and is wider at the end with no pommel.

Scabbard

The metal scabbard curves slightly at the point and has a simple throat-locket and three silver-gilt mounts. These are: (1) a simple band with a ring to take an end clasp of the baldric – in an old photograph this is some 8in from the mouth; (2) the broad mouth-locket, which has a frog stud and a ring to take an end clasp of the baldric; (3) the chape, which appears to be decorated with leaf-work and ends in quite a large finial. All three mounts have art- and leaf-work matching that on the quillon block and quillons. The mouth-locket and the band have been removed and replaced in the wrong order.

Exeter – The Nelson Sword – c. 1801

Length of sword	2ft 11½in – 0.902m	Weight of sword	1lb 13oz – 0.818kg
Length of blade	2ft 6½in – 0.774m – Single-edged	Width of blade	1½in – 0.038 m
Length of hilt	5in – 0.127m – One-handed	Width of guard	4½in – 0.114m
Length of scabbard	2ft 7½in – 0.800m	Weight of scabbard	12½oz – 0.354kg

Sword

The blade is curved in the style of a naval cutlass and is chased with foliage for some 16½in on both sides. It is now quite blemished with previous rusting which has obliterated some of the chasing. On the obverse are the royal arms, probably of George II, within the Garter and crowned, and trophies of arms. On the reverse there is a figure of a hussar, a crown with underneath very elaborate 'G' and 'R', and what appears to be the manufacturer's details, 'Wootter' and 'Street'. The hilt has on one side a turned-up quillon of strips of metal joined together, leaving holes, and the other side is a straight-forward knuckle-guard of similar style, looping into the pommel with a small ring for the sword knot. The grip is covered in leather bound with a spiral silver wire. It has the usual gilt plate running from the pommel into the guard. The pommel is in the usual form of a lion's head.

The sword was a presentation piece for Admiral Lord Nelson in 1801 on his being made a Freeman of the City. It is understood that after his death it has been sold on a number of times. Eventually it came into the hands of a local man, after whose death his widow gave the sword to the city.

Scabbard

The scabbard is curved and covered with black leather with three gilt mounts. These are: (1) the mouth-locket, which has on the obverse a second baldric ring, a frog stud and a large stylised italic 'N', and on the reverse the inscription 'Horatio Viscount Nelson (Vice Admiral of the Blue) enrolled as a Freeman of the city of Exeter, 21st January 1801. Thomas Floud, Mayor'; (2) a triangular locket (now rather loose), bearing a baldric ring, with two pairs of raised cables and the city arms on the obverse, the reverse being blank; and (3) the chape, which is plain except for two parallel lines on each side. The metal strip which passes inside the scabbard to secure the mouth-locket is broken, causing the locket to be very loose.

Liverpool – The Nelson Sword – 1805

Length of sword	2 ft 11⅝in – 0.905m	Weight of sword	1lb 9oz – 0.709kg
Length of blade	2ft 6⅜in – 0.771m – Single-edged	Width of blade	1⅛in – 0.029m
Length of hilt	5¼in – 0.134m – One-handed	Width of guard	4½in – 0.114m

Sword

This straight cutlass was made for ceremonial purposes only. The first few inches of the blade have at some stage been badly rusted. The cutting edge is quite sharp but not actually straight, with some shallow curves and nicks along its length. It bears some very simple gold leaf-work around an etched inscription 'THE SUBSCRIBERS TO A FUND FOR ERECTING A MONUMENT IN LIVERPOOL TO THE IMMORTAL MEMORY OF THE LATE RT. HON. ADML LORD NELSON, WITH EVERY SENTIMENT OF GRATITUDE TO HIS GALLANT SUCCESSOR THE RT. HON ADML LORD COLLINGWOOD, FOR HIS HEROIC CONDUCT IN THE EVER TO BE REMEMBERED NAVAL ENGAGEMENT AT TRAFALGAR, PRESENT TO HIS LORDSHIP THIS SWORD, EMBLEMATICALLY REPRESENTING THE GLORIOUS VICTORY OVER THE COMBINED FLEETS OF FRANCE AND SPAIN, IN THE YEAR OF OUR LORD MDCCCV.' The gilt guard is in typical naval style, with small protecting plates on each side bearing an anchor and a simple rather flimsy cross leading into an equally flimsy knuckle-guard. The grip is solid and engraved and ends in a lion's head, into the mouth of which goes the other end of the guard. On one side of the grip, under a trophy of arms and between laurel sprays, is a large cartouche with the stern of a man-of-war beside the head of a hart, above a crowned coat of arms of a lion guardant over three hart heads around a chevron over a motto, with an eagle and lion as supporters. On the other side, again under a trophy of arms and between laurel sprays, is a cartouche bearing the stern and side view of a man-of-war (probably the *Victory*).

Scabbard

There is no scabbard, and given the inscription it is unlikely there ever was one.

Preston – The Addison Sword – circa 1845

Length of sword	3ft 10½in – 1.181m	Weight of sword	2lb 4½oz – 1.038kg
Length of blade	2ft 10⅛in – 0.867m – Single-edged	Width of blade	1½in – 0.038m
Length of hilt	10⅛in – 0.257m – One-handed	Width of guard	4½in – 0.114m
Length of scabbard	3ft 0¼in – 0.921m	Weight of scabbard	13¾oz – 0.389kg

Sword

It has a straight blade with four narrow fullers for about 15in and one longer, wider fuller reaching nearly to the point on both sides. The last 4in of the blade is very rusted and pitted with a small hole near the tip. On each side of the blade are marks that could belong to makers or be metal imperfections. The blade on the knuckle-side is edged, as is the other side but for only the top half of the blade. The lower half has a blunt section as if for hammering. The blade is fixed to the hilt with two 5in-long protruding plates with side bars similar to short quillons. A simple one-piece basket is attached to these quillons with screws, and appears to have been gilt. The basket has a line of holes as a pattern. The grip, which is suitable only for a small hand, is leather-covered. The pommel is like a large, flat upturned saucer. In the base is fitted (screwed?) the tang cover, which is 4½in long, cylindrical and tapers to a blunt point.

The sword was presented to the city in 1845 by the then mayor, John Addison. It is claimed to be a Maharatta tulwar (a sabre from Maharatta in India). It is not a tulwar or a sabre, both of which are curved swords. It is more likely to be an infantry sword from one of the Maharatta infantry regiments of the Indian Army. This is the only non-bearing sword to be processed before a mayor. Carried by the beadle in 1895, it is now carried, incorrectly, against one shoulder, by a police officer in uniform.

Scabbard

The scabbard is covered with deep crimson velvet with a gold lace galloon running from chape to mouth-locket, and two brass mounts – the covering is coming apart on the reverse. These are: (1) the mouth-locket, which has a matching scalloped end, is plain on each side and has been cut on each edge to slide over the protruding plates and allow the quillons to engage. It has a long brass frog stud with minor decoration; and (2) the chape, which has an extended finial, is plain on both sides with a scalloped end.

Rochester – The Foord Sword – 1868–69

Length of sword	2ft 11¼in – 0.895m	Weight of sword	1lb 1½oz – 0.497kg
Length of blade	2ft 5in – 0.736m – Single-edged	Width of blade	0⅞in – 0.022m
Length of hilt	6¼in – 0.159m – One-handed	Width of guard	4½in – 0.114m
Length of scabbard	2ft 6in – 0.762m	Weight of scabbard	4¾oz – 0.131kg

Sword

The straight blade is damascened (blued and etched) for 15in and is well chased with leaf and scroll-work. It bears on the obverse two trophies of arms, and on the reverse the cipher of Queen Victoria and a trophy of arms, and under the protecting plate 'Firmin and Sons 153 Strand & 13 Conduit St London'. The hilt is silver-gilt, beautifully embossed with leaf-work and strap-work. The guard has an elaborate protecting plate and scroll-work attached over the position of the mouth-locket and bears a shield of the arms of the Admiralty Court and an oval cartouche of the city arms. The D-shaped knuckle-guard starts with a circular end with a recessed small flower, and has strap-work along the whole length, with on the obverse a cartouche with an ancient ship in full sail, and on the reverse a cartouche with a large fish with a long snout. The baluster-shaped grip has the same small recessed flower at either end and in the middle has raised images of Rochester Castle (O) and the martyrdom of St Andrew (R). The pommel is round and wedge-shaped, with the same small flower on four sides, and ends with a screw tang nut. The hallmarks are of London, 1868–69, the maker's mark 'P F'. The sword was presented to the town in 1871 by the then mayor, John Ross Foord. It used to be worn by the mayor as Admiral of the City and Constable of the Castle at mayor-making, but is now displayed in the town museum.

Scabbard

The scabbard is covered in dark tan leather with two silver-gilt mounts. These are: (1) the mouth-locket, which has a castellated edge, some engraving round a frog stud and is inscribed 'GIVEN TO THE CORPORATION OF ROCHESTER, AD 1871, By Alderman John Ross Foord, MAYOR AND ADMIRAL OF THE CITY AND CONSTABLE OF THE CASTLE'; and (2) the chape, which is plain on each side with a castellated edge, has a superimposed band with a castellated edge and a button finial – it is slightly split on one edge. The sword is designed to be worn with a baldric.

Crewe – The Watson Sword – *c.* 1877

Length of sword	3ft 3½in – 1.003m	Weight of sword	2lb 8½oz – 1.148kg
Length of blade	2ft 10⅛in – 0.867m – Double-edged	Width of blade	1⅜in – 0.035m
Length of hilt	5⅜in – 0.137m – One-handed	Width of guard	3⅞in – 0.099m
Length of scabbard	2ft 11⅛in – 0.892m	Weight of scabbard	12oz – 0.344kg

Sword

The sword was made in Germany. The blade, which has a very short ricasso, is decorated for some 18in from the hilt. On the obverse there is, appropriately, an etched train – a 2.4.0 steam locomotive with six-wheeled tender. It is inscribed on one side 'PRESENTED TO the MAYOR & CORPORATION OF CREWE by GEORGE WATSON Borough Surveyor Nov' 9th 1877'. On each side of the engraving is an abstract etching, roughly shield-shaped. The Crewe motto in a chevron, 'Never behind', chased with oak leaves and acorns, is included. On the reverse is similar chasing with a mace and sceptre in saltire under a crown, a large 'VR' cipher and some leaf-work. The hilt is gilt and elaborately chased. The quillon block has a small protecting plate and bears an animal head (wolf?) on each side. The quillons are extremely short and terminate with moustachioed male heads, with a very high forehead, long hair and quite a long beard. The grip is baluster-shaped and patterned. The pommel is somewhat bulbous and crescent-shaped, with a ram's head on each face and a male head, similar to the quillon ends, on each side.

The sword was presented to the town in November 1877 by the Borough Treasurer, George Watson, to mark the formation of the Borough of Crewe. It is not processed but is displayed unsheathed on special occasions.

Scabbard

The scabbard is made of black leather with two brass mounts. These are: (1) the mouth-locket, which is plain except for a long frog stud on one side; and (2) the chape, which is 6½in long, simple and plain on each side. The scabbard is extremely battered and bends in two places.

Exeter – The Buller Sword – *c.* 1901

Length of sword	3ft 2in – 0.965m	Weight of sword	1lb 9½oz – 0.723kg
Length of blade	2ft 7¾in – 0.806m – Single-edged	Width of blade	1in – 0.025m
Length of hilt	6¼in – 0.159m – One-handed	Width of guard	6½in – 0.165m
Length of scabbard	2ft 10½in – 0.876m	Weight of scabbard	1lb 15oz – 0.879kg

Sword

The sword is in the form of a cavalry sabre with a curved blade, with the top foot edged on both sides. The blade is etched with leaf- and scroll-work on both sides. On the obverse are a small city arms in a crowned star, the intertwined initials 'RHB', the battle honours of Natal, Relief of Ladysmith and Eastern Transvaal, a set of small motifs of crossed pickaxes and a shovel, '1900' above a pair of telescopes, and a crossed rifle and sword with a saddle, stirrups and binoculars. On the reverse are the Victoria Cross emblem, the intertwined initials 'RHB', the inscription 'PRESENTED TO RT HONBLE GENERAL SIR REDVERS H. BULLER VC GCB KCMG BY THE COUNTY OF DEVON IN RECOGNITION OF HIS GALLANT SERVICES IN SOUTH AFRICA 1899–1900', the battle honours of Natal, Relief of Ladysmith and Eastern Transvaal, and some leaf-work. The hilt is silver-gilt. The quillon block has a very pointed but small protecting plate in the form of a star with enamelled Tudor roses on each point on each side, and is decorated in a cartouche, on the obverse, with rubies forming the initial 'R', diamonds the initial 'H' and sapphires the initial 'B', and, on the reverse, with the city arms enamelled. The quillons are short, box-shaped, taper slightly, bear what seems to be a shamrock, a rose, a thistle and a leek on each side, and end in an elaborate fleur-de-lis. There are also several enamelled Tudor roses. The grip bears the figure of a soldier bearing a rifle on each side, with a pith helmet (O) and a slouch hat (R). The pommel is in the form of a lion's head with ruby eyes and a hole through the mouth for the sword knot of gold thread, picked out with red and an acorn. The blade next to the hilt is somewhat rusty. It was made by T. & J. Bragg of Birmingham in 1900–01. The sword is on loan from the Buller Foundation.

Scabbard

This is a very impressive example of ornate work. The highly polished metal scabbard is curved with three highly decorated silver-gilt mounts. These are: (1) the mouth locket, which is very long with a ring for a baldric attached. On the obverse are an enamelled shield of the Buller family arms and a Victoria Cross. On the reverse are the enamelled initials 'RHB' and the badge of the Devonshire Regiment; (2) the centre-locket, which has a baldric ring attached and bears, on the obverse, the King's Royal Rifle Corps (KRRC) badge, the enamelled arms of the city and the badge of the Devonshire Regiment. On the reverse are the Victoria Cross and the badge of the Order of the Bath; and (3) the chape, which is very long (9½in) with a long heel to protect it from the ground. On the obverse it bears an enamelled Tudor rose; the enamelled badge of the Order of the Bath; an enamelled crossed flags of the Union and the royal arms; a second enamelled Tudor rose; a third enamelled Tudor rose; the enamelled badge of the Order of St Michael and St George; and a trophy of arms. On the reverse is a Tudor rose (enamel worn off); the enamelled badge of the Order of St Michael and St George; a Tudor rose (enamel worn off); the badge of the KRRC; and a trophy of arms.

APPENDIX 8

THE CARE OF SWORDS AND SCABBARDS

Probably the most important aspect of looking after these very special swords is to remember that any finger- or handprints are highly corrosive to fine-polished metal and may leave irreversible damage.

Accordingly, anyone handling them should always, repeat always, wear gloves, preferably of white cotton, whenever the sword or scabbard is to be handled. It was very disappointing that during the visits to inspect each of the swords this happened in only about half the locations.

Certainly when bearing the sword and scabbard, white cotton gloves should be worn (in Bath, brown leather gloves are worn). Should the blade or any of the other metal parts be touched, a timely careful wipe with a cotton cloth or duster should remove the mark. Any cleaning should be done carefully and lightly, or damage will occur.

The Blade

If the blade is dirty, it can be degreased with acetone or white spirit on a soft cloth – when doing this, gloves must be worn and the room well ventilated. If the blade is blued or gilded, these can be affected by abrasion or oils. It is better to avoid these areas. If necessary, contact the Conservation Department at the Royal Armouries for advice.

Once clean and dry, the blade can be given a very light coating of microcrystalline wax, which is synthetic and does not become acidic with age. The wax can be applied cold on a brush or lint-free cloth, or hot with a brush using a standard hairdryer to heat the wax until it runs clear. The latter approach gives a better finish but requires more skill. When dry, the wax can be buffed with a soft cloth. If required, the wax can be removed later with white spirit.

The Hilt

The hilt may be of different metals and wood. Many of the swords described in this book have iron hilts – these can be cleaned by degreasing as described above.

Where parts of the hilt are gilded, these should be cleaned only if a build-up of dirt is present. In this case, a very gentle washing with soapy water is all that is required. However, it is essential that these parts are thoroughly dried. These parts should not be waxed.

If the grip is silver, it may become tarnished. Light tarnish can be removed with pure talc mixed into a paste with ethanol and applied on a clean cloth or cotton swab. A silver polish is suitable or a silver foam can be used, but moisture can be a problem. Both leave residues that must be brushed away thoroughly once the paste has dried. A silver polishing cloth can also be useful for this purpose. A silver dip is quick and easy but it needs to be washed off, which may damage other parts of the hilt. Heavy tarnish requires more complex treatments, and Royal Armouries' advice should be sought. Ethanol can be difficult to obtain in small quantities – try Amazon.com.

Many grips are wire-bound. It is probable that the grip itself is wooden. If there is obvious insect damage, proper preservation methods should be applied. If the wire has become detached or has moved, it will need retightening. This can be achieved by clamping the wire to the grip as it is re-formed, and then reattaching the loose wire end, either by an adhesive or by a small neat braze.

Brazing should only be done by a competent professional.

The Scabbard

The scabbard needs similar care. The velvet covering of many scabbards needs attention, as frequent handling has caused the velvet to become stained and worn. Straightforward replacement is relatively simple and not too expensive. However, in a number of cases the scabbard has been split at the side where the sword had been inserted/unsheathed at an angle due to the handler having shorter arms than the blade! A repair to the side of the scabbard can be effected when the velvet is replaced. In several cases the embroidery and/or the stitching has become loose. These faults need to be rectified before further damage/wear occurs.

The silver-gilt mounts may become tarnished. A very light washing with soapy water is the best answer; however, it is essential to slide a thin piece of protective plastic under the mounts so that the velvet covering does not get wet. In some cases the gilding has been worn away and the original silver has been exposed. Light tarnish can be removed as described above. If heavily tarnished, advice should be sought from the Royal Armouries.

Rain and Moisture

Should the sword get wet, perhaps in an outing in the rain, it is likely that water will reach the blade. Water will gather on the guard and penetrate the inside of the scabbard mouth. It is extremely important that the blade is removed from the scabbard immediately on return, and the whole sword dried thoroughly with a cotton cloth or duster. Any leather collar at the base of the blade should be removed and dried out, as this can absorb moisture.

If corrosion is present, use 3-in-1 mineral oil on a very soft 0000 grade wire wool. Always check to ensure no scratching is taking place. The wool and oil should remove the roughness of the corrosion without damaging the blade. Do not use a pin or needle, as these will cause extreme scratching. If the corrosion has caused heavy etching on the blade, it will be better, before proceeding further, to contact the Royal Armouries for advice.

The scabbard similarly needs to be dried, as the fabric covering will have absorbed moisture. The scabbards of most Swords of State and civic swords are made of wood (only a few are made of leather) and the vast majority of mounts are silver-gilt. All excess moisture should be removed from the scabbard, and it should then be placed in a warm environment to ensure that the velvet covering is dried out and that the wood or leather of the scabbard itself does not absorb moisture. The scabbard should not be placed on or next to a radiator. It may take as much as week for the scabbard to dry out sufficiently for the sword to be replaced in it. A daily check should be made for a couple of weeks to ensure that no residual moisture is transferred to the blade.

The mouth, in particular, needs to be carefully dried in case some moisture has built up here. Failure will result in a rusting of the blade in quite a short period of time.

Storage

Most of these swords are kept in cabinets on display. They are best displayed out of the scabbard to obviate the problems mentioned above. However, if this is not possible, then it is imperative that the sword be removed from the scabbard at regular intervals to inspect it and ensure that damage is not occurring.

Where swords and scabbards are in display cases, it is important to ensure that mounts and fixings are padded to avoid damage, and that they are acid-free.

Some holders of ceremonial swords have protective bags in which to transport them – these should be made of charcoal cloth or as supplied by Tarnprufe. The sword should spend a minimum period in such a bag to alleviate moisture.

Do not store swords or scabbards near felt or silk, or in a room with an open fire, as this increases tarnishing.

GLOSSARY

(h) Indicates an heraldic term

Types of sword

Arming sword   A sword used or worn with armour
Bastard sword   From the French word 'bâtarde', an irregular sword or sword of
                  uncertain origin. Also described as a sword midway between a long
                  sword and a short sword
Bearing-sword   A sword borne before a sovereign or mayor – usually two-handed
                  but four coronation swords are single-handed
Broad-sword   A long, heavy double-edged sword with a straight, broad, flat blade
                  held with two hands
Cutlass   A broad-bladed curved hanger with which sailors were armed. See
                  hanger below
Flamberg   A German style of sword – in some instances with a blade with a
                  wavy edge
Great sword   A large two-handed sword
Hand-and-a-half
sword   Having a grip which allows use by a second hand if necessary –
                  sometimes called a bastard sword
Hanger   A type of short sword originally hung from a belt
Long sword   A single-handed thrusting sword with a long blade similar to a rapier
Robe sword   A pseudo-medieval form of sword introduced as part of a revival
                  of chivalry that took place in the early seventeenth century. It later
                  became standard wear with ceremonial robes of all kinds
Sabre   A single-edged, curved bladed cavalry sword
Short sword   A single-handed sword with a short blade
Small sword   A light one-handed sword designed for thrusting; a dress sword
Tulwar   A curved cavalry sabre of Indian origin with a spike protruding
                  from the pommel; used for striking the opponent in extremely
                  close quarters

Other Definitions

Abjuration	To formally renounce something – in this case the Catholic faith
Acanthus	A leaf style from the Roman era but from a Greek word
Addorsed (h)	Letters turned back to back
Alto relievo	In high relief
Apparitor	An official sent to carry out the orders of a court
Basket hilt	A hilt with a basket-shaped guard covering the hand
Bally	A town-land – an administrative division (up to 7,000 acres) of land in Ireland (pre-dating Norman times)
Baluster	A 'pillar' which narrows at both ends like a pomegranate flower, or in the middle
Band	A flat strip of metal around the scabbard – sometimes decorated
Baldric	A diagonal sash or belt from which to hang a sword
Blade	The thin cutting part of an edged weapon
Bluing	To make, dye or become blue
Boss	A spherical ending or knob
Caboshed	Showing the full face of an animal. Borne as the head of a stag, full-faced and cut off close behind the ears
Calyx	A whorl of leaves
Canton (h)	A square figure positioned as the first quarter on a shield
Cartouche	A carved ornamental panel in the form of a scroll
Caryatid	A draped female figure
Chape (h)	The metal covering over the point of a scabbard, sometimes adorned with a crown or orb
Chappe	A flap of leather attached to the crosspiece (see also protecting plate)
Chased	To be adorned with work engraved or embossed in relief – a groove or furrow
Coat, Frock	A fitted, long-sleeved coat with knee-length skirt and central vent at the back
Coat, Morning	A single-breasted long-sleeved coat, the front parts curving away gradually into a set of tails behind
Coat, Tail	A knee-length long-sleeved coat with the front cut away square at waist-height leaving only the rear section as tails
Collet	A ring or collar
Commonwealth	The period between 1649 and 1659 when the monarchy was usurped
Cornucopia	A horn overflowing with fruit or vegetables
Crest	A heraldic device borne on the top of the helmet (sometimes a crown)
Crosspiece	See Guard

Cruciform hilt	A hilt with a straight guard to protect the hand
Cusp	The pointed end where two curves meet (i.e. the pointed ends of a crescent moon)
Damascened	Ornamented by etching or by inlaying other metals usually gold or silver (blued and etched)
Damask	A richly patterned fabric of cotton, linen, silk or wool
Damasked (h)	Decorated with a fine pattern, usually within a large expanse of a single colour
Desuetude	The condition of not being in use or practise
Dexter (h)	The right side of a shield but on the left as viewed
Diapered	A repeating pattern of diamond shapes
Dimidiated (h)	Two coats of arms on one shield
Écusson	A small shield-shaped extension from the centre of the quillons over the base of the blade
Electroplated	Coated with a very thin patina of gold, silver, rhodium or chromium through electrolysis
Engrailed	Having an edge formed by a series of raised dots or indented with notches (e.g. edge of £1 coin)
Engraved	Mark with incisions, carved upon a surface using a fine chisel
Escallop	A scallop or cockle shell
Escheator	A person responsible for recovery, to the Crown, of property for which there are no legal heirs
Escutcheon (h)	A small shield-shaped embellishment, usually on the shield of a coat of arms
Fasces	A bundle of rods, around an axe, carried by Roman magistrates as a symbol of authority – sometimes issued to flog criminals
Festoons	Chains or garlands (of flowers)
Ferrule	A metal cap placed at one end of a stick for added strength
Finial	The ornament at the end of an object – at the point of a scabbard or the tip of a hilt
Flash	A stripe of gold lace or braid on a hat, or a piece of material made up of five overlapping black silk ribbons hung from the back of a collar to protect the coat from a pigtail
Fleurons	Small flowers (French)
Fleury (h)	Flowered
Fluted	Round, shallow, concave grooves on a shaft or column
Forte	The first half of the blade from the guard to the middle
France ancient (h)	With several rows of fleur-de-lis (1340–99 in two different forms)
France modern (h)	With only three fleur-de-lis (1399–1801 in several different forms)
Frog stud	A small metal stud on a sword frog for attaching the scabbard

Frog-sword	An attachment to a belt into which a scabbard is placed for easy carriage and support
Fuller	A groove in a blade to allow easier withdrawal and give greater flexibility (also known as a gutter)
Gadroon	A set of convex curves or arcs joined at their extremities to form a decorative pattern
Galloon	A kind of narrow, close-woven braid or ribbon of gold or silver used for trimming
Garb (h)	A sheaf of corn
G(u)ardant (h)	Looking outward with the head in full face and the body in profile
Garter	Within the garter – encircled by the Garter ribbon including the motto
Girded/Girt	The action of attaching a sword around the waist
Grip	That part of the handle between the guard and the pommel
Guard	The part of the hilt of a sword across the base of the blade which protects the hand
Guilloche	An ornamental border with repeating pattern of two or more inter-woven wavy lines
Hanger	A device for hanging a sword from a belt (but see Frog above)
Helm	Helmet
High Constables	A small group of ceremonial guards at Holyrood Palace in Edinburgh
Hilt	The handle of a sword including the guard, the grip and the pommel
Hollowed shells	Metal pieces which form part of the guard – singly or in pairs – which protect the hand
Honour	A great lordship consisting of dozens or hundreds of manors
Ibid (em)	From the same place (Latin) (refers to the last cited source)
Impaled(h)	A way of combining two coats of arms
Inspeximus	A word in ancient charters confirming a previous grant
Invected (h)	Consisting of a series of small convex lobes or semi-circular bites
Jacobite Risings	These were a series of uprisings and rebellions occurring between 1688 and 1746. They were aimed at returning James VII of Scotland and II of England to the throne after he was deposed by Parliament. Ended in 1746 with the defeat of Charles Edward Stuart (The Young Pretender) at the Battle of Culloden
Japanned	Painted or coated with a glossy, heavy, black lacquer
Latten	An alloy of copper and zinc resembling brass
Lions/Leopards	Three lions are part of the England coat of arms. Sometimes they are referred to as leopards because early heralds described 'lion rampant' (rearing up – see below) as a lion but when walking along as a leopard. This was later altered to 'passant' (see below) to avoid confusion.

	Later still this became the term for a lion looking forward. The lions on the English coat of arms became known as lion 'passant guardant' (see above) because they look out of the coat of arms
Locket	An individual metal plate, ornament or decoration on a scabbard
Lozenge	A diamond-shaped figure
Magnate	A great nobleman
Mantling	Ornamental drapery issuing from a helmet
Martlet (h)	A swallow (without feet)
Matie	Majesty
Mordant	A tag of metal at the end of a pendant of a girdle (also an area etched with acid)
Mount	Used here as a generic title for all lockets and bands on a scabbard
Mouth-locket	The metal sleeve at the open end of a scabbard which protects the throat
Minerva	Roman goddess of handicrafts, the arts and the professions, and later of war
Miniscules	Medieval writing (mainly Greek)
Mullet	A five-pointed star
Op cit	*Opera citato* (Latin) – refers to 'the work cited' or a previous source
Ornament	An object used to decorate something
Pas-d'âne	Metal rings which form part of the guard to protect the hand
Passant (h)	Walking on three legs with the fourth raised
Passim	Here and there – throughout – frequently
Palatine	A territory ruled by a prince or noble possessing royal prerogatives
Personification	A dramatic representation of a person, usually in the form of a semi-clad female figure
Pierced (h)	With a hole so that another tincture shows through
Piety	In its piety – showing obedience
Plantation	See Appendix 5
Pounced	Powdered to prevent ink from spreading
Pommel	The knob terminating the hilt of a sword
Prerogative	An exclusive privilege or right (normally restricted to or given by a sovereign)
Protecting plate	A plate or locket, part of the quillon block, projecting over the scabbard to protect the mouth of the scabbard
Quarterly (h)	A shield divided into four quarters, each with contrasting arms or having two sets of arms each repeated in diagonally opposite corners
Quatrefoil (h)	A leaf composed of four leaflets
Quillon block	The centrepiece of the guard which abuts the blade and forms one end of the hilt

Quillons	The often decorated extensions of a cruciform guard from the quillon block – not so described before 1500
Raised cable	A decoration looking like a rope in relief
Rampant (h)	A beast standing on its hind legs, the right foreleg raised up
Re-curved	Where the two ends of the guard point in differing directions – one to the point and the other to the pommel
Regnum	Kingdom (Latin)
Reg(u)ardant (h)	Looking backwards over the shoulder
Repoussé	Raised in relief as a design on a thin piece of metal hammered through from the underside
Restoration	The restoration of the monarchy on the return of Charles II in 1660
Rococo	A style of architecture of the 1840s with conventional scroll-work and meaningless decoration – tasselled, florid, ornate
Ricasso	An unsharpened part of the blade just above the guard
Russet	A rough reddish-brown homespun fabric
Sacerdotium	The earthly hierarchy whose primary goal is the salvation of the soul, i.e. clergy (Latin)
Saltire	A diagonal cross (of Scotland)
Satyr	One of a class of lustful drunken woodland goat-like Greek gods
Scrollwork	Decoration consisting of spiral linear patterns
Shagreen	A rough grainy material; the skin of the ray (skinned and dried but not tanned)
Shield of pretence	A small shield in the centre of another shield
Sinister (h)	The left of a shield but on the right as viewed
Spandrel	A triangular space
Strapwork	Interlaced scrollwork ornamentation imitating pierced and interlaced straps
Tang	The pointed extension of the blade which forms the core of the hilt
Tang Button	The knob formed at the end of the tang by hammering, to secure the hilt to the blade
Tent – under a	Under a canopy
Terpsichore	A Greek and Roman muse of dance
Throat	The open end of the scabbard into which the sword is inserted
Top Nut	The threaded locking device screwed to the end of the tang to secure the hilt to the blade – see tang button
Triton	A Greek god, a merman – the son of Poseidon
Trophy of arms	A group of weapons splayed out as in a bouquet behind a shield or plate at the fixing point
Turk's head	A decorative knot with a number of interwoven strands forming a closed loop

Vallary crown	A circular gold crown, sometimes garlanded, bestowed on the first soldier to scale the enemy's rampart
Venus	A Roman goddess of fields and gardens but principally of love
Wolf mark	This mark, sometimes referred to as 'running', is found on many blades and is one of the most widely found of all marks. It apparently originated in the Middle Ages as the town mark of the city of Passau in Bavaria, but it was subsequently copied, especially by the blade-smiths of Solingen

NOTES

1 *The Corporation Plate and Insignia of Office of the Cities and Corporate Towns of England and Wales* (2 volumes) by Llewellyn Jewitt and W.H. St John Hope (London, Bemrose) 1895.

2 *The Crown Jewels* (2 volumes), Volume 2, *The Sword Catalogue*, edited by Claude Blair (HMSO Historic Royal Palaces) 1998.

3 *European and American Arms (c. 1100–1850)* by Claude Blair (Batsford) 1962.

4 *The Dublin Civic Swords* by Claude Blair and Ida Delame (Royal Irish Academy) 1988.

5 *The Sword in the Age of Chivalry* by R. Ewart Oakshott (Bordell Press) 1964.

6 *The Book of the Sword* by Richard Francis Burton (Cosimo Classics) 1884.

7 *The Engines of War* by Henry Wilkinson (Forgotten Books) 1841.

8 *European Regalia* by Lord Twining (Batsford) 1967, pp.227–51.

9 Proceedings of the Society of High Constables, 9 May 1892 (Edinburgh).

10 *Waterford Treasures: A guide to the historical and archaeological treasures of Waterford City* by Eamonn McEneaney and Rosemary Ryan (Waterford City Council) 2004.

11 Guildhall Historical Association, Transactions, 1965.

12 *Ceremonials of the Corporation of London: a handbook prepared by authority of the Court of Lord Mayor and Aldermen for the guidance of the Lord Mayor, Aldermen, Sheriffs, and Officers of the Corporation* by John Arthur Harris (Corporation of London) 1991.

13 *The Honours of Scotland: The Story of the Scottish Crown Jewels* by Charles Burnett and Christopher Tabrahon (Historic Scotland) 1993.

14 *Isle of Man Natural History and Antiquarian Society*, Vol. 11, No. 2, edited by Claude Blair, 2003.

15 *Studies in London History* by Philip Edmund Jones, edited by A.E.J. Hollzender and W. Kellaway (Hodden and Stoughton) 1969.

16 *A Record of European Armour and Arms* (5 volumes) by Sir Guy Laking (Benediction Books) 1920–22.

17 *Kingston upon Hull Insignia and Plate* by R.A. Alex-Smith (Driffield) 1973.

18 *The History of Drogheda and its Environs* by John D'Alton (Dublin) 1844.

19 'The Galway Sword and Mace' by G.A. Hayes McCoy, from the *Journal of the Galway Archaeological and Historical Society*, 1961.

20 *The Charters of Southampton* by H.W. Gidden (Cox & Sharland) 1909.

ACKNOWLEDGEMENTS

In addition to the many staff of (lord) mayors' offices up and down the land, my most sincere thanks go to: Bridget Clifford, Royal Armouries Keeper of Collections (South) at the Tower of London; Bob Woosnam-Savage, Curator of European Edged Weapons at the Royal Armouries Museum in Leeds; Keith Hanson, the Chief Exhibitor at the Jewel House at the Tower of London; Shruti Patel, Daniel Bell and Simon Metcalf of the Royal Collection at St James's Palace; Dr Tony Trowles, Head of Abbey Collections at Westminster Abbey; Michael Messer for the answers to heraldic queries; Michael Porteous for the Latin translations; Trevor Campan at Patey Hats, who have made many of these hats; Kate Hay at the Victoria and Albert Museum; Robert Wilkinson Latham for his guidance; Lieutenant General David Leakey, Gentleman Usher of the Black Rod, and his staff; Lieutenant General Sir Michael Willcocks KCB, CVO (former Black Rod); Helena Jaeske and Neil Bollen of Exeter City Council Conservation department; Keith McClelland for attempting to teach me how to use a camera and the art of photographing swords; Michael Rich and his daughter Sarah for guidance on editing photographs; Gill Carver for the onerous task of proofreading such a detailed work; and last but not least, the myriad of others who helped in my research and/or pointed me in the next direction.

You may also be interested in ...

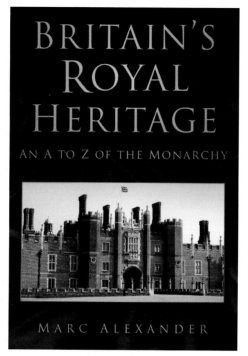

978 0 7524 5911 0

Royal scandals, wars, ceremonies, households, tombs and insignia make fascinating reading, and this book is the ideal reference work for all those who want to know more about individual monarchs and the impressive legacy of myths, traditions, beliefs and practices that have grown up around the institution of the monarchy.

You may also be interested in …

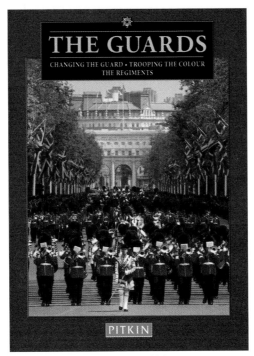

978 1 8416 5728 8

The seven illustrious Guards regiments, renowned and respected around the world for their self-discipline, smartness and reliability, are manned today by modern soldiers, equally at home on parade or on operational duty. See the Guards at their best in this superbly illustrated Pitkin Guide – a must for visitors to London or lovers of ceremony.